Sister in Sorrow

Sister in Sorrow

Life Histories
of Female Holocaust Survivors from Hungary

ILANA ROSEN
Translated and Edited by Sandy Bloom

Wayne State University Press
Detroit

12 11 10 09 08   5 4 3 2 1

Hebrew-language edition originally published by the
Ben-Gurion University of the Negev Publishers, 2003.

Library of Congress Cataloging-in-Publication Data

Rosen, Ilana.
[Ahot le-tsarah. English]
Sister in sorrow : life histories of female Holocaust survivors from Hungary /
Ilana Rosen ; translated and edited by Sandy Bloom.
p. cm. — (Raphael Patai series in Jewish folklore and anthropology)
Includes bibliographical references and index.
ISBN-13: 978-0-8143-3129-3 (pbk. : alk. paper)
ISBN-10: 0-8143-3129-7 (pbk. : alk. paper)
1. Jewish women in the Holocaust—Hungary—Biography.
2. Holocaust, Jewish (1939–1945)—Hungary—Personal narratives.
3. Holocaust survivors—Hungary—Biography.
I. Bloom, Sandy, 1955– II. Title.
DS135.H93A16713 2008
940.53′180922439—dc22
[B]
2007037111

∞ The paper used in this publication meets the minimum requirements of the
American National Standard for Information Sciences—Permanence of Paper
for Printed Library Materials, ANSI Z39.48-1984.

Grateful acknowledgment is made to the Mary Dickey Masterton Fund for financial
assistance in the publication of this volume.

Contents

Preface and Acknowledgments vii

1. Brainstorming about the Life Histories of
Women Holocaust Survivors 1

2. Mother-Daughter Discourse:
A Literary-Psychoanalytical Analysis of Five Life Histories 23

3. The Holocaust Experience of Its Listeners and Readers:
A Phenomenological-Hermeneutic Analysis of Ten Life Histories 83

4. A Journey without a Conclusion 127

Appendix: The Life Histories 135

Notes 223
Bibliography 233
Term Index 251
Name Index 265
Place Index 267

Preface and Acknowledgments

Sister in Sorrow: A Journey to the Life Histories of Female Holocaust Survivors from Hungary began as a PhD thesis that was written in the 1990s and devoted to the experiences and narratives of both male and female survivors living in Israel and in Hungary. At that time, the idea that Holocaust testimonies, as they were regularly termed, are narratives or stories with themes, structures, metaphors, and messages was not yet as widely accepted as it is today. Furthermore, the voices of women survivors had not yet started to receive the literary, artistic, academic, journalistic, and political attention they presently enjoy (if such a verb can be used in such a painful context). The present work is fortunate to have been part of these processes or developments, and to have been one of the pioneering projects in Israeli personal-oral narrative study. The following persons and organizations have a share in this accomplishment:

First and foremost are the Holocaust survivors in both Israel and Hungary who were willing to share with me their painful memories, losses, and grief, and also their remnants of hope, which they still had despite all that they had endured.

While carrying out this research project, I enjoyed the support of the Institute of Jewish Studies (now the Mandel Institute of Jewish Studies) and the Rosenfeld Research Project on the History of the Jews of Hungary and the Habsburg Empire, both at the Hebrew University of Jerusalem, as well as that of the World Sephardi Federation.

The adaptation of this work into a book more widely accessible to the general public in Israel was enabled by the support of the President, Rector, and Dean of the Faculty of Humanities and Social Studies at Ben Gurion University of the Negev (BGU) as well as the Esther and Sidney Rabb Center for Holocaust and Redemption Studies at BGU.

The translation of this work from Hebrew to English was supported by the Jewish Memorial Foundation at New York.

Throughout my academic career, I have benefited from the guidance, advice, expertise, experience, and critical eye of my PhD mentor, Professor Galit Hasan-Rokem of the Department of Hebrew Literature and the Program of Jewish and Comparative Folklore at the Hebrew University of Jerusalem, and I greatly appreciate the fruitful communication we have had and still have.

For this project specifically, as well as for others related to Hungarian Jewry, I thank Dr. Michael Silber of the Department of Jewish History at the Hebrew University for his advice and support. Likewise, I thank Dr. Gavriel Bar-Shaked of Yad Vashem, Jerusalem, for his help with Hungarian terms and the lore of Hungarian Jewry. The same thanks go to Professor Katrin Kogman Appel of BGU for her help with German and to Dr. Dalit Berman of BGU for her help with Yiddish.

Next, I am thankful to Professor Dan Ben-Amos of the University of Pennsylvania at Philadelphia, who is the general editor of the Raphael Patai Series in Jewish Folklore and Anthropology by Wayne State University Press. His trust and interest in this work and myself from a very early point have been invaluable.

Parts of this work were previously edited by Sarah Fine-Meltzer of BGU. More inclusively, my regular editor for abroad publications, Sandy Bloom, stands behind both the English edition of this entire volume and the translation into English of its analytical parts. (I am responsible for the translation of the oral-literary parts.) Shlomo Ketko has dexterously indexed this book. Finally, this work has profited from the thorough and professional treatment of Beth Ina, the freelance copyeditor hired by Wayne State University Press.

Last, but never least, all my projects are carried out and exist together with my loving and beloved family, my husband Michael and our three children, Yasmin, Oriel, and Itamar. In many senses, works such as this one are written for our children and future generations, for whom we wish a much happier history.

1

Brainstorming about the Life Histories
of Women Holocaust Survivors

And the poor, unfortunate one, this little sister
of mine, they took her away. All four of us
wanted to follow her. They beat us but would
not let us die. The poor one, they took only
her, and us they put on a transport, again on a
train. We marched, did not know where nor
why. We marched.

Rachel Markowitz, Szilágysómlyo–Petach
Tikva, 1991

In the Beginning There Was a Name

The beginning of this book is a name: Ilana, my Hebrew name, or Ilona,
the Hungarian name of two of my female relatives, one on the side of
each of my parents. Both women were murdered in the Holocaust. For
some reason, my parents named my sister and two brothers after their
own parents and other relatives who had died from natural causes long
before the Holocaust. Only I was given a "memorial candle" name, a
practice well documented in the study of the "second generation" of the
Holocaust in psychology and related fields.[1]

The first Ilona, or Ilush, was my mother's aunt on her mother's side.
Little was known about this aunt in my family except that she was very
religious and red-haired, as were some of her children. Along with them,

she was deported to Auschwitz (her husband's fate is completely unknown), and to the best of the family's knowledge, none of them ever
returned.

The second Ilush was also called an aunt, although she was in fact
my father's first wife who had died in Auschwitz, together with their son,
Péter-Pinchas. Until I reached adolescence, this distinction in status or
familial relationship did not matter. For me, this Ilush too was an aunt,
just like my other aunts and uncles whom I never met, either because
they had died long ago or because they never came to Israel like my
parents. Péter was, therefore, part brother, part cousin, though his very
existence was so vague to me that I never grasped the problematics of
defining our kinship. Only as an adult, while writing the PhD thesis on
which the present book is based,[2] was I at times lured to the fantasy that
my half brother was alive somewhere and that circumstances might still
bring us together, although I knew that the chances for that were nil.

During World War II my father served in the so-called labor battalions, or forced labor service within the framework of the Hungarian
army.[3] Once the war was over, he waited for his wife's return, but her
name never appeared on the lists of the survivors. Instead, at the office
where the lists were published, he met the woman who would be my
mother. The two married and started a new family.

In this family, whenever one of the deceased Ilushes was mentioned,
it was always with the emphatic adjective "poor," which is widespread in
the Hungarian language when talking about suffering and sufferers, in
the same way that the adjective *dear* (*drága*) (sometimes in the literal
meaning of *sweet* [*édes*]) is almost automatically attached to first-degree
family members. It is my clear recollection that my mother never expressed any resentment toward her predecessor, very much unlike the
treatment of such phenomena in world literature or in Israeli narratives
dealing with "second generation" and "second" families.[4] In addition,
Ilush's brother, Mishka, was a frequent and welcome guest at our home
who played and joked with us children just like a real uncle.

In spite of the burden of memories and consciousness of relatives
who "remained there," or perhaps because of them, my parents did not
tell us much about their past and families, let alone discuss meanings of
names or possible resemblances and differences between the two "aunts"
and their namesake. In our "family folklore," although the Holocaust was
not a taboo subject, it was dealt with as minimally as possible, a matter
brought up by the children in light of memorial events or information
gotten from the outside that aroused our curiosity.[5] Our parents always

answered succinctly, focusing on facts, dates, places, and names. Our father, so we were told, served in the Hungarian labor battalions; his wife and son "never returned"; our mother escaped to Rumania's rural areas and lived under a Christian identity.

These fixed and rigid repetitions, which I could eventually recite by rote, were in fact an unconscious proairetic ploy on the part of my parents.[6] They employed speech and silence together, or speech about a subject that they could neither completely suppress nor entirely reveal. As a child and later as an adolescent, I was satisfied with these bits of information; unfortunately, before I matured and realized my need to know more, both my parents fell ill and died within a year.

The memory of the Holocaust did not preoccupy me at the beginning of my studies at the Hebrew University in Jerusalem. My academic inclinations led me to English literature and to the culture of classical and Christian Europe. Toward the end of my MA studies, I became interested in the genre of autobiography, both historical and fictional, but the framework of purely literary analysis did not satisfy me anymore. Since autobiography is about an individual's life, one needs to know more about the context of the life in question, whether in terms of history, sociology, psychology, or philosophy. Only at a later stage did I become acquainted with folklore, anthropology, gender, and Holocaust studies. With this in mind, I began to look for a subject for a PhD thesis that would examine literary and other autobiographies in their cultural context. My search led me to Professor Galit Hasan-Rokem of the Hebrew University at Jerusalem, who encouraged me to strengthen and express the ties between the personal and the historical, the self-experienced and the academic. This was also the time at which I felt the need to turn from foreign cultures to the study of Judaism and Jews.

Until that time, the Holocaust did not interest me very much. It can be said that I was not encouraged to develop such an interest. On Holocaust Memorial Day, instead of watching Holocaust memorial programs on TV, I preferred listening to music or reading. Against this backdrop, the idea of documenting and studying the life histories of the Holocaust survivors of my parents' diaspora turned out to be a powerful combination of the familiar (or familial) and foreign, the known and unknown, the discomfiting and appealing, and the personal and professional. Needless to say, this enterprise also included the consoling and therapeutic element of "talking with the dead" and coming to terms with death and bereavement on a personal level.[7]

Thus, I found myself, at the beginning of my married life and during my first pregnancy, traveling to the homes of Holocaust survivors, listening to stories about suffering that words can hardly express and about the loss of meaning that follows having lost everything one cherishes in life. Sometimes I feared lest the child I was carrying would be affected by my distress, but I ultimately understood that together with the agony, there was also comfort in meeting survivors who had managed to rebuild their lives in spite of all they had gone through.

The interviews I carried out in Israel aroused my curiosity as to the Holocaust experience of survivors who had never left Hungary. It occurred to me that if the Israeli survivors told me the story of my "parents" (which they themselves never really told me), then the Jews still living in Hungary would tell me the stories of my "uncles" and "aunts," who had never emigrated, or made aliya, to Israel. Small wonder, then, that one of them happened to be a real aunt on my father's side. The stories of these people turned out to be pessimistic compared to the stories of the Israeli survivors, as their sense of persecution did not diminish with time but had in fact increased at the time of the interviews, in the summer of 1991. At that period, the collapse of the Communist regime unleashed a wave of anti-Semitism that had revived the horrors of the Holocaust for local survivors.

In addition to these two categories of survivors there is yet a third category, namely, that of Holocaust survivors who left Hungary but emigrated to the West (Western Europe, North and South America, and Australia) instead of to Israel. The scope of the present study does not extend to the experiences of this group, although I acknowledge the significance of considering their experiences as well.

Having completed the interviews, or "fieldwork," I had thirty-nine life histories: twenty-four recorded from Jews of Hungarian origins who had been living in Israel for several decades, and fifteen from Hungarian Jews still residing in Hungary and Rumania. Unintentionally, on my part at least, the number of women is double that of the men (twenty-six women as opposed to thirteen men). At the time that I wrote my doctorate, I did not attribute great significance to gender differences in terms of quantity or quality, other than remarking that they existed and duly noting them.[8] At that stage, I strove to achieve a general picture of the Hungarian Jewish Holocaust experience as it emerged from the life history corpus in its entirety.

To accomplish that goal, I examined in my doctoral thesis the life histories while employing research approaches from contemporary Western thought that relate to oral narrative, such as formalism, struc-

turalism, psychoanalysis, and phenomenology. I divided the life histories into subgroups according to their dominant features in terms of
theme, form, rhetoric, and ideology. This was done partly along the lines
of Roland Barthes' structuralist model as presented in *S/Z: An Essay.*[9]
There is an inevitable measure of imposition or artificiality in such an
emulation, but at that stage of mass and systematic analysis, this was
necessary to account for the many, long narratives. In retrospect, I see
that my choice of schools of thought and their implementation, as an
exercise in reading unreadable stories, produced some necessary obsta-
cles or failures. But owing to the poor, minimalist, or existentialist quality of many of the life histories, the so-called failure turns out to be consistent with the stories, much like the combination of negative forces,
which eventually creates positive results.

The Female Experience in the Context of Holocaust Literature

My work turned out to be of extensive volume not only in literary and
analytic terms, but also in its physical existence. Four hundred pages of
analysis based on a similar number of interview pages are more than
enough to limit the work's accessibility to audiences other than scholars,
students, and at times the narrators and their relatives. In attempting to
reduce this abundant material, I began to realize the extent to which the
female voice dominated the discourse of the life history corpus I had
recorded. I viewed this voice as a "natural choice" or main focus of the
present work.[10] The two exceptions are the husbands of two women,
who were interviewed jointly with their wives. In both these cases, interesting dynamics of support and subversion are discerned. I therefore
decided to include the life histories of these two couples on the assumption that their analyses would shed light on conjugal relations in this
corpus as a whole, since most if not all of the women had spent a lifetime
with their husbands at the time of the interview.

The female experience in the Holocaust is a relatively new and un-
explored subject in research, even compared to the experience of children, although this situation is changing rapidly in recent years.[11] The
reason for the void is that the war and the Holocaust, which affected all
sectors of population, are still considered primarily a man's domain.[12]
The research that does exist about women in the Holocaust deals more
with written and literary memoirs, such as the books by Livia Bitton
Jackson, Olga Lengyel, and Ilona Karmel,[13] than with folk or oral literature. In addition, in many cases the theories and tools for understanding

female Holocaust memoirs are not necessarily literary, but historical, linguistic, sociological, psychological, or various combinations of these. Often, these studies tend to highlight what is different or unique about the female Holocaust experience instead of examining the individual voices telling about it.

Myrna Goldenberg, for example, describes female prisoners in the camps as more resilient than male prisoners because of their training and skills in taking care of themselves and others, their ability to acquire food and prepare it, and their readiness to help and support others through empathy, talking, and listening. Likewise, Lillian Kremer, writing about Karmel's book, refers to these skills in terms of the capacity to create surrogate families, overcome loneliness, and preserve some sense of self-esteem through being vital to others.[14]

The historian Judith (Esther) Tydor Baumel, surveying the female Holocaust experience from an interdisciplinary angle, divides the publication of Israeli Holocaust memoirs into three periods or waves. The first occurred soon after the end of World War II; the second wave was during the 1950s and 1960s; the third was from the 1970s onward. The first wave is characterized by a focus on the Holocaust period itself, an emphasis on mutual help and support, a preoccupation with the female experience, and by a lack of moral reproach. It is significant that in many cases, the writers of the first wave were key figures in underground movements or camp leadership. The second wave appears to be too meager to evaluate, a "dead period," to use Baumel's phrase, between two periods of greater Holocaust consciousness. The third wave, beginning in the 1970s, is naturally enriched with perspective and communicative awareness, which were lacking in the previous two waves. While maintaining qualities such as emphasizing mutual help and concentrating on the female experience, this wave features additional traits, some of which are contradictory to each other. The more recent wave also presents a wider historical scope and expresses itself more cautiously about emotional and sexual matters. Nonetheless, it tends less to ideologization and more to focusing on the experience of ordinary women.[15] In her own more recent study of a group of ten women (the Zehnnerschaft) who maintained a world of their own within the world of the camps, Baumel shows how, according to present-day interviews with or written materials from the women, their previous Orthodox Jewish background (excluding one non-Orthodox participant) helped them preserve, create, and find meaning in life and survival despite the atrocious surroundings.[16]

Linguistics, which as we well know stands at the base of the structural approach and serves as the analytical impetus of literary studies and other fields from the second half of the twentieth century and forward, contributes a rigorously scientific tool to the understanding of Holocaust narratives. For example, Deborah Schiffrin performs a close historical-linguistic reading of a life history told by a woman who, as a child, was deserted by her mother in the Holocaust but who still refrains from accusing her mother in her life history. In her careful attention to issues of agency, self and other relations, and language and text types, Schiffrin illustrates the power of her discipline, combined with method-ologies from related fields, to expose the focal issues in the narrative she deciphers: mother-daughter relations and the complexities of rehabili-tated life after the Holocaust.[17]

In summary of the issue of women's unique Holocaust experiences, memories, and manners of narrating and conceptualizing them, it should be added that certain research trends put special focus on wom-en's sexual vulnerability in two Holocaust settings: in the world of the ghettos, which were usually run by prominent Jewish men, and the Nazi-German concentration or work camps and factories. In my opin-ion, however, the ability or readiness to shed light and discuss the (at times only hinted at) sexual abuse undergone by female Holocaust sur-vivors in both these settings has to be handled with great tact, taking into account the sensitivities of all involved—past and present—and, especially, the women survivors themselves. This will be at times at the expense of scholarly curiosity and the legitimacy of tackling every possi-ble aspect related to women in the Holocaust. This topic, including a fuller explanation of my reservations concerning it, will be further ex-plicated in chapter 2, which deals with the discourse of mothers and daughters about the memory of the Holocaust.

Scholars of Holocaust literature point to several recurring themes that are salient in the present corpus of women's life histories. Among them, one can count the dialectic view of the Holocaust as part of the known and therefore expected Jewish fate, another *hurban* (Destruc-tion) in a long chain of anti-Semitic events, on the one hand, and the Holocaust as a unique event, incomparable to any past Destruction, on the other. Alan Mintz and David G. Roskies tend to anchor Holocaust literature in a tradition of response to *hurban*, while Sidra de Koven-Ezrahi makes a distinction between communal memorial literature, which partakes of this tradition, and personal literature, which largely does not.[18] In contrast to these scholars, Lawrence Langer objects to clinging to the *hurban* tradition or paradigm, which he views as an obsolete terminology of martyrdom and redemption.[19] He argues that in previous Destruction events, Jews had choices: they could die for their religion and faith, thus sanctifying the name of God (*mavet al kiddush Ha'shem*), or they could convert, escape, or be expelled. But the Holocaust Jews were given no choice. Furthermore, even second- or third-generation converts, who did not consider themselves Jews at all, had no control whatsoever over the religious affiliation imposed on them and their ensuing fate.

Writers and critics pay special attention to the very language in which the Holocaust experience is transmitted. Langer discusses the loss of meaning of such otherwise everyday words as *hunger, cold, respect,* and *love,* while de Koven-Ezrahi discusses the assigning of special meaning to words such as *capo, selection, appell, smoke, deportation, cattle car,* and of course Holocaust or Shoah.[20] Beyond the language difficulties, there is the problem of relating to the Holocaust in cultural terms and thus integrating it into culture. In this context, some thinkers object to what they view as the "esthetization of the Holocaust" and prefer a writing style that is devoid of literary intentions and close to documentary or journalistic style.[21] Beyond this, one should point out the very difficulty of any communication concerning the Holocaust between survivors and their interlocutors. This is a major reason for the phenomenon, cited by Barbara Foley, of the preoccupation of Holocaust literature with difficulties of understanding by the survivors themselves even at the time of the events, not to mention afterward.[22]

As for the interlocutors, they face difficulties viewing events out of their own time, place, and fixed world, and the moral judgment that derives from them all. Thus, behind the language problem lurks the difficulty of the human consciousness to grasp and imagine the inhumanity of Auschwitz or Bergen-Belsen and then continue with normal everyday life as if such "planets" never existed. In addition, there is a derivative difficulty in telling about all of this to audiences who never even remotely experienced any of those "planets." In both the following chapters I pay special attention to inevitable barriers in the communication between the Holocaust survivors telling me their life histories and myself as part of the post-Holocaust era. Sometimes, the gaps between us are historical or cultural, deriving from our different backgrounds; at other times, we do not share the same codes regarding the Holocaust and its aftermath the way they were experienced personally, as opposed to the way they are described in history books. At still other times, we actually argue or bargain about disclosing specific information or incidents and their meanings to both parties.

In both these chapters, there are also instances of things untold that still call for human attention and analytical energy from the audience listening to the survivors or reading their accounts. Such are Rozsi Háger's remarks about things that cannot be transmitted as soon as she raises these issues, Aranka Friedmann's frequent requests to stop taping and let her regain her composure, the messages the mother Irma Fischer and her daughter Zsuzsa (Zsuzsánna) Faludi exchanged "over my head," and GZ's almost entire life history (as opposed to her mother's story, on which she dwells at length) in the second, psychoanalytical, chapter. Just as untold and still in need of interpretation are Rachel Markowitz's insinuation that Polish Jewish camp inmates had their own ways of getting extra food and better conditions in general, and their own reasons for maintaining their appearance; the refusals of both husbands in this work to go into details concerning their own suffering in the Labor Service or the loss of their families; and the entire "You Ask Me" section at the very ending of the third, phenomenological, chapter, which is an attempt to make me invoke the narrators to tell things they left out of their original succinct accounts told just beforehand.

What seems like an immediate solution to this problem, not to tell at all and let the events and memories sink into oblivion, is unacceptable even to those survivors who have a hard time relating (to) their own experiences and who have perhaps given up the attempt altogether. Even the most reticent among the survivors I interviewed agreed that the need to tell and commemorate is greater and more significant than their difficulty in expressing themselves. Therefore, it may well be that for these modest narrators, telling partial accounts is a way of compromise between the urge to talk and the compulsion to remain silent. As a result of the conflict between these two forces, often the narratives of such narrators, as will be shown in chapter 3 in terms of reader-listener response, are minimal or concise, yet hinting that there is more to them than meets the eye. At times, these narratives may also seem indecisive in terms of closure or moral judgment, to the point of suggesting that such decisions are beyond the narrators' capacities and are therefore left for their interlocutor or other audiences to deal with. In such situations, I found Shoshana Felman's and Dori Laub's use of the term "responsibility" helpful, although it still needed moderation in order to meet the specific needs of oral literary analysis of survivors' narratives.[23] For example, in addition to taking into account and explicating theme and content considerations, I also had to consider such linguistic aspects as language switches and intonation changes, as well as metalinguistic phenomena such as pitch, sobbing, or temporary inability to go on talking.

In *Holocaust Testimonies: The Ruins of Memory,* an analysis of Holocaust testimonies recorded at the Fortunoff Video Archives of Holocaust Testimonies at Yale University, Lawrence Langer deals at length with the conflict between the will and the inability to tell, or the inevitable "failure" of Holocaust narrators.[24] In the introduction to *Holocaust Testimonies,* Langer gives expression to the notion that the people telling about their lives during the Holocaust have in fact depleted their mental resources, so that only little is left for the future.[25] This claim serves to explain the tension between the sense of despair the interviewees feel and the way they are perceived by those in their everyday lives, in which they are surrounded by relatives, and especially offspring, who tend to stress the strength and durability of their parents or grandparents.

Langer's conclusion concerning this tension is that the Holocaust has created not one truth but many truths. In the life histories in my work, too, a sense of anticlimax is evident in the post-Holocaust period in the narratives. This sense is expressed by the brevity or shallowness of the text devoted to the longest and most stable period in the lives of the narrators. In the narratives analyzed in Langer's book as well, there is a weariness both in scope and in the attitude of narrators to their narratives. Weariness derives from, among other sources, the very act of telling, the revival of painful events and memories, and the need to supply explanations and even apologies, all in front of an excited and curious interlocutor.

Comparing the oral narratives with written ones, sometimes from the same narrator, Langer shows that the written narratives obey laws of order and literary principles in relating the events, while the video versions are characterized by disorder, lack of planning, immediacy, and directness. The adherence to literary principles is also expressed in the movement toward release and catharsis. Catharsis also derives from the very expression of things and their perpetuation in writing, yet, until this much-desired release, the stories fluctuate sharply between hope and despair. The oral narratives and narrators, on the other hand, are doomed to obsessive repetition of the imprisonment in the world of the camps. Release as a result of telling, as opposed to writing, remains unattainable for them.[26] Langer does not provide an explanation for this difference, but he gives the impression that the written story is a product that symbolically takes on the suffering of its creator, whereas in the case of oral narrative, the words remain in the air, as it were, with no possibility of symbolic containment. This perception seems to be negated by the observation that when formal interviews are carried out and recorded by academic or documentary institutions, the effect of the interview is close to that of a book. Yet even then, the interviewee or narrator experiences difficulty in dealing with the things told, and in the absence of a book—a tangible object—the narrator himself or herself remains the object of his or her suffering and is doomed to repetitious attempts to unload this burden. This might be the reason for the narrators' tendency to arouse strong emotions, even if by way of suppressed and seemingly neutral stories. This might also be the reason for the flourishing of written Holocaust memoirs in recent years.

In my own encounters with survivors, I often felt that just as I found them to be a kind of surrogate parents, the transmitters of narratives my own parents had spared me, so did they find me to be a willing listener replacing their own offspring whom they themselves had discouraged from developing interest in their Holocaust experience. Often, as will be shown in both chapters 2 and 3, the narrators relate their communication breakdown with their children around the Holocaust issue. This may be the result of the "melting pot (*Kur Hituch*)" and "Diaspora negation (*Shlilat Ha'Gola*)" trends that reigned in Israel in the fifties and sixties, or the Hungarian Communist prohibition, in effect until the beginning of the 1990s, of even mentioning anti-Semitism, let alone discussing the Holocaust and Hungarian Jews as its victims. But beyond political and ideological impositions or barriers, narrators simply preferred not to be exposed in front of their children in their utter weakness and helplessness. Or, as explained by a narrator in one of my later projects: "I didn't want to tell them. I wanted to raise normal children, like other people. Once they grew up, they weren't interested in hearing anymore."[27] Interestingly, time seems to have helped in making present-day survivors more willing to talk to both their families—albeit more often to their grandchildren than to their children—and wider audiences in memorial events, sites, and journeys. In addition to these general communication terms between survivors and listeners, our common Hungarian Jewish origins offered us a mutual familiarity with a common set of language (in its broadest meaning, including body language, for example), custom, history, and the need to fill in a void.

Needless to say, that empathy and eagerness to make our shared enterprise work and be known and appreciated by wide audiences are also
part of our implicit "contract."

Historical and Cultural Background of
Hungarian Jews in the Holocaust and Afterward

The narrators of the present work were all born in the last years of the
Austro-Hungarian Empire or shortly thereafter. After World War I, some
of them became citizens of neighboring countries such as Rumania,
Czechoslovakia, and Yugoslavia. Under Nazi occupation, some of these
areas were returned to Hungary and then back again to the neighboring
countries at the end of the war.[28] In spite of all these changes, many
Hungarian Jews retain their loyalty to Hungarian culture and language to
this very day, despite all the tribulations they endured in the Holocaust.[29]
In this regard, they are similar to the Jews of Germany in previous
decades, but unlike those of Russia and Poland, for example, who generally felt more alienated from their country's national identity.

From the time of the emancipation in the 1860s, Hungarian Jews
were divided into three communities according to their degree of religious adherence: Orthodox, Status Quo, and Neologist.[30] However, all
three groups viewed themselves as loyal to the Hungarian nation, and
many Jews of all persuasions took part in World War I, thus sharing the
defeat and humiliation at the rending of the empire. Ironically, this
national identification, with its physical signs in the form of medals and
injuries or handicaps, did not help these Jews later on, when the memory of defeat only augmented xenophobic and anti-Semitic sentiments
among non-Jewish conservative and right-wing Hungarian circles.

The fate of Hungarian Jews differed from that of their brethren in
other countries under German occupation because of the following
factors: Hungary's initial alliance with the Axis powers; the shortness
and intensity of the period defined as "Holocaust" for Hungarian Jews;
and the lack of a strong or effective Jewish leadership before and during
the Holocaust. Since these factors are interrelated, I will discuss them all
together.[31]

Hungary's initial alliance with the Axis put the Jews of Hungary and
its annexed territories in a delicate situation. On the one hand, the
Hungarian regime adopted Nazi doctrine as a necessary requirement for
belonging to the Axis, thus regaining the territories lost in World War I,
and also because it adequately expressed the atmosphere in the country at

the time. On the other hand, there were liberal and humanistic circles in the country that objected to the anti-Semitic policy. Until the German occupation in March 1944, rich and powerful Jews were themselves involved in these circles. But with the occupation, the liberal and influential Jews became powerless. Moreover, these influential Jews were then subjected to the same fate as the Jews in the rest of the country as well as the Jews of other occupied countries. It is true that Hungarian Jews witnessed an erosion of their status during the early years of the war, but their being earmarked for extermination so close to Germany's final defeat was still a shock. Because many Jews did not grasp the irrevocability of Germany's intentions even at this late date of March 1944, or the degree of Hungarian identification and cooperation with the Nazis, they failed to respond to the dangers inherent in their new situation.

Hungarian Jewry lacked a powerful leadership, perhaps owing to their strong identification with the Hungarian state even before the war; thus, when a real need for it rose, its absence was glaring. There is no indication that the Jews had a clear policy toward Hungarian and German authorities throughout the occupation period, except for attempts to come to terms with the new and constant demands that confronted them. Likewise, there was hardly any rebellion or abandonment of the basic sense of loyalty to the old regime that now forsook its Jews. There was some underground activity carried out by Jewish youth movement activists, who hid refugees coming from the east, manufactured forged documents for them, and smuggled them out of the country.[32] However, the total activity of the underground was small in relation to the number of the country's Jews, and what they did was often more criticized than appreciated by their fellow Jews, who still did not accept ways of coping that were different from those they were used to.

As a rule, Hungarian Jews preferred to cooperate with the authorities, be they Hungarian or Nazi-German, hoping that dignity, decency, productivity, and contribution to the war effort would improve the attitude toward them and eventually rescue them. Therefore, as a result, and owing as well to the brevity of the period of ghettoization in Hungary, there were no rebellions in the Hungarian ghettos, largely very little underground activity, and only minimal participation in the ranks of the partisans on the part of Jewish men serving in the labor battalions or service. The principal method for rescuing Jews before the deportations eastward was entreating the authorities and paying bribes or ransom when possible. It is well known that criticism and condemnation of such activities continued long after the events themselves. The Kásztner affair, and its echoes years afterward, serves as a prime example of the problematics of this method of soul-saving.[33] From a different angle, the pain caused by the criticism and countercriticism of Orthodox leaders, who escaped by themselves and deserted their communities while promising them salvation, also remains poignant and has continued to the present day for those who were involved.

The ghettos constructed in the provincial towns, that is, in cities and towns except Budapest, were soon decimated and their residents deported to Auschwitz. There, they went through the process known as "selection," in which small children with their mothers, the elderly, sick, and all those who did not seem fit for hard physical labor were sent to their death in gas chambers and then cremated. The remaining prisoners stayed in Auschwitz-Birkenau or were removed to work camps and factories all over the German-occupied territories, where the goal was to use them until they were completely exhausted and then exterminate them. The majority of camp inmates or prisoners did not survive imprisonment and perished of disease, cold, famine, or torture. However, most of Budapest's Jewish residents—around 100,000 people at that time—did survive thanks to the relatively early liberation or occupation of the city by the Red Army in January 1945. Until then, the Budapest Jews lived in its ghetto or in hiding, under Christian identity, or with ad hoc certificates supplied to them by foreign embassies and the Red Cross. At the war's end, out of about 800,000 Hungarian Jews (including those living in the areas ceded to Hungary in the war) almost 600,000 were murdered.[34]

After the war, the survivors, among them the narrators in this study, started a new life. Six of the narrators went back to live in Hungary or in those parts of it that now belonged to Rumania. The remaining nine emigrated to Israel immediately after the war or within a few years. All of them had new families. Some studied and all worked until retirement, at which time they told me their life histories. From this point in time, they bestride two different social and cultural frameworks as they view their past and relate it. The Israeli narrators include in their stories their exposure to Zionism, mostly after the Holocaust, and the change in their lives caused by their emigration to Israel. In contrast, the narrators still living in Hungary had no choice but to start a new life in the same place and within the same cultural framework that had abandoned and rejected them in the near past. In general, their narratives are more suppressed, implicit, and pessimistic, or less liberated and cathartic, to use Langer's terminology discussed previously. This may be due to the atmosphere of uncertainty in many East European countries around 1991, the time of the interviews with Hungarian Jews, and shortly after the collapse of the Communist regime in their country. In retrospect it turns out that the freedom to talk subjectively about World War II and the Holocaust became the privilege of other groups and circles as well, including neofascist ones. So the Jews were not all that mistaken in being cautious about manifesting their newly found identity as Jews and Holocaust survivors. As will be shown especially in the second chapter, Hungarian Jewish Holocaust survivors are well versed in repressive and totalitarian systems in ways that affect their narratives and determine their content, message, and tone, thus making them clearly discernable from those of their Israeli brethren.

Surviving Survival:
Characteristics of the Holocaust-Dominated Life History

In addition to the historical and cultural context, it is also important to consider the literary and discursive context of all these Holocaust life histories, Israeli and Hungarian alike.[35] The folklorists Barbara Kirshenblatt-Gimblett and Vilmos Voigt claim in their different works that powerful events create a flood of life histories and personal narratives.[36] Their assumption is that once people are past the harsh experience, they realize their need to tell and share their histories of the bad times that have just ended. However, most of the informants in my work contradicted this assumption and reported that until recently, almost fifty years after the events, they had never told their life histories to anyone, not even their children, for the reasons mentioned before in this chapter. Some of the narrators reported that only recently, in the Holocaust Memorial Day ceremonies held in the schools where their grandchildren study, did they tell *some of* what they had gone through during the Holocaust. It should be noted, though, that the silence of the survivors was mainly vis-à-vis the younger generation. When the survivors interacted in their own circles, in family or social gatherings, they could hardly avoid bringing up the memory of the Holocaust and stories of their experiences at the time.

This discrepancy between theory and reality can be explained by the difference between the nature of the experience of immigration referred to by Kirshenblatt-Gimblett and Voigt, and that of the Holocaust. There is no doubt that immigration, as difficult and painful as it may be, is not really comparable to living through the Holocaust, the enforced population movements of which could hardly be characterized as emigration or immigration. In addition, immigrants undertake the experience of their own accord (albeit with some degree of outside pressure) and with an awareness of the possibility of hardships. In contrast, the Holocaust survivors did not choose their fate and knew little about their future, and most of their experiences were sunk in their memory as traumatic, as will be further explicated in the second chapter.[37] This means that defense mechanisms and ways of managing and processing feelings work differently for them than for the immigrants in the works of Kirshenblatt-Gimblett and Voigt, although many of the survivors also became immigrants (even if some only for a limited period, as happens to GZ and her mother, as described in chapter 2).

It is important to mention that immigrants to the West often settled in communities consisting of previous immigrants, who were more open and understanding to the newcomers than the population in general. In contrast, the survivors who arrived in Israel in its early and highly ideological years were expected to merge with Israeli society, not necessarily among survivors or people of the same background or diaspora as themselves. Generally, until the Eichmann trial at the beginning of the 1960s, there was almost no public forum in Israel for Holocaust survivors to express their experiences and feelings about the Holocaust and their life following it.[38] The cultural atmosphere in those years encouraged repression of the Holocaust memory rather than its expression and emphasized the generalized Israeli experience and identity instead of highlighting those of various ethnic and Diaspora groups.

As a result, only rarely did works by or about survivors gain the attention of the Israeli public.[39] Very little was published in the fields of oral narrative, poetry, proverbs, and other oral literary genres, and there was little research in these areas. This situation persisted in spite of the fact that Holocaust memoirs and communal memorial books had been written and published since right after the Holocaust. One of the explanations for this may be that the field of oral literature research itself, as part of the study of folklore, was not considered serious or significant enough to deal with such weighty material. Conversely, history, with its adjacent documentary projects, and, to a lesser extent, the study of written literature, were seen as more appropriate for dealing with the Holocaust. Until recently, then, folkloristics did not develop research tools or a methodology to deal with these contemporary and at the same time postmodern materials.

It was only in the 1970s and 1980s that this situation started to change. Public interest became focused on "roots" and the uniqueness of Israel's different ethnic and diaspora groups. This process, in turn, brought home the realization that the survivors' pain did not disappear in spite (if not because) of repression but lingered and was even passed on to future generations. Finally, there was a renewed interest in Holocaust survivors and their offspring. This was also a time when additional fields, such as sociology and psychology, began to take an interest in the Holocaust as a social and cultural phenomenon. This birth or renewal of interest is the result of several factors, the most relevant of which is the realization that the Holocaust generation is soon to vanish and that their story or stories are of immense and critical value. To this one might add the increasing scholarly tendency toward interdisciplinarity as well as the recent favoring of ordinary people and the anonymous voice in the social sciences and humanities as well as in the arts and media.

Thus, Israeli Holocaust survivors such as the present narrators went through a period of silence after which their bonds of muteness were broken and their stories became part of Israeli and world Holocaust awareness and its oral lore. However, unlike the Israeli survivors, the survivors still living in Hungary continued living in silence and repression, except for the interviews conducted for the present work, and perhaps afterward. The reasons for the ongoing repression of the Hungarians are related to the political situation in their country and its ensuing cultural atmosphere, as has been explained. In addition, the survivors living in Hungary realize that there was and is a gaping abyss between themselves and their fellow citizens, who were and are indifferent at best and hostile at worst to Holocaust stories. At any rate, the postwar Hungarian public was busy with its own hardships.[40] Therefore, most survivors tended to suppress their wartime memories for years, as well as other aspects of their Jewishness, such as learning about Judaism, observing its dictates and customs, and exhibiting awareness of the existence of the State of Israel. In all these matters, the Hungarian Jews still maintain the same state of mind as before the war (with pride in Israel replacing Zionist awareness in the later period). While recording their life histories in the summer of 1991, I met Jews who expressed awesome joy and pride at the very existence of the Jewish State, as if this was a new revelation and not a fact of more than forty years standing. Only later did I realize that for these people, it was not the knowledge of Israel's existence that was new, but their right and ability to express satisfaction about it, which meant attaining and manifesting some form of self-definition and independence as Jews in Hungary.

In my doctoral thesis I examined, among other issues, the components of the life histories centering on the Holocaust, and especially the
relationship between these three main time periods: before the Holocaust, the Holocaust itself, and after the Holocaust. Biographically, the
first period includes the childhood, youth, and in a few cases the early
maturity of the narrators. The Holocaust period in the case of most
Hungarian Jews refers to the year between the German invasion to
Hungary in the spring of 1944 and the ending of the war in May 1945,
whereas for the Budapest Jews this period is shortened by half, as has
been explained earlier in the historical background section. The period
after the war had lasted for almost fifty years at the time of the interviews.

Nonetheless, in literary-psychological terms, as opposed to historical-
biographical ones, the single or even the half year of the Holocaust period
assumes a central or pivotal role in the life history as a whole in terms of
breadth, volume, detail, depth, and affect. In fact, when compared to the
short Holocaust period, the subsequent stages of the survivors' lives read
much like dry reports made up of names and dates, despite the fact that it
was during the post-Holocaust era that the survivors experienced the
more positive and constructive experiences of their lives. Likewise, they
might make anticlimactic remarks concerning their inability to feel joy in
their present life on account of their past experiences.[41] Furthermore, the
Holocaust "seeps through" into the periods before and after it, in the
form of insights concerning anti-Semitism on the eve of the Holocaust,
which the narrators now view as the beginning of the process that
reached its peak in the Holocaust. This model of attributing centrality to
the Holocaust and skimming over the other periods in life turned out to
be dominant in many of the life histories I recorded from women and
men alike.

Yet, in the life histories of the female narrators that are presented
and analyzed in the present work, there are interesting and intriguing
variations on this prevalent model in terms of the biographical and
literary relations between the three main periods in the lives of the
narrators. In the next chapter, which deals with the discourse of mothers
and daughters and its analysis according to literary-psychoanalytical
principles, the narrators tend to skim through the pre-Holocaust period
in their lives and dwell more on their Holocaust experience. Yet, the
post-Holocaust period receives just as much attention and development
as that of the Holocaust, as it is often conceived as no less excruciating
and demanding. In the third chapter, which deals with phenomenology,
or the response to the Holocaust on the part of both narrators and their

listeners or readers, the post-Holocaust life acquires even additional significance. Moreover, in some of the life histories in that chapter, the Holocaust may "disappear" from the narrative, or become a "darker text" lurking behind the "main text" and aspiring to eventually create a (or *the*) "valid text," to use Langer's more recent terminology.[42] Thus, they form significant or signifying stories for the narrators, albeit less coherent and tolerable for their listeners. At any rate, in the parts of these narratives that deal with post-Holocaust life, there are recurrent references, with varying degrees of explicitness, to the Holocaust and its negative imprint on the lives of the narrators ever after.

The language of recounting, as far as the Israeli narrators are concerned, is characterized by a paradoxical combination of lack of language and a multitude of languages, or muteness and verbosity at the same time. Owing to a variety of reasons, most of which have to do with the culture of immigration and immigrants in Israel to this very day, most of the Israeli narrators never attained full competence and fluency in Hebrew, although they had been living in Israel for most of their lives at the time of the interview. Therefore, some of them chose to tell their life histories in Hungarian, while others occasionally inserted Hungarian words or sentences into their Hebrew accounts. Also, as shown in the third chapter, many of the narrators insert words, idioms, sentences, and other language units from other European languages such as German, Yiddish, Rumanian, and French. This is often the result of having lived in areas that changed regimes between and during the two world wars. But it is also a unique trait of people who experienced the Holocaust, which often entailed forced exposure to or deportations across barriers of language and culture.

The result of all these is a paradoxical discourse that can be viewed as both all-encompassing and minimalist. It is comprehensive in its ties with a multitude of languages, idioms, and cultures. At the same time, it is a minimalist discourse, because many of the narrators were restricted by inevitable awkwardness in their use (or abuse) of Hebrew and thus had recourse only to a very basic and inarticulate manner of expression. Therefore, their language tends to be nonstandard in terms of discerning between tenses, pronouns, and genders, and unsophisticated in its scarcity of subordinate phrases. It should be pointed out that although the narrators were given the choice of telling their life histories in Hungarian, about half chose not to do so, despite the difficulties they encountered by communicating in Hebrew.

Notwithstanding all this, the seemingly meager language of the narrators, which is far from resembling the written discourse of Holocaust survivors whose stories were professionally edited, does not testify to poverty or shallowness of affect and certainly not of meaning and message. On the contrary, more often than not, the magnitude of the events related comes through despite all hindrances, and at times because of them, as will be demonstrated especially in the "You Ask Me" section of the third chapter. This kind of discourse with all its defects creates and transmits a sense of authenticity that has been lost from many of its written and edited equivalents.

From the point of view of research and methodology, the study of folklore—in contrast to its past image as too naive to deal with reality's hardships—has developed in the last few decades the research of the genre of personal narrative, which is strongly related to history and its study as well as to psychology and sociology.[43] Moreover, contemporary literary folkloristic methodology attributes great significance to authentic discourse, the precise recording of which includes "mistakes," thus enabling close attention to lingual and metalingual phenomena.[44] Only unprocessed discourse can yield valid analysis and response to both what exists and what is absent from it, starting with signs of hesitation and fragmentation, moving through imagery, and ending with explicit statements or "ideological discourse" of different sorts.

In addition, the study of folk narrative attributes no smaller significance to aspects of similarity and difference in relation to what is termed "the unity of misery," as expressed by many Holocaust survivors.[45] Despite the similarities of the narratives, many of them both create and preserve their unique characters and characteristics. To give expression to this uniqueness, the present work maintains a dual perspective. Chapters 2 and 3 are the fruit of research, analysis, and interpretation of fifteen of the life histories recorded in my doctoral thesis. They constitute a response and heuristic discourse inspired by the life histories, while attempting to reach some understanding of them. This discourse quotes and includes parts of the narratives. However, in order to establish, as directly as possible, a link to the narrators behind the life histories, the fifteen life histories are presented in their entirety in the appendix of this work, following their order of appearance in the analytical chapters.[46] Thus, different readers may approach these narratives from a variety of perspectives: academic, critical, experiential, or combinations of these and other stances.

With the same purpose in mind, of meeting the needs and interests of various readers of this work, the index is exceptionally detailed. Within the conventional categories of names, places, terms, and languages/identities, it also includes many items related to the life experiences of camp survivors, such as food, body ailments, the unique experiences of women in the Holocaust, the history of Hungarian Jewry, and the experience of new immigrants to the young state of Israel.

And last, throughout this work I use the term *life history,* which has become less popular in the last two decades compared with newer terms such as *life story, life narrative,* and *personal history.* All these newer terms express growing consciousness of the extent to which the lives in question are stories, narratives, texts, or constructs. Although I too acknowledge the necessary artfulness or contrivance of these creations, I still prefer the term *life history,* because it keeps alive the ties between history and story that are especially indispensable for the present subject matter. In addition, this term keeps more of a balance between the individual and the masses that he or she is part of and inevitably represents, and that, too, is an important part of the present project.

2

Mother-Daughter Discourse

A Literary-Psychoanalytical Analysis of Five Life Histories

> Angels on high, seventy pounds each angel
> She is there too, but what is her face;
> Just a block of fire, six million
> Identical lights that block her face.
>
> Magda Székely, "Mártir"

The five life histories to be analyzed in this chapter are unique in the importance they place on life *after* the Holocaust—that is, on the hardships encountered by these women survivors in rebuilding their lives in the void and emptiness left by the Holocaust. The post-Holocaust period in these narratives is fraught with struggles and difficulties that are viewed by the narrators as being just as arduous and significant as their experiences during the Holocaust. There are several possible explanations for this shift. One is the historical or "objective" explanation: of the five narrators in this chapter, three never left the borders of Budapest and were spared the horrors of Auschwitz. The remaining two narrators did undergo the horrors of the concentration camp but chose, nevertheless, not to dwell on the period they endured in the various work and death camps in any detail, although some of their scarce descriptions of this period are still very telling, as will be shown in this chapter.

It is important to add that the post-Holocaust period was difficult and even desperate for these narrators, who all remained in Hungary or Rumania, behind the "iron curtain" in the postwar years. Four of them remained there permanently, while the fifth, Rozsi Háger, immigrated, or made aliya, to Israel in the early 1960s. But Rozsi too describes the postwar period as being grueling, particularly in the first months when the way home itself involved many dangers, especially for women and Jews. These tribulations lend the period an Odyssean flavor, as these survivors attempt to turn the clock backward and rehabilitate their former lives, while gradually coming to terms with the impossibility of achieving this goal to the extent that they hoped.

The literary-psychoanalytical analysis in this chapter is based on the fact that the five narrators—Rozsi Háger, Aranka Friedmann, Irma Fischer,[1] Zsuzsa Faludi, and GZ (the last narrator prefers to remain anonymous)—all present in their life histories variations of mother-daughter discourse and relations. Háger and Friedmann, the first two narrators, assume a childlike or childish voice, in ways that will be explained later on. In addition, Aranka Friedmann is my father's sister and the only living representative of the previous generation in my extended family who is still in touch with me. Therefore, the discussion between us is an intergenerational family dialogue, even if it is not a mother-daughter dialogue.[2] The third and fourth narrators, Irma Fischer and Zsuzsa Faludi, are a mother and her grown daughter; the latter was a child of about eight during the Holocaust. The fifth and last narrator, GZ, experienced the Holocaust as a nine-year-old child who was protected and saved by her mother. As a result, her story is much more the story of her mother, who is no longer alive today, than her own life history. Thus, all five narratives and/or narrative characters present their stories either as mothers or daughters, and often refer to each other (mothers to daughters and vice versa).

Principles of the Psychoanalytic Textual Analysis of the Life Histories

The present literary-psychoanalytic analysis of the mother-daughter discourse presupposes a number of underlying premises that apply to psychoanalytic principles of literary analysis in general, folk narrative, or oral literature, and Holocaust testimonies or memoirs, in particular. Although there have been many changes in the relationship of psycho-analytic literary criticism vis-à-vis psychoanalysis since this criticism sprung up in the 1950s, the underlying assumption of the literary-psychoanalytic approach is still that, just like behavior and language, artistic expression is but the seen surface over deeper layers that cannot be exposed directly, because they include forbidden or unacceptable parts. Although it would seem that art itself is a refined expression of the forbidden or the unacceptable, in fact, because the work of art is a cultural product that has to be accepted as such, it necessarily involves hiding or camouflaging; hence its ties with artifact and artificiality. Therefore, just like behavior and speech, art is also greatly determined by unconscious forces.[3] To unearth these forces, psychoanalytic narrative analysis locates the hidden areas or issues as well as explains the motivation and manner of hiding.

Concerning the ties between folkloric expression as a unique artistic form and psychoanalysis, the psychoanalyst Ernest Jones claims that there are many parallels between folkloric phenomena and the mental processes that are explored by psychoanalysis, since there are essential analogies between ontogenetic development, of the individual, and phylogenetic development, of the human race.[4] Psychoanalysis studies the former (ontogenetics), while folklore contains aspects and remnants of the latter (phylogenetics). Therefore, psychoanalysis has much to gain from studying folkloric phenomena, as does Bruno Bettelheim with fairy tales.[5] It follows that folklore research is enriched when it adopts, in the appropriate cases, some of the principles and methods of psychoanalysis, as does the folklorist Alan Dundes in much of his work.[6] Both the psychotherapist studying literary-folkloric phenomena and the folklorist employing psychoanalytic tools deal with narratives or texts; both pay special attention to the covert or implied parts or aspects of the text; both account for the motivation and manner of covering or implying, or what we call defense mechanisms in psychoanalytic jargon; and both deal at length with the cultural implications of the phenomena they study.

In the five life histories presented in this chapter, the main literary-psychoanalytical issues are the stages of childhood or early maturity in— or in the shadow of—the Holocaust, the narrators' relations with their mothers or with the idea of mother they carry with them, and taboo or unacceptable issues concerning both their family or other relations and the Holocaust.[7] The mother-daughter relationship has three versions or variations here: (1) relations between real mothers and daughters (Irma Fischer and Zsuzsa Faludi); (2) relations between the mother or grown woman to the child within her (Rozsi Háger and Aranka Friedmann); and (3) relations between the daughter to the mother-figure she carries with her (Rozsi Háger, Zsuzsa Faludi, and GZ). To complete the family picture, relations with fathers are scarce to absent in these five life histories, for a variety of reasons that will be explored in the analyses, whereas other relationships are mostly in the background compared to those of mothers and daughters.

Concerning these mothers and daughters, as has been stated, some of their life histories share a "childlike" quality and can be described as unfocused and disorganized. In that, they tend toward the dream and other parapraxes and may be analyzed along lines parallel to those of such phenomena in psychoanalysis. Interestingly, these are not the narratives of those survivor-narrators who were children in the Holocaust (Zsuzsa Faludi and GZ) but rather of those who were in their early twenties at that time (Rozsi Háger and Aranka Friedmann). Their syntax tends more to coordinate than to subordinate structures, and at times to isolated phrases and words such as "my 'good' life," "who would imagine," "imagine," and "a tragedy." Likewise, their metalanguage may contain long intervals, sobs, requests to stop taping, or retreats to small talk. Often, the narratives are governed by a dynamics of free association leading the narrator from one scene or issue to the next, thus making the listener figure out the combining thread or principle. Accordingly, they contain many inner contradictions and can therefore be ascribed to Sigmund Freud's view of opposites or polarities. Freud held that seeming contradictions are in fact associated with each other and, paradoxically, are not really antithetical. We can point to many such contradictions in the present life histories: between idyllic childhood and painful maturity, between activity and passivity, between health and sickness, between movement and paralysis, between "good" and "bad" Jews in the Holocaust setting, between various versions of the same events as told by different narrators, and between inclusion of emotionally charged events and their partial or entire exclusion from the life histories.

The act of making meaning or of allowing the listener of the life histories to make out their meaning brings to the fore the significance of the role of "audience"—the one who hears, reads, experiences, and interprets the narratives. One of the focuses of literary psychoanalytic analysis is the measure of involvement of this audience—therapist, listener, reader, or researcher—in the phenomenon they are faced with. Their relationship is in fact part of a chain of parallelisms and analogies that typify literary psychoanalytic analysis, such as the dream and the artistic work or text, the creative process and psychoanalytic analysis, the patient and the therapist, the author and the reader or literary critic, and the text itself and the literary criticism written in its wake.[8] Whatever or whoever serves as the components or participants in these pairs, the principle of reflexivity or reciprocity connects to the essence of contemporary psychoanalytic "activity"—to borrow Roland Barthes' term describing the structural analysis of texts.[9] In addition, in the case of Holocaust narrative or testimony, which by now has a cultural status of its own, we may add the pair of the critical text and the response it evokes in its readers or the public, which may include the survivor-narrators who originated the initial narrative. This is a major point of difference compared to so-called traditional psycho- or literary analysis, which originally paid little to no attention to historical process or social context beyond acknowledging them as remote background to psychic phenomena. The Holocaust, like other mass traumatic events and processes of the twentieth century, has been significant to our understanding of survivors' symptoms and management of their curing process, as shown by Judith Lewis Herman in her study of trauma.[10] Moreover, Herman claims that the borderline between Freud's analytic method and those of mass or historical trauma researchers is located exactly at the point at which he was too alarmed and therefore reluctant to acknowledge the factual components of his patients' fantasies.[11]

Reflexivity may at times imply a kind of threat for readers, researchers, and the research establishment as a whole. These groups do not usually tend to relate specifically to their personal involvement in the text, as is evidenced by the most common form of expression—the first person plural—they use to describe their activity of literary textual analysis. In fact, Freud, the founder of psychoanalysis, initially put himself outside the healing and analytical process of his patients in that he did not relate in depth to his own pathology when he mentioned events from his own life, such as dreams or family scenes he was witness to.[12] This means that, historically speaking, psychoanalysis is not a reflexivist activity from its inception, but became so as it developed.[13] At present, and in other fields such as anthropology and folklore, too, reflexivity does not present a difficulty to contemporary scholars, who understand and accept the need to clarify their link to the issues and people that they examine, to the point of making this issue a main focus of their work. This approach appears, for example, in Robert Georges and Michael O. Jones's book *People Studying People*.[14] In addition, the relationship of the researcher and the researchee, and the form of communication between them, have themselves become an important research topic in the study of culture in the last few decades.[15] Therefore, present-day researchers include themselves—and the roles that they play in the narrations and narratives—within the domain of their analyses. My own analyses of the life histories in this work, too, include references to reflexivity and to the relationship between the narrators and myself, to our mutual expectations, as well as to the deeper layers of our communication. This is especially true for the life history of my aunt, Aranka Friedmann, or my deeper acquaintance with Zsuzsa Faludi. Therefore, my analyses also deal with the significance of the texts to me as audience, researcher, family and ethnic group member, and as an Israeli of the post-Holocaust generation, as described in the introduction.[16]

Regarding the narrators and their narratives, I adopt the following principles. First, my discussion attempts to process or "master" the texts only in as much as is necessary to understand their explicit and implicit meanings. In order to fulfill this goal, certain portions of the text are juxtaposed, compared, or cross-referenced. For example, I compare some of the narratives of Irma Fischer with those of her daughter Zsuzsa Faludi, or view them as parallel texts, especially regarding events that both experienced and mention both separately and together. This is done while bearing in mind that Zsuzsa Faludi was present during her mother's narration, but not vice versa. The purpose of this writerly reading is not to expose possible contradictions and inaccuracies, but instead to reveal the variations or different ways in which each of the narrators experienced, remembers, and described these events to me while bearing in mind the actual or psychological presence of her daughter/mother.[17] Second, I read these narrative portions, whether on their own or juxtaposed to others, as psychoanalytic texts such as dreams, free associations, slips of the tongue, and other such parapraxes. Within this reading, I pay special attention to outstanding linguistic, poetical, and cognitive phenomena, such as repetition, ellipsis, metaphor, metonym, and idiomatic or formulaic expression. Thus, I implement both Freud's fundamental view and Lacan's further elaboration concerning the centrality of language to psychoanalytic interpretation.[18]

Third and last, in the spirit of the parallels just described, I adopt the view of psychoanalysis as a form of healing in that it brings up the past to be analyzed and understood in terms of the present.[19] Another aspect of healing in these narrations and narratives involves bringing issues from the narrators' unconscious to their consciousness.[20] This aspect exists here only in an oblique or indirect manner, since this is an analysis of texts and not personalities. Still, we can assume that through narration, the narrators become more conscious of various aspects of their lives and stories, although they do not necessarily involve me in this process. Healing, then, is generally effected by the catharsis that at least some of the narrators attest to experiencing during the process of narration or as a result of it. In a more specific way, bringing up the past contains separate and unique significance for each of the narrators, although there are occasional similarities between them or their narratives. Healing, catharsis, or sharing are also part of the experience of the audience, who listens to the narrators or reads their narratives, shares their painful memories of the Holocaust, identifies with them, and eventually reaches a deeper understanding of their lives and the Holocaust.

The discussion of catharsis necessarily brings to the fore the pivotal term of *trauma* as a connecting issue or meeting point for axes between psychoanalysis and the Holocaust experience. Trauma is created as a result of an uncommonly negative experience that in many cases involves physical hurt or the threat of it. In fact, because of its weight, the event basically evades the person experiencing it and can only be grasped through reference to and treatment of its later results or symptoms, which are listed under the inclusive medical term of Post Traumatic Stress Disorder (PTSD), as coined by the American Psychoanalytic Association in 1980. These symptoms might include: psychic numbing, diminished capacity to feel, helplessness, depression, feelings of guilt, flashbacks, nightmares, and other repetitive phenomena.[21] It can be said that it is exactly the evanescent nature of the ties between these phenomena and their origin that attracts therapists, historians, philosophers, and literary scholars. These discuss memory and perception, or their absence or partial presence, in survivors' texts of all sorts, literary, memoirist, oral-testimonial, and therapeutic. It can also be argued, somewhat polemically, that scholarly discourse on trauma is inevitably touched by the kind of romantic fascination that is evident in Virginia Woolf's *Mrs. Dalloway* and similar turn-of-the-century and war literature, as well as in films about the Vietnam War and its effect on an entire generation.

Concerning the ties between the Holocaust and trauma, then, while it is clear that the Holocaust entailed tremendous suffering for large portions of many populations and especially those destined for destruction, it is less clear that trauma is necessarily the central term in relating to the ways in which the survivors experienced their suffering in real time and process or relate to it in retrospect. In fact, we should be careful about automatically attaching trauma scholarship to Holocaust studies and narratives exactly because: (1) trauma originally relates to psychic processes and patterns of individuals, whereas the Holocaust—just like other twentieth-century mass-violence events and settings that are often examined through the prism of trauma—engulfed masses, and (2) trauma is caused by abrupt and short-term terrible experiences, whereas the

Holocaust lasted for years and entailed many repetitions of atrocities that would each count as traumatic in their own right in normal situations. This last point connects to Laura S. Brown's claim against viewing trauma as *only* an event *outside of everyday life.* In her feminist view of trauma, such a definition is relevant only to white upper-middle-class males, whereas minorities, the working class, and women are dehumanized by this definition, as it rules out their everyday, secret, or insidious suffering.[22]

Brown's reservation concerning the uniqueness aspect of trauma holds good for the experience of Nazi camp interns and later survivors as well, for their suffering too lasted weeks, months, or years, and included many recurrent painful events that would each have counted as traumatic in their previous lives. However, in the camp setting, they overcame these—at least for the time being—in their overall effort to survive. In addition, they often saw their hurt reflected and repeated in the experience of others around them, which also helped to "normalize" the hurt and their perception of it, again, at least in real time. All this goes to show that in order to make the concept of trauma relevant to the Holocaust experience and its narratives, it needs to be redefined and broadened to include mass and long-term suffering. It must be admitted, though, that broadening in this direction changes significantly the original definition of trauma.

As for analyzing Holocaust narratives related to traumatic experiences, since the object for analysis here is not the souls of survivors but their narratives about events that took place decades ago, we have to acknowledge the degree to which these texts are "twice-removed" or remote from the experiences and their possible traumatic imprint. In other words, in the following analyses, trauma can only be traced speculatively and on the basis of literary phenomena that relate to the symptoms of PTSD such as numbness, amnesia, flashbacks, repetition, and guilt and their figurative, poetic, or generally symbolic representations in the narratives of the survivor narrators.[23]

In summary of this introductory section, I would like to point out that in addition to the relatively traditional literary-psychoanalytic approach I mentioned previously there are also more radical or ultramodern psychoanalytic approaches. These approaches are characterized by even greater self-awareness and exposure on the side of the researcher, greater preoccupation with language and its cultural components, and a more overt approach to sexuality and gender-related issues. In fact, French feminist-psychoanalytic critics, such as Luce Irigaray and Hélène Cixous, tend to deal in their works more with these theoretical issues than with literary and social ones.[24] However, my approach, which looks at the present female Holocaust survivor narrators as flesh and blood authors of their narratives beyond being imagined constructs or analytical units, will limit its reliance on these novel approaches, except for reflexivity and language issues, which I do endorse throughout this work. However, I make a point of paying special care and respect to sexual and other apparently bothering or problematic issues for the narrators. This topic will be further developed and explicated in my discussion of the life history of Rozsi Háger later in this chapter and will also apply to many of the other narrators in this entire work.

Rozsi Háger: Woman, Mother, Grandmother, and the Daughter Speaking through Them

The life history of Rozsi Háger (originally from Oradea, Rumania, resident of Hod Hasharon, Israel, at the time of narration) is characterized by a childish point of view or focus. This is expressed through, in addition to the linguistic aspects of this kind of narration already listed, the invariable dichotomy in her narrative between "good" and "bad," together with other significant oppositions. In addition, Rozsi's narrative is replete with formulaic folktale elements that are much more typical of traditional stories and serene settings than of Holocaust recollections. These two attributes are already evident in the first paragraph of her life history, which includes within it the period of her life that preceded the Holocaust and the deportations:

> When we were young, we had a very, very happy childhood. Not because of toys, which we didn't have, but because of the fresh air. The area was not built up yet, and all the kids from the neighborhood played outside, the poor just like the wealthy ones. From morning until evening we could play, and we had a happy and blissful childhood, until we had to go to school. The moment we started school the worries started; study, do your homework. And we could not play from morning to evening but had to go to school in the morning and do our homework in the afternoon. And so the time passed until there came the time when we had to learn a profession. Our home was warm and friendly although we did not have a big apartment. But in those days the parents were not greedy. They were happy if they had healthy children, and Mother was everything.

The expressions "a very, very happy childhood," "a happy and blissful childhood," "our home was warm and friendly," and "Mother was everything" serve as an introduction and backdrop to the events that occur later in the life of the narrator. The school years and the so-called worries of that period are but precursors to the following period in her life, for it was during the war years—the deportation to the concentration and work camps—and even the "rehabilitated" life afterward that innocence and happiness were irrevocably shattered. Thus, the happy childhood and all it involves are perceived as belonging to a past that is never to return and are therefore worthy of all the superlatives of bliss and perfection that the narrator attributes to it. In addition, since, as we shall soon see, she has trouble delineating the atrocities she lived through in later periods, the clinging to and dwelling on her earlier childhood is a compensation or an unconscious displacement mechanism through which she attenuates both the atrocities and her inability to speak of them.

But the narrator does not simply cling to the past in the elegiac *ubi sunt* tradition. She also uses the past as a sort of educational message that she addresses to me in the present, although it can be assumed that she has retold the same story many times, especially to her relatives, in particular her daughter and grandchildren, whom she mentions later on in her narrative. Her purpose here is to inculcate values of modesty and frugality, since happiness in her worldview is not dependent on or tied to economic prosperity. Her own childhood, for example, is happy not because of money or toys, which she evidently didn't have, but because of the carefree atmosphere in which she used to live. In addition, her parents were not "greedy" and did not have grasping materialistic ambitions, unlike other people that the narrator evidently knew or knows at present.

The intersection or meeting point between the children and parents in this idyllic description is expressed in the sentence: "and Mother was everything." It is the closeness to the mother and holding up of her deeds and personality as an example that are the epitome of the connection between children and their parents, or so it seems up to this point in the narrative. Accordingly, Rozsi Háger also views her own motherhood and fulfilling of the expectations of her offspring as the epitome of her aspirations. She sees this in contrast to present-day mothers, whom she feels are too busy fulfilling their own aspirations to care about their children's well-being and happiness and, ultimately, their own happiness. Rozsi does not mention her father at this point, and though she does at a later stage, it seems that her mother is the more dominant parent figure to her. This female dominance also appears later in the story, when Rozsi describes the way she courted her future husband immediately after the war, and incidentally, in all the other narratives in this chapter as well.

These two elements, the shattering of idyllic existence on the level of content, and the formulaic statements on the level of form, continue to dominate Rozsi's narrative. At times, the two converge. "When the Hungarians entered, everything changed."[25] Rozsi uses these words to open the second section of her story in which she describes the gradual deterioration in the status of Hungarian Jewry until their final deportation to Auschwitz in 1944. She dwells on the time period when the Jews from the provincial towns are forced into ghettoes. At this point their fate is in effect sealed, although most are not cognizant of this fact, as is evident in many personal recollections of the Holocaust. In Rozsi's narration, the lack of awareness as to the true severity of the situation is expressed in terms of hope, while the reality afterward is related by the shattering of this hope: "By [the Jewish holiday of] *Shavuot* we had been in the ghetto for a month. Since the Jews and Christians had their holidays at the same time, we hoped they would not put us on the trains to take us away, and that the Russians would come and bomb, so the deportation would be stopped. To my sorrow, it did not happen this way. On *Shavuot,* on a Sunday, they put us on cattle cars, on a train to Auschwitz."

The wording "We hoped . . . to our sorrow it did not happen this way" expresses a thoroughly unrealistic hope, or a delusion that could be termed childish or immature. The narrator describes a hope for solidarity from the non-Jews in light of the fact that the religious holidays of both groups fell on the same date. It would seem that all the Jews wanted was for the non-Jews to delay the deportation by one day, as if it all depended on the Gentile population of Nagyvárad and not on the Nazi occupation forces. The narrator presents a situation in which the Jews in the ghetto actually know that their fate is sealed and that they are destined for deportation. Therefore, they have no hopes for annulling the decree but only for delaying its execution, wishing that help would come during that time. As far as the first assumption, many contradictory testimonies make it difficult to determine to what extent the Jews in the Hungarian ghettos were cognizant of the fate that awaited them. It is also possible that the narrator ascribes this information only after the fact, as part of an unconscious attempt to heighten the dramatic impact on the audience. As for the second assumption, regarding the idea of delay, this is an unrealistic stalling tactic embodying the hope that rescue would come from a third agent such as the Red Army. Although there was some basis for this hope—since the Red Army was indeed winning the war at the time—the timing was not ripe for a full-scale invasion that would have saved Hungary's Jews. Therefore, it is more of a personal or communal fantasy—it is difficult to determine which one on the basis of a single text—of a Deus ex machine–style last-minute rescue, and not a hope truly anchored in reality.

This delusion or fantasy also represents another repetition of the theme of modesty, frugality, and self-effacement dealt with previously: the Jews ask *only* that the Gentiles delay their deportation by one day, with the hope that other Gentiles would come to their rescue in the meantime. It is almost superfluous to repeat that this form of expression demonstrates a lack of historical and political understanding of the events, a passive attitude, and an acceptance of the Jews' inability to prevent their doom, as often happens in traditional legends, which tend to end the way Rozsi hopes. Returning to real and harsh life situations, my purpose is not to claim that the Jews had recourse to a path of action at this stage but to shed light on the foundations of Rozsi's childlike point of view. This element of childishness is strongly evident in the structure of her entire life history, in its form as well as in its content and themes, despite the fact that the narrator was in her twenties when these events took place and in her seventies at the time of the narration.

The next stage of the narrative deals with Auschwitz and forced labor in labor camps and factories. This time period is characterized by another distinctive element in Rozsi's narrative: repression. The narrator tends to repress or exclude what cannot be told, yet at the same time, she hints briefly at the existence of the unspeakable. The narrator simply cannot tolerate, in her speech and in her consciousness, the awareness of certain significant events from her life in Auschwitz and the labor camps. Therefore she represses these events in various ways. At times, she employs a formulaic style of mentioning events without supplying sufficient details. For example, she describes the entrance into Auschwitz, the people and sights she sees, and the metamorphosis involved in this pivotal event as things that happen to *others*, whereas she herself is only a spectator and not one of the deportees. In addition, she chooses not to describe at all her own experiences, or those of her sister and friends, and instead says, "Of this there is nothing to tell, because it simply cannot be told." In this way she employs the proairetic ploy of revealing and concealing a focal and painful topic at one and the same time.[26]

Likewise, she represses or almost completely disregards two distinct time periods in the camps. She states that she was in Auschwitz until November (1944), but other than describing the camp's "routine," she does not describe any of her own experiences in Auschwitz. She indicates that she worked in an airplane factory until January of the year after, but again she does not dwell on the physical conditions, the work itself, or any significant events that she experienced during that period. By contrast, many other narrators direct much more attention to their analogous experiences in the camps and factories, to the work they did, to their relations with their supervisors, or with their "sisters in sorrow." Unlike these narrators, Rozsi Háger prefers to focus on communal rather than personal experiences in the camps and to discuss them in as general a manner as possible. Here, too, she employs formulaic language, or idioms, or common expressions that sound like them. These are some examples of her discourse: "We said to each other, 'Who are these people? Are they crazy, or are they thieves, scum, or what?' To this the German guard responded by saying, 'They are all of these' "; "and then the 'selection' started. For life or for death." The first quote relates to the moment of arrival at the depot in Auschwitz, an event that many other survivors describe. Some survivors recall that they, too, perceived the inmates as "insane" while others, consciously or unconsciously, also employ defense mechanisms to distinguish between themselves and the "crazy" ones. But Rozsi Háger goes even further to distance herself from the scene by focusing on the various conjectures that the viewers—"we" and the "German"—propose vis-à-vis the "crazy ones." It is as if she is describing a show or event that the viewers attempt to discuss and understand, and not an event in which she, the narrator, is part of the play, and will soon be numbered with those whom she has just labeled "crazy."

As for expressions such as "scum," "dirty," and "thieves," these are shameful epithets in the Hungarian culture of the period that were regularly used for minority groups such as Gypsies and Jews (these epithets also figure prominently in Irma Fischer's life history). Both groups are termed "thieves" as they are perceived as parasites that steal the livelihood from the nation in which they live. Similarly, "dirty" and "scum" denote dark and black and thus evoke the image of the negative stranger.[27] In this incident, however, Rozsi ranks the Jew as the lowest of the low in the Auschwitz universe, where even the Gypsies are ranked above the Jews, as they are not stripped of their clothes and hair like the Jews. In addition, the Gypsies are accorded positions of authority over the Jews, and this allows them to abuse the Jews as compensation for the abuse that they themselves suffer. In the context, then, of the arrival scene at Auschwitz, the answer of the German, "They are all of these," is a sign that heralds bad tidings for the fate of the narrator, who still lives in terms of the world she has just been torn from, and in which Jews are ranked above the Gypsies. At this point, though, it seems that she herself does not yet fully grasp the significance of this sudden change in hierarchy, or that she is too shocked to pay it greater attention.

The second quotation in this context, which includes the dramatic idiom "for life or for death," testifies to the narrator's gradual absorption of the meaning of the terrible scenes she sees when arriving in Auschwitz. Many narrators describe the "selection" that was held when they reached the camp, but only Rozsi Háger relates to it in this dramatic and explicit way, which demonstrates a deep connection to Jewish sources (the High Holidays prayers, and the blessing and curse of Deuteronomy 30:19). It is therefore ironic that at the same time she ascribes godly powers to Nazi German authorities, which, in this so-called theater of the absurd and the grotesque, is not far from reality.

Within this new order, the narrator, like other survivors who later convey their personal recollections of the Holocaust, is "condemned" to life in the camp. But the life she must live is a life that she finds difficult to describe. Therefore, from this point and on, she expresses over and over her inability to tell and reconstruct her experiences from the period of the camps, even when it seems as if she is just about to do so. Relating to trauma research, it could generally be argued here that these instances attest to numbness of feelings and to an ensuing inability of expression concerning these feelings. But beyond this general claim, each case of muteness carries with it unique meanings that are rooted in a specific narrative context. For example, a description beginning with "They took us to the showers, stripped us, and shaved us" is unexpectedly cut off by the following sentence: "There is nothing to say about this because it is impossible to talk about it." The text does not elucidate what, exactly, are the inhibitions of the narrator, but we may assume, from similar descriptions of other survivors who describe the public disinfection and penetration into the personal privacy of the female prisoners,[28] that Mrs. Háger still retains the same sense of humiliation she felt during the event itself, and that she is still unable to refer to it. The only way she is able to handle the experience is to declare that she will not describe it. This is another way in which we can view this narrator's life history as the narrative of a child who refuses to accept her femininity and maturation because in her traumatic experience these are tied to female vulnerability and to shame, and who therefore regresses back to childhood whenever these painful memories come up.

Similar expressions of inability to speak appear later in the narrator's speech and are linked to topical aspects of her yearlong life in the camps. For example, in her description of the routine existence in the airplane factory Rozsi says, "Even pigs wouldn't eat the food they gave us. There is nothing to tell about this, because it was clear that we were just prisoners who didn't deserve to eat." In this case, there is a different meaning to the repression, or the decision not to talk. This time she relates to the event in an ironic way and expresses a kind of acceptance of the viewpoint of the Germans who were in charge of her and her fellow or sister sufferers. In fact, the so-called identification with, or internalization of, the values of the oppressors is a way of coping with the reliving of the situation. Just like the talk about the "crazy" inmates at the arrival at Auschwitz, this ploy too allows the narrator to distance herself from her original and true perspective and from the pain that the recollection of the experience of hunger in the camps is still able to evoke in her even after so many years.

Another event the narrator is still unable to talk about relates less to the narrator and her memories and more to her relationship with her audience. This audience is constituted of myself as her sole listener as well as of the principle of "public opinion," which she is aware of throughout in a more general sense. The present unspeakable subject is the conduct of certain Jews, whom the narrator accuses of traitorous behavior toward other Jewish sufferers. For example, regarding the spoiled food—"not fit for pigs"—they received, Rozsi first indicates that the German work manager actually demanded better food for his prisoner workers so that they would be fit to work, and that the food should not be stolen from these workers. Then, to remove any uncertainties, Rozsi clarifies that it was the Jewish kitchen workers who stole the food from the factory workers: "The Jews behaved more sadistically than the Germans themselves, because for the Germans we were only workers. The Jews, by contrast, those who were transferred to the kitchen, they did their best not to be kicked out so they groveled and sucked up to the Germans. They did everything for the German women in order to keep themselves out of trouble." The narrator is well aware of the gravity of these accusations, and therefore defends herself a priori from disbelief or countercriticism by stating that she knows that she would not be believed if she were to speak. Despite this, or together with the apparent waiving of her prerogative to reveal these painful issues, she does tell about the offenses that she claims no one would believe.

As in the case of the entrance to Auschwitz, here too the narrator both states the existence of a painful issue and at the same time represses it owing to its gravity. Thus, she attains a kind of compromise between two conflicting urges or desires—to tell and not to tell—that are evident throughout her entire narrative. In addition, the narrator qualifies her accusations and ascribes them only to those Jews who were able to attain positions of relative power, such as those who worked in the camp kitchen. These are the same prisoners who are called *prominenten*, for example, in many of Primo Levi's descriptions of his experiences in the camps.[29] In contrast to these prisoners, the rest of the Jews, including the narrator herself, are described as harmless to their fellow sufferers, simply because they are "all in the same boat," meaning that they lack any special power or privileges. By making the distinction between this small, privileged group of prisoners and the majority of the camp inmates, Rozsi further moderates her accusation, as she makes it address or relate to but a small group out of masses of people.

Another group accused in Mrs. Háger's narrative, although it is not she who blames them, is the all-encompassing category of Jewish women. This group, which inevitably includes the narrator herself, is collectively described as injured victims and blameworthy or culpable at one and the same time. I am referring here to the stage of the immediate postwar period, when groups of women liberated from the camps made their way to their homes, as do the narrator and her younger sister. The narrator describes the first meeting of her group with the Russian army representative who liberated them:

> There we were liberated by the Russians. . . . A Russian officer came on the 8th of May, at eight in the evening. He got there on a jeep and asked us who we were. Some girls knew Russian and they said, "Jewish women." He said, "I wouldn't boast about it." One girl asked him, "And what are you?" He said, "As you can see, Russian." She said, "I did not ask that, I asked what *are* you." He said, "First of all, Russian, second of all, Russian, and third of all, Russian. Only afterward Jewish, but I don't boast about it. And another thing: If possible, don't move around in big groups, and leave immediately.

Because if you move in a group, the soldiers might notice you. These soldiers, I cannot speak well of them, because many of them are barely out of school, many of them are starved for women, so watch out for yourselves, because we cannot protect you."

Throughout her narrative, the narrator reveals the hostility that was displayed toward the Jews by all the various groups around them, such as Hungarians, Germans, Gypsies, other Jews in the camps, and Jewish soldiers in the Russian army, who did not see themselves as Jews at all. Hostility toward Jews, it seems, does not dissipate immediately at the war's end but remains the status quo to a large extent. In this section, the narrator discovers that she is not only lumped together with the despised Jews, but in addition, she is part of the subgroup of Jewish women who are subject to even more attacks and accusations as they try to make their way home. Hence the Odyssean flavor alluded to at this chapter's beginning, although the circumstances here are far from heroic.

For example, following the previous quotation, the narrator recounts how other women (an anonymous mother and her daughter) betray her group to the Russian soldiers in order to save themselves from the soldiers. In addition, although the newly liberated women have been through terrible experiences that left them unkempt, unattractive, and unfeminine in appearance, this does not work to their favor, because the Russians, "are looking for women. *Barishna* . . . is what they want, and they do not care if she is thin or fat, young or old, as long as she is a woman." Because of this, some women (including the narrator) try to align themselves with groups of non-Russian men such as Rumanian partisans. The women perceive the partisans as less threatening than the Russians but more able to defend them than the newly liberated Jewish men, who are too weak to defend even themselves. Indeed, the Rumanian partisans come to the defense of the narrator and her friends until they arrive at Budapest. Ironically though, the help and protection afforded them by the partisans give the group of women a bad name among still other Jewish women in Budapest. These faceless, anonymous women are taken aback to see the partisans buy blueberries—a dainty food, by all accounts[30]—for their female protégés: "Some Jewish girls saw this and shouted, 'Look, the soldiers are buying them fruit. Who accepts fruit from soldiers? . . . They must be loose women!' " The narrator immediately adds that after this incident, she and her friends agreed to separate from their protectors, although she does not indicate causality between the two events: "So, never mind, we parted from these

Tudor boys. They begged us to remain with them, but we only stayed in Pest for two days and then we headed home."

Here, again, we encounter an example of issues that are not explicitly stated but are nevertheless expressed in an indirect way. On the one hand, the narrator clearly transmits the message that the women's accusations are baseless, and therefore she does not object to repeating their crass words. Yet on the other hand, this expression of "public opinion" is important to the narrator and her friends, who cut off their ties to their protectors so as not to be subject to all sorts of false accusations. Years later, the issue of "public opinion" has become far less important to Mrs. Háger, as the phrase "never mind" clearly denotes. Therefore, she is able to surmount her inhibitions and actually describe this encounter in a way that stands in stark contrast to her continued inability to describe her previous life in the concentration camps.

As was mentioned in the introduction and in the preface to the present analyses, in Holocaust research, there has lately been a growing interest in gender issues and in the special vulnerability of women in the Holocaust. One research approach is to view the emphasis on the topic as an exaggeration or "myth" that is rooted more in fantasy than reality and is negatively influenced by the vulgarization and pornographication of the Holocaust in certain kinds of communication and art.[31] There is also a reverse approach that directs special analytic attention to the cases and stories of sexual abuse of Jewish women perpetrated by both non-Jews and Jews. This approach is motivated by the view that silencing these issues so far has in fact hurt women rather than protected them, as is well accepted with regard to present-day sexual abuse cases. But even within this latter approach, the question is often raised whether the special suffering of women is not outweighed by the universal horrors and atrocities of the Holocaust.[32] Research on women in the Holocaust also focuses attention on other womanly experiences in the camps, such as cessation of menstruation, or pregnancy and birth—which usually ended with the murder of the newborn.[33] Generally, however, these issues were connected to the initial period of the camps, since afterward the sexes were strictly segregated and menstruation had long since ceased, so we can say that these experiences did not constitute the major part of the camps period for the women survivors.

On the other hand, to be sure, experiences such as work, illness, hunger, as well as friendship and mutual help were far more common. Indeed, a great part of many personal memoirs deals with these experiences, while far fewer of them deal with the specifically feminine issues of incarceration just listed. Of course, it can be contended that this fact attests to the degree of inhibition of the narrators and the need to unearth and study exactly these repressed matters. However, as has been stated, this contention goes against my view of the proper relations between narrators and researchers, in which the latter should not strive to expose the former beyond their inclinations. In addition, bearing in mind the special sensitivities of Holocaust survivors in general, and traditional or conservative women survivors in particular, I consider delving too deeply in their intimate and sexual affairs a kind of betrayal of their trust—expressed by their agreement to tell me their life histories as fully and sincerely as they can—and a superfluous repetition of the initial assault on their privacy and lives.

Alternatively to this rather problematic analytical path, it can be argued that femininity has its expression not only in the type of experience undergone but also in the way the experience is felt and told by the female narrator after many years. Thus, even the more general experiences listed above may be experienced and recounted from a female or feminine point of view, much like what Hélène Cixous terms "feminine writing,"[34] albeit in the unique Holocaust context. In fact, research on women in the Holocaust points to the fact that the issues emphasized in women's Holocaust narratives—both written and oral—are the channeling of their traditional domestic skills as well as their flair for empathy, communication, and listening skills to coping with the hardships of camp life and to survival.[35]

Survival, it turns out, continues to preoccupy the liberated prisoners as they make their initial strides in the postwar world. Rozsi Háger too continues now to the next phase in her life and narrative and tells about her hope for the survival and return of additional family members, her efforts to rehabilitate her life, and her search for a husband. Her courtship story revolves around issues of food and work, and thus expresses the desire to return to some semblance of a normal life as well as reiterates issues of her previous camp experiences:

> A man walked into the cooperative dining room of the survivors. I went up to him and asked, "Where did you serve, maybe you met my father?" He said that no, he had not met my father. He had served in Bor. By then I had enough food with me and I said, "Sit down and eat." He said, "I am not hungry." I said, "Why pretend, you must be as hungry as we are." All those who came back from the camps of all kinds were hungry, could not be sated. We had

lunch three times a day and still we were hungry. We only worked
so we could eat. It was in June that I met the man from a labor
battalion, my future husband, and in December my sister and I
both got married. That day there were thirteen weddings.

The description of Rozsi's so-called courtship of her future husband
intertwines components of both the daughter and the mother in her
narrative character. This passage expresses a tension between passivity
and activity, stagnation and movement, in the struggle between the
forces of death, or Thanatos (passivity and stagnation), and the forces of
life, or Eros (activity and movement, or creativity).[36] The childlike or
regressive aspect of the narrator's character is evident in her passive
behavior, which in itself is another symptom of post-traumatic states.
She is fed in a communal survivors kitchen and does not take any
initiative except to maintain herself physically and eat as much as possible. The narrator is still in the "empty stomach" stage that dictates all her
actions, and which is similar to the situation that Elie Wiesel describes in
the world of concentration camps as well as in the early postwar period.[37] Alternatively, this behavior could be described as a form of regression to an earlier stage of oral development that verges on fixation.
This is comparable to Bruno Bettelheim's analysis of "Hans and Grettel"
(as well as a few other fairy tales), in which during the course of the story
the protagonist children overcome their desire to eat up the house made
of candy; at the end, they are cured of their obsession and thus reach
maturity.[38] If we, however, adopt Robert Darnton's interpretation of
many fairy tales that revolve around food and hunger, namely, that they
derive from real-life depravation situations,[39] we might view Rozsi's
hunger and inability to be sated as a life force that pushes her to con-
sume as much food as possible, as well as to secure future provision of
food and all that goes with it through marriage, which is the hoped-for
outcome of her act of courtship.

Still, as far as carrying out the act is concerned, even when Rozsi is
roused to search for a mate, the means that she employs to accomplish
this goal are childlike and naive. The topic she chooses to start conversation with her future husband is the common tribulations of Jewish men
in the Hungarian army. On the one hand, this topic is immediate and
self-evident, but on the other, it is impersonal and remote for her personally, because she is a woman and also because she has never mentioned her father so far. Indeed, the bombshell in the description of this
meeting is the very mention of her father. Until now, her father has been

completely absent from her narrative and her life, for after all, "Mother was everything." Therefore, up to this advanced point in her story we do not know whether her father was recruited to the forced labor service in the Hungarian army,[40] and if so, where to. Or, if he was too old for the labor battalions, was he instead deported to Auschwitz with his family? If he was in Auschwitz, was he sent to a work camp like his daughters, or to the gas chambers like his wife? All this information is missing from the text of the narrator, as is the father himself. If previously she spoke only her "mother's tongue," now she speaks also "in the name of the father," finally mentioning him as part of a conversation with a man who attracts her attention. Her question to the man of whether he ever met her father in the labor battalions seems immature and contrived, and she like a child who asks anyone in uniform whether they know her own soldier relatives. As expected in such cases, the man's answer is bound to be negative, and it may well be that he is not interested in this contact at all.

Yet, the narrator is undeterred by the man's negative answer and she turns to the next all-important topic in the world of the survivors: food. When the man declines her offer, she simply repeats her invitation more vehemently. This is the only point in the narrative in which Rozsi changes from a passive child to an active woman. In addition, she adopts here the presumed pattern of her own parents' relationship by assuming the more dominant role of the woman/mother in her dismissal of the man's refusal to eat with her. This may be viewed as the epitome of her daring or courtship, if we draw on the well-known link between eating disorders and gender relations,[41] as well as on the syndrome of the "empty stomach" pointed out previously. For Rozsi's invitation to the stranger to eat with her is, as becomes obvious soon after, an invitation to live with her and fill her empty stomach, meaning her desire for life, for a living, and for offspring. As for the man's response, we know very little except that he ultimately acquiesced to the narrator's courting, since the two were married about half a year after this initial meeting. At this point in the narrative, having achieved her goal for that period in her life, Rozsi returns to her formulaic style and says, "That day, there were thirteen weddings." Thus she departs from the unusual circumstances in which she actively courts a man back to her typical outlook and behavior of a passive child/woman whose life is accordingly anchored in verbal and numeric formulas, just like a fairy tale.

Parallel to Rozsi's regression from active to passive participant, her very next sentence after the wedding scene is: "On the same day I met my husband, on that day eleven years later he had a heart attack and died." Beyond pointing out that eleven years transpired between the two events, the narrator does not add any information about her life with her husband, except to state later on that they did not have children together and that she found, a year after the death of her first husband, another man who was as good as him. Her conduct toward this man is not as daring as in the first courtship, or at least she does not describe it as such. Instead, the second relationship is described as an attempt to realize the basic values that she expressed in the beginning of her account: living simply and frugally, and extending help to one's family and community. She marries her second husband, a widower with a daughter, so that she can mother the man's daughter and that in her old age, the stepdaughter "will give [her] a glass of water." Otherwise, she relates very little about the man himself, his personal qualities, or their relationship, except for the unusual fact that in this second marriage, at a relatively advanced age, she manages to become pregnant and have a child: "I was very lucky. I became pregnant. For four months I did not even know. When I had my daughter, it was a big miracle. Everyone said, 'Rozsi has a child, Rozsi gave birth!' True, I was not a young mother. I was not a mother to my daughter but a grandmother. I loved her."

This unexpected birth brings to mind the birth of Isaac, who was born to Sarah in her old age (Genesis 21:2), which explains why the narrator feels not like a mother but a grandmother to her child. She may also be saying that the experience of the Holocaust has made her more mature than her real age of thirty-four at that time. This feeling is strengthened by the description of "everyone" in her survivor community as a symbolic "public opinion" regarding the late childbirth. However, despite Rozsi's assertion, the picture that emerges from the story itself is that the daughter is clearly much closer to her than a granddaughter. In fact, in the framework of her mother's discourse, this daughter is part of her mother, or at least a fulfillment of a significant component in the mother's narrative personality, as the exclamation "I loved her" suggests. First, the very fact that Rozsi is able to conceive and give birth is a fulfillment of a major part of her femininity. Here we might appreciate her kindness, or naïveté, or cultural setup, which all prevent her from even hinting at her first husband's possible infertility and which result in her taking all the "blame" on herself, although we can at the same time view her stance as a continuation of her general dismissal of all men in her life and narrative, be they fertile or infertile, dead or alive. Second, it is an expression of her breaking out of the child's or the daughter's role, which is the main role she assumes for most of her narrative. Third, by the very act of giving birth, Rozsi approaches and attains the status of her own mother—the mother who is "everything" and who was lost to her in the Auschwitz crematorium. Thus, Rozsi attains a kind of closure that suits her formulaic mode of thinking and the values she expresses throughout her narrative. Closure and circularity are further confirmed by the concluding descriptions of her daughter and her family, which remind us of the opening with herself as daughter in her own family: "We came to Israel. She became a *sabra* [native Israeli], a graceful, pretty woman, thank God. She has three children. She has an excellent husband. I could not ask for any other happiness but to see her happy. She has everything. Her children study. What else does a mother need beyond seeing her children happy? What else can I tell you?"

The dominant theme in this latter part of the narrative is that of the mother/woman, as opposed to the child/woman that governs most of the narrative. This theme appears in the relationship between her parents as well as in her relationship with her own husbands, and is reflected in the secondary role that both her husbands and her father play in her narrative. Even in this last example, Rozsi first alludes to her daughter and her daughter's children; only afterward does she mention her daughter's husband. In addition, she describes her son-in-law in much the same way as she described her own two husbands: "a good husband" and "a very good man," which are essentially positive attributes but missing concrete and tangible elements beyond the rather vague compliment. Like the issue of family, happiness, too, harkens back to the beginning of Rozsi's life history and to her own childhood. The ending also reiterates this issue: the mother/grandmother is happy when she sees the happiness of her daughter/grandchildren. The expression she uses is phrased as a rhetorical question—"What else does a mother need beyond seeing her children happy?"—implying she needs nothing else and thus harkening back to her core values of modesty and frugality. The narrator now says that throughout an entire lifetime she never had or developed any materialistic aspirations or greediness. Motherhood is everything to her, just as it was to her own mother. Therefore, once she reaches the epitome of her aspirations in motherhood, she feels that she has nothing more to add.

Her inability to speak is evident in the continuation of the interview. When I asked her about the existence of anti-Semitism in her birth town and her attitude toward religion, she did not answer me directly, and toward the ending of her narrative it became clear that she was not interested in talking anymore. At this point her discourse became disconnected and especially biting and critical, a form of what Terrence Des Pres calls "excremental assault" in his work about survivors and their ways of coping in extreme situations.[42] In this case, however, it is the survivor who launches the verbal attack against me, and her purpose, evidently, is to conclude the narrative event, which she by now conceives as a kind of imprisonment.

Before that, Rozsi added details about her mother as part of her answers to questions I posed to her after the spontaneous part of the interview. The all-important mother figure is, first and foremost, the mother of the narrator, and the figure that the narrator-daughter has internalized into her own narrative character. Now, Rozsi explains that her mother had become an invalid and was confined to her bed for four years at the time of the Nazi occupation and just before the deportation to Auschwitz. However, the mother's disability, or what could be termed her inability to take action, is viewed as an advantage: as a result of the mother's infirmity, the family receives an additional room, which is very unusual for the overcrowded ghetto. In other words, the mother figure is helpful to the family despite, or because of, her physical helplessness. This principle will be repeated in the life history of another mother, Irma Fischer, as will be shown.

Rozsi's mother "dreams about Auschwitz," similar to Madame Schächter in Elie Wiesel's *Night*,[43] during three days of dying just before the deportation to the camps. The mother's daughters try to distract her from recounting her frightening dreams, similar to Mrs. Schächter's townspeople, but in this case they do so gently and respectfully. The result is the same: the significant fact is that the one who dreams knows things that others do not, and she is proven to be right and even righteous in terms of her "clairvoyance" or clear view of things that evade others. However, in this case there are no advantages to this righteousness or clairvoyance, and the dreamer is taken to the death camp together with the rest of the community, who refused to accept her prophecy.

This minimal allusion to Rozsi's mother and her image as remembered by her daughter give us an idea as to the extent to which Rozsi's narrative depicts not a real relationship with her mother (or her other relatives, for that matter) but a relationship with a figure she remembers from the distance of many years, and—alluding to the poem quoted at this chapter's opening—through the flames of Auschwitz. This figure, like the figures of her two husbands and son-in-law, is basically positive but shadowy and colorless beyond that. It is the image of saintliness and not of a real person. From this point of view, the mother as a real flesh-and-blood figure is missing from the narrator's text, despite the fact that she is ostensibly its central figure and idea. It can be assumed that this absence is connected to the salient dominance of the voice of the daughter—as opposed to that of the mother—that is expressed by Rozsi throughout most of her narrative. In addition, we should remember that the central figure in the text is the narrator herself—whether as daughter, mother, or grandmother, child or woman. Therefore, rather than characters that stand on their own, all the other figures and family members, women and men alike, are mostly reflections of aspects in Rozsi's own developing figure throughout her life history. Their limits are hers and eventually ours as we attempt to decipher and read her on the background of her family, environment, and historical setting.

Aranka Friedmann: Aunt, Informant, and the Child Underneath

The life history of Aranka Friedmann (resident of Nagyvárad, today's Oradea in Rumania) also contains childlike or childish aspects. However, unlike Rozsi Háger's narrative, in Aranka Friedmann's narrative these aspects are connected not only to the content or form of the life history but also or even more to the context of the narrative event and mainly its metalinguistic components. Aranka Friedmann is the only interviewee among all the narrators in my work who was not able to get over her "stage fright" or fear of the tape recorder from the beginning of the interview until the end. She notified me in advance that the presence of the tape recorder would make it difficult for her, and she was painfully aware of this difficulty during the entire interview. She requested frequent pauses in order to organize her thoughts and relax from the stress of the interview. These pauses were apparently an expression of the difficult emotions that flooded her from painful memories, which she could not express in words but only by their absence. Another expression of the tension that she was under was the weak, timid voice in which she spoke during the entire narration. This is not her natural voice but the voice of a small, bashful child. Moreover, this tension caused her to minimize or shorten the contents of her life history. For example, she did not develop certain events that she initially alluded to or mentioned, and it seems that she either consciously or unconsciously condensed her story so that she could finish it as soon as possible.

However, it must be emphasized that Aranka Friedmann, my aunt on my father's side, was definitely interested in being interviewed and expressed interest in my work from the time she heard about it, which was a great deal before the actual interview and the narration itself. Since she is a resident of Rumania, we coordinated our meeting far in advance to get together in Budapest. For the purpose of this meeting, Aranka Friedmann stayed in the house of a friend, Klára Nagy, whom I also interviewed. Moreover, both women attempted and managed to find additional appropriate interviewees for me during the time I stayed in Budapest.

Because Aranka and I are blood relations, she often referred to various family members in her narrative. Some of the people she referred to share the same names, and she assumed that I would understand whom she referred to, though she did not seem to be aware that these allusions would be lost on anyone else but me. For example, it is not clear, in her opening paragraph, how many brothers she has. She first says "the three of us" and after that, "No, us two," when in fact, she refers to her older brother and herself. At this point, she went to school with her older brother Miki (my father Miklós-Menachem), while her younger brother (Jenő-Yaacov) was not yet of school age. Later on, when she states "my brother went to an orphanage," the reference is to the younger brother, since the older brother was already married by then. Also, when after several sentences she describes how she met Jenő, she refers to her future husband and not her brother who has the same name. Somewhat later, she describes the circumstances of the death of her brother Jenő, and from thereon, all her references to "my brother" refer to her older and by now only brother Miki, and all her references to Jenő relate to her husband.

Aranka's voice is childlike not only regarding the metalinguistic aspects discussed previously but also in aspects of content and theme that are raised in her narrative. Her narrative is similar to Rozsi Háger's in that it is also characterized by a passive outlook regarding many events and people in her life—in fact, everything except her relationship with her husband. However, while Rozsi seems to entrench herself behind well-known formulaic blueprints according to which she leads her life, Aranka embraces a remote, rationalistic, and at times ironic viewpoint. In many ways, Aranka's narrative is a minimalistic one that does not presume to be a "story," or, as she herself describes her life at the conclusion of her narrative: "My life is not colorful at all." From a different perspective, Aranka's passivity and apparent emotional numbness can be ascribed to the trauma of the Holocaust she lived through. In addition, in Aranka's case, these traits may be related to her early loss of parents and support, as we shall see, and in that case "not colorful" also means unhappy. Either way, her narrative character is very inhibited and her narrative, as a result, is often ambiguous and enigmatic, and calls for rigorous interpretative efforts.

Aranka opens her story with a description of the family's genealogy. However, instead of describing her parents' lives and activities, she describes the circumstances of their illnesses and deaths, as both her parents died within a period of two years when she was a young teenager. The narrator's father (my grandfather Péter-Pinchas) evidently died of tuberculosis, while her mother (my grandmother Sarah) died as the result of an unsuccessful operation to remove a cancerous growth from her intestines. The common denominator between the illnesses and deaths of both parents is the impotence of the attending physicians. The passivity or powerlessness that the narrator later ascribes to herself, consciously or unconsciously, is also ascribed to various other persons who are fateful in her own life. In this case, these are the physicians who failed to save her parents' lives and left her an orphan at the beginning of her adolescence, between her thirteenth and fifteenth year.

The detailed description of the circumstances of the illness and death of both her parents attests to the fact that the knowledge of these topics, if not actual control of the medical details, is very important to the narrator. In fact, the entire physical-biological realm is very important to her. I discovered a similar phenomenon in the narratives of other interviewees in my thesis who describe nutritional and medical topics in detail during their life histories. Rika Salamon emphasizes the importance of a certain medication that she ingested in her childhood and ascribes to it her strength to withstand the rigors of the camps and of later years as well. Her husband, Andor Salamon, ascribes similar powers to certain types of food that he felt strengthened his body while he served in the labor battalions. One significant example he gives is the bone marrow that he found in a pile of garbage and lived off for many days.[44]

The existential nature of these almost "magical" medicines or foods is reinforced by similar descriptions given by Dora Ashkenazi, whose life history is analyzed in the following chapter. Dora describes a sewing needle that she finds in Auschwitz and manages to hide in her bread or personal effects during the entire period she spends in the camps. Of course, she finds many uses for this needle. Dora also tells us that a friend of hers in the camps hides a prayer book in a similar fashion, adding, "In this way she brought the prayer book home." The analogy between the needle (in light of the fact that Dora is by then an accomplished seamstress by profession) and the prayer book shows us that these survivors search for, find, and carefully guard objects that are most essential to their survival. Even after they survived the camps, the survivors continued to guard or at least remember the objects that helped them survive. Consciously or unconsciously, they ascribe almost miraculous powers to these objects—powers that far exceed their physical uses and characteristics.[45] In addition, it is clear that the attitude of the narrators to these objects tells us a great deal about their worldview and life in general. In this way, Aranka, who is a retired nurse, needs to understand the circumstances of her parents' deaths as information that she can grasp and control. These needs, to understand and control, at least mentally if not physically, are part of her life history and hence a central part of her narrative character. Perhaps this reliance on realism, objectivity, science, and laconism explains in another way why she views her life as "not colorful."

Regarding the next phase in Aranka's life, and in contrast to the decline and death of her parents in her youth, the period of the camps seems to be, strangely enough, the conclusion of the narrator's healing and rehabilitative process, following a sickly childhood and youth. This is so much so that the narrator later describes her return from the camps and reunion with her husband at the Nagyvárad train station as a surprising scene to her previous community members. "We were reunited right there in the middle of the street, and there was great joy. Many men whose wives remained in Auschwitz came too. Someone even said to me, "You? You came back and my healthy wife [grin] remained there?" Because they knew that I had been ill for a long time."

The expressions "remained there" or "did not return" are repeated in many Holocaust narratives. These are the familiar euphemistic expressions of survivors to convey that the people under discussion have in fact died. This very use expresses a desire or a need to avoid expressions directly connected to death, which Nachman Blumental terms "magical thinking" in the context of the Holocaust.[46] In addition, such phrases convey the uncertainty that was the lot of the survivors with regard to the circumstances of the deaths of their loved ones, and often even regarding the certainty of death. Since they were unable to conclusively determine the facts or circumstances of their relatives' lot, at least initially, they were unwilling to orally seal the fate of their loved ones. It is also possible that the use of such euphemistic terms, which are ordinarily used for daily activities, lessened the survivors' feelings of guilt that they alone survived. This is evident from the comment that Aranka quotes: "You? You came back and my healthy wife [grin] remained there?" and even more from her embarrassed laugh. As for guilt and inability to feel happy, these are evident from the impersonal description: "and *there was* great joy."

As mentioned, Aranka was weak and sickly in her childhood, probably with a tendency to tuberculosis. In my family they used to say that my aunt's work in the pine forests and the clear air she breathed there helped to strengthen and heal her. As is true of many family stories, this explanation was never subjected to the test of historical accuracy or reasonability but was instead accepted and even repeated verbatim. Thus, no one wondered how my sickly aunt was able to withstand the starvation, cold, and torture that decimated most of the forced laborers. The general arbitrariness of survival didn't count as much as my aunt's resilience and luck, for after all, the Holocaust was "brought home" to us via the stories of our relatives and not by history and statistics. I, too, even as a folklore researcher, never thought of asking my aunt more specifically about her health before, during, and after the Holocaust, probably because the "original" story was still so natural or axiomatic for me. In retrospect, though, it may be added that considering my aunt's old age at present, over a decade after the interview, and the fact that she is alone and in bad health in present-day Rumania, I am all the more convinced of her strength and endurance against all odds. Then again, knowing as I do about her delicate health in childhood, I invariably reach the conclusion that she must have developed stamina over the years and in response to life's hardships, whether early orphanhood, camp life, infertility, or chronic geriatric diseases and loneliness.

My aunt, on her side, felt the necessity to "justify" her survival by explaining that she and her friends in the camps did not suffer unduly since they met all the demands placed on them: "I cannot say that they were cruel to us, because we gave them no reason, we worked as they told us to." In addition, like other narrators, she mentions the contribution of the prisoners' work supervisor or meister, "who was OK," and made their work and living conditions tolerable. According to her explicit viewpoint, then, the behavior of the prisoners and the attitude of their meister were the major factors in the survival of the prisoners, herself included.

However, it soon becomes clear that the source of this narrator's strength is based not only on the physical conditions of the camps but also, or to a greater extent, on her own approach toward life, in the camps and afterward. The narrator has already presented herself as being passive: things take place around her and leave her no leeway for taking action. Her behavior can be viewed as a kind of shrinking of her existence to the bare minimum. She is inactive, never takes the initiative, and almost doesn't display any emotions toward the people and events around her. In the narrative section that follows, she describes an event, close to the end of the war, when it seems that the Nazis are about to annihilate her and the other prisoners who are locked in a barn for the night: "And then we walked, they marched us further down. At last we reached a farm, and I don't know how many of us there were, but there were many of us. We got there in the evening and they put us in a barn and, yes, they even locked the door on us. I was convinced that they were going to burn down the barn with us inside. I lived with this under-standing and thought. But in the end it did not happen. At night the Germans left, and we remained there. That is how we were liberated. Now, stop taping for a moment please, because I cannot talk anymore [short break]."

The narrator uses third person plural pronouns, such as "they marched us," "they put us in a barn . . . and locked the door," which express her own minimalist and passive attitude. In addition, her ap-proach is rationalistic and devoid of emotion. She relates to the event, including its dangers and meaning, not through her emotions but through her reason: she says she was "convinced " that they were going to kill her and she refers to her "understanding and thought," but she never describes what she felt at the time. In keeping with Aranka's presumable continuous traumatic numbness of feelings, it may well be that the emotions suppressed and verbally excluded from her narrative are channeled to its metalinguistic and contextual aspects, for it is evi-dent that the very recollection of this event drains much psychic energy from her, tires and causes her to take a break from her narration, as happened a number of times during the interview.

Aranka uses the same hesitant and minimalist style to describe an-other significant issue in her life, which at first does not seem to be tied to her survival. This is the issue of the children that she and her husband never had, and whose significance in the text is fraught with meaning precisely because of their absence. This is analogous to the Macbeth "children," or to Martha and George's "son" in Edward Albee's *Who's Afraid of Virginia Woolf?* Aranka says the following about this issue: "As for children, it may well be that the reason why I don't have any children is that I became pregnant when the Hungarians came in, and I then went to the doctor. After a short while, my husband was taken to the labor battalions, and I was taken to the ghetto. After the ghetto, where we stayed for a month, we were taken to Auschwitz."

It would seem, at first glance, that the narrator is simply telling us that she became pregnant at the time of the annexation by Hungary and had an abortion, because the times were difficult and the future seemed uncertain. Also, it seems that she was not able to conceive afterward because of this abortion. But in order to understand what she is really trying to say, we must compare her story with the events of other family members that she describes almost parenthetically, after she describes her own liberation from the camps. She now describes the circumstances of the death of her younger brother Jenő who escaped to the Soviet Union, the initial release of her older brother Miki from the labor battalions (in response to a question of mine after the narration, she remembered that he was re-taken to the labor battalion in the next draft). Then, and this is of great significance, she describes the circumstances of the deaths of her brother's wife and their child: "Then the deportations started. His wife Ilush and their son Péter, who was five or six years old, they went together to Auschwitz and they too never returned. The family was exterminated this way, you could say."

The comparison between the two young families in wartime elicits the following analogies: both men or husbands are taken to the work battalions and, though Aranka does not tell us now what happened to them there, they both survived the war. In contrast, the fates of the two women or wives differ significantly owing to the fact that the narrator's sister-in-law is the mother of a child while the narrator herself has no children. Mothers, as we know, were sent with their small children to the gas chambers and crematorium of Auschwitz, even if they were young and seemed fit for work, because the Nazis in most cases wanted to avoid the commotion and turmoil of trying to separate the mothers from their children. Young women who were not accompanied by small children and who looked fit for work were granted at least an initial chance for survival. These were usually single women or mothers of older children.

Most of the narrators I interviewed were single in Auschwitz. In contrast, Aranka Friedmann was married and could have been the mother of a young child, had she not aborted previously. In other words, when she talks about the abortion, she explains or justifies her survival in light of events that happened *after* the abortion. She does not claim to have anticipated Auschwitz like Rozsi Háger's mother, but that she did anticipate hard times and preferred to give up the baby because of this. Yet, in light of the fact that her fears proved true, and in view of the assumption that she would have died together with her child had she proceeded with her pregnancy, the abortion becomes the de facto reason for her initial survival rather than a mistake of the past that she is sorry about today. It seems, though, that the narrator is hard-pressed to say out loud a thing that flies in the face of humanistic principles and societal conventions, even though the times under discussion were not normal times. Therefore, instead of clarifying her meaning, she prefers to express it indirectly and through comparing her lot with that of her sister-in-law, who died together with her son.

Drawing on the parallels between the dream phenomenon and Aranka's life history, which, as stated before, is characterized by free association, lack of organization, and at times lack of order, we might infer that to a great extent, the logic of the dream governs her narrative, especially in its more problematic parts. The dreamlike quality is expressed in this section in two ways. First, the narrator does not explicitly articulate the norms of her ego, which fly in the face of the norms of society, that in retrospect it was better to destroy her fetus than to die together with her child in Auschwitz. Instead, she expresses this idea indirectly through displacement. She shifts the weight of her story from the circumstances of her initial survival, which stir up her feelings of guilt, to the issue of her childlessness, which instead stirs up her feelings of sorrow and which in turn arouses empathy in the hearts of her audience.[47] Second, she portrays a very limited microcosm, which includes only analogous family members, and especially her sister-in-law as opposed to herself. In the current narrow context, then, this sister-in-law is Aranka's reverse mirror image and represents the fate that Aranka would most likely have also shared if she had acted otherwise and had a child. In other words, Aranka brings up topics that are not necessarily directly related to her own life history (such as her sister-in-law's death) in order to give indirect expression to, and cope with, her own disturbing emotions regarding the fact and meaning of her own survival.

In the next stage of her story, Aranka describes her life in Rumania after the war just as briefly and concisely as she has described her earlier life. The central characteristics of her narrative mode are salient in this stage as well. Her description is still cold and seemingly devoid of feeling, and her passive outlook continues to remain at the foundation of her approach to life. She describes the professional and social life of herself and her husband in the following terms: "They included us, both of us were members of the party," "At a certain point they transferred me to the surgical ward," "They developed a new polyclinic and transferred me to there," and also, "They did not let a husband and wife leave together [to visit a foreign country]."

Another narrator, Klára Nagy, had also been an active member of the Communist Party (in Hungary), but she makes light of the importance of this activity, evidently because of the subsequent change in regime in her country at the time of the interview.[48] Aranka Friedmann adopts the same approach toward her past, in light of the change in regime in her country as well. It is probably true that what she says is grounded in reality, but beyond this and at the same time, her descriptions spring from her personal characteristics, her emotional makeup, and the way all these elements influence her view of reality. In her eyes, then, reality is a chain of events that she has no control over and that dictate how she must behave and react within the spheres of work and society.

But, like Rozsi Háger, Aranka directs her inner emotional resources to the one realm where the country and the party have no direct influence, namely, her relationship with her husband. In this realm, she shrugs off her passive approach and becomes an active figure that does everything in her power to save her husband's life in his old age. She describes her attempts to save him:

> When we retired, we came to Budapest in 1984 because my husband's sister had become ill and died. Jenő came first because they did not let a husband and wife leave together. So I arrived one week later. Already as I arrived from the station I saw that my husband was sick. He had had a stroke. Now with all the arrangements around my sister-in-law's burial, the lawyer and I don't know what, it all affected him. These things ruined him. In 1984, on the 20th of June, I took him home, and on the 26th, he died. I took him home for five days. I took him to a hospital, to the best cardiologist. But he did not want to stay there. The doctor said he should stay, but Jenő refused, and because of his stroke, his mind was confused and he started crying and saying he would not stay there. We did not want to force him, so as not to cause an attack, because I knew already: they did an ECG check here in Budapest and it showed that he was on the verge of an attack. That is why he lived for only five days more. Turn it off for a minute [break].

In this instance it is clear that the sudden active role she assumes is prompted by the intensifying powerlessness of her sick husband. In fact, this is the immediate reaction of anyone who is about to lose the one person they are closest to. They will do anything in their power to prevent the loss, as they instinctively realize that they have nothing else to lose. However, even this uncharacteristic description is toned down and anchored in the otherwise not too active life and rationalistic approach of the narrator, or, more specifically, in her need to master the knowledge of physical or medical issues. Because of her profession as a nurse and her closeness to hospitals and physicians, Aranka feels more empowered to take action for her husband than she would were the issue not a medical one. She knows that her husband should be under constant medical supervision, but at the same time, she knows that forcing medical supervision on him against his will is likely to worsen his condition, which is harmfully influenced by his emotional reaction to his surroundings. All this means that she has to pick the lesser evil between two difficult alternatives and assume responsibility for her decision. In the end, she brought her husband home, where he died after a few days.

Although there is no real significance to Aranka's decision in terms of external reality, as her husband was very sick and probably going to die anyway at that point, she at least feels that she did all she could to alleviate his physical and emotional suffering in his last days, though her narrative style does not allow her to enlarge on this topic beyond the pragmatic aspects. The emotional or mental aspects of the difficult circumstances she describes are again expressed in the difficulty she has in recalling and telling about it all, and in her frequent requests to stop the taping for a while so she can regain her composure, similar to what happened when she described the eve of her liberation, as has been discussed.

In concluding the analysis of my aunt's narrative, I will make three important points regarding the implications of her life history and its narration to me as her niece. The first point has to do with the genealogical aspects, or the family background material with which my aunt opened the story of her life. The early death of her parents, my grandparents, in Aranka's youth brings up the association of the similar fate that befell my parents, who also died of illnesses when I was only a little older than my aunt when she was orphaned. My aunt is surely aware of the parallel elements of our lives that unite the two of us, despite the fact that we never expressly discussed this issue between us. Bringing up this issue, then, strengthens the feelings of identification and kinship between the two of us, which exists anyway by virtue of our familial relationship and my express interest in Holocaust survivors. This can be viewed as a sort of "bargaining chip": my aunt offers me this indirect support and empathy at the beginning of her story in anticipation of the same kind of empathy and support she needs and hopes to receive from me in return as she embarks on the difficult mental journey into her life history.

The second point is connected to the first and can also be described in terms of support and "bargaining." The issue at stake here is the murder of my father's first family in Auschwitz. Here my aunt is trying to communicate or share with me part of the guilt she carries regarding this family of her brother or my father, since if his family had not been murdered he would not have created a second family and I would not have been born. This point is reinforced by the duplication of names in our family even to the present day. As explained in the introduction, I am named after Ilush, my father's first wife (as well as after my mother's aunt), and incidentally, my husband's secular name is the same as my father's, Miki (Miklós), as opposed to their different Jewish or Hebrew names (Menachem and Michael). Thus, my husband and I, completely inadvertently, perpetuate the existence of the original couple in my family who bore these names (my father and his first wife), and who no longer exist. In fact, when the two of us started dating, a few years before the interview, my aunt used to ask about my Miki, calling him Miki *Fiu* (Hungarian: boy, lad, or young man), although he was about thirty years old at the time. It may well be that this was her way of mocking or belittling her niece's potential mate until he deserved otherwise (possibly by marrying me). At the same time, this could also be an unconscious device of differentiation and distancing on her part between the initial pair carrying these names and their tragic life circumstances (which included a bad marriage and separation before the deportation and death of the wife/mother and child) and our prospective new relationship fifty years later.

To complete the issue of the intersections of my aunt's and my own life histories, my aunt mentioned more than once that her younger brother Jenő, who disappeared in the Soviet Union together with the brother of her husband Jenő, was regarded as the successful and learned child in the family. My aunt brought this up to offset her criticism regarding certain aspects of her older brother, my father, perhaps to show that although she speaks frankly with me, she does not only have critical things to say about her family but also some positive things. This may also be her way to tell me that she preferred her younger brother over the older one. In fact, supporting or encouraging and "bargaining" again, my aunt here makes a connection between my uncle (not my father) and myself. Thus, my aunt points out associations that were never made in my immediate family while I was growing up, perhaps because my father married at a young age and never had the opportunity to really get to know his younger brother as well as my aunt, the middle sister (there was a five years difference between each sibling and the next, and my father was already married at eighteen, whereas his brother was sent to an orphanage at about that time). And so, my instincts tell me, my aunt is "passing the torch" of my uncle to me, with the hopes that I will succeed in my scholarly endeavors and thus perpetuate the memory of her younger brother, who might have fared much better if it were not for the hard times in which he lived, and died.

Irma Fischer and Zsuzsa Faludi: Dialogue between the Life Histories of Mother and Daughter

The life history of the next narrator, Irma Fischer, is intertwined with that of her daughter, Zsuzsa (Zsuzsánna) Faludi; both of them were born in Budapest and still living there at the time of the interview. Irma Fischer opens her story along the same lines as Aranka Friedmann, describing the circumstances of her parents' deaths. These deaths turn out to be a premonition of the fate of Jews in general and in the Holocaust in specific, a link demonstrated by the narrator in different ways throughout her narration.

Mrs. Fischer's father was killed in the family workshop after it went up in flames and he rushed to save his children or workers, or both. Sometime afterward, her mother was burned in the bathroom while preparing for her bath before the Sabbath. The narrator seems to have absorbed from both tragic events that great devotion and great suffering are so closely joined together as to be inseparable. In her own life, too, this duality is expressed in her frequent efforts to sustain herself and her two children, especially during the war years when she was widowed. In addition, even long after liberation, she copes with illnesses—her own illnesses and her children's—that seem to plague all members of her family to this very day.

As was stated before, Irma Fischer narrated her life history in the presence of her daughter, who bridged gaps in the memory of her elderly mother and commented on and corrected her mother's story, sometimes even disagreeing with her. The mother's view of the daughter is generally revealed by indirect third-person descriptions and comments that are ostensibly directed at me. The attribute that is most emphasized regarding the daughter is her sustained excellence in school despite the difficulties of her childhood and youth. The second attribute is her devotion to her younger brother, whom she often took care of like a mother because of their mother's bad health.

Only once does the mother turn directly to the daughter, to remind her where she studied immediately after the war, and where she herself worked in the same time period. This ostensibly neutral comment opens the door to a disagreement between the two. The daughter, who is familiar with her mother's life history, knows exactly where this story is headed: to the description of her mother stealing food and hiding it in her underwear when she worked in the kitchen of the educational institution in which the daughter studied. The daughter is embarrassed by the mention of this incident and tries to prevent her mother from talking about it. She tries to convince her mother that the incident is not related to her life history, since "it was after the war." But the mother does not accede to the daughter's veiled request and tells the story despite her daughter's objection. She feels that it is the story of *her* life, which includes the period after the war as well as before it, and that only she has the right to decide what to include in or omit from her life history.

In retrospect, the mother's first comment to the daughter can be viewed as a warning that she intends to bring up a topic that the daughter is sensitive to. The mother insists on her right to bring up this topic nevertheless, perhaps as part of the mother-daughter power dynamics and perhaps to emphasize her devotion to her children, despite the embarrassment associated with the incident even so many years after the fact. It is important to comprehend these mother-daughter dynamics in order to understand the daughter's recounting of her own life history, which took place a few days later, and not in the presence of the mother. In her own life history, the daughter interspersed her reactions to and criticism of the way her mother had told her story previously; this time, she was the one who had the privilege of saying the last word.

Before embarking on an intertwined discussion of both narrators and narratives, it is necessary to focus on the basic characteristics of the mother's discourse, which resemble the life stories of the two previous narrators, Rozsi Háger and Aranka Friedmann. First of all, in terms of formulaic speech and narrative patterns, Irma Fischer's narrative is imbued with a "woe is me" or "misery" theme. Many of the characters mentioned in her life history merit the tag of "poor," "unfortunate," or similar labels, from her parents and the rest of her immediate family to her own children and, finally, herself. The theme of misery is presented almost as an inborn trait of the narrator, her family, Hungarian Jewry in general, and Jews wherever they lived during the period under discussion. Or, to phrase it in the words of another survivor-narrator I interviewed in my doctorate, "what a wretched generation we are."[49] Irma Fischer begins her story with the words "my poor mother," since for her, the fate of her unfortunate mother heralds wretchedness and bad luck for all the other characters within her life history. Therefore, her mother's death is the first thing that she recalls, but immediately, she realizes that since she is telling her own inclusive life history, she should tell it in an organized way and maintain chronological order. She therefore cuts off her discussion of her mother's poor fortune and talks, instead, about her father's death, which preceded that of her mother and which was also imbued with the misfortune and tragedy of fire.

This kind of self-correction occurs many times in her narrative: she starts talking about a specific topic and then stops herself in the middle because she is concerned that her words are not proper or seemly, somewhat like Rozsi Háger, as mentioned above. This happens, for example, when she starts to express critical comments about the behavior of Jewish power figures in the Holocaust. Previously, Rozsi Háger spoke about "bad Jews" in the camp's constellation. Irma takes a similar stance in her criticism of those Jews who were in charge of distributing the meager food supplies to the inhabitants of the ghetto in Budapest, and who abused their office by giving most of the food to their relatives instead of the ghetto inhabitants. Irma does not expand on this topic, or on the criticism she bears in her heart toward those Jews. Instead, she dwells more on describing the paltry food she had and prepared for herself and her children: potato peels for the children and the water in which these were cooked for herself. Then, she explains this by saying, "The reason that we had so little food is because, to my sorrow, some of the Jews who were in charge stole food from the ghetto for their relatives. They gave no food to the children." The abstract description of "Jews" or "relatives" or "Jews who were in charge" is not developed enough to imply or blame specific people and acts, as is done by other narrators in my work. Despite this vagueness, Mrs. Fischer achieves the same purpose as the narrators who were more specific in their accusations. Like the other narrators, Irma is able to obtain relief from her feelings of injustice and frustration at her failure to obtain food for her

children. She also involves her audience in empathizing with her situation—especially with regard to her daughter, who is present at the time
of the interview, and who was one of the children.

Another issue of criticism in Irma's narrative is the conduct of her
father-in-law, with whom she lived during a period of time after the war:
"Then later we returned home, to my father-in-law's home. May he rest
in peace, my father-in-law, but he was not a kind man. Although you
shouldn't say bad things about the dead, sometimes there is nothing
good to say." It seems, at first, that Mrs. Fischer wants to express her
criticism of her father-in-law, who evidently did not help her as she
expected from a financial point of view. But then, she immediately
retracts her criticism as she recalls that her father-in-law is dead and one
"should not say bad things about the dead." Therefore, her pronoun
changes into the second-person typical of imperative speech, as if she is
making a general statement to society at large as well as to herself. This
mode of expression evokes the genre of the proverb, which stems from
the voice of authority and maturity and which is characteristic of the
speech of the elderly.[50] However, her point—regarding her father-in-
law—has been made, and she achieves two objectives: she gets across her
message, and at the same time, she clears herself of any criticism of
speaking ill of the dead, since she doesn't go into details or say *everything*
she could have said on the topic.

To sum up the main points about Mrs. Fischer's discourse before
moving on to that of her daughter and to a joint discussion of the
mother's and daughter's life histories and relationship, it can be discerned that Irma's narrative contains a number of layers or levels of
meaning. These emerge through psychoanalytic analysis of distinctive
phenomena in her narrative, especially the tension between presence
and absence. First is the immediate or overt layer, which seems to spring
from inattentiveness or lack of concentration, free association, and a
kind of "stream of consciousness" style she seems to have. But a closer
look reveals that in most cases, these comments are not merely the result
of lack of control, although the narrator sometimes presents them this
way. Instead, the apparent "free association" is really a camouflage allowing the narrator to touch on topics that are sensitive or painful to her
or her various family members, alive or dead, present or absent, or even
to broader contexts. With this "technique," the narrator earns the right
to say what she feels and believes despite the anticipated opposition
from relevant family members, or any societal conventions or ethical
norms she might be violating. Thus, under the veil of free association is

a layer of painful issues whose expression needs camouflage and tempering. This is the second, hidden layer of meaning in her account.

The third layer is both thematic and modal. As has been stated, the central theme in Irma Fischer's narrative is the misery premise, which she sees as the key to understanding life—including the lives of most of the characters that are mentioned in her story, and even the essence of Jewishness as the narrator perceives it. This is also the key to understanding the concluding words of her narrative, which bring to mind a waking nightmare and ongoing anxiety. Parallel to the "wretched generation" mentioned before, here, too, the import of her words reflects not only on the narrator and the here-and-now in her life but also on everyone who is in her situation, past, present, and even in the future. The specific context of such utterances as "I don't dare to sleep at night" or "something will happen, I tell you," with which the narrator chooses to conclude her life history, is the political and social situation in Hungary at the beginning of the 1990s, the time of the interview, after the collapse of Communism and the reawakening of overt anti-Semitism in the country. Irma Fischer, as a member of a generation that experienced the horrors of anti-Semitism at its worst, is clearly afraid of the immediate future. These misgivings are not only on a personal level, as Irma is eighty years old when interviewed and surely does not expect to live long enough to suffer hardships in the more distant future. Rather, these are fears that she expresses in relation to her daughter, who sits opposite her, and her family. She also seems to symbolically address the younger Hungarian Jewish generations, who are meant to absorb the spirit of her prophetic words and "wake up" to a future whose exact nature she cannot foresee.

But she is clearly capable of remembering, in her unique way, the past, which makes her fear the future. The discussion of these memories will be intertwined with the parallel memories of Irma Fischer's daughter, who was a child at the time of the events, and is now a more lucid adult than her elderly mother and better capable of remembering and telling the events of the most significant and painful period in the lives of both mother and daughter.

Zsuzsa Faludi, Irma Fischer's daughter, was in her fifties when she told me her life history. At the time of the Holocaust, she was about eight years old. In her narrative she integrates the focus or point of view of the child she was, which includes the things she heard and assimilated at the time, and the present viewpoint of a grown woman recalling events of her childhood. At times she resembles Rozsi Háger in that she maintains a "formulaic" view of life. For example, she too maintains that child-hood is the happy time of life, and for a while after the war, she also maintained the belief that her missing father was still alive somewhere and that the family must wait for him to return. In both these cases, the starting point is the event that she experienced as a child, and as she transforms the experience into a story or text that she herself tells and hears at the same time, the viewpoint of an adult woman takes over in the description of the event. Thus, for example, the narrator does not express her view of her happy childhood as an absolute truth or value, as did Mrs. Háger, but instead she qualifies her assessment in the form of a condition: "And *if* there is such a thing as a happy childhood, *then* that is what I had." Her skepticism regarding her own happy childhood is the result of her later life experiences, but it also expresses her caution and awareness of the relativity of things, and as a result, her wish to be as accurate and credible as possible.

Zsuzsa is a friend of my mother-in-law's family, and as such she hosted me in her house during the whole period I stayed and worked in Hungary. Thus, we got to know each other more closely than I did most of the other narrators in my work (except perhaps my aunt, Aranka Friedmann), and as a result, she was more involved in and knowledge-able regarding my work. A clear example of our special relationship was expressed in the narrative of Zsuzsa Faludi, as well as in those of her mother and uncle, who was also interviewed for my doctorate. These narrators knew, as a result of some conversations we held during the time I stayed in Zsuzsa's house, that I was very interested in one question in particular: why did the Hungarian Jewish survivors return at the war's end to their former homes, to a hostile environment? Why didn't they leave their past behind and try to rehabilitate their lives in another milieu, such as the interviewees who moved to Israel, or those who left to Western countries? My interest in this question arose from the fact that the Israeli interviewees, whom I had interviewed earlier on, viewed the Holocaust as motivation for their aliya immediately after the war, or as early as possible under the circumstances. Of course, it is impossible to determine whether this is what actually happened, or if it is the way the Israelis see it in retrospect. Zsuzsa evidently interpreted my interest in this question as implied criticism on my part of those who remained in their country of birth. Therefore, she responded by justifying and explaining the situation. I would assume that this is also the reason for the apologetic tone and profuse explanations on this topic in the narra-tives of her mother and especially her uncle, and that Zsuzsa evidently involved her relatives in this concern of mine. As the one who inter-viewed this extended family and tried to account for their stories and expository discourse, I found that this experience was a very instructive lesson regarding the interviewer-interviewee or researcher-researchee relationship. The chief lesson I gained from this experience was to be very cautious of "leading questions," even at the level of tone of voice or facial expression. Interviewees, so I learned, are very alert to the ques-tions they are asked since, after all, they want to know what the inter-viewer is interested in and "supply the goods." I learned that it is best to "compartmentalize" or separate information amongst those who are interviewed, and especially among relatives or friends, at least until after the interview, so as not to influence the content of the narratives.

To return to Zsuzsa, among the other narrators in this chapter, she seems to enjoy a unique role as a knowledgeable or all-knowing inter-viewee because of her involvement in my project. She is also the one who evidently knows more today than she knew in her childhood, and who knows more than the previous three narrators in this chapter, who were characterized as having childlike voices and consciousnesses, at least partly, because of various forms of lack of knowledge and control that they exhibit in their stories. One example of Zsuzsa's omniscience is found in the issue of her father's death. The father served in the labor battalions inside Hungary and remained missing after the war. His death was not acknowledged by his daughter and family in the early years after the war, and Zsuzsa relates to this first with a general comment: "After the war, rumors spread that people were seen somewhere or other and then the relatives, who wanted to believe that their loved one was still alive, believed these rumors." Already in the next sentence she proceeds to a seemingly different topic and talks about her studies in a Jewish high school and about her joining the Zionist youth movement, which was still allowed in Hungary in those years. She also talks about her desire to move to Israel, a desire that she could not carry out because of her fam-ily's expectations that her father would return. After this sentence she re-turns to the issue of rumors about the return of those missing in the war:

> There were many "legends" in those days. One of my father's friends said he had seen him as late as December 1944. They met here in Budapest. My father was never taken out of the country to a camp like Auschwitz or Bergen-Belsen. So we thought he might be somewhere in the country, might have escaped the units made up by the Germans. For by December 1944, the Germans had fled.

They used my father to take apart the factory, and then the Germans took the machines. We thought my father might have disappeared somewhere. But they said there were rumors going on that if someone deserted, his family would be killed. People then believed in all sorts of things. I can imagine that my father, who did not live for anything else but his family, that he too believed these rumors and did not escape. So because of these rumors, these imaginary stories, we waited for him.

Zsuzsa mentions several types of "beliefs" that she criticizes and discounts post factum, even expressing anger for those who put their faith in them. She calls one such belief "legends" when she really is referring to rumors, which are a genre of oral lore in and of themselves.[51] The legends or rumors Zsuzsa encounters were regarding the survival of the missing men somewhere and their awaited return home. In the case of her own missing father, this belief does have backing in the words of one of the father's friend, who told the family that he had seen the father in the labor battalion at the end of 1944, very close to the liberation/occupation of Budapest by the Red Army and the withdrawal of the German army. It seems that Zsuzsa realizes, even if only in retrospect, that this is no proof at all that her father was not killed despite the withdrawal or during it.

Clearly, the narrator abandoned her hopes of her father's presumed survival many years ago, but only now, as she talks about these issues in a sober, distanced way, and with inner self-criticism, does she comprehend the extent to which this belief was groundless even in her childhood, and she is angry at herself and her family, who encouraged her to pin her hopes on an illusion. In fact, the discussion regarding the rumors of her father's return is another example of the defense mechanism of displacement, whose goal here is to explain why Zsuzsa and her family remained in Hungary after the war. But instead of saying outright that they stayed there because they awaited the father's return, she explains at length why the hope of her father's survival was misleading and erroneous. Thus, she shifts the emphasis from lack of rationale for remaining in the hated country to lack of rationale for anticipating the father's return. She may be doing it because it is easier to confront a conceptual error (the "belief" that the father would return) than an operational error of action or inaction (to leave Hungary or remain there despite the difficult emotions toward the country and the continuation of life in a hostile environment).

The other "belief" deals with the innocence or gullibility on the part of the men in the labor battalions—including Zsuzsa's father—who did not dare to desert, even when it was possible to do so, because they believed the threats of their commanders that their families would be harmed. Their "belief" stands in contrast to that of other men, such as Zsuzsa's uncle and his friends, who "hid, as Jewish deserters from the army." These men survived eventually, and it turned out that their families were never in danger because of them. Just as in the previous example, here, too, the narrator expresses repressed anger, only this time it is at her father and not just the family in general or, more likely, her mother. As opposed to his brother, the father was gullible enough to swallow the baseless threats of the Hungarians and the Germans and thus bring on himself his own death—according to Zsuzsa's theory.

But the anger directed at the father, who, according to her child's point of view, deserted her, is tempered by the father's faithfulness toward his family and his worries for their well-being, which the narrator understands in her mature adulthood. Zsuzsa tries to explain, in the name of her father as it were, his misgivings about deserting and thus causing harm to his family. Her father, who she says "lived only for his family," did not see any purpose in deserting and saving his own life if by doing do, he endangered his family. Zsuzsa understands today that her father really had no alternative than to act the way he did, and thus she excuses him from the guilt and the feelings of anger that she simultaneously directs toward him. If we accept Freud's ruling that opposites do not necessarily mean contradiction, and that dialectic choices reflect the reality of our lives better than the view that we choose among disparate options,[52] then we can say that Zsuzsa's anger about her father's death/abandonment on the one hand and her understanding of the possible reasons for his (in)action on the other are but two different aspects that coexist in her attitude toward her father. Zsuzsa's maturation, including the fact that she herself is now a parent, serves to temper her childish anger and strengthen her understanding of and identification with the father's deeds and considerations in the war period.

Unfortunately, suffering does not end for Zsuzsa Faludi when the war does. Her life after the war is depicted as a chronicle of various illnesses that plagued and continue to plague her. As a result of malnutrition and harsh living conditions during wartime, the narrator and her brother are both stricken by joint and bone diseases. In the unfolding of her life history she also directs much attention to describing a gynecological problem she suffered from, which she attributes to the trauma she endured in her childhood, and which threatened to make her sterile. However, as a result of a special surgery and after numerous complications, she does succeed in bearing a child and thus overcomes her malady and infertility, somewhat like Rozsi Háger did.

In describing the cause of her illness, Zsuzsa bases her explanation on the expertise of the doctors who treated her, in a way similar to Aranka Friedmann and Rika Salamon, who were mentioned earlier and who also brought medical "evidence" to support their stories. This "evidence" is composed of diagnoses and reports cited by the narrators to back up their assertions. In the present context, Zsuzsa's chronicle of maladies has a function in explaining why she did not leave the country at the end of the war or later on, a question that the narrator implicitly assumes I want an answer to.

In sickness as in health, Zsuzsa's story embodies the principle of stagnation versus movement as a constant conflict between her abilities and her desires.[53] This conflict has its roots in her childhood and adolescence, when she chooses to study in a Jewish high school since she "*cannot* look at the gentiles." Later on, when she wants to leave Hungary she cannot do so because she is dependent on her family, who still awaits the return of the missing father. Still later, in 1956, when political circumstances make it possible again to leave Hungary, the narrator is deep into medical treatments for her infertility. Again she hopes to leave, as many Jews did at the time, but her healing body and her intense desire to have a child effectively tie her to Hungary. As for today, when emigration is again possible, she is not capable of it because of her age, her present illnesses, and her daughter's family, who, as opposed to her, have no aspirations at all to leave Hungary. Zsuzsa summarizes this combination of circumstances and contrasts in her life by saying, "This is my bad luck: Every time the State is in trouble, and leaving it becomes easier, I too am in trouble and cannot leave." In other words, her bad luck does not allow her to rehabilitate herself from the crises and weaknesses of the country that had hurt her, because she herself suffers from personal crises at the same time. In addition to the practical implications of this uncalled-for identification, the narrator is troubled by the very analogy or similarity that seems to exist between herself and the entity (Hungary) that she feels so alienated from as a result of the Holocaust.[54]

Illnesses also have a central role in the life history of Irma Fischer, Zsuzsa Faludi's mother. However, whereas in the daughter's story, the illnesses represent stagnation and defeat, in the mother's story, the illnesses are constant companions of her life and pursuits, a combination that is synthesis and antithesis at once. While Irma Fischer's illnesses complicate her ability to work and support her family during the war and afterward, she does not give in but instead transforms her bad health into an adversary that she struggles against and ultimately overcomes. In conclusion, then, the mother's illnesses become a source of strength no less than they are a cause for her weakness.

The daughter, however, views her mother's work problems in a completely different light. She claims that the unprofessional and random jobs that her mother has always held and continues to hold even when she is eighty are not the result of her difficult life and the war that she endured but of her lack of proper professional training and qualification beforehand. The mother grew up in comparatively better economic circumstances than her children and did not imagine, nor did her parents before her, that she would need to work in order to maintain herself. This explanation of the daughter turns the tables on the mother by paradoxically viewing her suffering as the result of too "easy" a life in relation to the reality of the situation at the time and in the near future. It is hard to determine the extent to which the daughter is correct in her assessment. However, if we accept the assumption that no one could have foreseen the war and the Holocaust with the drastic changes that ensued,[55] we can safely assert that the daughter's arguments against the complacency and bourgeoisie of the mother are anachronistic. This view is likely to spring from the daughter's socialist-Communist education, which hailed professional training for both sexes and emphasized technology. Still, the factual explanation for the root of the mother's economic problems is, in and of itself, correct.

The most powerful instances of the implicit dialogue and dispute between the life histories of the mother and her daughter are found in their divergent descriptions of several life-threatening events and last-minute fortunate rescues. During the period of the Holocaust, the mother and daughter (and son/brother) were forced to hide and then flee from the Arrow Cross agents or guards, and their lives were in constant danger. One such incident took place even before Hungary was conquered by Germany, and it therefore reflects the depths of enmity and hostility the Hungarians held toward Jews regardless of the Nazi occupation. The following are the descriptions of the mother and the daughter concerning this event:

> Irma Fischer (the mother): Then there was this incident with my
> daughter. She went to school, she was very smart already when she

was in the first grade. My brothers and sister, my mother, everyone loved her because she was the first grandchild. Meanwhile, we were neighbors with this Gypsy couple, so then these Gypsies wrote a letter saying the child told them that the Americans [meaning, the Germans] are coming and then it will be bad for us Jews, and they will take us away. So the child . . . and the principal called my husband. They took my daughter to the cellar, and in the cellar they showed her the policeman. "Look, look over there, there is a policeman there. Now listen, tell the truth, did your parents say these things?" The child answered, crying, that she had not said or heard a thing. Then they also invited my husband to school. And he said, "The child and us, we don't talk about such things, we are happy just to be alive." But the poor child was beaten anyway. We wondered, she was just a child, maybe she did say it? But no, she did not. Then they told my husband that he should be happy that she stuck to her story, or else they would have taken away the whole family.

Zsuzsa Faludi (the daughter): I went to school in a working-class neighborhood and was quite a good pupil, meaning I was the best in the class. And since I was then the only grandchild in the family, the entire family, uncles and aunts, pampered me and gave me clothes and presents. I always had nice clothes to wear. This must have bothered many children in my class. At that time, 1942, the atmosphere was already very anti-Semitic. One girl in my class couldn't stand the fact that I was so special. So she and her family lied about me to the authorities, saying I said pro-Communist things in class. Had they proven it, then they would have arrested my entire family, because after all, a child only repeats what she has heard at home.

My father was called in for interrogation. This interrogation was carried out using a belt. My parents always believed that I told the truth, but the atmosphere was so tense that this time they doubted me. And this beating with a belt shocked me terribly, even more than the physical pain, although I will never forget that either —I screamed so loud that half the building heard me. Then it was found out that it was a lie. I was in fact guilty only of three things: I was Jewish, I was a good pupil, and my family dressed me nicely. Until the incident I could not grasp what it meant that I was of another religion. This first painful experience, at the age of six, made me realize that I was different.

The story is told by both mother and daughter as they experienced it and as it has resonated in their memories and consciousness over the years. The terms used in the narration of the experience naturally change in accordance with the identity of the narrator and her emotional baggage. The mother's descriptions and concepts are vague. She identifies the reason for the slander, as the daughter plainly calls it, as the "Gypsy" neighbors falsely maligning the daughter. She doesn't directly relate the reason for the act, which is their jealousy of her daughter, noting only that the daughter was especially cherished by her extended family since she was the first grandchild. It is only the daughter's account that directly connects the neighbors' jealous feelings with her Jewishness, her excellence in her studies, and her extended family's love for her. She also relates this one incident to the atmosphere of anti-Semitism that enveloped the country at the time.

The term *Gypsies* is probably not an actual description of the ethnic origins of the neighbors but an epithet used by the Jews toward others who harmed them in some way, as it appears in Rozsi Háger's narrative. This is similar to the derogatory terms used by the gentiles to refer to Jews, such as "dirty Jew," which could include not only Jews but also supporters of Jews and Jewish causes, somewhat like the term "Nigger lover" in American culture.[56]

The element of ambiguity or lack of clarity in the mother's story also finds expression in her use of the label "Americans" when evidently she intends to say "Germans," since if the family is accused of pro-Soviet incitement, then it is the Germans or their fascist Hungarian followers who would persecute them. At this point in time, somewhere in the years 1942–43, Hungarian Jews already had reasons for misgiving regarding the Germans, even if they knew nothing about concentration and death camps, which was often the case. The "policeman" in the mother's story is therefore a metonymy or extension of the authority represented by the Nazi Germans or Fascist Hungarians. It is this policeman who, according to the mother, was present during the first cross-examination of the daughter; only later on was the father summoned. This is one of the rare times that the mother expressly mentions her husband during her entire narrative, much like the first two narrators in this chapter. On this occasion, the mother describes her husband in a very positive light and emphasizes his resourcefulness and ability to respond to his interrogators satisfactorily. The mother also makes light of the whipping and its impact on the daughter, since she sees the punishment as part of the process of exoneration of the parents from the slanderous accusations supposedly attributed to them by their daughter.

The mother expresses an important principle at the end of her narrative: that in the framework of an oppressive power structure, strenuous denial is the only possible avenue to survival, no matter what the truth might be. Many other survivors have also expressed this rule in the Auschwitz "planet" as well. For example, in another interview I did for my doctorate, a prisoner nicknamed The Tall One denies that he has given food to his rabbi and is saved because of his denial, despite the admission of the rabbi that the man, in fact, gave him the food.[57] In other words, this cross-examination by the policeman is a kind of "introduction" to a totalitarian and oppressive world order whose ultimate extreme is the concentration and death camps and in which the truth is less important than the way in which issues are presented and received. It seems, therefore, that in this incident, the parents must flaunt their innocence even at the price of their daughter's beating. In contrast, from the daughter's point of view, this is a superfluous and traumatic punishment, as she claims that "my parents always believed that I told the truth." But from the mother's point of view, the incident is part of a long chain of similar life-threatening events throughout the prewar and war period, during which Jews needed to use every possible means to defend themselves in order to survive. For her, therefore, the whipping of the child, no matter how painful and humiliating, is a small price to pay for the survival of the entire family.

In contrast to the mother's description, the daughter's version is more exact, more accurately positioned in time and place, and creates a much more lucid and credible picture. The daughter mentions the anti-Semitic environment in Hungary even before the German conquest and thus emphasizes that the Hungarians are no less responsible for the suffering of the Jews than the Germans.[58] In the next stage, she indicates her excellence, the love that the entire family extended to her as the first and only granddaughter at that time, and that as a result of this and her attractive clothes, the jealousy of her non-Jewish classmates was aroused. In this way she reinforces the words of other Hungarian Holocaust survivors who describe anti-Semitic experiences of their youth, although in some cases hatred is directed toward the poor and less able among them as well as toward the outstanding ones. This makes them reach the conclusion that these incidents of blind anti-Semitism would have taken place regardless of the individual personalities or actions of the victims; they occurred simply because they are Jews.[59]

From this point forward in Zsuzsa Faludi's narration, her point of view in describing the event takes the focus of a child, as if she experiences the incident again while telling it. She dwells on the description of the flogging, although she does not actually mention who flogged her, despite the fact that when she discussed the incident informally, she specifically told me that it was her father. Evidently, however, in the formal and recorded version of the narrative, she prefers not to emphasize this fact. This is another attempt to defend her father from the unconscious anger she still feels toward him.

In addition, Zsuzsa does not expressly mention the existence of the policeman. In fact, the references to an impersonal third party such as "*they* said," and "*they* hit" in the daughter's story refer to her parents, while in her mother's account, this same pronoun refers to the authorities. In other words, in the eyes of the daughter, the abstract and external authorities do not exist or are not important in comparison with her own parents, who make up the rest of her so-called universe—besides herself—at that early age. She feels, therefore, that her suffering was not at the hands of the authorities, which she described earlier in neutral terms that evoke the scientific descriptions of her uncle, Sándor Fischer.[60] Instead, her suffering is delivered upon her by her parents—especially her father, to whom she assigns the same terminology as to the political authorities—because her parents depart in this instance from the relationship of trust that they formerly had with her, and thus deeply disappoint and betray her. The sentence "My parents always believed that I told the truth, but the atmosphere was so tense that this time they doubted me" is the essence of her attitude toward the incident then as well as today. Both as a child and as an adult, she bears a grudge against her parents, who did not believe her and preferred to "prove" their innocence and hers by whipping her. Thus, they acted like the hostile authorities and not like the loving parents she knew until then. However, in retrospect, she takes into account the influence of the oppressive regime on her parents and is capable of seeing their behavior not only through the eyes of a small child but also through the eyes of an adult and those of the regime. In light of all this, her account is in fact an attempt to bridge or reconcile two points of view: that of the child that she was then, and that of the mature woman and mother well experienced in oppressive regimes that she is today.

Another example of differing points of view between mother and daughter occurs at the height of the oppression, that is, during the period of the Nazi occupation. While the father was taken to the labor battalions, the mother and her two children stayed in a "protected house" under the auspices of the Swedish embassy, which issued them special life-saving documents called Swedish protection passes.[61] Afterward, they moved to the Jewish ghetto in Budapest. The mother describes three incidents in this context in which she and the children were saved, either by pure dumb luck or though her own ingenuity. These are: her foray to bring medicine for her sick son and an Arrow Cross man's turning a blind eye and letting her return to the "protected house" ("maybe he was a good man"); her success in convincing other Arrow Cross men, who came to take them away, that her children were sick with a contagious disease (it's unclear if that was from the "protected house" or the ghetto); and her escape with the children from the Arrow Cross men who led them to the Danube River, evidently to shoot them there. For her part, the daughter remembers two rescue events, one thanks to her father's intuition and one thanks to her mother's ingenuity, as described in the mother's last story. Following are the two descriptions of this last rescue, as outlined first by the mother and then by her daughter:

> Irma Fischer (the mother): When the Russians were approaching, there were air raid alerts frequently and the Hungarian guards rushed us out to the street, with our dead, and I took the children with me. I held my son in my arms. They even took us to this . . . what was the name of the street where the mayor lived? It doesn't matter. They took us and they wanted to take away the children, so I ran away and didn't care about anything. My daughter had a Star of David. I tore it off her. I held the boy [demonstrates how] and to . . .
> Zsuzsa Faludi: The name of the street is Szent István.
> Mrs. Fischer: Right. And they wanted to take away the children. And I said, Over my dead body. Only if I die. I went through a lot.

> Zsuzsa Faludi (the daughter): Finally, even the Swedish passes were no longer of help. One night the Arrow Cross guards came in, said these passes were forged anyway, and tore them to pieces in front of us. Then they took us out to this park, whose name I shall never forget, Szent István. They walked us to the Danube bank. I was

crying and a guard yelled at me. I remember he screamed that if I
didn't shut up he would hit me with his rifle. I remember the
weapon approaching my face. Then, in a second's flash of instinct,
my mother snatched me. With my brother in her arms, we sneaked
into the gate of one of the houses on the way. It is pure luck that
none of the guards shot us. My mother tore off her own star and
mine too, and we started wandering around, without any documents. Then my uncle found us and hid us for a while.

The mother's version brings to mind a dream, or more accurately, a
nightmare in which she is carried on a wave of associations that lead her
to the various stages of her story. Therefore, not surprisingly, her story is
not plainly fixed in time or space. When she starts talking about the
ghetto, at first she seems to want to tell about her experiences in the
ghetto *after* the stay in the "protected house." But then she recalls that
she has not yet explained the transition from the "protected house" to
the ghetto, and that this is a story in itself. She does point out, however,
unlike the daughter, that this happens at a later stage of the war, when
the Russian army is already at the entrance to the city. But she does not
stop to explain that it is not the Russians who are leading them, as it
would seem from her ambiguous wording, or even the Germans, but
instead the Arrow Cross militia men of the Hungarian Fascist Party. This
ambiguity may be the result of the intensity of her emotions while
recalling the incident, but it may also have deeper roots. These roots
would be connected to a denial mechanism that attempts to play down
the fact that the people who threatened their lives then, the Hungarians,
are the very people among whom the narrator lives to this day. This
perspective helps us understand the atmosphere of anxiety that is present in Irma's narrative as a whole and becomes overpowering especially
toward its ending.

In the same spirit, Irma Fischer both remembers and forgets the site
where they were taken by the Arrow Cross men. She tries to remember
the name of the place and does not succeed, but when her daughter
reminds her of the name it is as if she remembers it by herself, and thus
she integrates this detail in her story. She confirms that this is the place
by saying "right," but does not even repeat the name and instead continues her story. It is as if the two memories, the mother's and the
daughter's, are merged for a split second in order to complete the story
and then part again to create the two women's separate and distinct
versions.

The mother is not concerned with "orientation," or the anchoring of her narrative in time, place, or historical circumstance.[62] Instead, she is more intent on conveying the perceptions and emotions she experienced during these events and relives during their narration. These perceptions have been instilled in her from the time that the events transpired until the present, when she sums up the entirety of her burden by saying, "I went through a lot." She also highlights her despair and anguish in the sentence "and I didn't even care," meaning that she didn't care what they did to her as long as her children remained with her. This interpretation is reinforced in her words when she expressly points out that "they wanted to take the children away" from her and that she refused by saying, probably not aloud, "Over my dead body. Only if I die." This facet of Irma Fischer's narrative may remind us of stories of other women survivors who went through similar extreme experiences. Hilda Timar, for example, refused to hand over her baby daughter despite repeated orders to do so; and Ariella Greenfeld dashed out of a group of women destined to death in Auschwitz to join another group that had a chance at life. Ariella herself did not grasp the import of her actions in the first seconds afterward, but years later she describes her emotions as those of despair, courage, and indifference at one and the same time.[63]

To return to the present mother and daughter, the daughter's recollection of the same life-threatening event near the Danube River is more clearly anchored in time, space, and circumstances, a characteristic that runs through Zsuzsa Faludi's entire narrative. Although the daughter does not specify the exact time in which the incident took place, she tells us of the decision of the Arrow Cross militia to disqualify the protection passes as being no longer valid. This, in turn, enables us to connect the personal experience of the narrator with well-known historical events. In addition, we know from her mother's narrative that this took place when the Russian army was poised to conquer the city. Then also, the daughter clearly remembers the name of the square at which the Jews were gathered to be taken to the banks of the Danube River. Whereas the mother cannot remember the name of the site, the daughter, by contrast, cannot forget it. The emphasis in the daughter's narrative is on the positive or the existent, on what actually took place, and not on what is omitted or absent, or could have happened but did not happen. Therefore, in contrast to the mother's feeling of despair and passivity, the daughter emphasizes the mother's good instincts and the courage needed for the act of despair that she carried out. The daughter of course understands the arbitrariness of the success: she realizes that they could just as easily have been shot, as happened in many other similar incidents in the Holocaust. But the fact is that the family was saved just the same, and the daughter is alive today to speak about this rescue. She therefore feels that she owes her life to her mother's ingenuity and courage, and she takes advantage of the narrative event in order to express her appreciation for the mother's deed. On this occasion, the critical tone is totally absent from her narrative, unlike many other sections of her life history, which carry a residue of anger and criticism toward both her parents.

GZ (anonymous): The Daughter Who Narrates and Lives the Life (History) of Her Mother

GZ, resident of Budapest, a friend and contemporary of Zsuzsa Faludi, told me the story of her life in the house of her friend. This was the same house in which I lived during the month I stayed in Hungary for the purpose of collecting life histories. Since GZ was the one who took the initiative to come to me, thus clearly expressing her willingness to tell me her story, I found her hesitant behavior to be puzzling. First, she said that that she felt doubtful if she was a suitable candidate for my research since, unlike other interviewees, she experienced positive and humane treatment from the Hungarians. She felt that, therefore, she would not be able to indict them as much as the others could (she seemed to know about "others" although she never asked me anything about their life histories, so she may have thought of Zsuzsa's account, which she generally knew and in which Hungarians are indicted). In addition, she objected to the spontaneous nature of the interview and asked to plan and decide beforehand with me what she would talk about and only then tape her words. She said that she learned how to organize her thoughts this way from her mother, who was an author and a journalist, and that it would be difficult for her to be interviewed any other way. In light of her explanations, I let her say her introductory words, which included some of the "episodes" that she told me at length later on, and which usually ended in rhetorical questions such as, "Could such a man be an enemy?" or "Is this an example of human evil?" and the like.

After this long introduction, GZ told me her life history rather briefly, in flowery language and in a style that is far more common in written narratives than oral accounts. Most of her language is phrased in long, compound sentences with elaborate subordinate clauses that serve to describe reasons, results, or reservations, as I will soon demonstrate.

She also sprinkled her text with expressions such as "An example of this," or "In an interesting way," or "As a result of," which again characterize discursive rather than descriptive expression and attest to ostensible distance of the narrator toward the things narrated. Together with this, and inevitably, since all this was an oral interaction and not a written correspondence, her story contains some grammatical errors and lapses in style, which would not have been created had the interviewee not tried so hard to express herself in as sophisticated a manner as possible. Some examples of these kinds of expressions and sentences are: "Thus we had a roof and heat over our heads," or "The Gelért hotel had a spring, a medical healing spring, which also meant drinking water," even though water from healing springs is not necessarily also drinking water.

A close analysis of GZ's narrative shows that the form and substance of her life history reflect two main themes. One is the narrator's strong identification as both a Jew and a Hungarian, or a "Hungarian of Moses' religion" despite her experience of the Holocaust. The second is her relation to her mother, in whose shadow she took refuge during the most difficult period of her life, and whose figure continues to influence, shadow, and even oppress her over thirty years after the mother's death.

The first theme is rather unique in the corpus of life histories I collected. All the other survivors I interviewed identified themselves unequivocally as Jews, albeit with no emphasis on religion or nationality in some cases. In contrast, GZ bears a complex or divided identity, and thus identifies with and relates herself to a larger circle of artists and intellectuals of Jewish birth who stood out in prewar Hungary and today as well. An outstanding example of this dichotomy is the poet Miklós Radnóti, who died while serving in the labor battalions, despite the fact that he never identified himself as a Jew. Even in his autobiographical poems, which were written soon before he died in the labor service, Radnóti did not recognize the "Jewish problem" as concerning him.[64] The topic of GZ's Jewish identity is not our chief concern here, owing to its rarity in the inclusive life history corpus, and it is certainly secondary compared with the narrator's recurrent allusions to her mother. But it has to be stated as background to some of the incidents that appear in GZ's life history and the explanations she supplies for them.

GZ begins her story by reciting her birthplace, Budapest, and the year she was born; then, she tells us the story of her mother's life and her mother's career before and after the war. During the German occupation, the mother and daughter wander from one hiding place to the other, while the mother uses her connections with well-known Hungarian cultural personalities in order to find hiding places for her and her daughter. GZ also tells us about her father and the crisis in her parents' relationship at the beginning of the war. While her mother is described as a person who, though fragile, has great resourcefulness, her father is described as an irresponsible man who allows his stamp-collecting hobby to impoverish the family, thus causing the inevitable breakup. Although the father comes from a wealthy and well-known family, he loses his job as an accountant even before the war and his family somewhat later. It seems that he even symbolically loses his blood relationship with his family since the mother, who "anticipates the future," decides to change the family name to one that has a more Hungarian ring. The daughter summarizes the issue of the name change and its implications in this way: "Her far-sightedness proved itself useful in the future as well, because after liberation our original, German-sounding name would have also been problematic under the Communists. The family used to be very rich once and even owned a factory in Hungary. Even though we never enjoyed this wealth—my father was already a poor man and his hobby only plunged him even deeper into poverty—the Communists would have still persecuted us for belonging to the upper class in the prewar period. Therefore, the name change turned out to be very advantageous for us."

In this passage, the narrator describes the complex relationship between her parents as well as exhibits her dense and often problematic style. As is the case in many of the narratives of other narrators in this chapter, here, too, the mother is described as active, full of resourcefulness and ingenuity, and clearly dominant in her relationship with her husband, GZ's father. And here, too, the mother is realistic and sees what the future holds, while the father does not even grasp the significance of the present. Instead, he withdraws from the world and immerses himself in his hobby.

The daughter, our narrator, is clearly on her mother's side throughout her story. However, she herself is absent from most of the narrative, which ostensibly is the story of *her* life. She hardly describes her own actions and her own life, not during her mother's lifetime or after her mother's death, just as she does not describe her relationship with her mother by way of conversations that they had or things that her mother did with regard to her. What emerges, then, is that the mother, who erases her husband from her own life and the life of her daughter, does something similar with her daughter as well, although, of course, it is the daughter who does it to herself in the narrative she tells and by the way she tells it. Thus, the daughter is mostly and paradoxically missing from her own life history, except for a few occasional remnants, as we shall soon see.

There is a symbolic aspect to GZ's "disappearance," which is also expressed in her name. GZ chose to tell her story anonymously, along with only three additional narrators from a total of thirty-nine people whom I interviewed for my doctorate. Since the very act of relating a life history involves the creation of an identity and the establishing of one's presence on the stage of history, especially in the context of the Holocaust, the decision to remain anonymous within this context arouses surprise. The significance of the anonymity in this case is explained and explicated within the life history itself. The disappearance or erasure of GZ's name is part of her tendency to disappear under the shade of her mother, to scrutinize the history of her life—actually, the history of her mother's life—from the side, and to remain uninvolved and unidentified as much as possible.

Yet the narrator's disappearance is not total. GZ singles out her studies as the one constant in her inconstant and irregular life. This is similar to the previous narrator, Zsuzsa Faludi, who is described by her mother as one who never stopped studying and excelling in her studies despite the difficulties of her life. GZ, too, starts to study right after the end of the war, although unlike Zsuzsa Faludi, she exhibits no interest in the subjects of Judaism and Hebrew that she is forced to learn in the town of Pécs, and therefore does not succeed in them. This issue is connected to GZ's complex identity as a Jew and Hungarian, as has been discussed, and to her refusal to become more Jewish by learning about Judaism. Next, she enrolls in engineering "for pragmatic reasons, because that is the quickest route to a good salary," and manages to graduate and obtain a good job, to her mother's gratification. Her mother dies at a young age just shortly afterward, from "the great suffering she underwent in her life and her chain smoking." The daughter does not interrupt her studies even in her short exile with her mother in France, or after their return to Hungary as a result of this failed attempt at emigration. Close to the end of her narrative, she summarizes her achievements and mentions that she has earned four degrees; yet despite all this, her salary or pension "is barely enough to cover basic living expenses."

GZ's scholastic and professional achievements might seem an attempt to escape the financial constraints and pressures that characterized her mother's life and her own life alongside her mother. As opposed to her mother's more spiritual and "fluffy" pursuits in journalism and literature, she does succeed in achieving a technological career. Nevertheless, she too is unable to escape the financial pressures that characterized her mother's life, with or without her husband, before the war, during the war, and after it, until her death. In light of her mother's great influence on her, it is possible to read GZ's financial hardships as a sign of similarity between the two, in spite of the fact that externally, GZ's life is completely different from that of her mother's.[65]

The daughter resembles her mother in other ways as well and cannot help but follow in her footsteps. On the one hand, the mother is described as a very practical person who knows how to do the right thing at the right time, to "foresee" the future and, ultimately, to save her own life and the life of her daughter. On the other hand, the mother is not able to create the basis for a normal, relaxed family life even after the war. She joins the Communist Party, then condemns the injustice in the regime and is fired from her job in journalism—a cycle that repeats itself after the revolution of 1956. She then tries to emigrate to France as a dissident but meets with an official representative of the Hungarian regime in Paris and is subsequently returned to Hungary by the French authorities. In this context, the daughter mentions her refusal to leave Hungary and accompany her mother, despite the fact that she is passively dragged along with her mother, against her objections.

Considering her entire life cycle then, the mother emerges as an innocent and idealistic figure who is also unstable and unable to foresee the future, despite the fact that she is described as having exactly that trait. The daughter, like her mother, also fails to read the future, at least as far as her professional life is concerned. Thus, the daughter, like her mother, is an anxious and haunted figure, despite her attempts to overcome her "demons" and present herself in a different light. This facet of the daughter's figure is mentioned only at the end of the interview, as an answer to my question about the influence of the war on her life. Although my question related to her feelings of identification, she chooses to answer from a different viewpoint entirely, evidently of greater importance to her. These are her words: "If it were not for the Holocaust, I would have experienced a much more relaxed childhood and my nerves today would be in a much better state. Since one's childhood affects one's nervous system and entire life, no doubt I would have had a happier and more balanced life . . . All in all, I was left with very bad nerves and an empty life."

This is an unusual admission for the narrator, since here she talks only about herself and does not mention her mother. She relates to the influence of her childhood on her entire life, a topic that she has not dealt with before. Yet, even now, she does not cite any specific incidents in her childhood that subsequently affected her nerves, unlike Zsuzsa Faludi, who demonstrates her contentions through several incidents in her life history. Thus, the end of GZ's narrative could also be the beginning of another narrative, a second version, since this version does not really tell the story of her life. Her concluding sentences are a tantalizing invitation to ask her more regarding the reasons for the status of her nerves and her "empty life," but it is doubtful whether her answers to these questions would produce anything different than what she has already told, and whether, in fact, she is able to relate to her own life, apart from her mother's life, on any level.

3

The Holocaust Experience of Its Listeners and Readers
A Phenomenological-Hermeneutic Analysis of Ten Life Histories

> And in accordance with your point of view,
> you identify with some of them. When you
> encounter insolvable questions, you surely
> offer a number of solutions, then with great
> refinement you select one, and circle the
> square to create the perfect picture.
>
> Shoshi Brainer, *Ariadna*

The life histories that are presented and analyzed in this chapter are divided into two major groups. One (including the life histories of Dora Ashkenazi, Rachel Markowitz, and Ruth Matias) presents a mosaic of languages and cultures, and the second (including the accounts of the Heiman and Bihari couples and those of Berta Wazner, Esther Israel, and Piri Meister) is characterized by a tension between revealing and concealing, or presence and absence, and is further subdivided into two subgroups. The narratives of the first group resemble those in the previous chapter in that the pre-Holocaust period in them is relatively short and presented as an introduction to the Holocaust chapter in the lives of the narrators. The Holocaust period is central in terms of both its length and its thematic breadth, while the post-Holocaust period is no less significant and demanding.

The second group of stories differs in significant ways from the two previous groups (the first group and that of the previous chapter). The period preceding the Holocaust is presented briefly in this group, too, with the exception of Dr. Ernő Bihari, who dwells much on this period.

The Holocaust is described in abbreviated form (sometimes in just a few sentences), with only a general description and listing of names of places or dates, instead of descriptions of the unique experiences that the narrators themselves underwent during this period. In contrast, the post-Holocaust period is described in much more detail. Yet, some of the narrators refer back to the Holocaust period while they describe the post-Holocaust period in their lives, and all of them were willing to elaborate on the Holocaust period when I posed questions for clarification at the end of their spontaneous narration. Concerning this rather reticent group, I will analyze the tension between revealing and concealing in the discourse of its narrators, though the "revelations" of these narrators are limited in scope. Therefore, in this group, the interpretative or hermeneutic activity is that of those who listen to or read the stories, while in the first group of life histories in this chapter this interpretative activity is carried out also by the narrators themselves and even by figures in their narratives, as we shall see.

The Phenomenological Approach and
Its Application in the Analysis of the Life Histories

Before I enter into a discussion of the narratives, it is necessary to enlarge a bit on the principles of the literary phenomenological approach and the hermeneutic activity that is connected to it or results from it. I shall start with hermeneutics. Hermeneutics, as defined as far back as the nineteenth century by the German philosopher Wilhelm Dilthey, is the study of the processes of understanding (*Verstehen*).[1] This is a scientific and systematic process, and as such it also enables the scholar to generate predictions on the basis of phenomena that have already been recognized and studied.[2] Hans Georg Gadamer relates to play in all its forms, including acting, performance, and the work of art, as objects with a consistent structure that can therefore be studied scientifically and systematically.[3] Furthermore, the very process of understanding is often a presentation or revelation of the object's own rules and innate consistency.[4] This principle is further explicated and demonstrated by the work of literary scholars such as Stanley Fish from a predominantly stylistic aspect, and Umberto Eco, Wolfgang Iser, Paul Ricoeur, and others from narratological and philosophical ones. Whatever the specific perspective, all these scholars tend to display their analytic tools and methods through their application while reading and

experiencing various literary texts, as will be done in my own implementation of the work of these scholars.

The activity of understanding and its pursuit fill an empty void or
deficiency in our consciousness, since often the true nature of things is
unknown to us, and all that is left for us to do is suggest interpretations
or explanations.[5] Hence the connection of hermeneutics to Hermes, the
messenger of the gods, and hermeneutics as an activity of interpreting
signs from unknown worlds or distant times.[6] This situation, in which
all that is left in the search for understanding is to suggest interpretations, is key in the present corpus of narratives, despite the fact that in
essence, these are verbal accounts created by immediate interaction and
live communication between contemporary narrators and myself. The
very nature of this interaction, then, would seem to give me an immediate opportunity to examine and answer the questions that arise from the
stories of these narrators. However, the reality of these narrative events
proves to be much more complicated. Apart from the fact that the
nature of the narrative event is such that I, as listener, cannot always fully
comprehend it while it takes place, we must also consider the fact that
the content and substance of these narratives are often difficult to recall,
tell, and absorb for both narrators and listener. In addition, the written
texts in front of us are not the exact same accounts as told by the
narrators, as anyone who has ever dealt with collecting and transcribing
narratives and discourse well knows. Therefore, the texts are often vague
and obscure or raise even more questions than the narratives did when
told to me originally. These difficulties arise on a linguistic, psychological, and ideological level. It follows, then, that despite the fact that the
narrators ostensibly have a chance to explain themselves more than
equivalent narrators and narratives in written literature, this is not accomplished solely by the act of narration. The narratives still need an
additional layer of interpretation and decipherment, or creation of
meaning. This interpretation does not profess to reach the *only* possible
truth (if such a thing exists) regarding these life histories but to present
one or more possible understandings that rise from the way one interpreter's consciousness operates.

In the same spirit, according to Georges Poulet, while the meaning
or the outcome of the interpretation does not belong to anyone, not
even the interpreter, like a coin, it may be passed "from hand to hand."
Gadamer too holds that a text's meaning is "owned" neither by its reader
nor its writer.[7] To be more exact, and in the spirit of reader-response

criticism, the meaning or implications that may be in a text are not realized until the text is read, heard, or experienced in some way by some kind of audience. It is the interaction between the text and its audience(s) that allows the text's more latent or implicit significance to gain expression and realization.

The relationship between the phenomenological approach and the hermeneutic activity, or the uniqueness of phenomenological hermeneutics, is based on the view that there is a connection between understanding a text—and, we may add, creating a text—and self-understanding. This does not refer to understanding in terms of personal psychological or psychoanalytic notions but rather to a more general process that the consciousness of every reader undergoes when he or she encounters a text or a phenomenon. The consciousness of this implied reader and the meaning encoded in the text are at the foundation of the phenomenological literary analysis. Jurgen Habermas explains that in this process, the "I" (of the reader) becomes an external entity, so that an external or historical event can become part of this same "I." Paul Ricoeur describes the reader's broadening of consciousness and its modifications, and claims that the process of experiencing or interpreting a text causes the reader to interpret her or himself and thus understand himself or herself better, or differently than before. Edmund Husserl formulates these changes in awareness in phenomenological terminology as the transition from a "natural attitude" to a "phenomenological attitude." The "natural attitude" is also called "life world." In "The Reading Process," Iser describes these transitions as a process whereby the reader leaves his or her familiar world to take part in the "adventure" extended to him or her by the literary text. At the same time, through experiencing a different reality, the reader gains insight into aspects of his or her own life. Later on in the article, Iser again relates to this paradox or presumed contradiction and claims that this process involves or results in an abolishing of the distinction between subject and object, at least temporarily.[8]

Gelya Frank's conclusions are of great significance to the auto-biographical narratives in the present work, in which the Holocaust plays a central role. She concludes that the life history created by the interaction between researcher and narrator contains a double auto-biography; that is, the autobiography of both of them, separately and as one.[9] This may seem an overstatement, but Frank draws our attention to the degree to which the researcher becomes a partner, so to speak, in forming the biography of someone else's life by virtue of listening to and understanding the story and thereby undergoing processes of identification and internalization.

A number of literary scholars address the experience undergone by the listener, reader, or any interlocutor of a text in and through the act of experiencing it. As has been explained, these scholars focus on the presumed persona of the reader or audience according to their understanding of the author's perception of this audience. Tzvetan Todorov, for example, claims that the character of the reader is always present in his analyses.[10] Other scholars also relate to the reader, albeit indirectly, and make mention of him or her in their analyses. Their approaches may differ, but they agree that the reader's understanding of the text is affected by both the text itself and the reader's intellectual and emotional background.[11]

However, we must keep in mind that these contentions are based on the study of written works, while in the case of oral narratives the concept of the audience is more complex or problematic. Our audience is an entity split into (at least) two: the listener (me), who listened to the narratives while they were being created and contributed to their creation by carrying on a dialogue, and finally transcribed and turned them into texts; and the reader (myself and any other reader), who experiences the narratives and the dialogues that took place within the narrative events. Thus, we deal not only with a narrator or author and their implied reader(s) but also with flesh-and-blood narrators and readers whose actions can be studied and referred to in empirical and experiential terms more easily than would be possible with written texts. In addition, my presence at the time of narration is a central factor in the creation of context, or the process of contextualization. The analyses of these narratives must then relate to the situational context as well, as was done in the analyses of the narratives of mothers and daughters in the previous chapter.

The discussion of context leads us to consider the more general or cultural contexts of these narratives, such as their literary, historical, social, and psychological background. For example, Rachel Markowitz relates her life history in Israel during the Gulf War of January 1991, and this affects the conclusions that she reaches at the end of her story. Similarly, Ernő Bihari tells his story in the Hungary of September 1991, in the shadow of the Yugoslavian civil war—a war that threatened neighboring Hungary and Dr. Bihari himself as a citizen of Hungary. Another citizen of Hungary, Károly Krausz, tells his story during the intermediate days of

the Jewish festival of *Sukkoth*. This makes him recall an "act of faith" that
he carried out during *Sukkoth* many years ago, on the eve of the Holocaust of Hungarian Jewry, when he brought home a *lulav* [palm] branch
from the synagogue to his sick mother and thus proudly demonstrated
his Jewishness in public.[12] These examples show that in the sort of oral
narratives analyzed here, it is important to pay close attention to a number of elements and factors: the text or work that is created by the interaction between the narrators and the researcher; the processes that take
place in the consciousness of the participants, be they the narrators, the
researcher, or the readers of the narratives; and in addition, all the components of the narrative event, including their narrow and broad, or
situational and cultural, contexts.[13]

Let us now turn to the principles of the phenomenological approach
and their application by the scholars mentioned thus far. First, we recall the
practical instruction of Stanley Fish that when we read phenomenologi-
cally, we must ask and answer the question "What does this [sentence/text]
do?" In other words, we deal not with aesthetics or evaluation but with
rhetoric and close analysis of the text and its effect on the reader.[14] The
attempt to describe the text's activation of its reader must be firmly rooted
in time and attentive to diachronic considerations, unlike structuralist
analyses, which tend to be more synchronic or nonhistorical and uncon-
textualized. This analysis must show awareness of the fact that reading and
interpretation are in themselves temporal processes and that there are
therefore significant differences between the first reading of a text and any
subsequent readings.[15]

The reader must also take action to understand how the text affects
him or her. Umberto Eco and Christine Brooke-Rose categorize literary
texts according to the measure in which they invite or allow the reader to
create meaning while reading. Eco distinguishes between "closed" and
"open" texts, which either hinder or encourage the reader's chances of
deciphering and realizing his or her role in the (p)act of reading.[16]
Brooke-Rose also discusses examples of "closed" and "open" texts,
which she terms "over-determined" and "under-determined," respec-
tively. In addition, and in accordance with these categories, she distinguishes between the "sub critical" reader, who does not have enough
data and tools to operate vis-à-vis the too "closed" text, and the "over
critical" reader who is given—at times excessive—data and tools to interpret the text.[17] Here, too, we should remember that all this is not about
the differing abilities of various real readers but about implied or encoded readers built into various texts by their authors. From this per-

spective, Brooke-Rose's view of the reader is close to that of Tzvetan Todorov and thus more attentive and relevant to written than to oral literature.

A reasonably open text, which is optimal for phenomenological interpretation, enables the reader to realize his or her function in creating the text's meaning. A too open or avant-garde text disturbs the balance between the contribution of author and reader and their sharing of consciousness. According to Eco, the reader of a reasonably open text is invited or encouraged to create "ghost chapters," that is, to fill in the missing parts of the text on the basis of information given in it.[18] Wolfgang Iser, in his various works, describes the process by which the reader creates and "fills in the blanks." First of all, the reader must maintain open vistas as it were, to be able to "skip" backward and forward in time within the text, reconstruct its past, and foresee its future. Second, the reader must create, complete, or explain the text's consistency or, rather, its inconsistency, as we shall often see later in this chapter. In addition, the reader must cope with what Iser calls "blockages," or instances in which the reader has difficulty in connecting or bridging consecutive sections of the text.[19]

All these actions of the implied reader are grouped under the heading of "picturing." Picturing is the ability of the reader to imagine or reconstruct things that are not directly expressed or explained by the narrator, thus enabling the reader to complete the "ghost chapters" or sections of the text through an implicit sharing of consciousness between reader and narrator.[20] This act of imagination results in, according to Eco, an entire system of possible, imaginary, or desired worlds. Iser, on the other hand, characterizes the process of reading as a dynamics of creating illusions and shattering them, again and again: "We look forward, we look back, we decide, we change our decisions, we form expectations, we are shocked by their non-fulfillment, we question, we muse, we accept, we reject; this is the dynamic process of recreation."[21]

In his later studies, Iser turns to what he terms literary-anthropological readings of narratives, texts, and in fact the historical and sociocultural settings in which they are produced, read, and rooted.[22] This turn is part of a more general readmission of history and historical and cultural considerations into literary interpretation. This stage heralds the rise of new historicism,[23] or the opening up of literary studies to social sciences and vice versa, at first methodologically and then philosophically and politically as well. This is also the stage—mostly during the 1990s—at which all sorts of not strictly anthropological "anthropologies" began to appear.[24] Currently, fields such as anthropology, sociology, and psychology welcome and embrace textual analysis and what they term "qualitative" methods, whereas literary cultural studies at present perform interdisciplinary readings of literary as well as historical, legal, political, commercial, and popular texts.[25] This broadening of analytical method and scope entails an extension of the concept of genre to include different kinds of discourses related to these texts, such as film or cinematography, television documentary or docudrama, soap opera, court and political speeches, advertisements, and persuasive language in general. The present study participates in these developments through its ties with historical study and more specifically the study of personal testimony, which in the context of the Holocaust gains special magnitude and calls for a combination of analytical approaches and tools related to the previously listed disciplines and their meeting points.

In my analysis, then, of the life histories of the first out of the two groups in this chapter, which display what I called "a mosaic of languages and cultures," I demonstrate some of the principles of the phenomenological-hermeneutic analysis of texts, while paying special attention to the ways in which the narrators themselves see and explain their stories and cause their audience to respond to their interpretations. In other words, in this group, the narrators' knowing and understanding of events when they occurred and while narrating them are the object for the phenomenological-hermeneutic analysis by both the narrators and myself. Then, I turn to the issue of the various languages that crop up in the narratives in this group. I discuss the role of languages in the cultures of the narrators (who spent most of their lives in Israel) during the time of the narrated events and today, and the function of these languages as an object of interpretation.

In contrast, my analysis of the life histories of the second group in this chapter, which I called reticent, focuses on the tension between revealing and concealing. The narrators in this group avoid explaining their life histories in any detail, and some of them almost avoid telling at all, thus leaving interpretation of their stories solely to the audience. Therefore, the audience is forced to supply their own interpretations for these two aspects: topics that are only alluded to or hinted at in the narratives, and the contribution of the interaction between husband and wife and between narrator and listener to the creation of the stories and their meanings.

The Analytical Activity of the
Audience vis-à-vis the Life Histories

The narrators of the first group in this chapter, Dora Ashkenazi, Rachel Markowitz, and Ruth Matias, all integrate their life histories into the general and generally well-known history of the period in question and especially the Holocaust. However, this integration is not done explicitly, and external events are not specifically mentioned, because the narrators assume that their audience is well versed in the history of the time period and familiar with its associated terminology. Therefore, they freely use terms such as *appell* and *selection* without explanation, since they are confident that their audience is familiar with their meanings. Accordingly, many of their cryptic descriptions of events rest on the assumption that their audience can "fill in the blanks," to use Iser's term.

Examples of these descriptions include the arrival of the deportees in Auschwitz, the process of being directed "to the right and the left," the tension that accompanies each entrance to the "showers" and "disinfection" rooms, and the repeated "selections" that the prisoners are forced to undergo. In some of these descriptions, gaps of understanding may appear between the narrators and their audience or readers, whether because of the narrators' excitement and inability to hear their own narrations and process them, or because things are not clear even to themselves. An example of this kind of gap is demonstrated by Dora Ashkenazi (originally from Dunaszerdahely, resident of Bazera, Israel, at the time of the interview), in her description of the "selection" event in which she is forever parted from her older sister. Soon after, this pregnant sister is taken with her nine-month-old son to the gas chambers and crematorium: "My older sister had a small child when we reached Auschwitz. She had a nine-month-old baby boy, and she was also six months pregnant. I was holding her baby in my arms. In the distance I saw my best friend, who had already passed the 'selection,' whereas I was in the next-to-the-last row. I saw that women with small children were sent in another direction, so I told my sister, 'Take the child, for the child could have stayed with me.' Then Mengele said to me in Hungarian, 'Hand over the child quietly, you'll see each other again on Sunday.'"

The source of the confusion in this passage is that the word *not* seems to be missing between the words *could* and *have* in the next-to-the-last sentence. It is clear that Dora realizes at this point that the child can *no longer* remain with her, and that she must hand over the child to its mother, who will then join the group of mothers and children in "[the] other direction." Mengele's comment, as quoted by the narrator, also strengthens this understanding of the situation. Yet the "not" is missing. It is perhaps accidentally omitted, but perhaps there is another explanation for its absence, one related not to content but to form and performance of this burdened narrative section.[26]

When I listened once more to the tape of the narrative, it became clear to me that Dora did say the exact words that I recorded; there was no mistake about that. Now it was also clear that the key to the misunderstanding lies in the change of volume and tone in the narrator's voice when she utters the two parts of the sentence in question. Listening again to Dora's words, which is analogous to rereading a difficult text, involves not only the things said and the way they are said but also my way of grasping them when told me and transcribed by me. When Dora reconstructs her words to her sister, "Take your child," it sounds as if she is reproducing her shout to her sister in the loud tone of voice that would have been necessary to rise above the noisy, tumultuous, and panicky background of this scene in Auschwitz. But in the next part of the sentence, when she says, "for the child could have stayed with me," there is a sharp drop in her tone and intensity, as if she returns to the present and directs this part of the sentence to me again. In other words, the two parts of the sentence are directed at two different addressees or audiences and belong to two different contexts. Accordingly, the word "for" (in Hebrew, *shç*), which connects between the two parts, serves here to describe not a reason but a possible alternative, such as "*otherwise*, the child could have stayed with me." In this instance, Dora turns to me to say that had she not handed the child to his mother, the child would have stayed with her, and she, like her pregnant sister, would also have died in the gas chambers. Thus, in effect, the narrator describes how her instincts and intuition led her to save her own life. This way of relating (to) the event serves to protect her from possible pangs of conscience, as she ostensibly does not know what is about to happen— or rather, that she instinctively knows and does not know at one and the same time.

Dora's allusion to her best friend, who is constantly mentioned throughout her narrative, is just as pertinent to the way Dora captures reality at this point. The narrator sees her friend, who is a sort of mirror or parallel image of herself, on the safe side of those who made it through the "selection," and she, too, wants to reach that point. Instinctively, she realizes that the nephew in her arms will prevent her from reaching her friend, even if only because of the rigid principles of sorting and classification employed by the Nazis, who dictate that mothers with small children must be in a separate group. Therefore, the narrator conforms to this world order, which rules her life from this point and on, and hands the child over to his mother and to the fate awaiting both. Viewing Dora's narrative thus, we come to realize how her choppy, disconnected descriptions are joined into an apologetic account, or explanation, according to which Dora feels the threat of impending doom even though she cannot express this fully and verbally in retrospect.

Likewise, Dora does not expressly refer to the subsequent death of her sister and nephew, but it is clearly implied in her earlier words concerning "my older sister with her baby boy . . . and another sister, who survived," and the knowledge of her audience concerning the slim odds for survival of infants and young or pregnant mothers in Auschwitz. In terms of the phenomenological-hermeneutic negotiation for the understanding of her life history, Dora clearly lets her audience reach their own conclusions about the events that she describes, and perhaps reformulate her account to clarify this event in which she was saved while most of her family members were sent to their deaths. Being heavily burdened with the memory of this event, Dora avoids formulating its description more lucidly so that the "responsibility"[27] for (re)-phrasing and creating meaning in this scene is thrust only on the immediate listener and later readers of her narrative.

Another incident in which Dora lets her audience "picture" the event occurs in her description of the improvement in her living conditions after she was transferred to work in a "factory for fine mechanics." Just as the abrupt entry into the world of the camps is accompanied by a confiscation of personal belongings, impinging on the privacy of the deportees, and a general deterioration in their status as human beings— as many survivors repeatedly describe—so the improvement in their clothing, personal hygiene, and food signify for them a rise in the value of their lives in the eyes of their jailors, even if only partially and temporarily. In this instance, Dora relates how the engineer in charge of the prisoners "sent us to wash. I shall never forget it. They brought us to the factory's shower house, with real ceramic tiles and hot water. Oh, *Hamechaye* [Hebrew: thank God]. We washed. We hadn't washed this way since June, and by now it was September already. Then we stood in line and were given small white bowls and spoons. Now we saw . . . And we received peeled potatoes and a piece of meat. That was paradise."

The obvious questions concerning this excerpt are, What does Dora mean when she says "Now we saw," and why doesn't she continue her line of thought to explain what it was that she and the other women saw or understood at the time? It is clearly not the improvement in their living conditions, for this is explicated with great feeling and emotion that has not dulled over the years, as phrases such as "*Hamechaye*" and "paradise" express. The issue at stake then, or the thing that Dora cuts herself off from explaining, is the meaning of these improvements as she saw it at the time; namely, the assumption that these improvements signify a rise in the evaluation of the prisoners' lives in the eyes of their jailors and subsequently, an increase of their chances for survival, eventually. Here, too, it is possible that the narrator did not finish her sentence simply because she lost her train of thought and her concentration, something that can easily happen during oral narration when the narrator has no opportunity to prepare or edit her words. However, we can just as easily ascribe a more specific meaning to this lapse, as to other lapses of this kind in other narratives.

We have already seen that when narrators touch on sensitive issues, they often cut off and do not dare continue a painful line of thought, as happened with Rozsi Háger and Irma Fischer in the previous chapter in their descriptions of nakedness, bad Jews, and painful memories concerning family members, and with Aranka Friedmann throughout her narrative. In the present case, then, it seems that the reason for Dora's self-censorship is the tension between her information at the time that the events transpired and her knowledge post factum up to the present. During the actual events, the prisoners had no recourse to reliable information, and they were forced to rely on rumors from their fellow or sister sufferers or to glean scraps of information from their German guards, whose credibility they learned to doubt.[28] Thus, the prisoners tend to interpret various "signs" in the camps as significant omens of the future, both for good and for bad, and an improvement in their living and work conditions seems to usher in a general improvement in their situation and chances for survival. This is the point of view from which Dora expresses the satisfaction that she and other prisoners felt at the time. From the perspective of the present, she knows that these assumptions were later proven completely groundless. She remembers that the "paradise" did not last long and was followed by the infamous retreat and forced "death march" in which many of the prisoners died. Therefore, her evaluation of "paradise" is qualified in hindsight, and she does not even finish her thought to explain what the prisoners "saw," since it soon became clear to them that what they saw and felt did not last and was therefore misleading.

A different example of the need for interpretation by the listener or readers is the use of formulaic terms or code words to describe the period of the Holocaust. For example, Ruth Matias (originally from Sziget, a resident of Kfar Sava, Israel, at the time of the interview) says in the very beginning of her narrative, "None of the men ever returned and I never heard anything from any of them again." Similarly, Rachel Markowitz (originally from Szilágysomlyo, a resident of Petach Tikva, Israel, at the time of the interview) tells how a group of sisters who are being taken to the crematorium turn to their friends and say, "If you return home and find someone from our family, tell them not to wait for us." Possible explanations for the use of euphemistic expressions such as "did not return" or "remained there" are raised in the previous chapter regarding the life history of Aranka Friedmann. However, in the present context, these expressions have an additional meaning that is tied to the interaction between the narrators and their audience. Just as the narrators presuppose that their audience is familiar with the historical facts that provide the basis for their life histories, so too do they assume that the audience is familiar with the victims' terminology or code words used during the Holocaust. Of course, the veracity of this assumption is not obvious, and the narrators themselves never check the accuracy of their assumptions. In fact, the listener or readers may only begin to understand the meaning of these expressions ("did not return," "remained there," or "were deported") by encountering them over and over in the various narratives and within very specific contexts.

I conclude this discussion of the terminology used in these narratives by citing some of the experiences of Rachel Markowitz and examining the ways in which we may interpret them. Rachel describes the procedure of the entrance to Auschwitz as she experienced it: "We arrived at Auschwitz. There were many men there wearing what looked like striped pajamas. They started to yell at us in Yiddish that we should hand over the children to the old people. 'Hand the children over to the old.' No one knew what this was supposed to be. There were some people who did give over their children. There were some."

The narrator obviously knows at the time of telling that the "men wearing striped pajamas" are the Jewish Sonderkommando men whose job was to take the Jews to the gas chambers and their dead bodies to the crematoria. Therefore, she also knows why they turn to her group in Yiddish and urge them to hand over the children to the old people. But

Rachel chooses to tell the event not from the perspective of hindsight but rather as she experienced it at the time it transpired. Thus, her point of view is completely different than that of Dora Ashkenazi, whose description of the arrival at Auschwitz intertwines both these frames of reference, then and now. Rachel Markowitz aligns herself in her narrative with those who did not know "what this was supposed to be." Her stance is much like that of Imre Kertész in his Nobel Prize–winning Holocaust memoir, which preserves a sarcastic, naïve stance throughout.[29] Here, this perspective turns Rachel's narrative into a kind of riddle whose solution lies in the audience's knowledge of the historical background of the events, familiarity with similar stories of other survivors, and, again, readiness to assume responsibility in pronouncing the actual and terrible meaning of these otherwise vague descriptions.

However, Rachel Markowitz also tells another story, in which general knowledge of the Holocaust or familiarity with the milieu is necessary but not sufficient to understand its import. Close to liberation, Rachel and a group of fellow women prisoners decide to hide out in one of the villages around the camp to avoid the women-hungry Russian liberating soldiers: "But the Russians, they said, it wasn't advisable for so many girls to stay at one place when the Russians came." The prisoners therefore find refuge with a Hungarian-speaking Czech woman from the countryside. The Czech woman manages to drive away the Russian soldiers that reach her house in the village, and then all the women together decide to escape before the soldiers return at nightfall. The Czech woman provides food for her "guests" and even invites them to take anything they want from her house. The only thing she asks in return is that they give her a prisoner's uniform with the number on it, so that she too will be considered a former camp prisoner. The Czech woman then takes with her only a small pillow, in which, as it later turns out, she hides jewelry and money. Later on, one of the ex-prisoners steals the pillow from her.

The interesting and intriguing issue in this story is the attitude of the narrator to the Czech woman and the way she describes this event. The narrator and her friends suspect the woman of having collaborated with the Germans, although their only "evidence" is the following: "All the men in her family were gone, hiding, and she was the only one around, so we suspected her of being a big Jew-hater, maybe someone who survived by betraying Jews." Accordingly, Rachel relates sarcastically to the woman's need at this point to be identified as a liberated Jewish prisoner. "Fine, you too are Jewish, come on. One girl gave her her own number." Similarly, Rachel belittles the stealing of the pillow with jewelry and money from this woman: "So some of us condemned her [the thief], and some said, 'To hell with the Czech woman. She must have been a big Jew-hater, if she escaped like that.'"

Throughout this incident, the narrator ascribes hatred of Jews to the Czech woman and her family. She theorizes that the males of the house escaped because they had collaborated with the Germans, and that the woman went suspiciously out of her way to befriend the Jewish women survivors in order to protect herself from reprisals. Rachel mocks the woman's request to take on the identity of a Jew, since it is clear to her that neither the uniform nor the number on it will fool anyone into thinking that the Czech woman is really a Jewish survivor of the camps. Rachel also seems to think that the source of the woman's wealth is tied to corrupt or dishonest deeds, and therefore, she does not condemn the person who stole the woman's pillow. Yet these accusations are not substantiated in the narrative and are based only on general theories regarding the hostility of the villagers toward Jews; there is no textual evidence that this specific woman was a collaborator or Jew-hater. At any rate, Rachel does not take the trouble to try to find out the truth, and the truth about the Czech woman does not really concern her. As a result, those who hear or read her story are left with the disquieting impression that cause and effect are not sufficiently related or explicated, so that the hatred of the narrator toward the woman remains inexplicable.

Rachel does include in her narrative a number of background descriptions of an indirect nature that can explain her hostility to non-Jews in general and thus to the Czech village woman by extension, though the hostility is not directly connected to this specific incident. Rachel's audience here is expected to connect the dots and uncover the relationship between Rachel's generalized anger and hostility and this incident in particular. When she returns to non-Jewish society after liberation and after the horrors of the Holocaust, Rachel cannot forgive or forget and does not take into consideration the change in attitude that this society presents or extends to the Jews after the war. In the following example, the narrator and her sisters live in the house of other villagers for a while after the war; the sisters work as housekeepers, and in return, the villagers feed and house them: "They treated us very well. They weighed each one of us when we arrived, and two weeks later they weighed us again. It is unbelievable how they fed and stuffed us. We all worked. One of us did sewing work, another sister worked with the ducks. I had to take care of the child, a brat. I felt such anger and hatred that I couldn't stand it. I said, 'They killed our beloved children, and I have to play with this child?' I pinched him, and he cried. Then they took him away from me and I had to tend to the chickens. They didn't deserve it, really, because they were very kind."

The narrator also describes two other incidents involving her sisters and herself vis-à-vis the outside world in their journey home after liberation and back at home. In Budapest they confront a streetcar driver about payment for the ride. The older sister of the narrator defies the driver by saying, "You go to Auschwitz, that's where our money is. You took us there; you can go there for the money, we have no money." An argument ensues and is resolved only when one of the other passengers pays for the sisters to board the streetcar. When the sisters return home, they retrieve family possessions that were stolen by one of their former neighbors. In the same context, the narrator describes how her brother had to use threats to get back the family sewing machine from the same neighbors.

In three out of four of these confrontations involving the narrator and her sisters in the outside non-Jewish world (excluding the incident involving the possessions stolen by the neighbors), the narrator and her sisters do not seem to react to the non-Jews they meet as individuals— the Czech village woman, the family that takes them in, and the Hungarian streetcar driver—but instead relate to them as representatives of a hostile non-Jewish world. They view this world as the extension of the Nazi German and the fascist Hungarian regimes that annihilated their families and would have murdered them as well had the war not ended. The narrator has lost her faith in non-Jewish society (or *goyim*, in biblical Hebrew) as a whole and is not able to show gratitude to members of this society even when she rationally realizes that she should, as in the case of her behavior toward the child, the "brat" she is supposed to take care of.[30] Similarly, she exhibits animosity toward the Czech village woman, though she has no proof that this specific woman is indeed a "Jew-hater." Rachel's hatred is neither personal nor connected directly to this woman's deeds but is part of her general attitude to Gentiles as a result of her experience of the Holocaust.

Considering the interpretative activity of Rachel's listener or readers, then, this incident shows that often, the answers to questions that come up while listening or reading are found not within the specific incident that is described, as happens with Rachel's hostility toward the Czech village woman; instead, the listener and readers must take into account the history, personality, and worldview of the narrator, as these are described throughout her entire life history, as well as the narrative's historical context. Thus, to use Iser's terminology, the audience must "skip" backward and forward in the text: forward to the incidents with the kind village family, the streetcar driver, and the neighbors; and backward to the terrible experiences endured in the concentration and work camps.[31] The reader then assembles the information garnered from these various incidents and arranges them coherently to explain and resolve, for example, the hostile attitude of the narrator and her sisters and friends to the village woman who hosts them with kindness and generosity.

The Analytical Activity of the Narrators
Regarding Their Own Life Histories

The narrators themselves also carry out activities, such as "skipping" or "information gathering," to cope with "blockages" and fill in "ghost chapters" in their lives. These cognitive activities all reflect the narrators' difficulties in understanding the reality they faced during the actual unfolding of events. In this section, I analyze the various modes in which they do this during those periods of time when their lives were in constant danger and their consciousnesses in utter lack of certainty. At times, some of these incidents recur in the narrations of several narrators, with slight variations.

Dora Ashkenazi describes a typical scene in Auschwitz when a large group of women prisoners wait to be transferred to a work camp. The prisoners have already endured the roll call or *appell* and the showers, both of which are nerve-wracking since the women do not know whether they will survive the *appell* or be taken to the gas chambers instead of the showers. Now they wait for the cattle cars that will transfer them to the work camp. But the cars do not arrive and this delay engenders rumors and doubts as to the uncertain future that awaits the prisoners. Below is Dora's description of one such scene:

> Finally, the *appell* was over and they took us to the showers. We showered. We finished and there were no cattle cars waiting for us. We stood half the night. It rained. My poor sister . . . I'll tell you about her later. They gave us different clothes, gray clothes. Everyone. In the end we saw that no trains were coming and it was still raining and raining and raining. We stood in the rain. Then they let us go into the shower rooms again, to get out of the rain, and the

girls started to say, "It's the gas chambers and crematorium," and this and that. But it wasn't. We went in, we dried ourselves. In the morning the train came. Each one of us received half a loaf of bread. They took us to Plaszow.

This portrayal of uncertainty and fear of imminent death is repeated in a similar episode later on in Dora's narration, in which she describes an incident that took place when the prisoners are returned to Auschwitz and before they are taken to a work camp in Augsburg:

On September 5, again we had roll call. To work, they said. I passed the roll call and went through two fences. Then we saw two electrical fences guarded by dogs and a path going between them; you might have seen this on TV. Our Blockälteste [block commander] was with us, so while we were walking, we asked her in Czech, "Elsa, where are we going?" So she said, "To work." Then one girl said, "Don't tell us stories, we are being sent to our deaths." I overheard that exchange. They put us in a small room, there were benches there but nothing else. A girl whom I met, originally from our town, had a small prayer book. She had a prayer book, and I had a needle. I don't know how I got this needle, but I got it from someone. We used to pull threads out of our blankets and sew or make things we needed. I kept it all to myself, didn't say anything about what I had overheard to anyone. It was enough for me to know where we were headed. While we were waiting in the room, we received some bread. My friend took out the inside part of her bread and put in her prayer book instead and covered it up by some of the bread. In this way she brought the prayer book home. We sat down there, and I awaited death, I simply awaited death. Suddenly the door opened. We didn't know that the gas chambers looked like showers. We already knew that [unclear]. Water came down on us. We remained alive. . . . They took us to work in Augsburg.

In the first episode, the prisoners are showered several times. First they are taken to the shower room, then they get soaking wet in the rain during the *appell*. This evidently continues all night (excluding the time during which they are sent back to the shower room) while they wait for the train, which arrives only in the morning. The second episode, on the other hand, is characterized by a lack of water as the prisoners wait in the small room in front of the shower room and anticipate the gas chambers. In both cases, whether because of too much water or too little, and at any rate owing to the abnormality of the situation, the prisoners reach the conclusion that they are being taken to their deaths, and in both cases they are proven wrong. In the first episode they are even fortunate enough to receive bread, as they are very hungry, and when the cattle cars finally arrive, they are taken to Plaszow. In the second episode, they are given bread from the beginning, even before they enter the showers. The Germans would not have wasted bread on prisoners condemned to die, yet even so, the passing of time shakes the prisoners' confidence that the Germans want them to live.

The preoccupation with the objects hidden by Dora and her friend while waiting serves the purpose of maintaining the suspense in both the narrated event and the narrative event. The purpose of suspense during the event is, as the narrator phrases it, to "keep it all to myself," "it" referring to both the hidden object and the sense of approaching doom. In contrast, in the narrative event, "it" refers to the knowledge of the group's rescue or escape from death this time. Naturally, the success—in both dramatic and linguistic terms[32]—of creating suspense in this regard is only partial, for the very act of narration includes within it the realization that the narrator was eventually saved, or else she would not be here to tell about it all. Yet, her listener and readers are gripped with suspense and uncertainty, at least temporarily. We identify with the narrator's tension and fear as well as with her overwhelming relief at the end of this scene. In this way, we implement the notions of Habermas, Ricoeur, and Iser, mentioned before, concerning the leaving of our own world behind us as we enter the world of the experience told us, all the more so when this experience is so total and extreme.

Dora Ashkenazi herself goes though various stages in analyzing the unfolding of this event while going through it and while telling it. At first she, too, believes in signs like the distribution of bread before the showers, or rumors gleaned from other prisoners, and sees them as positive omens that she and her friends will be saved. Evidently, she acts this way on the basis of her previous experience and information from other prisoners. In this way she, too, "skips" backward to experiences in her past and forward to her hopes for the future. Other survivors also describe their reliance on signs such as these. For example, Andor Salamon wants to ascertain whether the Germans intend to kill him, so he devises a "test": he asks the guard in charge of the showers to allow him to take in his boots, in which he keeps his shaving equipment and other personal effects. When the guard answers in the affirmative, Andor interprets this to mean that his life and personal cleanliness are still important to the Germans and that they do not intend to kill him.[33]

But during the long wait for the next unknown stage, the prisoners start doubting the meaning of the signs they hitherto believed in. Now, they tend to ascribe the reverse meaning to these signs and see in them acts of deceit perpetrated by the Germans to mislead them and eventually kill them. Thus, for example, Rachel Markowitz describes a similar situation: "Again they put us on cattle cars and gave us some food. This time they said we were going to be liberated. Well, I knew this meant death, because they always said the opposite of what they meant."[34] Finally, the prisoners come to understand that neither of the two explanations is necessarily true: the signs have no connection to reality at all, despite all their hopes and efforts to create such a connection. Applying deconstructionist terminology in the context of the Holocaust survivors' narratives, we might say that the prisoners experience sheer "differance," namely, a complete shattering of the link between cause and effect, signifier and signified, or the very adequacy of signs and signifying systems in the world of the camps.[35] This world's reality and rules turn out to be completely arbitrary, and the intentions of the German persecutors remain incomprehensible and unfathomable to the end.

It is only the act of narration that allows the survivors to survey the events of the past and thus connect the various events or incidents that brought them, step by step, to the present time in which they narrate their inclusive life histories. The very act of narration, then, is the closest they can get to applying meaning to their survival. Yet, even through the process of narration, they cannot fully understand or really explain why things happened as they did or why they are the ones who survived in the end. In that sense, narration is both an act of protest and a coming to terms with the painful past.

The Function and Meaning of Languages and Cultures in the Act of Narration

The three narrators in the present group bring to their narratives a multiplicity of languages and their corresponding cultures. The interplay of languages is a significant component in these narratives as it reveals the narrators' unique and vital conception of major events in their lives.[36] The speech of all three narrators is an amalgam of Hebrew, Hungarian, and German, while some of the narrators also use additional languages such as Yiddish and French. Dora Ashkenazi recounts her life history in Hebrew, but she integrates quotes and expressions from other languages. Ruth Matias starts her narration in Hebrew but then turns to her native Hungarian when the terms that she needs to express herself become more sophisticated and less available to her in Hebrew. Rachel Markowitz speaks primarily in Hungarian, though she, too, like the other two narrators, incorporates quotes or direct speech in German. The source of the multilingual roots of these women is the Austro-Hungarian culture from which they sprang. Despite their Orthodox Jewish religious upbringing, these women were strongly influenced by their primary education in Hungary. Jewish girls, as opposed to boys, did not delve as much into Judaic religious studies and, therefore, participated more in the general culture of their locales. Dora Ashkenazi discusses her proficiency in the German language in her narrative: "Usually, Hungarian Jewish girls only spoke Hungarian and didn't know any German. I knew German because my mother spoke German, and at the salon where I learned to sew, the teacher was from Mattersdorf, Austria. I learned to speak German well there."

It should be noted that Dora's comment that "Hungarian Jewish girls only spoke Hungarian" is not accurate. Perhaps it was true for Dora's personal or regional environment, and she mistakenly extrapolated that all or most Hungarian Jewish girls spoke only Hungarian and no German. In general, though, many Jewish girls and boys were exposed to German and other languages spoken in their close environment. In addition, in the rural areas or in the regions that were cut off from Hungary in the interwar period (such as Transylvania [in Hungarian, Erdély] or Carpatho-Russia), many Jews spoke Yiddish, which helped them later on to understand German in the camps.

Ruth Matias is also representative of the milieu of linguistic and cultural pluralism in which she was raised. She describes her father's educational background, scholarliness, and personality, and then her home: "I remember that in our home we had a bookcase with *Gemara* and other sacred books on one side, and all the great writers of German culture on the other side. Schiller, Goethe, Heine, Nietzsche, and the rest of them. We all received an education. I went to a rabbi to learn Hebrew, to read and pray, and I also studied German. In school I studied the languages then taught in foreign schools."

Later on I asked Ruth about the source of her strength and resilience in the face of adversity, and she explained how her proficiency in many languages contributed to her survival during the Holocaust: "In the hard times, do you know what helped me? For one, the fact that I speak and write German and French. I can write German with Gothic letters. One day, when I was working in Bergstadt, doing welding work . . ." At this point she reverts to the Hungarian language and describes an incident in which her knowledge of German and her ability to write in Gothic letters led to a drastic improvement in her status and living conditions. She stresses that she did not take advantage of this to improve her chances of survival during the forced retreat but instead insisted that "Whatever happens to the others will happen to me as well, I shall not part from them."

It is interesting to note that this narrator uses the German language to reconstruct the conversation that she exchanged with the German work supervisors only when she quotes *them* directly; but she always reports her answers to their questions in Hungarian. We might conclude from this that although she prides herself on her knowledge of German, she seems to avoid using this language unless absolutely necessary. Her pride at being fluent in German is tempered by her reluctance to use this language beyond the necessary, since she is aware, at least partly, that it is the language of the oppressors. Thus, we see how the shifts from language to language, which are part of the linguistic component of the narratives, also represent cultural contrast and psychological struggles concerning the very use of the languages in question.

Dora Ashkenazi's narrative also exhibits similar linguistic-cultural struggles. Following are three examples of the clash of languages and cultures as they appear in one consecutive section of Dora's narrative:

> We were working there, and Yom Kippur [Hebrew: Day of Atonement] came. How did we know Yom Kippur was approaching? We knew that it was approximately the time for Rosh Hashanah [the Hebrew New Year Eve] and Yom Kippur. Once, four of us were sent to bring supplies of meat and bread. We walked down the street and then waited outside the shop, for we weren't allowed to enter. Suddenly a man riding a bicycle passed us shouting, "*Kinderlach* [Yiddish: children], in two weeks' time it's Rosh Hashanah." When we heard this, we were standing in *achtung* [German: attention] and couldn't move.
>
> Then, later, two women passed by when we were speaking Hungarian. They said, "Magyarok vagytok? Honnan jötetek? Mit csináltok? [Hungarian: Are you Hungarian? Where do you come from? What are you doing?]" Then our guard yelled at them, "Weg von hier [German: Go away]," she didn't let us talk with them. But

we did learn that there were other Hungarian women there. We even managed to tell these two that we worked in the local factory.

There were soldiers there, Hungarian soldiers, who passed by the factory. When they passed by the factory they sang this song: "Kinek Zsidó lány a babája, kösön kötelet a nyakára [Hungarian: If you have a Jewish girlfriend, you might as well tie a rope around your neck and strangle yourself]." Are you familiar with it? No, you weren't born there. But they used to sing, "Kinek Zsidó lány a babája, földi menny-ország a hazája [Hungarian: If you have a Jewish girlfriend, your home/homeland is a Paradise on Earth]." Now they changed it to mean that to have a Jewish woman was bad.

Dora starts by mentioning the Yom Kippur that she spent in the factory, and this reminds her of how she found out that the Jewish holidays were approaching. The encounter between the prisoners and the "man on the bicycle" is so sudden and abrupt that even the German guard does not come to her senses in time to prevent the transmission of information from the man to the women prisoners. However, she becomes sufficiently wary to cut off the dialogue between the prisoners and the next passersby, the two women who speak to them in Hungarian. To us, the audience, it is not clear who says what in the exchange before they are abruptly cut off by the German "Weg von hier" or "go away." However, what is clarified or reinforced in this scene is the superiority of German over Jewish Hungarian, with all the ensuing implications concerning the respective speakers of these languages in this scene.

This seems to be Dora's conclusion as well, since her next spontaneous association is to a clash of words and values around a popular Hungarian song of the era. The song used to be a song of praise for Jewish women, but by now it has turned into a derogatory song. The metamorphosis of this folk or popular song, from praise of Jews to an act of anti-Semitism, well represents the social and political deterioration in the status of Hungarian Jews during World War II and the years preceding it. In this instance, we might say that the German prevails over the Hungarian not only on the level of the languages spoken and their respective speakers, but also on the cultural, social, and political levels. As explained in the introduction, the rise to power of Fascist and pro-German sectors in Hungary on the eve of the war and during the war greatly influenced the social and cultural state of affairs in the country. This, in turn, was expressed by the creation and dissemination of derogatory expressions, jokes, and songs that denigrated the Jews.

True, some of these had always existed among the Hungarian underclass or in its street lore, but the recent political developments and changes in the social milieu further legitimized these jokes and songs and made them far more blatant and widespread.[37]

During the period of the Holocaust, then, the general appearance of Jewish women camp prisoners who survived the initial "selections" and were employed in exhausting and menial jobs truly reflected their degraded and desperate circumstances. Thus, they became "deathlike," just as they are depicted in the words of this song. In this case, therefore, it is not only the German language and culture that overpower the Jewish milieu, but in addition, the pro-German Hungarian essence defies the vitality of the Jewish Hungarian women. Accordingly, in contrast to the mention of the Hungarian language in the previous incident, which was the language of the Jewish Hungarian women in the camps, in this case, Hungarian represents Hungarian men who desire Jewish women only when they are at their best, not when they are oppressed and robbed of their femininity. Needless to say, the sentiments expressed in this song reinforce national and religious oppression by adding to it sexual humiliation, albeit only verbally, as contact with such women seems too revolting (or "strangling") to the Hungarians of the time. To come back to Dora, who remembers this song, only the passage of time and the fact of her rescue from the "rope" allow her to describe this scene as one who survived both the patronizing affection of the Hungarians and the murderous intentions of the Nazi Germans aided by their Hungarian henchmen.

However, during the time that the events actually transpired in Dora's life, it seems that there was no clear-cut conclusion to the struggle between languages, cultures and worldviews. Throughout her narrative, therefore, Dora uses such German terms as *appell, lager,* and *achtung* almost unconsciously, even when we can safely assume that she is aware of the translation of these terms into Hebrew or Hungarian. Unlike Ruth Matias, who partly quotes and partly translates, Dora relates the events as close as possible to the way in which she experienced them in real time and in the language mostly spoken at that time, which is necessarily German. In fact, only one survivor in my entire work expresses awareness and sorrow at the very fact that she has to integrate German words in her life history: "It was just before supper, when the huge pot called 'kübel' was brought in. I am forced to use words from the camps, German words. This 'kübel' was a huge pot so heavy that two women had to carry it."[38] Dora, however, is not aware of such subtleties. Even when she works in the factory, as has been mentioned, she is proud of the fact that she "taught" her German meister that "Jews know how to work hard." Thus, she internalizes, at least partially, the German outlook regarding Jews, the self-image of the Germans, and their perception of the relations between themselves and Jews. Below are some sections from Dora's narrative that touch on these issues:

> My meister, I shall never forget it, he told me that within three weeks we were already doing all the work in the factory, work that only men had done before. So my meister said, can I say it in German? "Jetzt verstehe ich warum man die Juden hasst [German Now I understand why people hate the Jews]. The Jews are so [unclear]." He said that now he finally realized what they had been taught in the Hitler Jugend about the "real nature" of Jews. He said "They taught us," which was true, "that the German Jews were rich, they had a lot of money, they filled the theatres. There were rich Jews everywhere and that caused hatred." He said, "Never in my life did I imagine that Jews knew how to work hard. And not just regular hard work, but work like this."

To this we may add Dora's recollections from a later stage, close to liberation:

> They caught us. We ran away. They caught us. Then I said, "No one else here knows any German, so I'll go to this German and ask him." I went up to him, and said, "Tell me, Sagen Sie mir, wird man uns erschiessen? [German: Tell, are they going to shoot us?]" He said, "Warum, was haben Sie gemacht? [German: Why, what have you done?]" I liked that answer. He then went on saying German proverbs, that I always tell everyone [unclear German], how do you call it, don't let people step on you. I use it now with our politics [in Israel] to say that if we show only a little bit of weakness, we are lost. I learned that from the Germans.

Whereas after liberation, she says the following: "The Germans were afraid of the released Russian prisoners of war, they feared them like death. But they weren't at all afraid of us [the Jews], for they knew we were weak fools, we wouldn't do anything to them. And we really didn't do anything to them." In the first two quotes from Dora's narrative, she shows how she has internalized the Germans' antipathy toward Jews by quoting German expressions and views about Jews and by accepting them. In the third section she demonstrates this again by comparing the recently liberated Russians and Jews. Concerning the first excerpt, Dora is proud that she and her friends learned the work in the German factory in record time and thus proved to the Germans, represented by her meister, that they "knew how to work hard." Her pride comes in sharp contrast to the attitude of other survivors, who are proud of accomplishing the exact opposite, namely, sabotaging the German war effort.[39] By contrast, Dora's need to prove her hard work in its literal sense shows that she and her friends were influenced by the way in which the Germans perceived the Jews: "German Jews were rich," meaning exploitative, unproductive, lazy, and parasitic. Dora, on her part, fully adopts and never questions or counters this stereotypical assertion of the meister concerning Jews.

The second and third excerpts further illustrate Dora's adoption of the German worldview regarding the weakness and defeatism of Jews. Although it is not clear which "German proverbs" the German man quotes, it is evident from Dora's paraphrase that he talks about acting assertively and not showing weakness, since any weakness only strengthens the aggressiveness of the opposing side: "If we show only a little bit of weakness, we are lost." In addition, Dora contends (in the third paragraph) that, unfortunately, the actions of the Jews seem to confirm the words of the German. Her proof is the comparison between the postliberation behavior of the Russians and the Jews toward their former persecutors, the Germans, which is reflected in the fact that the Germans fear the Russians but not the Jews. Just as in the first paragraph, here, too, Dora does not notice the distortion implicit in this ruling, for the Russians under discussion were trained soldiers who were imprisoned under far better conditions than those of the Jews. By contrast, the Jews imprisoned in the camps were men and women who had never been trained in warfare. Still, as far as Dora can see, these Jews act as what she calls "weak fools," although, by using this almost affectionate term and by including herself within this group, she injects a modicum of forgiveness or self-acceptance. Thus, she leaves a so-called escape hatch big enough for those who do not agree with her and would hold that the behavior of the Jews is to be preferred over that of the Russians. Had she used a more scathing term, she might have alienated her audience; this way, both she and her audience accept the behavior of the Jews with sympathy despite the fact that we might not agree about the possible alternatives for the postwar Jewish reaction.

The third narrator in this group, Rachel Markowitz, also relates differences of mentality and culture, but in her case it is about the differences between the Polish and Hungarian Jewish female prisoners. As we know, there were reasons for differences of opinion and even animosity between the two groups, for the Hungarians were spared the horrors of the concentration and work camps until the last year of the war, as opposed to most of the Jews of Europe, and especially of Poland, who suffered in ghettoes and camps for a much longer period of time. In the present context, then, Rachel expresses her criticism of the Polish Jewish women who, when offered incentives and bonuses for their work, ask for " 'Lipstick, powder,' and who knows what." When I hypothesized that perhaps they weren't that hungry, as they were well versed in camp life and therefore better at attaining extra food than the novice Hungarian camp prisoners, Rachel answered in an unclear manner, saying, "I don't know." This leaves open the possibility that the Polish women had ulterior reasons for asking for makeup over food. But since Rachel chooses not to develop the subject, we have no way to draw reliable conclusions in this matter beyond her rather enigmatic words. Implementing the terminology of Christine Brooke-Rose, we might say that this is a case of an excessively under-determined text, which therefore leaves us no access to further, or sufficient, interpretation.

To return to the issue of languages, both Dora Ashkenazi and Ruth Matias, whose descriptions are more detailed and explicit than that of Rachel Markowitz, seem to use German mainly to reconstruct conversations and events from the past as accurately as possible. After all, oral lore tends toward drama in its preference of direct speech and showing over reported speech and telling.[40] As a result, the live storytelling event enlivens the content of the narrative as well. In addition, both narrators tend to characterize themselves through their descriptions of encounters and even direct confrontations with their German jailors. Ruth Matias emerges from her dialogical accounts as a brave and altruistic woman who refuses to benefit from any special privileges more than the basic minimum needed to stay alive. Dora Ashkenazi emerges as a woman full of life, courage, and a sense of humor that does not abandon her even during hard times.

Apart from ideology clashes and characterization, these multilingual passages reflect another aspect, which in my opinion is less conscious to the narrators, although certain folkloristic approaches might claim otherwise.[41] This aspect is the need or even compulsion of the narrators (and others who have undergone similar traumatic experiences) to describe several different points of view of an event at one and the same time. This is the flip side of the loss of individuality and erasure of personal identity that were endured by millions of deportees during the war and displaced persons in its aftermath. In Primo Levi's book *The Truce*, which depicts the lives of the newly liberated camp prisoners, the survivor-narrator describes the sick and decimated survivors as "begging for help in all the languages of Europe."[42] Even during the war, many languages and cultures were intermingled and created a sort of "Tower of Babel," to use a paradoxical metaphor of both construction and destruction. This situation can also be labeled, following Mikhail Bakhtin's work, a "polyphony" of cultures and ideologies.[43] As has been shown earlier, this polyphony may be expressed even by a single narrator describing an uneventful incident—like Dora Ashkenazi quoting and responding to Nazi-German views of Jews—that still gives expression to contrasting and conversing ideologies at one and the same time.

However, in light of the uniqueness of the Holocaust and the horrific experiences of the narrators, the term "polyphony" cannot fully describe the multiplicity of voices, events, and layers of meaning that are expressed in these narratives. Or, in Bakhtin's terms, carnival expresses and obeys rules that world wars necessarily destroy or deconstruct. The search for an alternative term leads back to notions springing from mythic or ancient sources, precisely because these—like the terminology born of the Holocaust experience—are obscure and incompatible with contemporary concepts. It follows, therefore, that only expressions such as "Tower of Babel" or "chaos" can replace more neutral or positive terms, such as "pluralism," or Bakhtin's "polyphony." In these narratives, postwar Europe is indeed considered analogous to the primordial world just before the Creation, since both suggest a kind of death before birth or a void to be filled by presence. Indeed, many of the narrators describe the postwar era in terms of emptiness and primacy, to be followed by the descriptions of their rehabilitated, but not necessarily rebuilt, lives.

Revealing and Concealing in Holocaust Memories and Narratives

The stories of the second group of narrators in this chapter are salient in their difference from all the life histories discussed previously. These narratives are outstanding in their brief reference to the period of the Holocaust, although some of the narrators were willing to discuss the Holocaust again in their answers to my questions following their narration. Despite their rather transparent desire to repress the memory of the

Holocaust from their narratives, these narrators cannot help but indirectly give expression to the Holocaust period in their post-Holocaust lives, if only through intimation and allusion. It is necessary, then, that we read the narratives of this group with an eye to uncovering those places in which the narrators open a small window, as it were, into painful and latent memories, and explain the "view" from this small aperture based on their overall life histories.[44] The justification for my hermeneutic intrusion into the narrative consciousnesses of these narrators is that they themselves are willing to tell their story, tolerate certain exposure, and pass responsibility to their audience.

The analysis of the present group of seven narratives is further divided into two subgroups. The first subgroup analyzes the narratives of two married couples (Heiman and Bihari) in which the husbands' narratives are dominant, although the comments and stories of the wives enrich the narratives of both couples and the interaction among us all during the narrative event.[45] The second subgroup, whose heading is "You Ask Me," deals with three life histories that develop as a result of a series of questions and answers between each narrator (Berta Wazner, Esther Israel, and Piri Meister) and myself.

Shared, Separate, and Dominated Life Histories: Two Examples of Married Couples Telling Their Life Histories Jointly

Yoseph and Leah Heiman (originally from Szolnok, residents of Jerusalem at the time of the interview, though the interview itself was held in a hotel in Netanya, Israel) are the first narrators I interviewed for my doctorate. Therefore, our meeting was somewhat less polished than subsequent interviews and occasionally characterized by a lack of self-confidence on the part of both the interviewer and interviewees. However, to balance the awkwardness of entering uncharted territory, there was also a feeling of comfort and hominess in the event, since I had known the Heimans previously as good friends of my departed parents. My parents had lived in Israel for a number of years when the Heimans arrived and were thus able to help the newcomers, as Yoseph Heiman mentions in his narrative. Later on, the situation of the Heimans improved and they were able to extend aid to my family in return. In short, the Heimans and my parents experienced together many periods of difficulty during their absorption in Israel. For a survivor family cut off from its original ties abroad (for a variety of reasons, as explained in the introduction), the Heimans were more like an uncle and aunt than just friends or acquaintances of the family. Since the Heimans were something between family and strangers, meeting them was in the juncture between the familiar and unfamiliar (or familial and nonfamilial), from an academic and methodological point of view as well as from the personal one. However, I was not familiar with their life histories until I interviewed them, and the content of their narratives is therefore of equal import and status for me as those of the other interviewees, except my aunt Aranka Friedmann and to a lesser extent Zsuzsa Faludi, whose narratives are analyzed in the second chapter.

Yoseph Heiman opens his narrative with a general description of Jewish life in the city of his birth, Szolnok, and pays special attention to the opposition to Zionism in his community, which was similar to many other Jewish communities in Hungary of the time. He doesn't talk about himself or his family at all until I draw his attention to the fact that he hasn't said a word about his childhood. To this, he responds by asking if the story of his aliya is relevant. In other words, he still avoids talking about himself. Only after I answer that he is welcome to discuss his aliya later on in the narrative does he summarize the earlier years of his life in a few sentences. He explains that he was weak in all his subjects except for Judaic studies. His wife Leah adds here, "He was bad in mathematics," and Yoseph dismisses her comment the way he does her other comments throughout the narration, by saying "Right, but that's not relevant now." However, it must be said in his defense that Yoseph is the "owner" of his life history and only he can decide what is relevant and what is not. This is similar to the interaction of the mother and daughter in the previous chapter, where Mrs. Fischer is often interrupted and corrected by her daughter but sticks to her version or words.

Yoseph then describes his professional training and the fact that he still practices the same profession to this very day. Then he turns to the Holocaust, which in his case is represented by his service in the labor battalions. He cites several names of places in Hungary he reached during the retreat from the Russian army but does not tell us even one incident from his life in this period. All that he is willing to say, in summary of the war period, is, "I went through so much torture and trouble," to explain why he did not want to remain in Hungary after the war. Even when I asked him to explain what he meant by "torture and trouble," he skirted my question and simply reiterated, "the labor battalions" and again emphasized that his family wanted to leave Hungary and move to Israel. In other words, Zionism represents the aspects of Yoseph's life that he chooses to reveal, in order to shield or conceal the unmentionable period of the Holocaust, which he prefers to conceal, as will be further exemplified later on.

The next chapter in Yoseph's life deals with his attempts to leave Hungary for Israel. In this period of time Yoseph is already married and, therefore, his wife starts to participate more and more in her husband's narrative. Whereas Yoseph usually speaks in Hebrew, Leah Heiman interjects her comments only in Hungarian and thus brings to mind the chorus in classic drama in the ways she transmits insidious information, or represents the unofficial truth, or raises issues that her husband either conceals or considers irrelevant. For example, when Yoseph summarizes the story of the family's aliya to Israel by saying, "We even received a welcome gift, another daughter," his wife adds in Hungarian, "but she went far away from us." Thus, she responds to the fact that this Israeli-born daughter is the one who left Israel to live in the United States when she married, since for Leah, the sadness at the daughter's physical distance is more real and relevant at present than the joy of her birth about thirty years earlier.

Leah continues to comment on her husband's words when he says that the postwar Hungarian authorities claimed that Jews had no reason to leave the country since there was no anti-Semitism in Hungary any longer. Leah immediately interjects in Hungarian, "but there *was* [anti-Semitism]." Then, when Yoseph asserts that there were Jews who dared escape with small children by giving the children sleeping pills, Leah retorts, "And some children never woke up." Her comment here seems to reflect an old disagreement the couple may have had about whether to cross the border illegally, as well as a response or retort to her husband's labeling her "a coward wife" in that context (eventually, the couple and their two children were able to leave the country legally in 1956). After this, Leah does not intervene in her husband's narration almost to its ending.

At this point, I asked Leah to recount her life history and she did this very briefly. Now it is the husband who interrupts the wife, ostensibly to guide and direct her in her narration. For example, he dismisses her comment about her family's poverty by saying that poverty isn't relevant. He does this in an amusing way, with an off-the-cuff translation of a common Hungarian proverb that says: "If two poor people give birth to a third and a fourth, then that's success." This is analogous to the Western idiom, "The rich get richer and the poor have children." In this way, Yoseph expresses his discomfort with regard to the mention of their low socioeconomic background. His reaction to his wife's story may well explain why he avoids giving details about his own childhood, which was probably characterized by the same poverty as that of his wife.

It follows that Yoseph's outlook on life is to emphasize the positive—or the positive results of his actions—and minimize the negative—the difficult situations from which his rebirth after the Holocaust sprung. For him, then, this central meaning of his life history is at least as important as the life history itself. Accordingly, Yoseph views his identity as a Zionist Israeli as more significant than his identity as a Holocaust survivor, as the Zionist in him has long since overcome and overshadowed the Holocaust survivor. Therefore, he emphasizes his affinity for Zionism even from early childhood, despite the fact that Zionism was very unpopular in Hungarian Jewish communities at the time. This, evidently, is also the reason he chooses to tell his life history in Hebrew, despite his difficulty in expressing himself in this language. Leah Heiman's account, as opposed to her husband's, is direct, personal, and devoid of explicit ideology. Yet, in view of her husband's corrective comments throughout her brief narrative, it seems that she starts feeling insecure and, therefore, concludes her story quickly, saying that she relies on her husband's version of events, as she herself is not a good interviewee.

At this point the microphone returns to Yoseph, who describes the initial difficulties of the family's absorption in Israel. Now it is Leah who uses flowery, pompous language in her interjections, while Yoseph is more realistic, and we the audience engage in a process of "cross-referencing" and comparing the content and meaning of both accounts. An example of these dynamics is the way they say something and its very opposite at the same time, she in Hungarian and he in Hebrew. She says "we had great expectations," and he says "before we came, we didn't have many expectations." Perhaps they have different views about the absorption process they underwent in Israel, or maybe each has a different perception of "expectations." Yoseph seems to refer to more concrete issues, such as finding a place to live and a means of livelihood, while Leah, who has just been instructed by her husband to rise above her poor roots, now expresses the abstract notions of religious and ideological freedom that her husband stressed previously. In addition, Leah knows that she has finished her narrative and will not have to explain her words, so she allows herself the luxury of figurative and ambiguous expression, as opposed to her husband's more pragmatic recounting at this stage.

From this point and on, Leah intervenes less and less in her husband's story and when she does, she tends to strengthen his words from her own point of view. Her last comment refers to "contacts" that other people had when the Heiman family was sent to live in the development town of Beit Shemesh as new immigrants. While other people left this place almost immediately after arriving there, since "everyone had someone to go to," in Leah's words, they themselves were not able to leave until much later. As far as regarding friends and supporters, it is clear that Yoseph Heiman wants to take advantage of the narrative event to mention the much-appreciated help that my parents extended to them when they first came to Israel. He cites the help of "Mrs. Rosberger"—my mother—in translation and taking care of official arrangements. He also cites the help of my father, whom he simply calls "Father," who worked at the same hospital in which Leah gave birth to her Israeli daughter, the one who "went far away."

Yoseph Heiman concludes his narrative with an indirect reference to the Holocaust period of his life. He explains that although the family was recommended to live on a kibbutz, he turned down the offer for the following reasons: "I could accept anything, except for living on a kibbutz. No way. My nature is such that I hate crowds, I can't be around more than three people in my close environment without getting nervous. It is a nice place, the kibbutz, no problems, nothing to worry about. But everything is always the same, the same people, all is the same. For me it is like a labor camp, everything is always the same. It is good to visit the kibbutz, stay for two, three, four or five hours, and that's it. It's a psychological thing I have since the Holocaust. I don't like to live in a cooperative framework, and I don't want to live in such a small community." Thus, Yoseph, who did not enlarge on the Holocaust period of his life or the brutalities he endured in the labor battalions, hints only now at the effects this period had on his life in later years. To Yoseph, the kibbutz is a type of work camp in terms of its limited scope: "everything is always the same, the same people, all is the same." He prefers to forgo the financial security of the kibbutz lifestyle so that he does not have to live in a framework that continually reminds him of the Holocaust period of his life—which he is unwilling or unable to face directly to this day. To return to the phenomenological terminology of interpretations given by both the narrator and the audience, here Yoseph "skips" from the present, which he is willing and capable of speaking about, to his past during the Holocaust, which he is not willing and able to reveal, and explains the present in terms of the past by means of a very brief and general reference to this past. This way we, too, as

Yoseph's audience, gain a glimpse of understanding (even if no further information) of his "torture and trouble" during the Holocaust and the ways in which these terrible experiences shaped his viewpoint up to the present.

The Bihari couple (originally from Szombathely, residents of Budapest at the time of the interview) also told me their life histories jointly, but the nature of their interaction is different from that of the Heiman couple. Here, too, the husband, Dr. Ernő Bihari, gave a detailed life history, while the wife, Anna, gave a very abbreviated one, and here, too, the wife felt that her story was less compelling and less important than that of her husband. However, the degree of intervention of each spouse in the other's narrative and the nature of the interventions are very different than those of the Heiman couple. Dr. Bihari does not intervene at all in the life history of his wife, while Mrs. Bihari intercedes in her husband's narration to insert scraps of information that he seems to be unable to recall—such as the name of Georges Clemenceau, or the number of grandchildren that they have from their oldest son. Apart from these factual details, Mrs. Bihari interrupts only once during her husband's narrative, when he goes off on one of his many historical tangents, and she asserts that he is talking too much about issues that are not related to his life history. In my analysis, I show that in many cases, Ernő Bihari uses these tangents to conceal difficult issues that he prefers not to reach or touch on too closely.

Indeed, Ernő Bihari's narrative embodies a dialectic tension between his readiness to express himself through the narrative event and his tendency to repress issues that pain him. He repeatedly reminds himself of the essence of the narrative event, in statements such as: "Now, since I concentrate on myself," and "I turned around a minute so as not to talk into the microphone." He also accords special significance to our meeting by mentioning the State of Israel and its importance to the diaspora Jewry. In fact, these tangents are delay tactics that Dr. Bihari employs with varying levels of self-awareness to repress or avoid the painful topic of the Holocaust as he and his family experienced it. Throughout most of the narration, then, Ernő prefers to hover over the story, remain at the metanarrative level and not delve into the painful subjects revealed toward its ending. In a similar way, he also reiterates autobiographical details such as the year of his birth and the year he began studying in school.

However, the most obvious proof of his unwillingness to touch on the Holocaust is the fact that he skips over this period in his spontaneous recitation. He talks about the completion of his studies and the opening of a dental clinic in his hometown on the eve of the war, and then he moves directly to the present period, in which he again has a private practice after years of working in a government clinic. His profession as a dentist is a thread that ties together the prewar and postwar periods, while skipping the significant interceding years. He then proceeds to his present family, which includes two grown sons and their families. It is only when I inquire about his years during the war and his service in the labor battalions that he is reminded that he has not yet discussed that time.

He now dispatches with his labor-battalion era in a few terse sentences. Still, he seems determined to stop the painful memories of this period from breaching his conscious mind and active memory by talking in the most general terms about "very bad conditions" or stating that "it was quite horrible because we lay on the earth and in the dirt." However, he does not specify what were the "bad conditions" or what, exactly, was "horrible"—just as Yoseph Heiman limits himself to code words like "torture" and "trouble" to sum up his brutalizing experiences in the labor battalions. In addition, he prefers the first-person plural in talking about himself as an individual.

In fact, Ernő Bihari goes through a gradual process of penetrating into the depths of his most painful memories during the act of narration. This process is occasionally interrupted by "skipping in time," a technique Ernő uses to give himself breathing space between one painful event and another. For example, after briefly summing up his service in the labor battalions, Ernő immediately skips to the period after the war and says, "Suddenly it was all over and we came back home." Now he talks about the difficulties he encountered in putting his life back on track, and his ultimate success in doing so. The dental clinic, like his profession as dentist, is central in illustrating the extent of his success in rehabilitating the life that he had created for himself before the war. In fact, it sometimes seems as if the dental clinic assumes the role of an actual character in the narrative, through which Ernő talks about and characterizes himself, since it is so hard for him to talk more directly about himself. This phenomenon is analogous to the centrality of the synagogues in the narratives of two other narrators, Károly Krausz and Ármin Földvári,[46] who also live in Budapest as does Ernő Bihari himself.

The description of Ernő's recovery and rehabilitation after the war brings him to his present family and his decision to move from the town of his birth, Szombathely, to Budapest, some time after the war. The reason for this move was because he had no family left after the war. This mention of his family finally and inevitably sends Ernő back to the war period and the fact that his family members were all killed, except for his father, who passed away earlier. Now he lists, one by one, how each family member died: his brothers died in the labor battalions in Hungary, while his mother, his sister, and her children died in the gas chambers of Auschwitz. Ernő Bihari is on the verge of tears when he says, "I reached a sad part. And to talk about it, honestly, makes you cry." But he overcomes what seems to him a moment of weakness by this metanarrative comment, which distracts him from the painful content of his words, and also by letting me speak for a while.

In terms of the communication and interaction between the narrator and myself, we seem to be in a constant movement to and from a "secret" or "grave"—to use metaphorical language—in the consciousness of the narrator and in the atmosphere of the narrative event. The same phenomenon can be depicted in this entire group, which includes the two couples and the three women in the "You Ask Me" section. On the face of it, it would seem that I am the initiator of the movement or advance toward the "secret," as I am the one who is trying to delve into that which is concealed, while the narrators are the ones who draw away from the "secret" or shield it. According to this viewpoint, the narrators are the "patrons," who "own" the "secret," while I am the "client" who seeks to obtain it from them.[47] Accordingly, the event of the narration, the narrators who speak and respond to my questions, and I are all in bargaining terms regarding the "property," "secret," or "grave" in question.

However, reading the narrative transcriptions carefully, or even listening closely to the narratives themselves, is enough to reveal another pattern of movement, which is less abrupt and more wavelike or rhythmic, especially regarding the narrators. First of all, even the most withdrawn or inhibited narrators are interested in telling me about their experiences; otherwise, they would not have agreed to be interviewed as Holocaust survivors. Second, even those narrators who self-censor their stories because of all kinds of inhibitions or mental blocks at the same time invite me, more or less directly, to ask them further questions. Thus, they leave open a window of opportunity to reexamine their censored accounts in order to weaken the blockages that prevent them from discussing problematic issues in the first place.

All this is not to say that my questions always lead directly to an abolishing of the narrators' inhibitions and total revelation of their "secrets." What is true, however, is that the interaction between the narrators and me leads at least to an acknowledgement, in varying degrees, of the "secret" and the difficulty of referring to it, depending on the personality of the narrator and the dialogue that develops between us. A similar process is demonstrated in Claude Lanzmann's movie *Shoah* (1985) in the dialogue that the director initiates with the survivor Abraham Bomba, who is called Abe. Even though Abe, a former member of the Sonderkommando,[48] has been open and revealing in his interview so far, now he reaches a breaking point where he cannot continue with his story and expose a "secret." The interviewer, Lanzmann, does not leave him alone but prods him to go on while telling the survivor that he "must" tell all. Abe hesitates, the signs of an internal struggle obvious on his face, then finally continues his story. Similarly, the interviewees in the present research respond to my questions following their spontaneous narration, although I do not prod them as Lanzmann does. However, as in Lanzmann's film, it is not clear whether the survivor-narrator does, indeed, face the issues that he hitherto repressed or finds a way to circumvent them. Still, the outburst of emotions that the narrators often experience during the stage of hesitation or immediately afterward means that they choose to confront at least some aspects of their painful and repressed memories.

Another aspect in which we see the wavelike or rhythmic movement regarding the "secret" is the narrators' repetition of themes or keywords that are connected to the problematic topic. As has been shown, Yoseph Heiman summarizes his experiences in the labor battalions with the keywords "torture" and "trouble," although he does not elaborate on them any further. But when he describes, later on in the narrative, his opposition to living in the kibbutz collective framework, he uses the terms "labor camps" and "Holocaust." This is his way of making a connection between the two different ways of life in collective frameworks, thus propounding similarities that kibbutz residents, for example, might not think relevant or apt, but which are nevertheless powerful and relevant for him as a Holocaust survivor. Concerning the wavelike movement, then, this is a return to the source of his pain and the "secret" that he did not want to divulge earlier. At this point in his explanation of his aversion to kibbutz life, the same keywords that stand for the maximal exposure of which he is capable still allow him minimal expression of the pain that he endured in the Holocaust and in its aftermath. In Ernő Bihari's narrative, the turning point or the wavelike movement occurs when Ernő talks about his wife and children, and this, in turn, reminds him of his original nuclear family that perished in the

Holocaust. During the first time he discusses his family, he tells about his sons and even his grandchildren. It is only when the topic comes up a second time that Ernő finally cannot avoid remembering his original family and the fate that befell them. This time, the narrator conducts a patron-client relationship not with me but with himself and his memories, since he is the only one who understands or anticipates where his life history will take him, while I have only intuition to fall back on at point like this.

The life history of Ernő Bihari's wife, Mrs. Anna Bihari, is the shortest interview that I conducted and reached only about a page and a half of text. As mentioned before, Mrs. Bihari perceives herself to be in her husband's shadow, just like Mrs. Heiman. Mrs. Bihari also feels that her husband's story is important and interesting, while hers is the opposite. While Mrs. Heiman claims that she is not a good interviewee, Mrs. Bihari clams that "there were no big upheavals in my life." She uses a slightly apologetic tone to express the fact that, unlike many others in her generation, she did not endure the horrors of the camps, or those of forced labor, as did her husband, as she hid in Budapest during the time of deportations.

Another issue in which we see that Mrs. Bihari is influenced by her husband is in her attitude toward anti-Semitism. In general, Ernő Bihari's comments and evaluation of anti-Semitism simply do not tally with the reality that was experienced by his generation. It is clear that he tries to play down the intensity of hatred for the Jews throughout his entire narrative, probably as part of his tendency to repress painful issues in his life. Similarly, his wife also claims that "as a rule, no, there was no hatred. No one ever hurt me personally." To validate this assertion she says that when she was sick and hospitalized while working in a factory, many of the non-Jewish workers from the factory came to visit her. The problem with this validation is that this must have happened only before 1942, because, as she stated previously, she was not allowed to work in the factory from 1942 and on. The main period of suffering for Hungarian Jewry did not come until two years later, in 1944–45, when they were deported to the concentration camps and there was much less support from the Gentiles in their environment, for many reasons.

However, Mrs. Bihari chooses to discount or minimize these facts in her narrative, and in the end she summarizes her life in this sentence: "I personally was hurt only, well not *only*, by the loss of my father and my first husband. It is a loss which hurts me to this day." Here, finally, Mrs. Bihari becomes aware of the contradiction in her account, or, rather, the inconsistency between her account and life experience. She tries to resolve this by ameliorating her own minimization of the Holocaust, represented by the word "only," as she understands (probably by hearing her own words while uttering them) that the murders of her father and first husband are no trivial matters and should not be dismissed with "only." On the contrary, these losses are an important part of her life, and any other attitude toward them puts *her* in an inhuman light. And all this, while the thrust of her narrative is to belittle the atrocities inflicted on herself, her family, and community. It is important to repeat that the Biharis, like most of the narrators in the previous chapter, still live in Hungary and must cope with the fact that they live in the same nation that assisted the Germans in annihilating their families. The complexity of this predicament must, inevitably, be expressed in the texts that these survivors create, at times even through a single and seemingly innocent quantifier like *only.*

In summary of the life histories of the Bihari couple it may be said that the narratives of both husband and wife embody a relationship of revealing and concealing on two levels. The first is the external and explicit discourse between them and me, their full narrations, my following questions, and their answers. In the framework of this level, or discourse, I consciously held back from trying to "outwit" the narrators and "trick" them into talking about things they seemed reluctant to discuss. Therefore, the thrust of my interpretation regarding shadowy or murky areas on this level is done retroactively, after the event of the interview, and only by me. The second level is more latent or implicit. This is the dynamics of revealing and concealing between the narrators and their narratives (or themselves) with the mediation of the interview event and myself. Here, the narrators confront and cope with their most difficult memories and determine, while recounting, the extent to which they are willing to relive their memories, and thus perhaps view them in a different light than they did before. This level affords only minimal exposure to external eyes and remains largely with the narrators and in their control.

You Ask Me: The Role of the Interview in the Evocation of the Life Histories

Strong structural similarities exist among the life histories of the last three female narrators in this book, Berta Wazner, Esther Israel, and Piri Meister. All three life histories are very short, and the Holocaust appears in them in only a few sentences, as was the case with the two married couples just discussed. When they do talk about the Holocaust period, Berta Wazner and Esther Israel list the names of the places and camps to which they were sent and state the dates or duration of time they stayed in these places, but they never describe their thoughts, feelings, or even what they did during this period. Piri Meister expresses herself in even more general and vague terms. As a result, the perception of the three narrators at the end of their spontaneous narration, and my feeling as well, is of frustration or "failure in performance."[49] The story is told, yet it remains untold. Therefore, the narrators now ask me to ask them questions about "what I am interested in." As a result of these question-and-answer sessions, some narrators further develop parts of their life histories, while for others, additional difficulties arise as a result of the question-and-answer dynamics. At the end of the event they all feel relieved, whether because they have unloaded and discharged the burden of their memories, or simply because the event that they had feared, the meeting with me and their memories, has finally reached its conclusion.

In the end, despite the question-and-answer sessions, my overall perception concerning these narratives (and especially with regard to the last two) is still one of nonfulfillment. The "ghost chapters" remain unwritten and we (the audience) are not able to plumb the issues discussed in depth, either from an informational point of view or from the psychological and communicative points of view. We only manage to touch on the difficulty of penetrating these depths. This raises the question of whether Holocaust survivors in general experience a sense of success or accomplishment in or through the act of narrating, or what is linguistically termed the "felicity" of successfully carrying out the task or performance. Although the answer to this question was not checked empirically or directly in my work, my intuitive perception is that there is a strong correlation between the degree of openness and responsiveness in survivors' narrations and their sense of success and relief at having told their story.

The sense of a "secret" or "grave" that was brought up in the previous section regarding the narratives of the two married couples is further developed in these three narratives. However, only Esther Israel comes close to the issue of her "secret": she retains the specter of the bodies of those who died from typhus piled on top of each other. Berta Wazner and Piri Meister do not even approach this measure of detail regarding their memories from the Holocaust era. Instead, it seems that the central issue in the life histories of these two narrators is memory itself and the terms of their communication, or lack of communication, with their memories. Alternatively, we can say that their narratives express the great tension between memory and repression, or speech and silence, existing in their consciousnesses.

Berta Wazner (originally from Somorja, a resident of Bazera, Israel, at the time of the interview) expressly discusses at several points the way she represses her Holocaust memories:

> I'll tell you frankly, ever since we came to Israel, I think of the past only very rarely.
>
> I became part of life in Israel very quickly, and thought very little about life there.
>
> Yes, the past is dead, just as you say. I always feared this encounter with my past: the cemetery, the whole town. I don't know, I didn't want to go at all, it was my husband who pushed me to go. I didn't want to visit the old community, I didn't want to see where my past is dead and buried, where my terrible memories are from. It's true that I have good memories from my childhood, but those years are gone, and only the bad years remain.
>
> Here in Israel, I have my children and grandchildren, and my bad memories have somehow quieted down. But going back there seems to have stirred up the memories again. Sometimes at night I have terrible nightmares.
>
> We didn't discuss these things with the children. But, if friends came over we did talk and our conversation always ended up in those years, what happened to this person or that.

Berta flatly states a number of times in her narrative that she has tried not to think about the Holocaust period of her life ever since she came on aliya to Israel in 1949. As far as her conscious mind is concerned, she tries not to talk about the past and not to talk about the Holocaust in front of her children. Despite this, she admits that with fellow survivors, it is impossible not to talk about the Holocaust. In addition, just recently she has reluctantly agreed to accompany her husband on a trip to their places of birth in the former Austro-Hungarian Empire, and as a result, she suffers from the intrusion of unwanted memories that burst forth from behind the dam that she maintained for so many years since she left Europe.

The key term of this narrator regarding her memory is *control*. Berta tries as much as she can to control her memories: she blocks them from her new life in Israel and her relationship with her children, but she lets them cross the threshold into her life circle when she is with fellow survivors. Likewise, the specter of the past confronts her on the trip with her husband to their hometowns in Europe. It seems, then, that Berta understands that it is impossible to totally repress the painful memories or make them disappear completely, and therefore, she must give them some small measure of expression so that she can successfully block them from other aspects of her life. This is why she chooses—largely unconsciously—to face these painful memories only when accompanied by her husband or by fellow survivors.

At first it seems that Berta mentally assigns me, the interviewer, to the same category as her children and her life in Israel, with whom she prefers to repress her Holocaust memories. That seems to be the reason she tells her story as briefly as possible and especially avoids the Holocaust period in her life. However, as a conversation develops between us, and as a result of the questions that she encourages, Berta gradually removes the defense armor from her memories and is willing to relate (to) her life history more inclusively. Yet even now, her memories do not deal with the horrors of the Holocaust itself but only with the difficulties she encounters in returning to what was her hometown before the Holocaust. The town still exists today but looks completely different; the Jews have disappeared as well as anything that evokes Jewishness. Berta tells us that in her journey to her past, she managed to find her mother's grave in the destroyed Jewish cemetery, but in her dreams she still searches for the grave and cannot find it. This contradiction is expressed in the paradox of her relationship with her memories as well. She reluctantly agrees to physically return to her hometown and relive her memories, while at the same time, she still mentally refuses to really confront her past. She vacillates between acceptance and rejection and is not really comfortable with either of these alternatives, as the repeated references to this issue clearly show.

Yet in her conscious and controlled mind, Berta comes to some terms with the past, at least in contrast to her friends who still live in Slovakia. She says about them, "I see our friends there in Slovakia, still suffering, still having a hard time psychologically. There is no real release there." Berta's own audience may well wonder if she herself has had "real release." After all, her frightening dreams persist despite her method of alternatively locking up and freeing her memories. The answer to this question tilts toward the negative side of the pendulum as far as Berta's world of emotions, thoughts, and dreams is concerned, and toward the positive side as far as her daily life and explicit reference to her past and especially the Holocaust. According to Berta's life history and perception (or perception of her life history), in order to proceed with her life and live in the present after the Holocaust, she finds it necessary to control her past and memories. She tries to censor them as much as possible, but occasionally she opens "air vents" to let off excess steam by discussing the Holocaust with fellow survivors, traveling to her hometown, or agreeing to be interviewed.

For Esther Israel (originally from Dunaszerdahely, a resident of Hod-Hasharon, Israel, at the time of the interview), the root of her difficulties in telling her life history hinges on the central Holocaust memory that haunts her, the memory of piles of corpses. Finally, she does mention this memory and reveals some of it to me, saying, "the corpses were piled up like a mountain, they weren't buried at all. It was horrible." At the same time, she declares that she never wanted to tell her children about her experiences in the Holocaust, even though they are adults today, because these memories are "scary," and she does not want to instill fear in her children. She is willing to talk in detail about more impersonal events, however, such as the incident she likens to a "pogrom." Here she describes how hooligans attacked the dining room of the survivors in Bratislava after the war and would have killed them had the Jews not escaped in time.[50] It seems that Esther is able to obtain some emotional release, as well as the ability to speak more freely, when she shifts from her personal experience of the Holocaust to the more general history of others apart from herself, and after the Holocaust.

Piri Meister (originally from Gyergyóvárhegy, a resident of Ra'anana, Israel, at the time of the interview) expresses misgivings before the interview that she may not succeed in telling her life history. At the end of her narrative, she summarizes her difficulties by saying, "It's not hard to tell, as long as I don't tell about *all* we went through. That is why I say that it's no use to tell people how much we suffered." In essence, she is telling us that in the life history she has just narrated, she has not touched on the "secret" or "grave" that she carries with her, since only by avoiding these painful areas is she able to tell her story. We might conclude from her words that had she attempted to discuss these painful areas, she might have not been able to tell any story at all. Her own conclusion is that "it's no use to tell people how much we suffered," meaning that she is unable to tell *everything* and thus obtain the kind of release that other survivors attain by narrating their life histories.

This conclusion concerns not only the narrator, who is left to cope with her largely untold story, or whose story remains locked up in her, but also her audience. For us, her assertion that "it's no use" is also the corollary of "you won't understand no matter what I say." This view of our interaction evokes Dora Ashkenazi's attempt to describe a concentration camp to me by remarking, "You might have seen this on TV." Both Dora and Piri express their awareness of the enormous, perhaps unbridgeable, gap of understanding between the inner world of Holocaust survivors and that of their nonsurvivor audience. These observations imply that no one but a survivor can understand the world of the camps or the tremendous suffering of its inmates. Otherwise, phrases such as "how much we suffered" are shown to be but worn clichés that have no power to convey the horrors imprinted in the souls of Piri, Dora, and other survivors.

To return to Lawrence Langer's terminology, cited in the introduction, concerning the kinds of texts generated by the Holocaust, it may be concluded that for most of the narrators in this chapter, although the existence of a "darker text" lurking behind the "main text" is clearly evident, neither the narrators, nor the narrative event, or myself as a curious interlocutor can fully reach or create the wished-for "valid text."[51] Moreover, most of these narrators wish to do just the opposite, namely, to evade the "valid text," suppress the "darker text" as much as possible, and remain with only the "main text" exactly because of all that it excludes.

4

A Journey without a Conclusion

It's not hard to tell, as long as I don't tell
about all we went through.

Piri Meister, Gyergyóvárhegy–
Ra'anana, 1991

As mentioned in Lawrence Langer's *Holocaust Testimonies,* cited in the introduction to this book, narratives about the Holocaust generate not one but many truths.[1] Among them is, first and foremost, the truth of the narrators, which often includes their conflicting accounts or viewpoints about how and what to remember and tell. Then there is the truth—or truths—arising from the interaction around and interpretations of these narratives.

Two of the narrators in this book exemplify this process in their life histories and in the afterlife of the narrative events in which these were told. Human and professional sensitivity regarding the issues that will be discussed dictate that I do not reveal their names. The two women, distant relatives, used to live in the same town and in the same street in Europe. One of the women was particularly expressive and recounted her life history with great detail and relish. Therefore, when I was invited in 1994 to lecture on the topic of my research at Yad Vashem in Jerusalem, I saw fit to invite this narrator to join me and tell her story. Despite some initial misgivings, she agreed and came to the event accompanied by her granddaughter, a high school student. Before the event, when we prepared our presentation, she asked me whether to include certain incidents in her speech. Among them, she mentioned her suicide attempt soon after liberation, an event she had not referred to in the life history she had told me previously. I advised her not to bring it up in public. When we appeared in Yad Vashem, she spoke about her experiences with great confidence and zeal. Needless to say, she did talk about her suicide attempt and even joked about it, as if to say: I survived that as well.

This woman then asked me if I had turned to the other survivors that she had recommended to me during our previous meeting. She mentioned her relative and former neighbor, whose narrative is extremely brief and obscure, and asked me if this woman had mentioned certain experiences. For example, she told me that this woman had had the task of evacuating the dead bodies in the concentration camp, and that in return for dragging them to the collection spot by their ankles, she received extra portions of food. No, the woman in question had not revealed this to me. Instead, she had tiptoed around the whole issue and avoided describing her Holocaust experiences in detail.

The fact that I encountered these "postscript" stories only through accident made me realize that many more such hidden or side stories might exist in the minds of other interviewees and Holocaust survivors in general, as the epigraphs to this conclusion and to the appendix to this work well exemplify. This brings home the message that the Holocaust experience cannot ever be truly fathomed or exhausted. Of course, all narratives contain within the potential for a multiplicity of versions and interpretations, but it seems that in relation to the Holocaust, there is special room for thought and discussion of the factors working to conceal or reveal, dismiss or stress, exclude, include, or hint at significant portions of the lives and life histories of its survivors.

This work presented a reading of life histories of elderly Hungarian Jewish female Holocaust survivors currently living in Israel and in Hungary. Although I approached these women mostly through the "snowball" or "friend recommends friend" networking dynamic, which usually creates an arbitrary group, it eventually turned out that these subjects do share a set of personal traits and cultural characteristics related to their places of origin. Born in most cases in the 1920s, these women are still part of the Austro-Hungarian mentality and cling to its memory and remnants. That Jews were by the 1920s accused of the Empire's fall or of Communism does not seem to affect these women and their families. The Hungarian Jews of this time were proud of their participation in World War I, and of both the handicaps and the medals they accrued. They identified themselves as Israelite Hungarians and were sure that anti-Semitism was but a passing cloud on the skies of Hungary as of the 1860s (when Hungarian Jewry was emancipated) and on.[2]

Concerning the family portraits of many of these women, since birth rates in the interwar period were still relatively high, moreso among Orthodox and middle- to working-class circles than among secular and upper-class ones, they are often part of so-called series of siblings, at times with barely a year between one and the next. In World War II and the Holocaust, therefore, while their brothers were usually drafted to different Labor Service units within the Hungarian army and rarely enjoyed each other's company and support, sisters were able to cling to each other in the framework of camps and forced labor factories and to create "teams" consisting of up to five sisters (as in the case of Rachel Markowitz in the third chapter). These groups of sisters stuck together in the face of atrocity and were devastated when any of them were lost (as happens to Rachel and her sisters).

Cousins, friends, neighbors, past members in youth movements, and at times complete strangers also formed meaningful groups to help them in the struggle for survival. As pointed out in the introduction, the phenomenon of womanly friendship and bonding was widely stressed both by women survivors and in research about them, because of its ability to supply the women with mutual physical help, psychological support, verbal and mental communication, a sense of family, and because it added meaning to their effort to survive. Years afterward, in their narratives and discourse, the women still remember their "sisters in sorrow" as such. For example, my aunt Aranka Friedmann, living in Rumania, to this day refers to three Israeli sisters she befriended in the camps as her "camp-mates," and the four have maintained ever since a decades-long correspondence between Oradea and Yavne.

Notwithstanding varieties of social and financial status, most of these women received professional training in their youth as seamstresses of varied expertise, teachers, nannies, and so forth, or joined the family workshop or business. Concerning this background, Zsuzsa Faludi's criticism in the second chapter of what she considers her own mother's overly delicate upbringing, which did not include professional training, becomes an explanation for the mother's harsh life circumstances in her postwar widowhood and older age, when she is forced to take menial jobs to support her orphaned children and herself. As for the other narrators in this work and in equivalent corpora, initial professional training prepared them for the demands of the work world in relatively peaceful times and even in poverty and war, but not for the extreme conditions of forced labor camps and factories, where work is the easy part compared to the hunger, cold, sickness, and harassment they had to endure.

Above all, these women came from protective homes in terms of both the central European middle class in general and the Jewish ethos of any of the three streams of Hungarian Jewry specifically. Coming from Orthodox, Status Quo, or Neologist circles, Hungarian Jewish girls as a rule "were brought up strictly and received a good education. None of us were allowed to go out alone at night. We had to do our share at home too. One did the cleaning, another the cooking, helping at the shop, setting the table, etc."[3] Added to the aforementioned aspects of the upbringing, surrounding, and cultural milieu of these women, such and many similar descriptions give us a sense of the total collapse and loss of an entire world they experienced during World War II and the Holocaust.

It has to be clarified that my claim that *these* women were unprepared for the Holocaust is not at all intended to imply that anyone, anywhere, no matter how hard their life, upbringing, or circumstances, could be prepared for such an event. To claim so would belittle or humanize (or rehumanize) the Holocaust. Rather, my intention in this work was to portray the world of one specific group, with its inner varieties, on the eve of a universally shattering event, stressing the unique aspects of this group in terms of both the experiences they went through and the ways in which they remember and recount them decades afterward.

As pointed out in the introduction, the central aspect of the Holocaust of Hungarian Jewry is its intensity and abruptness so close to the war's ending and to the final defeat of Nazi Germany. This blow is added to that of Hungary's readiness and even eagerness to implement the "final solution" on its Jewish population. Remembering Hungarian Jewry's high degree of identification with first the Austro-Hungarian Empire and then the Hungarian State, we must realize this Jewry's dismay at being rejected by and eliminated from a country they truly believed they were part of, up until March 1944. This is the backdrop against which we should listen to and understand seemingly absurd accounts, such as that of Dora Ashkenazi in the third chapter, about the motivation of Jewish women camp prisoners to show their German meister at the ammunition factory that "Jews too could work" and thus contribute to the German war effort. This is also the backdrop against which we should read Dora's descriptions of language and culture "battles" between German and Hungarian, or German and Yiddish, and all they stand for in their context. German in the war and Holocaust years becomes for Dora and her friends the language of orders and horror, whereas beforehand, it used to be the language of refinement and culture. Hungarian stands for treachery at the same time that it is still their own language, and Yiddish is at times a reminder of one's family and community, at times a language of secrets and intimacy, and at times a signifier of wretchedness and helplessness.

Unlike survivor authors writing Holocaust fiction (which may be related to their real-life experiences), the present narrators do not consciously invest artistic effort in making their accounts literary. On the contrary, they try to convince their listener and readers that their stories are part of reality and known history, in addition to being private stories that have never before been shared with the public. Therefore, in my analyses of their inclusive life histories that focus on the Holocaust, I tried to respond to their stance by a combined literary and historical-cultural reading. Such a reading takes realistic data and events into account as if they were part of the narrative, as well as vice versa, and views these narratives as part of known and formal history, although that, too, can be told in several ways. In fact, such a reading focuses on the meeting points between history and story, and examines the ways in which one is expanded, enriched, or contradicted by the other. All this without, of course, seeking one ultimate "truth" but rather exploring varied conceptions of truth by different narrators, be they ordinary people, renowned writers, researchers of different disciplines, or interdisciplinarians.

To some extent, this is a new historicist reading, except that it does not deal with specific historical documents but with historical accounts in their entirety, that is, with well-known and widely renowned relevant studies. Thus, the present reading avoids the flaws of eclecticism or of a fragmentary treatment of elements that should be viewed in their inclusive framework, while still keeping alive dynamics between (personal literary or testimonial) text and (historical) context.[4] In the present narratives, side-by-side with the principle of "the unity of misery" as experienced and shared by millions,[5] we also encounter the phenomenon of "many truths" quoted earlier from Langer's work. The accounts and counteraccounts of mother and daughter (Irma Fischer and Zsuzsa Faludi) in the second chapter, for example, provide a series of fascinating illuminations to both these views at one and the same time. Both mother and daughter were part of the crucial events they describe, and although they generally agree on the essentials of these life-threatening events, they still disagree on points that may look trivial to others but are utterly significant to them. The mother remembers that the daughter was beaten in the "slander" incident (as termed by the daughter) in order to prove her innocence and show that despite the flogging, which resulted from the accusations of neighbors, she stuck to her claim that she had never said any pro-Communist things. For her part, the daughter avoids the issue of *who beat her*, only to finally and painfully disclose that it was her beloved father, the same father she so misses since his disappearance at the war's ending, and who was and obviously still is her favorite parent. Although the mother generally sympathizes with the daughter's pain and insult at being "exonerated" in such a rigid manner, she too avoids or neglects the issue of the beater's identity, to the extent that we might gather from her disorderly account that it was the guard or policeman sent to interrogate the family. The daughter here faces her complex and mixed feelings concerning her beloved father and much-criticized mother, whereas the mother neither fathoms the depths of all this in the eyes of her daughter nor deals with her own responsibility as parent to her daughter's ever-lingering hurt.

A similar thing happens to their descriptions of a successful escape attempt from a raid that would otherwise have ended with their being shot on the banks of the Danube. Here again, it is the daughter who remembers while the mother forgets the name of the square they are led to. Only this time, the mother is aware of her lapse of memory and confronts it by asking her daughter for the missing detail, momentarily letting the daughter into her narrative before going on by herself. The daughter, who otherwise criticizes her mother's conduct and reflections throughout her narrative, here embraces her mother's view of herself as an ultimate earth mother ready to sacrifice herself for her children's safety. Thus, in a rare moment of reconcilement between the two, the daughter expresses her gratitude for the mother's altruistic act in this case and her general devotion throughout their life together.

Another example of many truths, or varied and intriguing versions of events, is my aunt's somewhat naïve depiction of her period of forced labor in an aircraft factory amid pine trees somewhere in Eastern Europe. Curiously and unlike most survivors, Aranka Friedmann describes the work routine and all that goes with it as a strengthening experience for her, in contrast to her sickly childhood and young adulthood. In fact, even the abortion episode, if read from this angle and not the one chosen in that chapter (that of the analogy with her sister-in-law's fate), is just another illustration of her pre-Holocaust weakness and inability to face hardship. Here the contradiction is not between the versions of two narrators, like those just cited of the mother and daughter, but between this specific narrator's view of the forced labor experience and its historical documentation and recurrent testimonial description as excruciating and decimating rather than rehabilitative. Still, this has been her way of living and viewing this experience ever since. Aranka then continues to surprise those around her when she finally returns to her town after liberation, while other women, known to be much healthier and with greater stamina than she, never return. Her survival is so unexpected in her previous environment that one expectant husband expresses to her face his surprise (or anger) at this weird reversal of fates. Aranka does not disclose her response to this welcome but chooses to describe this scene in retrospect with a partly bitter, partly embarrassed grin, keeping it all to herself.

Paraphrasing Tolstoy, we might conclude that the stories of (or about) those exterminated in the Holocaust are eventually all the same, no matter how strong or feeble they were in the first place, simply because, sorrowfully, these individuals are not here to tell them, make variations, or explicate difficult points. Nor can others, however well meaning or informed, do it for and instead of the dead. By contrast, the stories of survivors are remarkably varied, not only in relation to each other, but also in regard to the light they shed on their entire lives in the world before, during, and after the Holocaust. These stories continue to grow or shrink with every telling—as do the accounts of the two relatives at the outset of this summary—and call for our attention, interpretation, participation, and empathy, although at times it seems the narrators want none of these. As for the listeners, readers, and audience in any sense of these and similar Holocaust narratives, we find it hard to let go, although much has been done and said already. We delve ever deeper into the depths of these unfathomable experiences and inexplicable accounts. We hope to come to an end. But at least for the time being, as we continue, we find that ours is but a small contribution, and that much has still to be done and said.

Appendix: The Life Histories

I remember a lot of things, but you can't tell it all.
Dora Ashkenazi, Dunaszerdahely and Bazera, 1990

Rozsi Háger. Originally from Nagyvárad, Hungary/Rumania.[1] Interviewed in Hod Hasharon, Israel, May 1991

(Translated from Hungarian)

Rozsi Háger[2]: When we were young, we had a very, very happy childhood. Not because of toys, which we didn't have, but because of the fresh air. The area was not built up yet, and all the kids from the neighborhood played outside, the poor just like the wealthy ones. From morning until evening we could play, and we had a very happy and cheerful childhood, until we had to go to school. The moment we started school, the worries started: study, do your homework. And we could not play from morning to evening but had to go to school in the morning and do our homework in the afternoon. And so the time passed until there came the time when we had to learn a profession. Our house was warm and friendly, although we did not have a big apartment. But in those days the parents were not greedy. They were happy if they had healthy kids, and the mother was everything. At age thirteen I went to learn a profession. I learned sewing at a first-class salon. I graduated from there. Then I worked there for ten years and became a cutter.

When the Hungarians invaded, everything changed. They started harassing the Jews. They raided the city. Came from Hungary. Bought everything. Then they gave us coupon rations for food. I cannot say that we were hungry, because with these coupons we received what we could, Jews and Hungarians alike, flour, sugar, bread. So I cannot say we starved, until the Germans came in. When the Germans came, the persecution of Jews really started, and they started harassing the Jews in a very harsh way. Then they started the ghetto. We did not know at first where the ghetto would be. We were lucky because by chance, my uncle's house was included in the ghetto. And since my mother was

135

sick by then and bedridden for four years, we had a room for ourselves. We were granted this special privilege on account of the bedridden ill woman.

By [the Jewish holiday of] *Shavuot,* we had been in the ghetto for a month. Since the Jews and Christians had their holidays at the same time, we hoped they would not put us on the trains to take us away, and that the Russians would come and bomb so the deportation would be stopped. To my sorrow, it did not happen this way. On *Shavuot,* on a Sunday, they put us on cattle cars, on a train to Auschwitz. They put eighty, a hundred people in a cattle car. We received no water; we could only tend to our needs in a bucket. There was such a stench. On Wednesday we reached Auschwitz at dawn, and by that time, there were some dead people among us. It is better not to talk about the way we looked. We look out of the window, we see the people there are naked, bald-headed, and they shout to us: "Throw everything out, throw everything out." We said to each other: "Who are these people? Are they crazy, or are they thieves, scum or what?" To this the German guard responded by saying, "They are all of these." But we did not understand what he meant, because the Germans we had known in the past—the ones who came to Hungary to work and study—had always been polite and kind, not sadistic as these were now.

When we arrived, they took us down, separated the women from the men, and the "selection" started. For life or for death. They stripped us naked, took us to showers, stripped us, shaved us. Of this there is nothing to tell, because it simply cannot be told. We entered the showers through one door and came out from another. They took away everything we owned, we received nothing back. We had no personal belongings anymore. Those who were lucky got some clothing and those who weren't lucky got nothing. They took us to a block. They put in it more than a thousand people. There were no beds. We slept on the ground. At night, if we happened to touch each other we screamed, because wherever you touched it was shaven, naked. We did not even know if it was a man or a woman, we knew nothing. Early in the morning they sent us to roll call, where we stood for hours. If in the meantime someone died you could not break the line; we had to hold the corpse up from the sides, from the back, it couldn't be otherwise, because they had already counted us. Then, when the Germans had counted us all, when the counting ended, we had to go get our food. It went on this way until November, always the same. Then we found our aunt and cousin, who asked us not to go to work so that we could remain together. But in the end we had to leave them because we could not stand the "selections" three or four times a day, with Mengele. It was terrible.

In the end they chose us from among the whole group, took us to work in an airplane factory. We walked six kilometers. We worked there from November to January. It might have been a labor camp that had been turned into a factory. We worked for twelve hours and had twelve hours to rest. Even pigs wouldn't eat the food they gave us. There is nothing to tell about this, because it was clear that we were just prisoners who didn't deserve to eat. Once we received such bad food that even our engineer and the factory manager both came to see and ask that they give us food so that we can work, that they shouldn't steal our food. But, it was the Jews who stole and gave it to the Germans to send to their families. A thing like that, if you tell it, they would say it couldn't happen. The Jews behaved more sadistically than the Germans themselves, because for the Germans we were only workers. The Jews, by contrast, those who were transferred to the kitchen, they did their best not to be kicked out, so they groveled and sucked up to the Germans. They did everything for the German women in order to keep themselves out of trouble.

Then the Russians were approaching, so the Germans took us to another factory, to "Telefunken." There, we were liberated by the Russians. They gave us each a certificate that we were ex–concentration camp prisoners who had been liberated. A Russian officer came on the 8th of May, at eight in the evening. He got there on a jeep and asked us who we were. Some girls knew Russian, and they said, "Jewish women." He said, "I wouldn't boast about it." One girl asked him, "And what are *you*?" He said, "As you can see, Russian." She says, "I did not ask that, I asked what *are* you." He said, "First of all, Russian, second of all, Russian, and third of all, Russian. Only afterward Jewish, but I don't boast about it. And another thing, if possible, don't move around in big groups, and leave immediately. Because if you move in a group, the soldiers might notice you. These soldiers, I cannot speak well of them, because many of them are barely out of school, many of them are starved for women, so watch out for yourselves, because we cannot protect you."

Some Czech partisans came by our camp. They were very good to us. They noticed that our camp was mined, that it was going to explode. And they were the ones who saved us. When we remained there in the camp on the 8th of May, liberated, we dived into heaps of potatoes like animals and could not eat enough. Then we left on the following day.

We started on our way, we left and reached Pozsony [Hungarian name of Bratislava, in Slovakia]. When we reached Pozsony there were some Jews who had been in hiding before and were now trying to help the returning deportees. They asked us, because there were many of us, they asked us where we were from. We said, "Nagyvárad." They said, "Come into town, do not stay here at the station, for there are many Russians here and they are looking for women. *Barishna* (or *woman* in Russian) is what they want, and they do not care if she is thin or fat, young or old, as long as she is a woman." We said, if this is the situation, then we will head toward home. We caught a train to [Buda]Pest that had a few stops on the way. In Pozsony, as we got on the train, there was a woman who told the Russians that there were women there. There were some Rumanian partisans there, belonging to the Tudor Vladimiresku movement [anti-Fascist Rumanian Socialist movement], who had access to everything, just like the Russians. These men saw us and asked us in Rumanian where we belonged. We said, "Rumania." They asked, "Which part, because you speak in a Hungarian accent." They were three young men. One was a lawyer, the other a university teacher, and the third one I cannot say because it happened so long ago that I have forgotten. These three walked us to the train station. They were carrying beds with them. A Russian soldier came and asked, "Where are the *barishnas*?" They replied, "Gone, *barishna nyet, barishna nyet.*" That's how they protected us until we reached Budapest.

In Budapest we got off. There was a Jewish organization there that took care of Jews. They said we had to be disinfected. We saw girls with bald heads. We asked them, "Why are you bald?" They said, "Those who go to disinfection also get shaven." Well, our hair had just started to grow, it was one or two centimeters long. But we did not want to be bald again, so we decided we wouldn't go, we wanted to be left alone. We left and went further. These Tudor boys now bought us blueberries, because they had money. Some Jewish girls saw this and shouted, "Look, the soldiers are buying them fruit. Who accepts fruit from soldiers? They must be loose women!"

So, never mind, we parted from these Tudor boys. They begged us to remain with them, but we only stayed in Pest for two days, and then we headed home. When we came home to (Nagy)Várad we did not find anyone, nor did we have the strength to go back to our old apartment. We just approached the building where we had lived, because we had hidden our sewing machine in a place which used to be a stable. That way everyone thought that a machine that was in a stable was not worthwhile taking because surely it was broken. Now we brought it back home, repaired it, and started to work. My sister, who was younger than I, met a man who used to date one of our friends, and they were later married. I, on the other hand, got to know two brothers who lived in our building. For a whole month, they gave us food and clothing and helped us with whatever we needed.

Now, a man who had been wounded on the Russian front also came to this house. He was not a soldier but served in the labor battalion of the Hungarian army, and he was injured while taking apart a hand grenade. An acquaintance of his sent him from Pest. He had been in Yugoslavia and suffered a great deal. He walked into the cooperative kitchen of the survivors. I came up to him and asked, "Where did you serve, maybe you met my father?" He said that no, he had not met my father. He had served in Bor. By then I had enough food with me, and I said, "Sit down and eat." He said, "I am not hungry." I said, "Why pretend, you must be as hungry as we are." All those who came back from the camps of all kinds were hungry, could not be sated. We had lunch three times a day and still we were hungry. We only worked so we could eat.

It was in June that I met the man from the labor battalion, my future husband, and in December my sister and I both got married. That day there were thirteen weddings. On the exact day I met my husband, that day eleven years later, he had a heart attack and died. I was very bitter and did not believe in anything anymore. I said to myself, here we came home from the camps, had no aspirations, we worked, we lived, and God took away such a good man. I had no parents, no children, I was very bitter. Nothing.

Then, almost a year later, I got married again. I again found a very good man, a widower with a daughter. That is why I married him. I thought, If I myself cannot have any children, I shall at least raise this orphan so that in my old age someone will give me a glass of water. I did not expect her to support me, just to give me some attention.

I was very lucky. I became pregnant. For four months I did not even know. When I had my daughter, it was a big miracle. Everyone said, "Rozsi has a child, Rozsi gave birth!" True, I was not a young mother. I was not a mother to my daughter but a grandmother. I loved her. We came to Israel. She became a *sabra* [a native Israeli], a graceful, pretty woman, thank God. She has three children. She has an excellent husband. I could not ask for any other happiness but to see her happy. She has everything. Her children study. What else does a mother need beyond seeing her children happy? What else can I tell you?

Ilana Rosen: I would like to ask you about the existence of anti-Semitism even before the Hungarian and German eras. To what extent could you sense it?

Mrs. Háger: There was no anti-Semitism then because you could not even tell who was Jewish and who was Gentile. Moreover, there were many Christians who hid Jews. But today, they would not save Jews again. The reason for this, among other reasons, is the following story. One of our apprentices hid our manager. After liberation, this man came up to the manager and said, "Mister manager, you know very well that I was never anti-Semitic, and you know very well that if I had gotten caught for hiding two Jews, they would have deported me too. All I ask now is a letter certifying that I am not anti-Semitic." To this the manager replied, "How would I know that you're not an anti-Semite?"

I.R.: Can you return to the issue of religion we discussed before and tell me if anything changed for you in that regard?

Mrs. Háger: As a child, I was raised by parents who grew up in very religious families. My grandmother on my mother's side was so observant that she never wore a wig but only silk head scarves. She also never learned Hungarian. She came from Galicia, she spoke only Yiddish and never learned Hungarian, she was very religious. My mother kept a hundred percent kosher house. She taught us girls how to kosher our meat. She demonstrated it on a pigeon. When I first went to work, I had to work on the Sabbath or else they would not have hired me. I did not eat any unkosher food there and just waited to see when the Good God would make a miracle and the needle would fall out of my hand on the Sabbath.

My father was a very wise man. He said, "My daughter, if you learn a profession, you should do your best. As long as you are at work, concentrate on your work; you have to practice in order to learn it well. But the moment you leave your work, as soon as you close the door, leave it all behind you. Only this way can you be relaxed and happy." Then, when we came home . . . My mother, just before they deported us, she was dying for three days and three nights. While dying, she dreamed of Auschwitz. How they put us on cattle cars, how it all happened. And we said to her, "Mummy, do not talk like that." She was so afraid that her dreams would come true. When we returned from the camps, my sister and I, we became completely secular. We said, if there was a God, He would not have let it happen that such an ill person, who could not take one step, would die in the camps. At least we should have been able to bury her in a cemetery. Even that was not possible, for she was taken to the gas chambers. They burned her and spread her ashes on the water.

I.R.: Now I would like to ask you about language. How were you, Jews coming from many different countries, able to understand each other, or did you stick with other Hungarian Jews in the camps?

Mrs. Háger: The Czechs were the first. When the Germans took over, they deported all the Czech students from the universities, doctors, etc., and they were the ones who built Auschwitz. They sent women to the front, inscribed "Front-Line Whores" between their breasts. They removed the women's wombs so they could not give birth, could not become pregnant. There were people from many places, Poles, Greeks. The Germans deported people from wherever they set foot. We were in Block C, for the camp was made of Blocks, A, B, C. Opposite us were Gypsies. They were allowed to keep their clothes, their hair. When we said, "Look, Gypsies," they answered, "Yes, Gypsies, but not Jews."

I.R.: By then, it was better to be a Gypsy than a Jew. You mentioned earlier the way certain Jews mistreated other Jews. Did all the Jews act that way, or just those who had important jobs, like the Capos?

Mrs. Háger: Listen, we the ordinary people could not cheat each other because we were all in the same boat. Our greatest enjoyment was to have our piece of bread, sit in the toilet, excuse me, and eat it there. There at least we remained seated. We always looked for pieces of coal, for almost everyone suffered from diarrhea. All of us women, after we arrived to camp, had our periods only once and not anymore, because they put bromide in our food, which calmed us down and stopped our menstruation. Many suffered from diarrhea, and we ate these pieces of coal instead of coal-dust.

Aranka Friedmann. Originally from Félegyháza, Hungary/Rumania. Interviewed in Budapest, September 1991 (Lives in Oradea, Rumania)

(Translated from Hungarian)

Aranka Friedmann: I was born in Félegyháza. I lived there with my parents and three, no, two brothers. My parents had a grocery store and a few other businesses and we had quite a good life. I went to school, all three of us did. No, not all three, just the two of us. Miki, my big brother, he was older, he already attended high school. Whereas I, it was exactly when I had to start high school that my father became ill, so I could not go to Nagyvárad to high school. What now?

I.R.: He got ill and what happened next?

Mrs. Friedmann: Well, for a while he remained in the village, sick as he was. Then we brought him to a sanatorium for people suffering from lung illnesses. He became ill because he used to travel to Várad to purchase merchandise for the store. Once he was late for the train, so he started running, and probably from the effort a blood vessel in his lung was torn. That was how the illness started. When the village doctors could not do anything beyond worsening his situation, we brought him to this sanatorium that was very expensive at the time. But by then he could not be helped. My mother stayed with him, and he died in 1930. Shall I talk about my mother?

I.R.: Yes.

Mrs. Friedmann: My mother, my older brother Miki, my younger brother Jenő, and myself were left with the store, and our grandmother also stayed with us. About two years later, my mother died too, in the following circumstances. She had been suffering for years from digestion problems and later, I don't know how, she became dependent upon drastic laxatives, which caused her a tumor. Then we brought her too to Várad, where they operated on her, and nine days later she died too. So my father died in 1930, and my mother in 1932. The three children remained at home. We had to give up the store, as we could not keep it anymore. Then my older brother got married, received a dowry of 10,000 leis [Rumanian currency], and they remained in Félegyháza. Whereas I, after my younger brother entered the Jewish orphanage of Nagyvárad, I found myself a job at this crafts shop. However, I earned very little there, so I moved to a company that manufactured toothbrushes. I was then fifteen-and-a-half years old and had to wait until I became sixteen to start working at this company. I was working there when I met Jenő, my future husband. We went out together for a year, got to know each other, and after a year, we got married.

Now, shall I turn back to the family? Well, my husband Jenő worked as a street-sign painter. He had good hands and he made street signs for stores, as well as drawings. What can I say? We lived well enough. Now, again I am not sure what to talk about. As for children, it may well be that the reason why I don't have any children is that I became pregnant when the Hungarians came in, and I then went to the doctor. After a short while, my husband enrolled in the labor battalions, and I went to the ghetto.

After the ghetto, where we stayed for a month, we were taken to Auschwitz. I did not stay long in Auschwitz, only three weeks or so, for we were taken to Riga, the capital of Latvia. There in the woods there was a camp. Underneath us was a weapons factory. We did not know it then. Later, as the Russians approached, we were moved to Stutthof, another camp from which they sent out transports. I got there, joined a transport that was sent to Gutava, where we worked in digging antitank bunkers and carrying heavy stones, this was the kind of job we were given. Of course, I was thin, as were all the others, and there was very little food. I cannot say that they were cruel to us, because we gave them no reason; we worked as they told us to.

There were quite a lot of us when we were liberated. It happened like this: When the Russians approached, the SS took us away from there and put us in a barn, after marching for maybe two days without any food or anything, in a big snowfall. People, meaning the women who were with me, ate the snow, they were thirsty, and they suffered from the cold too. One SS man was OK; we entered a village, and he went up to the commander saying we should get some food. And really, we entered the village and received cheese and bread. And then we walked, they marched us further down. At last we reached a farm, and I don't know how many of us there were, but there were many of us. We got there in the evening and they put us in a barn and, yes, they even locked the door on us. I was convinced that they were going to burn down the barn with us inside. But it did not happen. At night the Germans left, and we remained there. That is how we were liberated. Now, stop taping for a moment please, because I cannot talk anymore [short break].

My younger brother who was in an orphanage left the orphanage before the Hungarians came. Together with my husband's brother and with a group of people they went to Marmarossziget, where they joined still many others and all fled to the Soviet Union to try to save themselves. They had a tough life there, as I learned later. To my sorrow, both died. Neither of them returned. Now, my older brother Miki and his family stayed in the village for a while and after that they too came to town. Miki worked here as a helper in a shop until the deportation. He was first taken to the labor battalions. He went together with my husband, Jenő; they were taken to Nagybánya. Jenő stayed there, but my brother was exempt because he was too short. They had such criteria. He came home and kept on working at the shop. Then the deportations started. His wife Ilush and their son Péter, who was five or six years old, they went together to Auschwitz and they too never returned. The family was exterminated this way, you could say. And now I shall return to . . .

I.R.: After the war.

Mrs. Friedmann: After the war. Yes, turn it off for a minute [short break]. Well, after returning from the deportation, I mean it was an excruciating journey until we came back. In the end there was a difficult period because a group of Polish survivors switched our camp number and assumed our identity to make their way to Hungary and from there, to escape Europe to Israel and other countries. Meanwhile, because the other group had pretended to be us, there was a lot of confusion and we, instead, were taken to the Soviet Union, to Minsk. We stayed in Minsk for at least six months and only when we passed the border did I learn about the reason for the mix-up, that in fact we could have returned much earlier. But it happened on both sides. On the Rumanian side the Rumanian-Jewish leaders were arrested, and so were the Russians, those who were responsible for it all.

Then I came back, in a rather big transport. Eighty of us came home to Várad. Now they were supposed to transfer us officially, but we saw on the previous stations what a circus they made with other women, how they taunted them and made them cry. So we were already forewarned and we decided to escape from them. Some four or five of us dismounted at the station that was before Várad, and everyone threw them their things, backpacks or whatever they had. When we came to Várad we went out to the toilets. The Russians thought, why is everybody going, but they did not say anything. But we did not come out until the train left. We went out to the street and waited there. They thought we were going to the toilet so they did not say anything when we came in. And we did not leave until . . . Then we gathered in the street.

Now, the news spread in Várad that a train came and the Jews hurried to the station with Jenő among them. Standing in the street I saw the streetcar coming and Jenő jump off it. We were reunited right there in the middle of the street, and there was great joy. Many men whose wives remained there in Auschwitz came too. Someone even said to me, "You? You came back and my healthy wife [grin] stayed there?" Because they knew that I had been ill for a long time before deportation. Then Jenő and I went home to our apartment, which remained as we left it. I cannot say it was great, but at least we had that.

I.R.: Did Jenő serve in the labor battalions?

Mrs. Friedmann: Yes, he was in the labor battalions, but when the city was freed, he came back, one day later. Now, he came to the police, worked for a while at the police. When I became stronger, I took a course with the Red Cross and became a nurse, *achot*, in Hebrew [laughs]. We both worked, and we were like everyone in the working class, I can say. Jenő worked as a painter in a streetcar workshop, and naturally we enrolled in the Communist Party. They were very fond of him at work, so he even became a functionary in the Party. I first came to work in a hospital, not with the patients, but as a receptionist in the office. After a while I was moved to the surgical department, to the same function as a receptionist, and worked there for ten years. After ten years I moved to a bigger clinic, where I worked for a few years and then moved to another clinic. I worked there until I retired.

I mentioned my illness, but in the meantime Jenő got sick too. I recovered and he became ill, so he had an early retirement. When we were pensioners, we came to Budapest in 1984, because my husband's sister had become ill and died. Jenő came first because they did not let a husband and wife leave together. So I arrived one week later. Already as I arrived from the station I saw that my husband was sick. He had had a stroke. Now with all the arrangements around my sister-in-law's burial, the lawyer, and I don't know what, it all affected him. These things ruined him.

In 1984, on the 20th of June, I took him home, and on the 26th, he died. I took him home for five days. I took him to a hospital, to the best cardiologist. But he did not want to stay there. The doctor said he should stay, but Jenő refused, and because of his stroke, his mind was confused, and he started crying and saying he would not stay there. We did not want to force him, so as not to cause an attack, because I knew already: they did an ECG check here in Budapest, and it showed that he was on the verge of an attack. That is why he lived for only five days more. Turn it off for a minute [break].

We buried him and I, too, was in bad shape. Three weeks later I also had a ministroke. My present life is hard, because it is difficult to live on your own. I should add that I suffer from a certain illness, but my medical situation is relatively stable. The conditions in Rumania are hard. But I, I don't complain about not having this thing or that. Not a colorful life, my life.

Irma Fischer. Interviewed in Budapest, Hungary, September 1991

(Translated from Hungarian)

Irma Fischer: My poor mother. We were five brothers and sisters. My father worked as a mechanic and died at a young age from an accident at the workshop. The gas container exploded near some children, young workers. My father rushed to save the children, and instead, he himself was killed. I had three brothers and a sister, and I was the youngest. So we were seven family members until my father's death, and after he died we remained with our mother. My older brother already worked as a mechanic's helper, and the other two brothers were still apprentices. My poor mother . . . Then I went to school but missed a lot because I was anemic and had many other health problems.

My mother was very religious, and she used to take a bath for the Sabbath. The bath and the toilet were in the same room. She was there, and we did not know how, probably her dress caught fire from the gas used to heat up the water, and she too was killed. I was already married and pregnant with my son when this accident happened.

Then there was this incident with my daughter. She went to school, she was very smart, she was in the first grade. My brothers and sister, my mother, everyone loved her because she was the first grandchild. Meanwhile, we were neighbors with this Gypsy couple, so then these Gypsies wrote a letter saying the child told them that the Americans [meaning the Germans] are coming and then it will be bad for us Jews, and they will take us away. So the child . . . and the manager called my husband. They took my daughter to the cellar, and in the cellar they showed her the policeman. "Look, look over there, there is a policeman there. Now listen, tell the truth, did your parents say these things?" The child answered, crying, that she had not said or heard a thing. Then they also invited my husband to school. And he said, "The child and us, we don't talk about such things, we are happy just to be alive." But the poor child was beaten anyway. We wondered, she was just a child, maybe she did say it? But no, she did not. Then they told my husband that he should be happy that she stuck to her story, or else they would have taken away the whole family.

My husband was working at the time in a military company as an electronics technician. My daughter was a very good pupil. Then we had to leave the house, had to leave everything behind. They took us all to the ghetto, and from there they then took my husband to the labor battalions, and I remained alone with the children. It was terrible, the ghetto, because we were surrounded by a fence. I tried to escape from there, just to be out, go anywhere. But I did not succeed. Then my brother-in-law, Sándor Fischer, I don't know if you heard about him—

Zsuzsa Faludi (Mrs. Fischer's daughter): Yes, she did.

Mrs. Fischer: He got me a Swedish Protection Pass. I went to Katona Jozsef Street, to the Protected House, to the shelter with the children. And my son became very ill. I had to go to the pharmacist for medicine because the child was very ill, even though I wasn't supposed to leave the Protected House. I went out during an air raid. I left the children there and did not know how I would return. The Arrow Cross guards came, and I wrapped my shawl around my head. I did not care what would happen to me, but come what may, I knew I had to return to the children, because I left them there alone. This guard may have been a kind man, I asked him if I was near the Protected House, and he helped me return. My daughter was sure I was not coming back. She was six years old then.

Then the Arrow Cross men came another time and wanted to take us away. I again put the children in a separate room to lie there, so I could say they had a contagious disease. They were as red as crabs. So they let us stay there. Then I escaped and went to my brother-in-law, Sándor Fischer, who was then in the labor battalions, I went there. They were very kind to me, the labor battalion men [crying]. But my son was still in diapers and my daughter [unclear] and we had nothing. So I could not remain there, without diapers and food for the children. Then the men had to leave, and I remained with the children. I came back to the Protected House. I did not know anything about my husband. My brother-in-law came to see what was going on with us in the Protected House. Then, the children became sick, so I had to leave the Protected House and move into the ghetto again, for medical care. Afterward I couldn't leave anymore.

In the ghetto I tried to get to the hospital with the children. The ghetto was surrounded by a fence. We entered the hospital, they took us in, and I knew nothing about the others in my family. They took us in to a house where I had to clean, do the laundry, and everything, so that I could stay there with the children. I remained there. When the Russians were approaching, there were air-raid alerts frequently and the Hungarian guards rushed us out to the street, with our dead, and I took the children with me. I held my son in my arms. They even took us to this . . . what was the name of the street where the mayor lived?

It doesn't matter. They took us and they wanted to take away the children, so I ran away and didn't care about anything. My daughter had a Star of David. I tore it off her. I held the boy [demonstrates how] and to . . .

Mrs. Faludi: The name of the street is Szent István.

Mrs. Fischer: Right. And they wanted to take away the children. And I said, "Over my dead body. Only if I die." I went through a lot. Then we came back to the ghetto, where we either got some food or we didn't. I cooked potato peels for the children, and I drank their water, so that I could get some nourishment to go on providing for them. The reason that we had so little food is because, to my sorrow, some of the Jews who were in charge stole food from the ghetto for their relatives. They gave no food to the children. Then, after the end of the war, with great difficulties, I returned home. Empty. With nothing to come back to. Whatever I now have, I got on my own, all by myself.

I sent the children to study. I went to sell lottery tickets, whatever work I could find. I put my daughter in [unclear] Street, in the dorms. My son went to another day-care center called Makarenko in the Zuglo neighborhood. Then, there was a notice at the National Theater saying that war widows could get a job there. That was how I got a job as an usher, as well as kept on selling the lottery tickets, night and day, and I washed and cleaned to buy the children food. In summertime, I went to do agricultural work, to dig. My poor daughter, she kept waiting for her father. She always said, "Let me be the first to know when he comes back."

You [turns to Mrs. Faludi] studied in Tetk at that time. It was there that I went to work. And I went out to . . . steal, because they wouldn't let you have enough food. This Red Cross woman, she acted like a Nazi and wouldn't let me have anything, so I got up—

Mrs. Faludi: But that was already after the war.

Mrs. Fischer: So I got up early, put on stretchable underwear, and I stole tomatoes, peppers, onion, and hid them in my underwear, so I could take it to the children. I also worked in the kitchen there, where my daughter studied for a year, right? And my son contracted diphtheria, so the woman there asked me to leave because the boy was contagious. They came with a car and took us to the hospital, and I was lucky to have a very good Jewish doctor. We could not even enter the community offices with the sick boy. This doctor gave the boy an injection, extracted from a horse. They usually made a cut in the patient's throat, but in this case they didn't have to. This Jewish doctor also arranged for the children to receive some clothing, and I went to sleep there, in the hospital. My daughter was in Tetk at the time. I didn't know how she was doing, we couldn't even correspond. But she, her grandfather lived here in Pest, so she could write him that her brother was taken away and she didn't know if she would ever see him again, for he was so sick. Then later we returned home, to my father-in-law's home. May he rest in peace, my father-in-law, but he was not a kind man. Although you shouldn't say bad things about the dead, sometimes there is nothing good to say.

Then I went to work. I sent the children to boarding schools. First I worked in a sanatorium where I worked in the kitchen. I got up at four or five at dawn every day to bake bread, make a dough of I don't know how many kilograms, to be able to provide for the children. Then, with great difficulties, we came back home, and I was given the job at the theater, where I work until now. I was ill many times. I had an eye operation because of glaucoma. Then I had paralysis of the vocal cords. I was hospitalized, almost died there. I fainted four times, and my daughter was my son's little mother. She didn't let him go anywhere, took care of him, kept studying. This is how we struggled.

My brothers and sister also hid during the war. We didn't know anything about each other. They had a workshop. When my mother died, they continued with the workshop. Later they left to Israel, to Nahariya, where they died, all three of them. They wanted me to come to Israel too. But I would not leave the children behind. They wanted me to leave the children and come. It would not have been looked upon well for me to flee the country while leaving behind my children who went to boarding schools. I too wanted to leave after liberation, go to a kibbutz, but the government did not let us. They didn't care. We couldn't leave. So the children studied, despite great hardships, both of them.

And now again we are afraid of the future, of what's to come. I dare not fall asleep. We went through 1956, that was terrible too. Something is going to happen, I feel it in my bones.

Zsuzsa (Zsuzsánna) Faludi. Interviewed in Budapest, Hungary, October 1991

(Translated from Hungarian)

Zsuzsa Faludi: I was born in 1936 in Budapest. My father came from a Neologist family. My mother was Orthodox. I learned all about religion from my grandmother on my mother's side. Every Friday evening the family gathered and held the religious traditions and had a special meal. We visited my other grandmother on other occasions, but not on holidays. We were a big family with many uncles and aunts, and if there is such a thing as a happy childhood, then that is what I had. I was the first grandchild, everyone loved me. That is also why it was so hard for me to adjust to the terrible changes and the shortages we suffered in the forties. My family belonged to the middle class, the working class. Not poor, not rich, but we had everything we needed. My mother did not work; my father supported the family. This became a problem later on in our hard life because my mother had no profession besides being a housewife. After the war she became a widow, which meant that she had to work, and since she wasn't skilled in anything, she had to take any job offered. That usually meant unskilled labor like cleaning, kitchen work, etc. Later she managed to get a relatively better job as an usher, which she keeps to this day.

In 1944 I experienced the first bad incident that made me realize what it meant to be a Jew. It was in the first grade that I realized I was different, after being badly beaten. We lived in a working-class neighborhood then. My father was an engine technician, worked for a military factory where they manufactured repair parts for airplanes for the Germans. My father was good at his profession. That is why he was exempted for a while from being drafted to the labor battalions. I went to school in this working-class neighborhood and was quite a good pupil, meaning I was the best in the class. And since I was then the only grandchild in the family, the entire family, uncles and aunts, pampered me and gave me clothes and presents. I always had nice clothes to wear. This must have bothered many children in my class. At that time, 1942, the atmosphere was already very anti-Semitic. One girl in my class couldn't stand the fact that I was so special. So she and her family lied about me to the authorities, saying I said pro-Communist things in class. Had they proven it, then they would have arrested my entire family, because after all, a child only repeats what she has heard at home.

My father was called in for interrogation. This interrogation was carried out using a belt. My parents always believed that I told the truth, but the atmosphere was so tense that this time they doubted me. And this beating with a belt shocked me terribly, even more than the physical pain, although I will never forget that either—I screamed so loud that half the building heard me. Then it was found out that it was a lie. I was in fact guilty only of three things: I was Jewish, I was a good pupil, and my family dressed me nicely. Until the incident I could not grasp what it meant that I was of another religion. This first painful experience, at the age of six, made me realize that I was different, and from then on, I looked at things differently. It may sound unbelievable, but it is true that the war and its terrible experiences made everyone older. The children turned into grown-ups, the grown-ups became old.

Then the war events started. First, we had to move into houses called "marked houses" in the ghetto. They were marked by a Star of David, and we moved into my grandfather's house. We had seven people in one room and a kitchen. Then, family members started to disappear. First one uncle was called to the labor battalions, then another uncle. Slowly, the family grew smaller. We never knew where everyone was. They took away my father, because the factory was closed. Then we couldn't go to school anymore. We had to wear the yellow Star of David. My space for moving around at the age of seven was a room of four by five meters, day and night. Adults were allowed to go out during the day to buy food with special tickets. Jews of course received smaller rations, to make them starve. Then we left this place.

Once my father appeared unexpectedly and took us, my mother and the children, to a certain synagogue, to be safer. Then at night, he came back and took us out of there. The day after, we heard that at night the Germans raided the synagogue and killed everyone who was there. My father took us out because he had a premonition. At one point, my uncle came out of the blue and was able to get us Swedish Protection Passes. Then we moved to another house. In this house, they once came at night to check our papers. Meantime, I didn't even mention that we always remained in our clothes, because you could never know when the next air raid would be and you had to rush to the shelter. I do not remember how we were fed and what we ate, but I am sure we had little to eat.

Finally, even the Swedish Passes were no longer of help. One night the Arrow Cross guards came in, said these passes were forged anyway, and tore them to pieces in front of us. Then they took us out to this park, whose name I shall never forget, Szent István. They walked us to the Danube bank. I was crying and a guard yelled at me. I remember he screamed that if I didn't shut up, he would hit me with his rifle. I remember the weapon approaching my face. Then, in a second's flash of instinct, my mother snatched me. With my brother in her arms, we sneaked into the gate of one of the houses on the way. It is pure luck that none of the guards shot us.

My mother tore off her own star and mine too, and we started wandering around, without any documents. Then my uncle found us and hid us for a while. He couldn't really help, because he too was in hiding as a Jewish deserter from the army. My brother was a year and a half. He had to be diapered. I remember the men there tearing pieces of cloth from their shirts to be used as diapers.

When my mother couldn't take it anymore, and it became difficult to take care of us, it was decided that we would move into the ghetto. That happened in the beginning of December. We went in, and I don't recall much from this period. I do remember that we were among children. My mother tried to get a job there in return for our staying. We were in the shelter and slept on the floor. This period lasted for about seven weeks, so they said, until the Russian army units came in and liberated us.

I was nine years old. My brother was a year and a half. Before these terrible weeks started, my brother could walk and talk. When everything was over, he couldn't talk, walk, sit, or stand. He only knew these words: "give me." He became sick with rickets, and not many people thought he would live. Everyone who survived in the family, besides my uncle, rushed to the ghetto, found us, helped us. My grandparents survived too.

Of all the relatives, the two of us were the only children who survived. We had nothing at all except the clothes we were wearing and lice. I had a long beautiful braid. It had to be cut off because I was full of lice. They now brought us food, clothes, heavy and light blankets. My brother was sick with rickets, I with the mumps. Sicknesses came one after the other once the war was over.

These are the memories I have from the age of nine, as well as chronic arthritis and ensuing bone illnesses which harmed my spine.

I also had a gynecological problem. I underwent all kinds of medical tests and exams for years, but they couldn't figure out the problem. Two American doctors finally discovered the cause when I was twenty. In Hungarian it is called the Stein-Lowenthal Syndrome. It meant that I had to be operated on on October 1, 1956, for five hours and then hang between life and death for months. I was twenty at the time. The professor prepared me for the seriousness of the surgery, for I was the first patient with this problem. We knew the operation was successful when later I was able to conceive and then give birth to my daughter. The problem was, so they explained, that my brain suffered a shock which caused it to manufacture both masculine and feminine hormones. This meant that I could not conceive. After my marriage, and since I had gynecological problems beforehand too, the professor who checked me recommended that we do the operation, if I agreed. Of course I agreed. He said they would have to cut through the belly, reach the ovaries, and peel them. If that worked, then the ovaries would start functioning regularly and create eggs. This was in 1956, and a year later I became pregnant for the first time. Then we knew for certain that the operation had succeeded. Until then, we couldn't be sure.

Now, I am telling you all this to show that I had two opportunities to leave this country, the country which had hurt me so badly as a child. The first occasion was when I was nine. But a nine-year-old girl cannot leave the country on her own. The other thing was that I loved my father very much, and for three years I waited, we all waited, for him to return. We did not believe he was dead. We waited because people told us that they saw him here or there. After the war, rumors spread that people were seen somewhere or other, and then the relatives, who wanted to believe that their loved one was still alive, believed these rumors. Myself, after 1945 I went to a Jewish high school and couldn't bear to look upon Christians. I said I would only go to a Jewish school, and then I joined a Zionist movement. I wanted us to leave very much. But my mother also waited for her husband. My grandmother was still alive—she died of cancer in 1946—but she was waiting for two of her sons, we all waited for them.

There were many stories and legends in those days. One of my father's friends said he had seen him as late as December 1944. They met here in Budapest. My father was never taken out of the country to a camp like Auschwitz or Bergen-Belsen. So we thought he might be somewhere in the country, might have escaped the units made up by the Germans. For by December 1944, the Germans had fled. They used my father to take apart the factory, and then the Germans took the machines. We thought my father might have disappeared somewhere. But they said there were rumors going on that if someone deserted, his family would be killed. People then believed in all sorts of things. I can imagine that my father, who did not live for anything else but his family, that he too believed these rumors and did not escape. So because of these legends, these imaginary stories, we waited for him. After two years when he did not return, the borders were closed, and by then it was too late to leave the country legally.

I became very ill. I suffered pains in my joints. I had to be hospitalized because I couldn't move my arms, and my legs swelled up. The professor said it couldn't be cured and it would always return. So my mother did not dare to embark on an unknown journey with a sick older girl and a very small boy, aged three or four, while at the same time she had her family around, which helped her support her children.

Then in 1956, when the border opened up again, I was operated on. The following year I had to be hospitalized two or three more times because of all kinds of gynecological complications. I couldn't go out to the big world in that condition. I also hesitated to leave the doctor who took care of me. How could I be sure that I could proceed with this process that I started only because I insisted upon having children? I couldn't be sure about having that done elsewhere. In addition, I was hospitalized again in December after having lost fifteen kilograms. In that condition, I couldn't make the journey.

This is my bad luck: Every time the state is in trouble, and leaving it becomes easier, I too am in trouble and cannot leave. This is how I experienced my Jewish identity, by being hurt by it, in my childhood and in my youth. But I realized that you do not choose the identity that you are born with, and I tried to live with that.

I.R.: Were there any incidents after the war in which you realized that your schoolmates had belonged to the same families that persecuted you before?

Mrs. Faludi: Not in my childhood or in school. They were so repressed that if anyone would as much as dare say "dirty Jew," or something like that, and two people would testify to that, they would be put in prison for years by the Communist regime. Now, this did not help to prevent anti-Semitism but only worsened it. It went underground, it was stifled, while the official viewpoint was that the whole Hungarian nation was guilty. But you cannot attribute such a thing to an entire nation, it's impossible. You can imagine that most people were not guilty. Although Mihály Babits, one of Hungary's greatest poets, said that whoever kept silent was guilty. And the Hungarian people, unfortunately, did remain silent. Out of fear and intimidation. But it was impossible, and still it was the official viewpoint, that the whole nation was guilty.

My classmates, young people, after the war they all tried to forget. Not only did they not dare to start up with us, but they didn't even want to notice us. Only after 1956 did anti-Semitism appear again, and then I said we should leave. Only physically I wasn't able to. Now that it has become possible again to emigrate, I am already too old, too sick for a new place. After a certain age, it is just too late.

Mrs. GZ Interviewed in Budapest, Hungary, September 1991

(Translated from Hungarian)

G.Z.: I was born in 1935 in Budapest. My mother was a journalist and she also had a teacher's diploma. My father was an accountant and worked in the field of finance. In 1938 he lost his job and had to subsist on an unemployment pension. My mother, on the other hand, was a writer and a freelance journalist. She wrote novels. She always used pseudonyms, such as Baron Jozsef Miklós; frequently, she used her typist's name as a pseudonym. Once, in a novella-writing competition, my mother's novella won the first prize. Since it was under the pseudonym of my mother's typist, which was a woman's name, they asked her to change it into a man's name. When it came out, the book carried the name of a fictional literary persona as the author.

When the war broke out and the situation worsened, the family's financial state deteriorated. Since my father would not give up his stamp-collecting hobby to support the family, my parents parted. I lived with my mother under difficult financial and housing conditions that only became worse with time.

The German invasion in 1944 caught my mother working in room service in a pension. We got an apartment in the pension, which turned out to be a dangerous place to live, because it was known that Polish refugees were living there too. After the 19th of March, the Germans came in, checked our papers, and took away the Polish people but not us. We barely escaped from that pension, and after that, until the war ended, we moved around every day or every other day. We stayed with friends, sometimes even with strangers who risked their lives to save us by letting us stay with them.

There was one typical example in November 1944, when we were under curfew for the night. Unfortunately, the friend we intended to stay with was not home. Since there was an air raid, we couldn't leave the house, and after the curfew began we realized that we were stuck in that building for the night. We searched the names on the apartments in the entire apartment house and looked for a familiar name. My mother recognized the name of an actor, since she was a theater reviewer, although she didn't know him personally. We rang their bell, explained who we were, and the actor and his family accepted us for the night. They risked their lives for us: if we had been caught there, this family would have also been executed. In fact, we owe our lives to complete strangers.

Before the siege on Budapest I became ill and needed to recover in a heated house for a few days. A woman who had gone to school with my mother and was now the wife of the manager of the Gelért Hotel arranged a room for us at the hotel. This way we had heat and a roof over our heads for two days. Meantime, the siege had begun, and a Hungarian army hospital opened in the hotel so that they could take advantage of the hotel's water supply. As a result, hordes of German soldiers came to the hospital, and we spent our time in the hotel in the company of German soldiers.

Neither my mother nor I were religious. This means that we were persecuted solely because of our identity as Jews, not because of our religious beliefs. According to Nazi law, a person couldn't choose his or her religion but had to have three Christian grandparents to be considered non-Jewish. Thus, we were persecuted because of our very identity, over which we had no control [asks for a break in order to arrange her thoughts and plan the continuation of the interview].

Because of her work in journalism, my mother knew all about Adolph Hitler and Nazism even before they were well known in Germany. Therefore, the events were not totally unexpected to her. In a sense, she suspected what could happen. Therefore, she changed her original German-sounding name to a Hungarian name that meant one of the days in the week. Thanks to her old connections, she was able to obtain an international passport but did not have the money needed for leaving the country. Also, I was only three years old in 1938, and she did not dare to leave with such a small child. So, unfortunately, we could not leave the country.

The changing of our name became very significant in the long range as well. During 1944, when we spent every day in a different place and had no documents, my mother made up a story that we were refugees from the bombed Erdély [Transylvania] region. My mother knew that changing a name with a small child can be dangerous, so it helped a lot that we already had a Hungarian-sounding name. Her farsightedness proved itself useful in the future as well, because after liberation our original, German-sounding name would have also been problematic under the Communists. The family used to be very rich once and even owned a factory in Hungary. Even though we never enjoyed this wealth—my father was already a poor man and his hobby only plunged him even deeper into poverty—the Communists would have still persecuted us for belonging to the upper class in the prewar period. Therefore, the name change turned out to be very advantageous for us.

In the hard times of 1944, there was an interesting episode in my life. It happened right after the seizing of power by the Arrow Cross Party in the fall of 1944, exactly when I was sick and had a high fever. In this situation, it was dangerous for me to move from place to place every day, so we found a room and spent a few days in 102 Király Street, which was part of the ghetto. During those days, my mother was once caught and brought to the Nyilas, or Arrow Cross headquarters, where they gathered people to send them to work. Since she came without a bag, the guard asked her why she did not have a bag, and my mother replied that she was a poor Hungarian writer who couldn't afford a bag. Of course she could not tell him the real reason—that she meant to escape at the first opportunity. They started talking, she asked him where he worked, and he said that he used to work as an announcer at a park. This way my mother softened him up, and he moved aside to let her escape. Two other people escaped too, but after a few hours of searching she was the only one who was not caught. The others were marched to the brick factory, and to the best of my knowledge they never returned.

By contrast, the following is an example of human cowardice. I mentioned before that we spent the siege days at the Gelért Hotel, where in addition to German soldiers there were also Hungarian policemen. We started talking with one of them and realized that, although Budapest was a city of a few million people, we knew this man and had met him somewhere before. He also knew who we were. Now when this was going on, the Soviet units were five hundred meters away from the Gelért Square, at Moric Square. Although he knew we were Jewish and could just shoot and kill us on the spot, he probably did not harm us because he was already afraid of the Soviets. This might have also been because there was a Soviet agent, a "mole" in the shelter. We found out about this later, and the policeman probably suspected as much too. When the Soviet units reached the shelter two days later, this Hungarian policeman suddenly changed his uniform, as did other guards as well, from that of a Nyilas, or Arrow Cross guard, to a regular army uniform, to save their lives. Years later, I bumped into this commander in Budapest. He worked as a lawyer, because army officers had to have academic degrees. Thus, he used his education in a later period.

After liberation my mother weighed only thirty-six kilograms; she had lost a lot of weight and her health was poor. She decided that we should move to Pécs, where her father's family came from, so that if she died, then our relatives could raise me. However, it turned out that none of the Pécs relatives survived; they were all taken to German concentration camps. We could not understand why they did not act like us, hiding and changing places every day, and instead they let themselves be taken to the camps. For two years I went to school in Pécs, in the local Catholic convent, where I became acquainted with the Bible, from a Christian point of view of course. At that time religious studies were still obligatory and they insisted at the convent that I be examined in the Jewish religion. The teacher on his part insisted that I learn Hebrew, for him that was the only important thing. But I never really mastered the Hebrew language.

My mother became a party member, first of the Socialist and then the Communist Party. She worked for the Communist newspaper. Later, in 1945, we returned to Budapest until the "witch hunt," which started in the fifties. My mother criticized injustice in her articles, so in the end, they threw her out of the Communist Party and she lost her job. She again started working as a freelance journalist, this time using her real name and writing not literary pieces but news items, and thus she supported me. I chose the technical field for pragmatic reasons, because that is the quickest route to a good salary. I finished high school at the Technikum. By then my mother was already very ill, but she insisted that I continue studying. She did not interfere in my choice of profession, but she expected that just as she had studied at the university and earned a teacher's certificate in hard times, so would I. The great suffering she underwent in her life and her chain-smoking had damaged her health, so she died at the age of fifty-seven. By then I had finished studying, so she was still alive to see me graduate and make a living for myself. Unfortunately, though, she did not really live long enough to see me with my husband and enjoy family life.

There was another shock that brought her death closer. These were the 1956 events. I mentioned earlier that she had been kicked out of the Party and lost her job at the beginning of the fifties. In September 1956 she was exonerated and got her job back. But the stormy political events in October, which included armed battles, made her lose her job again. Then she had an opportunity to renew her ties with some Parisian relatives who had emigrated there [to France] in the twenties. So in January 1957, despite my reluctance, we left illegally in the direction of Yugoslavia. We arrived at a United Nations camp where she was able to declare her Parisian relatives, and these people sent our train tickets to Belgrade. The camp officers collected some money for us to reach Belgrade, and from Belgrade we reached Paris, to stay with my mother's cousin. He was a wealthy man, but his family was French, and they did not like the Hungarian side of the family. Still, they gave us food and housing. I was admitted into a French university and was able to continue studying. I did not want to go there in the first place, and then an unfortunate incident ended our stay there.

This is what happened. As a freelance journalist, my mother had worked in the past for the Foreign Affairs office, and now an old friend from there was the chief consultant of the Hungarian embassy in Paris. When we came to Paris as dissidents, she thought it natural to renew her contact with this person, and we did meet in a restaurant in Champs-Elysées. The following day, we were invited to the political department of the French police. It turned out that Hungarian diplomats reported this meeting to the French authorities, who thought it very suspicious for Hungarian defectors to meet with an official representative of the regime from which they escaped.

My mother was then subjected to a long interrogation in the political department of the French police, where they suspected us of being "agents provocateurs," maybe even spies. Now, sick of the constant moving, we became disillusioned with this aspect of the free world. We waited for an opportunity to leave, which came by way of the Amnesty organization [Amnesty International], and in March we returned to Hungary. We were back again in Hungary after only six weeks.

Upon our return, I went right back to the Technological University of Budapest without losing any time and received my diploma about a year and a half before my mother's death. First I worked in a company; then, I taught at the university. In fact, I worked at the university until I retired. I married one of my colleagues. At the university I was expected to make academic progress, so that over time I earned four diplomas and even passed a national grammar exam. Still, with all this, my pension hardly reaches the minimum needed for basic living expenses.

I.R.: In what ways did your Holocaust experience change you, what would be different had it not happened?

Mrs. G.Z.: If it were not for the Holocaust, I would have experienced a much more relaxed childhood and my nerves today would be in a much better state. Since one's childhood affects one's nervous system and entire life, no doubt I would have had a happier and more balanced life. In fact I went through a war-and-a-half: after the events of World War II, I also endured the 1956 events, which were very much like a war, and I went through a hard time again. All in all, I was left with very bad nerves and an empty life.

Dora Ashkenazi. Originally from Dunaszerdahely, Hungary/Czechloslovakia. Interviewed in Bazera, Israel, February 1990

(Translated from Hebrew)

Dora Ashkenazi: I was born in Czechoslovakia to a religious family of seven children. I was the sixth. No, not the sixth, because my mother had twins before, so mine was the sixth birth, but I was the seventh child. My mother had two sets of twins, and of the twelve children, seven survived. I had a nice childhood. My father made a good living. We all received a good education. I finished elementary school and then went on to junior high school. After three more years, I wanted to continue studying, but there was nowhere to go. So I had to move to Bratislava [Hungarian: Pozsony] to study there. One of my brothers studied for a teacher's certificate there, but he couldn't complete his studies. In 1938 the Hungarians took over. My mother sent me to learn sewing. I learned and started working in sewing. Meanwhile, in 1939 I intended to come to Israel, but that didn't work out either.

We were taken to the ghetto. The ghetto area included our house, and several families now had to share our house. Then they moved us to a place near the big synagogue. In a yard nearby, they crammed more than 4,500 Jews of the entire area. They brought all the Jews of Dunajska Streda, an area which by then had become Hungarian and was called Dunaszerdahely. Finally, we were deported to Auschwitz in 1944. At first we stayed there for eight days, and then they moved us to Plaszow, where we stayed for five weeks.

I.R.: Who is "we"?

Mrs. Ashkenazi: There were five of us when we arrived at Auschwitz: my mother, my older sister with her baby boy, her mother-in-law, another sister, and myself. My older sister had a small child when we reached Auschwitz. She had a nine-month-old baby boy, and was also six months pregnant. I was holding her baby in my arms, the baby was with me. In the distance I saw my best friend, who had already passed the selection, whereas I was in the next-to-the-last row. I saw that women with small children were sent in another direction, so I told my sister, "Take your child," for the child could have stayed with me. Then Mengele told me in Hungarian, "Hand over the child quietly, you'll all see each other again on Sunday." But on the other side I saw my father looking at his little grandchild, I can't forget the picture of him [weeping], with tears in his eyes. And he said, "Oh, *tatele, tatele* [Yiddish: Daddy, and also an affectionate address for a child], will I ever see you again?" This was his first grandchild. And I, I didn't even get to say good-bye to my father. I saw my friend and followed her, running. We still had some bread that we brought for the way. When they led us on, bald-headed people stood behind the fence and reached out like this [demonstrates begging gesture]. We thought they were insane. I said to myself, I'd better find my sister [very excited].

I.R.: Don't push yourself, Mrs. Ashkenazi.

Mrs. Ashkenazi: It's this image I still have in my mind. Then they made another "selection." Now, as a child, I had contracted chicken pox, and although it healed it still left some scars, some small marks. Now they started to say that if they see the slightest defect, they will send you to the other side. Every "selection" was a trauma. Thank God, I passed all of them, and the fact is that I am here today.

Next we arrived at a big big hall. SS men came in, they said, "Take all your clothes off." A Jewish girl? Entirely naked? But we had already endured our first trauma when they put us on the train. Then, too, they checked us "there." Our mother was an elderly woman and they checked her inside to see if she hadn't hidden some gold in there. Now, in Auschwitz, my best friend and I were together, and we had to undress in front of a man. My friend and I had lived in the same street, we had been together in the ghetto as well.

Well, we started taking our clothes off. At first, I did not take them entirely off. I undressed slowly and didn't want to take off my underwear. Then I got a "welcome" greeting; the German came with his whip and [Unclear, quick and undecipherable German]. We came out on the other side. They threw us some clothes. One piece only, without any underwear or anything, just that one piece.

We went out and had to stand in lines of five. We were standing in roll call, and I was looking for my sister, "My sister, my sister, where is my sister?" My sister was standing right next to me, and I didn't even recognize her! Then I got the second "welcome" greeting for moving during the *appell*, the roll call. Then my sister said, "See what an idiot you are, I am standing right next to you!" I didn't recognize her. Then they took us to a "lager," a camp, where we stayed for eight days. Among us we said that this was our *shiva*, our mourning period.

We stayed in a room just a bit bigger than this living room, for two hundred women. We sat down like this, with legs spread out and one behind the other. We weren't allowed to drink any water. They said there was typhus, that you could contract typhus from the water. I remember it rained heavily on the roof, on the tar. It rained heavily, and we stood under it to catch a few drops. We were afraid to drink from the water tanks they brought us because of the typhus. We stayed like this for eight days. Some of the women went mad, they started to scream at night, Anyukám, Anyukám [Hungarian: Mommy, Mommy].

One day, it was raining and they did the roll call in the room. Everyone was hungry, because we received very little food. And I didn't have anything to eat. My friend stood before me. She saw how pale I was and said, "You fool, do something: if you the strong are so faint, then what will happen to the truly weak ones?" No sooner did she say "what will happen to the truly weak ones" than she fell down and fainted. Fine, the *appell* was over and they took us to bathe. We bathed. We finished and there were no cattle cars waiting for us. We stood half the night. It rained. My poor sister . . . I'll tell you about her later. They gave us different clothes, gray clothes. Everyone. In the end we saw that no trains were coming and it was still raining and raining and raining. We stood in the rain. Then they let us go into the shower rooms again, to get out of the rain, and the girls started to say, "It's the gas chambers and crematorium," and this and that. But it wasn't. We went in, we dried ourselves.

In the morning the train came. Each one of us received half a loaf of bread. They took us to Plaszow. There we had nothing to do. We carried stones from one place to the other and back again. I don't know how many people we were there, and we were put in five big barracks. I will never forget. All this time I was with my best friend and another cousin, together all the time. Then they sent us back from Plaszow in cattle cars. It was the beginning of August. Now the return took three times the time it had taken us to get there. Someone stole my bread and I had no bread, we had no water. This is how we arrived back in Auschwitz, to lager A.

There was a girl, a friend, who just as we received our bread, she said, "Girls, I can't take it anymore." She distributed her belongings. She gave her shoes to her best friend and said, "Good-bye to you." She jumped at the electrified fence [claps once], just like that, and she was killed.

From there they moved us to [unclear]. I still didn't have any food. We came there in the morning and had to stand there until they gave us our "numbers." I was lucky. There was a girl there who told me to stretch the skin on my arm with my other hand. She said, "Hold it tight and you won't feel it." Each hole they made started bleeding, but she told me to tighten the skin so I didn't feel the pain. I wasn't so fat then [laughing]. It went on until evening, and our soup stood in the sun and got spoiled and we couldn't eat it.

The next morning they gave us something to eat and put us in the barracks. We had nothing to do there. At two in the morning, they threw us outside. We stood there until eight or nine in the morning, and then they let us go without doing anything. They gave us clothes: I got a black dress with white speckles and a collar. It was too hot during the day but fine at night. But my poor sister wasn't so lucky. She received a short dress full of holes, and she trembled with cold.

One day they came to tell us that there was typhus in lager A, so they delivered the food through our camp. Now, girls who came back from delivering food in the men's lager said they met men from our town. I asked one of them, "Switch with me, I'll go instead of you, for I want to see these men from my town." They led us out between these gates. They already counted us, and after they counted us then you couldn't go back, only with a special pass. Suddenly one girl says to me, "Here's your brother." He was fifteen years old. "Here's your brother, and he is looking for you!" Now I recognized him. Instead of the child I knew, a man stood in front of me. I started to cry. I said, "Yonah, don't you know me?" He recognized me by my voice; he couldn't recognize my appearance because I was as red as a tomato from standing in the sun all day without anything to protect my skin. He told me that it was only by my voice that he recognized me.

I was outside the fence and he was inside. In order to meet me, he switched with someone who had to clean up and take the garbage out. One girl saw my meeting with my brother, and so did the guard. She said, "Oh, Dora, what am I going to do with you?" My brother had already gone through the gate, so she took me to the Germans with the excuse that my number had to be fixed. The German did see that there was a meeting, but I was lucky; he didn't punish me, don't ask.

Finally, finally, I met with my brother. When he saw my sister with the torn dress, he went into the bathroom and took off his shirt and his underwear, and gave them to me for my sister so that she could cover her breasts. To this day she has a skin blemish made by the sun during the days she wore that torn dress. I said to him, "But what about clothing for you?" He said, "Don't you worry. Our town doctor works at the clothing warehouse, he'll give me something." I still remember that her birthday was on September 2. My brother managed to send her a gift, his ration of bread with margarine and salami.

On September 5th, again we had roll call. To work, they said. I passed the roll call and went through two fences. Then we saw two electrical fences guarded by dogs and a path going between them; you might have seen this on TV. Our Blockälteste [block commander] was with us, so while we were walking, we asked her in Czech, "Elsa, where are we going?" So she said, "To work." Then one girl said, "Don't tell us stories, we are being sent to our death." I overheard that exchange. They put us in a small room; there were benches there but nothing else.

A girl whom I met, originally from our town, had a small prayer book. She had a prayer book, and I had a needle. I don't know how I got this needle, but I got it from someone. We used to pull threads out of our blankets and sew or make things we needed. I kept it all to myself, didn't say anything about what I had overheard to anyone. It was enough for me to know where we were headed. While we were waiting in the room, we received some bread. My friend took out the inside part of her bread and put in her prayer book instead and covered it up by some of the bread. In this way she brought the prayer book home. We sat down there, and I awaited death, I simply awaited death. Suddenly, the door opened. We didn't know that the gas chambers looked like showers. We already knew that [unclear]. Water came down on us. We remained alive.

They took us to work in Augsburg, where [unclear]. I remember traveling in coal trains for three days. We arrived at a station, far away from the factory. We scared them because we were bald-headed and black from the coal. We heard someone asking our German guards if we were insane women from an asylum. We reached a yard, walking. They asked us, "Where are your bags?" We started laughing. Which bags? Just as we reached the factory yard, there was a bombing. The workers ran outside, they were terrified by the bombing. All of us were standing: what a motley group, five hundred women looking as though we came from an asylum. But they were scared by the bombs, so they kept running.

Meantime, they sent the factory's engineer to receive us. He gave each of us a gray shirt or dress and even underwear, and they sent us to wash. I shall never forget it. They brought us to the factory's shower house, with real ceramic tiles and hot water. Oh, *hamechaye* [Hebrew: thank God]. We washed. We hadn't washed this way since June, and by now it was September already. Then we stood in line and were given small white bowls and spoons. Now we saw . . . And we received peeled potatoes and a piece of meat. That was paradise. They took us upstairs, where there were three rooms with bunk beds in them. Do you know what these are?

I.R.: Yes, bunk beds, one above the other.

Mrs. Ashkenazi: Those were wooden beds in three levels, with straw and quilts on them. In Auschwitz we had to share each such bed among twelve women. Now we started learning the work. They put us in a factory where women had never worked before, except in inspection. Now we worked in precision mechanics. Some of the girls were sent to another section of this factory outside the city, in a suburb. I joined this group that traveled each morning in a streetcar to work. We rode, and we marched, and we sang with all our might. We cleaned the factory from the mess made by the bombings.

There were two women who were pregnant. They were pregnant when they came, but now it started to show. These poor ones tried to hide their growing body shape with blankets. Once a Blockälteste asked one of them, "Éva, are you pregnant?" She was afraid to say so. Finally she said, "Yes." The engineer arranged that they get milk every morning and evening, and an extra meal every day. One soldier kept calling them "whores," but despite everything, they managed to keep their babies alive and, eventually, to bring them home.

We worked in the factory, and there was a yard leading to a vegetable garden. I shall never forget my best friend, who is dead for nine years now. She was more courageous than I. I was brave too, but she was braver. Once she said, "Dora, come with me to steal some kohlrabi now." It was foggy and we couldn't see anything, so we crawled on our stomachs to the kohlrabi, we reached the kohlrabi. Suddenly the fog disappeared and we saw that the field was filled with workers. We thought, now they have caught us! But they didn't do anything to us, we even kept our kohlrabi. We ran home with it and never stopped until we reached the camp.

Our meister was very good. Usually, Hungarian Jewish girls only spoke Hungarian and didn't know any German. I knew German because my mother spoke German, and at the salon where I learned to sew, the teacher was from Mattersdorf, Austria. I learned to speak German well there, so now I was able to speak to our meister. My meister, I shall never forget it, he told me that within three weeks we were already doing all the work in the factory, work that only men had done before. So my meister said, can I say it in German? "Jetzt verstehe ich warum man die Juden hasst [German: Now I understand why people hate the Jews]. The Jews are so [unclear]." He said that now he finally realized what they had been taught in the Hitler Jugend about the "real nature" of Jews. He said: "They taught us," which was true, "that the German Jews were rich, they had a lot of money, they filled the theaters. There were rich Jews everywhere, and that caused hatred." He said, "Never in my life did I imagine that Jews could work. And not just work, but work like this." And what did we get after twelve hours of work? At night we got some black bread they said was made of sawdust. At noon we got some soup. In the morning we got some bread and margarine and salami. As our hair started to grow, we spread the margarine on it instead of on the bread. After all, we were still women.

Well, our engineer, the meister, arranged things so that the person in charge of the night shift always brought us leftovers from the kitchen. He said he needed workers, not hungry people who couldn't work. Hungry people are unable to work. Toward the end of 1944, November 1944, all the workers suffered from the shortage in food. Now, our meister received bread and meat every Saturday. The meat he kept for his children; he said he had two children, aged six. And the bread he gave me. Once, I wasn't there on the Saturday shift, and still he sent me bread with another girl. I had to share it with her in return, but it didn't matter. I had the extra bread. All this to say that I had a good meister.

We were working there, and Yom Kippur [Hebrew: Day of Atonement] came. How did we know Yom Kippur was approaching? We knew that it was approximately the time for Rosh Hashanah [the Hebrew New Year's Eve] and Yom Kippur. Once, four of us were sent to bring supplies of meat and bread. We walked down the street and then waited outside the shop, for we weren't allowed to enter. Suddenly, a man riding a bicycle passed us, shouting, "*Kinderlach* [Yiddish: children], in two weeks' time it's Rosh Hashanah." When we heard this, we were standing in *achtung* [German: attention] and couldn't move. Then, later, two women passed by when we were speaking Hungarian. They said, "Magyarok vagytok? Honnan jötetek? Mit csináltok? [Hungarian: Are you Hungarian? Where are you from? What are you doing?]" Then our guard yelled at them, "Weg von hier [German: Go away]"; she didn't let us talk with them. But we did learn that there were other Hungarian women there. We even managed to tell these two that we worked in the local factory.

There were soldiers there, Hungarian soldiers, who passed by the factory. When they passed by the factory they sang this song: "Kinek Zsidó lány a babája, kösön kötelet a nyakára [Hungarian: If you have a Jewish girlfriend, you might as well put a rope around your neck and strangle yourself]." Are you familiar with it? No, you weren't born there. But they used to sing, "Kinek Zsidó lány a babája, földi menny-ország a hazája [Hungarian: If you have a Jewish girlfriend, your home/homeland is a Paradise on Earth]." Now they changed it to mean that to have a Jewish woman was bad.

In the factory we had to work with rubber aprons, since we worked with water. The screw machine I worked with was full of water and grease, so I used newspaper to clean and dry it. My meister left his newspaper on his desk every night, so of course we read the paper first, before we used it on the machinery. But the newspaper was full of lies, just like here the paper is full of lies. Finally, though, they couldn't deny it anymore, we knew that the Americans were getting closer. One day my meister came and said, "I heard they are taking you away. It's a pity, because the Americans are only thirty kilometers away from here." Anyway, he gave me a note with his address on it. He told me, "Dora, nach Deiner Befreiung, komm hierer mit Diner Schwester, nicht allein [German: Dora: When you are liberated, come here with your sister, not alone]." He said, "You come to me, and I will help you with everything." I had my "number" sewn onto my shirt, and I stuffed the note under it.

Well, they made us board the train, and we started riding. We had a guard and a commander. The guard was very kind to us. You know, he wasn't an SS man, he was a Wermacht soldier. He arranged things for us and didn't let the commander do as he liked. For example, one night there was a bombing. We were working upstairs, and it was dangerous. The factory was dangerous. Still, the commander wouldn't let us go down to the shelter. There was a bombing. We knew the bombing meant that the Americans were approaching. The commander came and yelled at us, "What do you want?" We finally went down to the shelter.

That night a bomb fell on the factory but it didn't explode. The Germans said it was thanks to us, that God saw we were there, and the bomb didn't go off. I remember the sappers came to take the bomb away. Well, it's all a long story; I remember a lot of things, but you can't tell it all. The point is that they did take us from there. We rode back and forth, for the Americans and the partisans had already exploded all the bridges. I was on my way to get some bread when I met my uncle, my mother's brother. I had met his daughter earlier on. They drove us further and let us off in Landsberg. There I saw a Muselmann [victim of the camps who has lost the will to live] for the first time. Do you know what that is?

I.R.: Yes, I do.

Mrs. Ashkenazi: You heard of it. They were Hungarians. They asked us, "Where are you coming from, home?" We looked good, much better than the survivors of concentration camps. We said, "No, we've been in camps for almost a year now." And they told us about themselves too. There was no more room in this camp, so they took us to Waldlager. There my cousin met with her father. I didn't see it, because I was a bit further away. Just as we arrived there, a young man came to me and said, "Two days ago they took your brother to Landsberg." I started crying, for he said, "Your older brother Yossi," when actually it was Yonah. All I knew about my older brother Yossi after he had been called to the labor battalions was that he disappeared. We received a message from the army that he was missing. We thought maybe he was a war prisoner. Now I started crying, Oh my God. I didn't even suspect that it was my younger brother Yonah who was taken to Landsberg.

We stayed with these men there. Then, we had to board the trains again, where I met my uncle. We drove for four days. During this time, they only gave us bread once. We couldn't find a place to stop, for all the bridges were bombed. On the way we even had an American air raid. I shall never forget that. We were together with these French men for three days already, and for the last two days we hadn't had anything to eat. Suddenly, one of them asks, "Who is hungry?" We started laughing, what a silly thing to ask. My head hurt, so I leaned on my sister's back. Suddenly airplanes were shooting at us and I heard a bullet pass by my ear. A girl was sitting right behind me, and she got it straight in the forehead, straight in her head.

Then they opened the cattle cars, calling, "Out, out." I shall never forget it. We had to squat on the earth; over our heads the airplanes were coming down low and shooting, they shot at us with machine guns. One of the French guys jumped up, took off his striped jacket, and spread it over a barn that was close by. He put it there so the Americans could see we were prisoners and stop shooting at us. Now it turned out that these vile Germans had attached some five ammunition cars to our train. The Americans saw these and thought that all the cars of the freight train carried ammunition. So they shot at us too, even though they saw the striped jacket.

Then they put us back on the cattle cars, the dead apart from the living. Now there were many of us and it became crowded. Suddenly, the Germans said, "The war is over, you can leave, go wherever you want." This French guy came to me and said, "Dora my love, let's go to a big city, where we can easily disappear and never be found." We got together, some five girls who were friends and four French guys. One of them, this one, knew Hungarian, for he was originally from Ungvár. His family had emigrated to France three years ago, and his friends didn't even know he knew Hungarian. I didn't know it either as long as he only spoke French. Now he said, "Be a városba [Hungarian: Into town]." Some other guys ran away into a nearby woods. The nine of us headed to the open field.

It was spring already. It was the beginning of April, just after Passover. In Passover I didn't eat any of the bread my meister brought me. He said, "Du verflucht, wo ist dein Gott? [German: Damn you, where is your God?]" Well, I come from a religious family. "Where is your God?" This is what they asked us when they saw our red eyes in the morning from crying all night. Right after Passover, it was the beginning of April. Right after Passover, they took us away. Now we were walking through this field and I saw the farmer plough. We asked him where we were. He looked at us, insane people with numbers painted on us. He said, "Ihr wisst nicht, dass der Krieg geendig ist? Ihr seid frei [Don't you know that the war is over? You are free]." He also told us that Munich was just a few kilometers away.

Suddenly, a car full of soldiers came by. They stopped to pick us up and they took us to the train station. It was night and it was raining, so we spent the night in the train station. There were Italian ex–war prisoners there. They heard we were coming, so they brought us a heater, for it was raining hard. One of them brought us the heater, another one brought us some potatoes. We told them we hadn't eaten anything for three days. They brought us coal too. We were with the French guys. We lit the heater and started slicing the potatoes when we heard knocking on the wall [knocks on table]. One of the station workers asked, "Hol vannak a magyarok? [Hungarian: Where are the Hungarians?]" Now they brought us a pitcher of warm milk and five big pieces of bread, only for the girls. The guys didn't get any. Later, this man told us he had been a prisoner of war in Hungary and the Hungarians treated him well, so now he wanted to return the favor. Do you know what that meant for us, hot milk and bread? We ate and drank. One of the French guys started chanting the *Kol Nidrei* prayer [weeping], what can I say?

I.R.: A French Jew?

Mrs. Ashkenazi: Of course, all of them were Jewish. In the morning we wanted to board a train. Then we learned that some four hundred prisoners thought they were free and took the train into town, but there they were caught and imprisoned again. So the other prisoners were afraid to take the train, and they stayed right there. Now they boarded the train cars with us. I knew one of them, he was with us throughout. It was so crowded, people all but fell off the cars. I kept repeating, "I am not boarding those train cars, I am not going in there because they will catch us and imprison us again!" The guard started to shout at me [unclear German]. Suddenly the train started moving and leaving us behind. My sister said, "Dora, why do you have such a big mouth?" That man now shot in the air to make the train stop. Another uncle of mine, whom I hadn't met since before the deportation, was on the train. He heard my sister screaming, "Dora, Dora," then he heard the shooting and thought I was killed. You know, I was mourned several times.

I.R.: Was she already up?

Mrs. Ashkenazi: What do you mean?

I.R.: I mean, did your sister board the train by then?

Mrs. Ashkenazi: No she didn't, because I refused to go. I said, "I am not boarding the train." We were five girls. Almost all of us fell over on each other because it was so crowded. My poor sister was very sick by then. They said they were going to shoot us. They caught us. We ran away. They caught us. Then I said, "No one else here knows any German, so I'll go to this German and ask him." I went up to him, and said, "Tell me, Sagen Sie mir, wird man uns erschiessen? [German: Tell, are they going to shoot us?]" He said, "Warum, was haben Sie gemacht? [German: Why, what have you done?]" I liked that answer. He then went on saying German proverbs, that I always tell everyone [unclear German], how do you call it, don't let people step on you. I use it now with our politics to say that if we show only a little bit of weakness, we are lost. I learned that from the Germans.

Well, after all this, I finally did get on that train. We rode a while, and then the train was stuck and couldn't proceed. One day, after several days, we received some bread. I was walking with the bread I got when suddenly someone calls my name, "Dora, are you alive?" That was my uncle. He told me that people heard the screams of my sister—she was always hysterical—they heard the screams and the argument and they thought I was killed. Then, one morning, the train stopped at the Sassen station, and the Germans just disappeared. Our French fellows told us not to leave the train, and then they left themselves. Now, these French men were well versed in camp life after three years. They disappeared and came back later, came back to sleep. They found a plce where a hot potato pot was on the stove, still warm. We hadn't eaten anything for a few days at that time. There was also a bottle of wine, and we were thirsty. Our French Hungarian friend brought the wine to the nine of us, for we still remained together, the four guys and us five girls. We started to drink on an empty stomach and got drunk, oh, and we ate the bread and waited.

Suddenly, there were screams. It was my friend. Suddenly, she screams. The American tanks arrived just then. I will never forget this sight. My friend tried to jump over the fence, but she couldn't manage it, so she remained hung on the fence. Then one American got off and took her down. By that time we were all together. They asked us to remain near the train, as they were coming to take care of us. I went out for a walk with my friend. It was April, the end of April, April 28. It was snowing, there were flowers in the fields. We are free, we told each other; let's pinch ourselves to make sure this is real and not a dream! We are strolling all by ourselves, how wonderful, all alone. We saw white sheets. On every house a white piece of cloth of whatever they could find, underwear, whatever.

Then we were taken to Feldafing. My sister and I settled in a very beautiful house. The Germans were afraid of the Russian released war prisoners, they feared them like death. But they weren't at all afraid of us, for they knew we were weak idiots, we wouldn't do anything to them. And we really didn't do anything to them. Well, we stayed there, but my sister was sick. She had pneumonia so they took her away. God, after all these years, throughout the last year in the camps we were together all the time and now, now they took her away! There was a young man from Bratislava who knew English. He found out for me that she had been taken to the hospital in Feldafing, whereas we, our gang, were supposed to be sent to Munich. I said, "How can I leave now, how can I leave my sick sister?" Then this guy, the translator who knew English, brought me to the hotel where he stayed. I shall never forget, I had to sleep in his room, and I said, oh my God, how can I be alone with this man all night long. No man has ever touched me even with his little finger. God, what will happen, what will happen now? He said, "If you want, you can sleep in another room, but the Russian ex–war prisoners rape everyone, you can scream all you want but they do as they please." So I stayed in his room. He asked me if I had ever been with a man. I said, "No, I come from a religious home, and my mother always told me to watch myself." So he didn't touch me, just protected me from the Russians.

The next day we were taken to Feldafing, where I joined my friend, and we met the French guy I had met before. Finally, I was reunited with my sister. We only stayed in Feldafing for a few days, until my sister recovered, and then the Americans took us to Pilsen. In Pilsen we were handed over to the Czechs, and rode in Czech trucks. We reached Bratislava. In Bratislava, we had to wait for a train that would take us home. There my sister and I stayed in a small hotel run by the Joint [Joint Distribution Committee]. Meanwhile, my sister was still weak after her illness. I went out for a walk alone and found a cousin who told me, "Your brother Shlomo is at home." God, my brother Shlomo is at home! He was the first to be deported when the Germans invaded Hungary. He was taken by train to the Kistarcsa camp. Have you heard of this camp? It doesn't matter. He is at home, God, I am here and my brother is at home.

We stayed there for two more days. There was a Joint dining room where we met a cousin of my father who brought meat to this kitchen. He had a carriage. A bunch of people originally from Somorja, did she [Berta Wazner] tell you about this? Well, this man was her uncle, and this bunch started walking home following his carriage. The uncle was on the carriage, and they walked beside him. I had two packages of clothes I had taken from the Germans. I put those packages on the carriage with the intention that later on, my brother would pick them up from Somorja, which wasn't far away from our town.

Then I said to my sister, "I am not staying here anymore. Whether you are weak or strong, we are heading toward home now. They couldn't have gone very far, they have only been on the road for an hour; we'll catch up to them!" So we left Bratislava. As we were leaving Bratislava, a truck with Russian soldiers passed us. The cap of one of them fell out of the truck, so they stopped to pick it up. I knew Slovakian well, so I understood Russian and I asked them where they were going. They said they were going to Komarno. Oh, surely God sent us this truck, we are also going in the direction of Komarno! You had to pass through

Dunajske Streda to reach Komarno, so I thought, great, hopefully we'll meet up soon with our relatives' carriage.

We boarded the truck and started riding. There was a barrel of vodka in the truck. The soldiers were drinking and offered us a canteen of vodka too. God, soldiers drinking like this, and we two girls are all alone, what have we done? They started flirting with my sister. Then God gave me brains. I said, "Leave her alone, she is still sick with typhus." They were afraid of typhus, so they left us alone. We stopped; I went up to an officer and I said, "Listen, I survived the German camps. The Germans never touched me. I don't want any of your soldiers to mess with me." The officer helped us and warned the soldiers saying, "If anyone of you does anything to these two girls . . ."

We ride and ride. Where is Dunajske Streda? Where are our relatives with the carriage? Gone, gone, gone. They drove a different route, which I didn't recognize, and I was worried. We drive on. It's almost evening. Now, our truck was part of a convoy of trucks, and occasionally they had to stop and wait for the others. A guy on a bicycle passed by. I knew they were speaking Hungarian in this region, so I asked him where we were. He said, "Close to Galanta." What are we to do? I thought. It's nighttime. They stopped in Galanta. I said to my sister, "When the truck stops, the two of us will get off, and we will start running with all our might. I will not spend the night on this truck, come what may." I got off and held my sister. The soldiers started laughing at us. I said, "Drop dead."

A cousin of mine had married a man from Galanta. I met a girl and asked her if anyone from my cousin's family came back after the war. She said the husband was home. "Where?" They showed us to his house, and we stayed there for the night. It was Thursday night. On Friday morning, we wanted to leave. My cousin's husband, the smart guy, said, "Wait for the Russians, they can give you a ride." Well, we had certainly seen enough of the Russians and the way they treated women. I didn't want to meet any more Russians, I didn't even want to hear of them!

We started walking. My father had been a cattle dealer. This was the area where he had always bought calves and cows. We walked and walked. I wasn't ashamed to enter houses and ask for some food. I went in and introduced myself, mentioned my father. They said things like, "Oh God, but why do you have this look on your face? What has happened to you?" I said, "Do I know what an expression I have?!" My sister, the poor one, she was tired. I asked for some food for her too, for my sick sister. They always gave me something. One day, we entered a yard where they knew my father well. It was Friday noon. They had cheese pie and bean soup. Now you can't carry soup outside, and they didn't give me any pie either for her. They only gave me a piece of bread. I said to my sister, "You fool, you see? I had bean soup and a cheese pie and you only got bread." We walked and walked. Cars passed us like this.

I want to tell you something, something in which I believe as sincerely as I believe in the Torah. When I was in the camps, I used to dream how I would come home. There was a flour mill opposite the train station, on the other side, and I used to dream that I would come home that way. Now, walking, that's exactly how it happened. We came home. A friend of my brother saw us and said, "Your brother heard some guys were coming to Somorja, so he went there." Us, to Somorja? I later told the whole story to my brother, once he returned home. When he finally returned we were so happy to see each other, we kissed each other and cried; people said that they had never witnessed such a dramatic reunion even with lovers.

We stayed there in Dunajska Streda, and I started sewing. This very morning I thought, I still can sew, and I still have this tablecloth that a young man gave me for taking in some old shirts of his father. The shirts were too big for the son, so I took them in for him. That was my first work, making small shirts of big ones. He didn't have any money, so he paid me with a Damask tablecloth. If you want, I can show it to you. That was the first time I was paid after returning home.

Then others started to return too. My brother had already prepared a house for us. We had a house in town. Then, our cousins started coming back. Among them were three sisters, two of them twins. One of them was sent to Sweden to recover, for she was very ill. She had been in Bergen-Belsen. Luckily no one identified them as twins, when Mengele asked for twins. Now the twins joined us, as well as our cousin who had been with us throughout, and three more cousins. We all lived together in one room now. My brother worked to earn money. He earned some money, and I worked and earned too. The rest of our family was very weak. This is how we lived for a while.

One day it was written in the paper that Shmuel Fuchs was coming home. That was my father's name, so we were very excited and went out to welcome each train. But the newspaper wrote Shmuel instead of Yonah Fuchs by mistake; they must have mistaken my father's name for his son. It was my brother that came home, not my father; we never saw my father again. My brother told us that initially, our father was sent to work, because he looked strong. However, in the same section was a man, a neighbor of ours who was younger than our father but looked older, who was sent to the other side. Then my father told my brother, "I am not strong enough to work like you and the other young men. I will go with this neighbor, at least I'll be with someone I know." And he joined that man. Had he stayed with my brother, he might have survived.

We all stayed home together. Then, my younger brother, the one who was the last to return, received a call-up for the Czech army. He didn't want to serve in the Czech army, so he enrolled in the *Hashomer Hatzair* youth movement and Youth Aliya [youth emigration organization], and he came here, to Israel, with Youth Aliya. Then, another brother was also called to service in the Czech army. I told him, "Don't you go."

Now, you remember I told you I was a Zionist since youth. I had gone to *hachshara* [preparation course for emigration and agricultural work], to a *Hashomer Hatzair hachshara*. I wanted very much to come to Israel, because my younger brother, now my late brother, may he rest in peace, was already here. My sister left at that time to Switzerland to work as a housemaid. I didn't want to go to Switzerland, I only wanted to come to Israel. My best friend and I, while we were in the camps, we planned how we were going to come to Israel. We planned to open a hot dog stand for a living, and we talked about it all the time.

Once back home, I went to *hachshara*, and in *hachshara*, I developed a skin infection that wouldn't heal. So I came home from *hachshara* for vacation and never went back, you hear me? I never went back. I started working and my sister left for Switzerland. My brother received a call-up notice from the Czech army, so he decided to emigrate illegally. He joined a group, and unfortunately, they were caught on the way. They were taken to Italy and Belgium, they sat in prison, and finally he arrived in Israel. But at this point, at the point that this brother also left, I was alone in Czechoslovakia.

One day I was riding a bicycle and I fell off. Our town doctor was Doctor Hershkowitz, a devoted Zionist. When I went to him to tend to my wounds from the fall, he said, "Dora, I know that you are dying to go to Israel. There's a last transport being organized these days, but you have to go to Bratislava and make arrangements. I myself am leaving with this transport." So I immediately took the train to Bratislava, just as I was, with bandages and iodine. I went up to the Palestine Affairs Office and said I was Zionist ever since 1938. I said, "I don't want to go to Switzerland, I only want to go to Israel. Whenever there was fund raising, I was involved; in short, I deserve to go." I didn't mention the doctor's name, because he had told me not to say that he sent me. The man from the Palestine Affairs Office said, "My dear, this is the last transport. If you can somehow get a passport, like the ex-members of the Czech Brigade have managed to do, then you will be the first to go."

I thought, how can I get hold of a passport? I went out looking. My aunt was living in Bratislava and I stayed the night at her house until the morning train. My aunt said to me, "You are lucky, I have a tenant who bought a passport in Prague, and he is coming back here tonight." So instead of returning home, I waited for him. He came in a taxi, don't ask. He said to me, "I bought the passport for 20,000 kronas, but I already gave it to the Palestine Affairs Office. If you want, go there tomorrow and try to get it." I went to the Office and took the tenant's passport number with me. I didn't have a picture. I said, "Look Mr. Rosenthal"—that was the name of the man in the office, may he rest in peace—"Look Mr. Rosenthal, I have a passport issued in Prague." He said, "Bring me two pictures, I'll see what I can do." I rushed to Bratislava, had the pictures made, and took them back.

It was Sunday. On Monday, I came back home. The man from the Palestine Affairs Office had told me to call him on Wednesday evening, and he would tell me whether I was going or not. On Wednesday I called him, I remember. He says, "Dora, start packing. On Sunday morning you have to be in Bratislava." Now, I didn't have any money, and I had to pay half the price of this passport, I promised to pay for it. It was a so-called couple's passport, but I'll tell you about that later. I had a radio set, a closet, and a few other things that I now sold within three days. My brother who had emigrated illegally left me ten English gold coins and a diamond ring. I asked him then, "If I have a chance to leave the country, may I sell the ring?" He said, "It's yours. You can do with it as you like." Now I sold everything and collected the 10,000 kronas, and didn't even have to sell the gold coins.

On Sunday morning I made my way to Bratislava, and then to Prague. They organized us for the transport by creating "families" out of total strangers. Each "couple" or "family" also got a "child." Older people got two children. The man I met at my aunt's house became my "husband"; he and I were a "couple" and we were assigned a fourteen year old "son" called Mishu, who didn't even know my name, so he called me Mamichka.

We started our trip. In three days' time, we arrived at Marseilles. The doctor who advised me to join the transport was there, he met me and said, "Well done, Dora." At Marseilles, our ship was already waiting. There I met friends from Youth Aliya and also two cousins who were in *Hashomer Hatzair*. It took us a week to get to Israel. After all the excitement I had, I was sick for the whole week on the ship. We had a doctor on the ship, and he was very nice.

We arrived at Alexandria. The ship stopped there for a day to load coal. Black Sudanese workers were working there. I had a piece of cake I couldn't eat, so I threw it to the workers. The doctor came and hit my hand, saying, "Are you insane, throwing food to our enemies? Don't you know who these people are?" Now our ship also had students coming back to Israel from England for their summer vacation, for it was June. Among them were women too. In the evening they gathered all of us and announced that any woman who dared to talk to these Arabs would have her head shaven, as in the camps. "Do you want to start relations with Arabs, our greatest enemies?"

Well, we arrived at Haifa on Saturday afternoon. The *Sochnut* [Jewish Agency] people weren't there because it was Saturday. My "son" Mishu said, "Mamichka, I am leaving." I said, "Where are you going, for God's sake, you are my responsibility now!" He said, "I am going to my grandfather and uncle in Haifa." Well, you can't stop a fourteen-year-old boy. He left. Within two hours he came back with his uncle. I asked him, "Mishu, how did you do it?" He told me that he left the ship, left the port, met a man who knew German, and showed him the address of his relatives. Mishu said, "I am looking for this address." The man saw a boy all on his own and asked, "Where have you come from?" Mishu said, "I just came with this ship." This Jew then got a taxi and took the boy to his grandfather! Mishu told his grandfather he had come with me and my pseudohusband. So, later on in the evening they came back to visit us on the ship and took us to spend the night in a hotel in Haifa.

I got up the next morning in Haifa and went to a coffee house to have breakfast with my pseudohusband. I decided that I wanted to find my brother who was living in Karkur. I hadn't told him that I was coming; I wanted to surprise him. How does one get to Karkur? People told me this funny sounding word *Tachana Mercazit*, which means Central Bus Station; they told me that I had to get to the Haifa Central Bus Station and look for a bus to Pardess Hana, and then get another bus from there to Karkur. People asked me, "How are you going to get there on your own?" I said, "I know the person I'm looking for and somehow, I'll manage." I get to the Central Station and take the bus to Pardess Hana, and get off by a kiosk. I asked, "Where is the bus to Karkur?" People answered, "It left five minutes ago." "When is the next one?" "Only late in the afternoon." "Is it far away?" "Not so much, half an hour's walk." What is half an hour's walk for me? I was a young woman, what was the big deal? They told me, go straight and then there's a crossroads. But they forgot to tell me which way to turn, so when I came to the crossroads, I stood there like a fool. It was nighttime.

Suddenly a man comes, wearing a strange hat. I stopped him and asked, "Sagen Sie mir, wie kommt man nach Karkur? [German, Tell me please, how do you get to Karkur?]" He looked at me. "Du wilst gein in Karkur zu fus? [Yiddish: Do you intend to walk to Karkur?]" I said yes. He said, "You can't walk there, there are two Arab villages on the way, it's too dangerous." There was a tree there. I stopped by it and started telling him how I got there. Suddenly an old woman came by with two girls. He stopped them and asked them in Hebrew where they were going. They said, Karkur. He told me, "Izt kanstu gein [Yiddish: Now you can go]. Go to your brother in peace." I joined the old woman and soon I arrived in Karkur. Some girls originally from Dunajske Streda saw me and took me to my brother. What a joy to see him again!

Together with my brother I went back to Haifa. Now I went with my pseudohusband again and had the brains to announce the *Sochnut* people in time that "Ich Bin Nit Farhiret mit im [Yiddish: I am not married to him]." I had a friend who didn't tell them, and went through many *tzures* [Yiddish: troubles] in the community because it said in her I.D. that she was married. I had to go and testify for her, and what trouble they caused her.

I received seven liras from the *Sochnut* for housing in Hadera. I spent one night there. They said it was a room with a kitchen. The room was very small, and in the corner there was a bowl. That was the kitchen! What to do now, how can I find a job here? I had a cousin in Givat Shmuel, they had been here for half a year before I arrived. I decided go to my cousin's. Next day, I traveled to Tel Aviv. I walked to *Tachana Mercazit* to catch the bus to Givat Shmuel. I met my past pseudohusband there and he told me he heard of a room that could be rented for twenty-five liras in the Montefiori neighborhood. Suddenly, someone calls my name, Dora Fuchs. God, I am in Israel for one day only, who would know me? In *Tachana Mercazit*, there was a small restaurant. A young man I knew in my town was standing there. We were in the same class. He came here in 1939, when I wanted to come too, before the War. He recognized me; I was among the first to come after the camps. *Simcha* and *sussen* [Hebrew and Yiddish: great joy].

He asked me, "Where do you live?" I said, "Meanwhile, I don't have a place." I told him how I came to Israel. He said there was a man there in Montefiori Street with an apartment for rent. "Go there, look at it, and if it's any good, come back to me, and I will give you the money." I said, "Lajos, how can you? You work hard for your money." He said, "Of course I will help you, who should I help if not you?" I remember my brother also came with me to see the place. The room belonged to a man of Turkish origins, a bird and plant dealer. We went in. You had to go down three stairs into a yard, and then into the room. It was an elongated shabby room. The man refused to let me cook in it. I started crying, and I said to him, "Are you a Jew? How dare you be like that?" My brother already knew Hebrew so I asked him to tell the man that we are two orphans, our parents died in the camps, we have the twenty five liras and I promise not to cook anything in there. What could I have cooked? Eventually, he gave us the place for twenty-five liras. I went back to Lajos and he gave me the money. I really didn't want to sell my brother's gold. I told him, "Look, Lajos, I've got some gold, but it's not mine, it's my brother's. He should be on his way here, I don't even know where he is right now. I want to give you this gold to watch over it for me, because where I live, it won't be safe with strangers."

Believe it or not, after all that, I didn't even stay in that apartment for a day. How come? My cousin from Givat Shmuel, who was very religious, said, "I will not let you sleep there, no way." So I joined them in Givat Shmuel. They had a room and a half, with a nine-month-old baby. All I had was one *Sochnut* bed. I lived there for half a year, until later I found a room with my friend in Montefiori. I still came to my relatives for the weekend. Once I met an old friend of mine there, who now lived with her mother. We also went together to greet those coming in on the ships.

I, who had a profession, was the first to start working. Once in Givat Shmuel a fellow told me he read in the paper that on 20 Allenby St. there was a store in need of a tailor. I went there and the owner asked me to sew something. That was the first time I worked on an electrical sewing machine, and I had problems with it, because it stopped whenever it wanted, not when I wanted it to stop. He saw all this, and despite my inexperience, he treated me to coffee in a nearby coffee shop and told me to start working the next day. I wouldn't have hired myself for this work! I worked there for a few months and earned well. At noon, when he closed the place and went home—there were only three of us working there—I went to Rothschild Street, sat on a bench, and made buttonholes. This way I was able to earn some extra cash. I earned well, and within three months I was able to return the twenty-five liras I paid for that room in which I never lived. Later on, my brother started working while living in that apartment; then my sister got married there, and finally she left it too.

I enlisted in the army in 1948. I volunteered. My other brother, who came illegally, arrived at Cyprus. When they let the pregnant women leave and come to the country, he too jumped and swam to the ship. He arrived in Israel without my knowledge and immediately joined the *Palmach*. Then he disappeared in Manara. Meanwhile, I hadn't heard anything from him and knew nothing about his whereabouts for seven months, except that the newspaper said he "disappeared." So I worried about him.

When I was in the army they even took my picture for *La-Isha* [Hebrew: For Women] Magazine. By then, I already met my future husband, and I was corresponding with my sister in Switzerland. Suddenly, for a while there was no answer from her. Then a letter came from her from Dunajska Streda. How did she get back to Dunajska Streda? Well, she didn't like it in Switzerland, so she went back to Czechoslovakia. I couldn't believe she did that—after all, from Switzerland you can go anywhere, you can go to the Joint and say you want to come to Israel—but Czechoslovakia?!! Finally she arrived from Czechoslovakia in 1949. I received a letter from her to my army base. I was a cook. By then I already knew Hebrew well, and I received a letter from her saying she was near Haifa. My sister was here! I went to see her and returned.

Upon my return, a telegram awaited me saying my brother, whom I hadn't heard from in seven months, was wounded and hospitalized in Bilu Hospital. I ran to my officer. She says, "What am I going to do with you? Try and go to Kfar Bilu." Where is Kfar Bilu? No one knew where it was. Finally, someone advised me to go to Herzl Square, where I was bound to get a ride with someone to Kfar Bilu. So that's how I got to see my poor brother who was hurt and in bed. Then he was moved to Sarafend [Hebrew: Zrifin]. By then, I was engaged to be married. My sister married five weeks before me. When I was in the army, I lived in an apartment from the army in Jaffa. Two or three months after I was released from the army, I got married, and then we shared an apartment with my two brothers. Then, my older brother got married, and finally, we moved here to Bazera.

I.R.: When was that?

Mrs. Ashkenazi: We married in 1949. In 1951 my older daughter was born. In 1953 we came to Bazera. Eight years later, my younger daughter was born, and we have been living in the same place since then. In 1974 my older daughter got married, and four years later, her younger sister got married. I have six grandchildren, thank God. But ever since I came back from the camps, I have high blood pressure and I have to take medicine, but I live on.

I.R.: May I ask you if you always remained religious, even during the War?

Mrs. Ashkenazi: Certainly. On Yom Kippur, we had this prayer book that one woman managed to hide, so we took turns praying with it. We told our guard we wanted to fast. He said, "Do whatever you want, but you still have to work as usual." I shall never forget, I closed my machine, so the meister came up to me. I told you how kind he was to me. Now he said, "Dora, Was hast Du

gemacht? [German: What have you done?] They might accuse you of sabotage."
I told him about our holiday. Again he said, "Du bist verflucht, wo ist Dein
Gott? [German: Damn you, where is your God?]"

Still, as I told you, we kept *Pesach* [Passover] as well, I told you how we
avoided eating *hametz* on Passover. I shall never forget. On the last day of
Pesach, our only food was potatoes, and on Saturday we got soup with noodles
in it, and bread in the evening, things we couldn't eat on *Pesach*. I remember
feeling that I couldn't take it anymore. After returning from the camps, our
rabbi told us that in fact we sinned by refraining from eating, because we
jeopardized our very lives, which was more important than *Pesach*. There was a
girl from Nagymegye with us. She was the rabbi's daughter. She didn't eat any
nonkosher food for the whole year we spent together. She didn't eat any meat,
no blood sausages or frankfurters, just bread and margarine. I was observant in
my youth, and to this very day.

But I'll tell you another thing. When my older sister got married, she cut all
her hair and started wearing a wig. I wasn't like that. I used to slip out of the
house after the Shabbat meal, I was wild. I had a friend who covered for me and
said I was with her. But in fact I went to the *Betar* Zionist movement. Now when
my sister got married, I told my mother I wouldn't do like her. My mother told
me, "If you want your mother to visit you and eat at your house, you should keep
a kosher house, wear a wig, and act like all Jewish women." Well, I don't have a
wig, I used to lie about going to the *mikve* [ritual bath], for my husband isn't at all
religious, but I keep kosher. At first I didn't even ride in a car on Saturday, but
that caused many arguments with my husband, even though his father was so
religious that he wouldn't eat anything at our house. I had a religious friend who
then told me, "Dora, to achieve peace between you two, you have to compromise." Now my husband says *kiddush* [blessing over wine and/or *challa*] every
Friday evening, and I do travel by car on Saturdays. What can one do? But in here
[points toward her heart], I will always remain religious.

Rachel Markowitz. Originally from Szilágysomlyo, Hungary/Rumania. Interviewed in Petach Tikva, Israel, February 1991

(Translated from Hungarian)

Rachel Markowitz: I was born in Szilágysomlyo in 1923 to a big family. We had
twelve brothers and sisters, and many uncles and aunts. My father was a mover;
we had a moving company. We were brought up well and had a good life until
the Hungarians came in 1941 or so. Then they started persecuting the Jews.
When Jews would come home from the synagogue they were beaten, shouted
at. Jews had to wear the yellow star. Jews weren't allowed to go out to the street

after eight in the evening. Even though we were born there and we felt we were integrated into everything, and we were loyal citizens, we still were different.

Until one day they came at dawn and said, "Within two hours you must be out of the house." Just the way we were, they almost didn't let us take anything with us, except for a few things. They told us to take off our jewelry. Things that our parents collected during a lifetime, for six girls, many, many things, all was gone. We had to give everything to these snot-nosed youngsters. And we went out to the street, old people, children, nobody cared about us. We were arranged in a row and marched three kilometers to the local brick factory called Sziládicse, where they crammed us together in terrible conditions. They almost didn't give us any food. People were filled with lice. And they tortured the Jews. The local Hungarians, the well-known acquaintances with whom we grew up, now tied up Jews with their heads faced down. When the Jews lost consciousness, the Hungarians poured a bucket of water on them and started interrogating them again about the valuables they had supposedly hidden. My father was smart. He didn't let us hide anything. He said, "If we shall remain alive after this, we will replace everything."

We lived there in the brick factory for about a month. And one fine day they put us onto cattle cars of a train. They stuffed some eighty people in each cattle car. Children, old people, everybody. We, the young ones, I was twenty-one years old, couldn't even sit down anywhere. We let the older people sit. There was one bucket they gave us as a toilet. After I don't know how many days, we left. I had a sister, aged seven or eight. She said to my father, "I have some toothpaste in my pocket, can I eat it?" My father said she could; there was no other choice.

While we were on the way, they never opened the doors. We arrived at Auschwitz. There were many men there wearing what looked like striped pajamas. They started to yell at us in Yiddish that we should hand over the children to the old people. "Hand the children over to the old." No one knew what this was supposed to be. There were some people who did give over their children. There were some. There were other mothers who wouldn't let go of their children. We marched forward, the whole family, and reached Mengele. Mengele pointed with his stick, Right, Left. Young mothers or old grandmothers who had children with them went to the left. We, who were young and capable of work went to the right. We didn't want to part with our parents, but they said we shall meet each other later.

We went into the camp. We entered a big space or hall, full of soldiers, and all of us had to undress completely, and they started to shave all our body hair. They shaved each person completely and gave us some rags to wear. I had a pair of good sport shoes. Of course they took them away from me. I was very sorry then, they meant a lot to me. Then, just as we were, in rags and bald headed, they made us stand outside in the rain. The rain came down on us, and we had nothing. We took a piece of a rag, tore it off our dress, tied it on our head. From here we reached Auschwitz, the inside of the camp.

The camp had thirty barracks like ours. A thousand women were in each one. In the middle of it there was a heater they did not turn on, and there were very large bunk beds in three levels. On these we had to lie, some twelve or thirteen women divided into six and six, or six and seven, lying in the opposite direction to the one next to you. While we were sleeping, if one of us wanted to roll over, all the others had to roll over too. These bunks were made of thin logs which left their marks on my body even long after I came home from there. I still had stripes made by the logs I used to lie on. Life there was very hard. The place was in fact an extermination camp, and every day Mengele came there to pick up people and send them to the crematorium.

We, the five sisters, remained together all the time. We didn't tell anyone that we were sisters. Had they known it, they would have immediately separated us. There was this Blockälteste, a Polish Jewish woman, she was the only one we told about us. And we asked her to let us know if they were going to send everyone, without "selection," on a transport, that she should tell us so that all five of us could go together in that transport.

We stayed there for about five months. Every day this Mengele came, with his cane, and we had to pass naked in front of him. If he laid his cane upon a woman, that woman was doomed. There were four sisters of one family in Somlyo, the Weiss family. Mengele chose one of the four, and the other three, even though they knew she was going to die, joined her. While being marched, running, they managed to tell us, "If you return home and find someone from our family, tell them not to wait for us." Even though they were healthy. We, the five sisters, also agreed that we would all go together to wherever any one of us would be sent. I had a younger sister aged sixteen. She was skinny and tall, and we always worried that she would be taken. We always arranged it so that she wouldn't get to the "selection," although during the "selection" there was also a block curfew.

Not to mention the toilets. This was a long hall in which we had to sit side by side. It was a terrible situation. We didn't get any water so we couldn't wash. We were full of lice, something terrible. Food was allotted per bunk, for the thirteen women sharing the bunk. It was some green grass full of stones, and each girl could only take one gulp of it in her turn. Then, like animals, they snatched the bowl from one mouth to another. This is how they fed us. They also gave us a small piece of bread, so that we would have something more substantial. And they always took us to disinfections.

When they took us to disinfection we never knew what to expect, water or gas. We lived in fear. We had to hand in our clothes just before it started and get them back right afterward. Once, I didn't get any clothes at all afterward. For five days I stayed naked as on the day I was born, and every day they dragged us out to roll call, in rows of five. We had our own row, and my sisters kept me warm on both sides. We stood there waiting for hours. It was raining, then the sun shone, and we were left there like dogs. One cannot describe the suffering and fear we experienced.

When the Russians approached, the Nazis started burning entire camps. The camp opposite us, they liquidated it overnight. Then the Blockälteste called us and said, "Die funf Schwestern, geht jetzt weiter, jetzt machen wir keine elektion mehr, denn Mengele hat keine Zeit [German: The five sisters, go now, there aren't any "selections" now, as Mengele has no time]." And they put us in a transport. We left the camp. Many acquaintances saw us leaving, so they joined us. When we reached the showers, there were too many of us, so again they made a "selection." And the poor, unfortunate one, this little sister of mine, they took her away. All four of us wanted to follow her. They beat us but would not let us die. The poor one, they took only her, and us they put on a transport, again on a train. We marched, did not know where nor why. We marched.

We reached a camp with two hundred Polish Jewish women. We were two hundred Hungarian Jewish women. There also, there were bunk beds with three levels, but the barracks weren't so crowded, and each woman had her own place. From this place they sent us to a factory, an airplane repair–parts factory. That was in Silesia, Mittelstein. We worked there in two shifts, night and day. At night they gave us some food, and we worked hard by the machines. There too we had roll calls. They went searching in our rooms. You weren't allowed to own anything. We were cold. We received Dutch wooden clogs, but the snow entered them. We bumped and fell over, but they didn't let us cling to each other. "Los, los," they hurried us. It is impossible to describe the suffering a person went through there. We finished working, we were tired, we fell asleep. One of my younger sisters, she once fell asleep during work. She found a place where they were drying up some repair parts. She went in there and fell asleep. The Germans searched and found her there. The poor one, she started crying and begging them not to kill her. They pitied her.

In the factory, if you had to go to the toilet even, you had to report to the woman in charge. When you returned, you had to report again. It all went on this way for several months. We were brought there in October. There was a different Blockälteste for the Hungarian women and the Polish women. We didn't mingle much. Why? Because, for example, once they wanted to give a premium to those who exceeded their work ration and asked us what we wanted. We said, "Food, soup." The Polish women said, "Lipstick, powder," and who knows what. So we couldn't get along with each other.

I.R.: Maybe they weren't that hungry?

Mrs. Markowitz: I don't know. There too you had all kinds, I don't know. I had a very good meister, a work supervisor. He asked me in German if I liked the Russians. I said, "How do I know whether I like them or not?" He said, "Listen, the Russians are getting closer. You are very tired. They are going to take you away. They are going to march you all the way. You have no strength, so they are going to shoot you." This German, who was from the Wermacht, also said, "Run away, there is a forest nearby, hide there. The Russians are going to liberate you." Of course, we didn't have the courage for that. But next to my machine there was a small closet, and every day, this meister put into this closet slices of bread as thin as cigarette paper. This in itself was very kind of him. And he also told us the latest news. So that this Wermacht man was very good to us.

Now, what did God do? This man ran away, my meister ran away. Then my machine had no meister. Next to me there was a war prisoner, Dutch or French, and he worked by the very difficult machines. The work he did was dangerous and physically hard. This man died, and now that I was without work, they wanted to put me instead of him. But I knew, if I worked there, I'd drop dead, because I didn't have any strength anymore. So I refused to work there. They came and said, "Komm, wir werden Dich lehren [German: Come, we'll teach you]." And they taught me. I knew how to handle the machine better than they, but I didn't want to do it. I went mad, I didn't want to. They came every day and instructed, and threatened, said that if I didn't start working they were going to make me lie down on the snow and shoot me. My sisters were crying, the poor ones, and they said: "Don't be so stubborn, maybe we will be liberated soon." But I said, "I will not let them kill me with this job."

When they threatened me this way, I went to the camp doctor. I knew that she wasn't allowed to exempt anyone from anything, that's what they told her. But I also knew that she was of Hungarian origins, and I had this instinct which made me go to her. I told her, "Doctor, the chief inspector wants you to give me a note that my legs swell up; they are in such bad condition that I can't work while standing." I was lucky enough to find her in a good mood and she actually gave me such a note. For a few good days, I carried this note on me all the time. The minute I entered the factory, all the meisters and the SS men were already waiting for me, accusing me of refusing to work, of sabotaging the factory, and whatnot. Finally, I managed to get an easier job, which was done while sitting. Well, for a few days I worked in this job, and it was very good for me.

Not to mention, which I forgot before, that there were air raids and sirens throughout, and they had to go down to the shelter. They, the Nazis, went down and left us upstairs. During these times I asked the good Lord to make a bomb fall on us, finish with us, but it never came. The worst times were the Friday nights. Everyone remembered the way they spent Shabbat at home with their families, and they cried at the comparison.

Suddenly they came, "Los, los, los. Clean up the machines and back to the camp." We took apart the beds and everything. We didn't know where they were taking us. We started crying, because again they started with "selections." There, too, they separated the strong from the weak. They wanted to kill the weak and us they meant to move further away. We arrived at the Sudetenland.

Again they put us on cattle cars and gave us some food. This time they said we were going to be liberated. Well, I knew this meant death, because they always said the opposite of what they meant.

We reached the Sudetenland, so they called it. There was a big camp, called Weisswasser, with a big cable factory. There were six hundred Jewish women working there when we arrived. They were brought there from the nearby camp. I didn't tell you yet that at night the women went out to "pinch" potatoes from the warehouse. I was such a coward, I was so afraid that I said, "I am not going, I don't want to die." My sisters, the poor ones, they always went out and brought me potatoes. I didn't want to take it from them, I said I didn't need it. Until one night, when we were supposed to be asleep they told me, "See, everyone is going out to find some potato peels and stuff. Why don't you go too?" So, this time I went out too. It was raining, and I slipped and fell. I was covered with mud and had no way of cleaning myself. I told my sisters, "Now are you happy? I went with you and still didn't get any food." I was very afraid.

Here, too, in the Sudetenland, my sisters were sent to work in the factory, and I was sent to dig the frozen ground. It was a sort of a lavatory, and you had to dig out the frozen dirt and then put it back. There was no point to the work, it was only to torment us. It was snowing, we were cold, we had nothing. In the factories, they were working with French men, partisans. Every Sunday in this camp, they woke us up, sent us out for roll call, and went searching in our rooms, so that no one could hide a comb or a piece of paper or anything on Earth. Still, in the factory we always used newspaper to wrap up our feet, for they were frozen.

Well, one Sunday morning we were waiting for the Germans to come and wake us up, and no one came. Some girls went out to search in the camp and saw that the French partisans had kicked the SS men out of their room. Of course, all the Jews went out to see what they could get, once they saw the SS had been kicked out of there. They opened up stocks of potato, sugar, margarine, and everything. And they started to fry and cook everything. Not fry, really, they only made a fire and went into the SS room, and whatever they could find, they took, grabbed everything. By the time I got there, there was nothing there, just broken pieces of wood. One of my sisters was coming out carrying a big quilt just as I was trying to go in. Everyone else said, "Who is this fool who is taking a quilt?" And they pushed her. When I came back to our room I found this big quilt that my sister brought on our bed. She said, "Even you pushed me!" I said, "Why on Earth did you take the quilt, do you want to bring it home?" She said, "It doesn't matter what it is, as long as you have something, something of your own."

My older sister, who now lives in Nahariya, didn't let us eat a lot at once. She said, "I will give you some food, a little bit of it, every hour." People died by eating too much. They were just liberated and they started to eat a lot, out of hunger, potatoes in margarine and everything, and they died one after the other. They got diarrhea and died. My sister took care of us. If it weren't for her, we too would have died.

They started saying that the Americans are fifty kilometers away and the Russians, eighty. Those who arrive first would conquer the place. But the Russians, they said, it wasn't advisable for so many girls to stay at one place when the Russians came. Where shall we go? What should we do? We went on our way. There was a Czech village close by, and we headed there. As we were going toward the village, bullets flew around us like this, fewww, fewww. There were air-raid shelters with people inside, but they didn't let us in. As we were walking, evening came, and we didn't have a place to hide. That is why I say, it is fate that we remained alive.

We walked on and suddenly we saw a light. It was a flour mill. Five girls from the camp were sitting there around a table. We said, "Are you still sitting here? Don't you hear the shooting outside? Go away." All five girls and the landlady, a Hungarian-speaking woman, went down to the shelter. They went down, and we ate up whatever they left on the table. We weren't afraid of anything. We just came in from the outside. Then, we too went down to the shelter. Toward morning, it all quieted down and we went up.

Now, the landlady, a Czech woman, took good care of us and fed us; she let us sleep there, together with the five girls. But all the men in her family were gone, hiding, and she was the only one around, so we suspected her of being a big Jew-hater, maybe someone who survived by betraying Jews. Then some Russian soldiers came, and the Czech woman was so strong that she pushed the door on them and didn't let them in. But they said, "Now that we know where the barishnas [Russian: women] are, we'll come back in the evening." I said, "We must leave, we can't stay here for the night." She said she would take us to another village, seven kilometers away, but that she too wanted to have a "number" like the Jewish women. "Fine, you too are Jewish, come on." One girl gave her her own number.

The woman said, "Take anything you want from the house." We took some food, because of our hunger. We swelled up from hunger. I weighed thirty-five kilograms when I returned, with all this height. We went out like this, without any strength. The Czech woman didn't take anything with her except a small pillow. We reached a village. They put us in the village school, poured some straw on the floor for us. The woman went to her relatives, and we were put under watch. In the morning, they divided us among the local Czech families. Meantime, we heard that this girl who knew Russian stole the woman's pillow. The pillow was stuffed with a fortune. Dollars, jewelry, everything, everything. There was everything in that one pillow. She stole it. So some of us condemned her, and some said, "To hell with the Czech woman. She must have been a big Jew-hater, if she escaped like that."

The next day they divided us among the local families. We joined a

German-speaking family with a small child. They treated us very well. They weighed each one of us when we arrived, and two weeks later they weighed us again. It is unbelievable how they fed and stuffed us. We all worked. One of us did sewing work, another sister worked with the ducks. I had to take care of the child, a brat. I felt such anger and hatred that I couldn't stand it. I said, "They killed our beloved children, and I have to play with this child?" I pinched him, and he cried. Then they took him away from me and I had to tend to the chickens. They didn't deserve it, really, because they were very kind. They took us to plant some vegetables, and I didn't have patience to finish the work, I wanted to finish it as quickly as possible.

After two weeks we left. It was difficult to leave this place. They gave us food for the way. They were very kind. We wrote them when we arrived home, but they weren't there anymore. We left this place and headed to the train station. There was no more room in the train, so we rode on the roof. We rode about ten kilometers and got off. We reached a place where there were Jewish men. They gave us some money, and what did we buy with it? Cherries. We bought some cherries and slowly we made our way to Budapest.

In Budapest we boarded a streetcar and were asked to pay. My older sister said, "You go to Auschwitz, that's where our money is. You took it from us; you can go there for the money, we have no money." The driver started arguing with us, until one man, maybe he was Jewish, paid for our four tickets. We went to my father's cousin in Budapest. The cousin's family gave us clothes and everything. Then, with great difficulties, we boarded a train and headed to Rumania, for by the time we returned from the camps, our region had become Rumanian again. We got off on the Seklers Road, and they told us that there would be no further transportation until five o'clock that day. The local Jews hosted us. There was a special dining hall there for those returning from the camps. We spent the night there too, and in the meantime they called the Somlyo municipality and told them about us, the four sisters. My older brother was at home, he was already working, and we arrived home in a carriage full of Jewish young men. We were the first women to come home. That was a big sensation, because we knew about many others and we brought news.

The next day they bought shoes, clothes, and brought it all to us. So, slowly, we started life again. We used to have a maid before the war, but when we weren't allowed to keep her anymore, she went to work at our neighbors' house. Now she heard that we returned, and she came to see us. She told us that at our neighbors' house, she once went up to the attic and saw a big box there. She asked them what was in it, and was never allowed to go up there again. We got a search warrant and went there. We found many of our valuables there, our parents' wedding gifts, Rosenthal houseware. We found everything.

Another brother of mine, who served in the Czech army, came home once but didn't find anybody, so he returned to Czechoslovakia. While home, he learned that our German neighbors, with whom we used to have good relations, took our sewing machine. He went over to them and told them, "If you don't give me back my sewing machine right now, I shall make a sewing machine of you." Within one hour, the machine was back.

An ex-servant of us now took care of our garden, cooked and did everything for us for three weeks. During this time, we went out to eat at this public kitchen or dining hall for the survivors, as well as ate at home. We were so famished we couldn't be sated. For a year we didn't get our periods, because they used to put bromide in our food in the camps. I once got to the hospital in the camp. I had a lung disease, and I had fever. My meister kept sending me slices of bread with my sister, and he told her, "Don't you eat it, Das ist für die kranke Schwester [German: This is for the sick sister]." That was very helpful then. Now, too, we felt very good, after all the unbearable things we went through.

We came home. I started to be active in the Mizrahi Zionist movement. I was a "Mizrahic." I also had to be a member of the Communist party, and they started using me as a spy in the Mizrahi. When I realized that, I said, "No more." I signed up for the first aliya that was supposed to arrive in Israel in 1946. But the person who arranged the papers took my place, and I had to wait some more. Finally, in 1947, I came here, to Israel. When we arrived, two big British ships caught our ship. We were some fifteen hundred people.

I.R.: Did all the sisters come?

Mrs. Markowitz: No, only I came then. I was the first. My sisters stayed home. Then one sister married and left to Chile, where she lives to this day. Our ship was caught and brought to Cyprus. When I saw a gate and a camp again, I said, "I am not going in." I used to have this close friend in the camp; she was my "camp sister," and the two of us swore after the war that we would never again enter any camp. Let them kill us first; we will not go through this again. When I came there and saw a camp with closed gates, I said, "I am not entering this place." But how can you not enter? One of my brothers was there with my sister-in-law, and I said to them, "I am not going in." They argued and argued with me, but I refused to enter the camp. Suddenly, I saw this "camp sister" I just mentioned. I said, "Éva, what? Are you here too?" She said, "Yes, come on in, this is not like Auschwitz used to be. Here there are no roll calls, you get food regularly, and you can come in peacefully." Had I not seen her, I wouldn't have gone in.

We went in there and they divided us up. Not to mention the searches and the things they took away. I had a small medicine box. They took it away. When we left Rumania, they let us leave with fifteen kilograms per person, so my bag weighed fifteen kilograms. Then the British took everything away again, so that again we had nothing. There in Cyprus the weather was the same as Israel. We wore out our clothes. They became rags. Luckily, some people left and we could use their leftovers to make ourselves clothes. Men made needles, tools, and everything we needed. I can show you. For example, we received plates, and they made pots of them, everything. People were organized. The Jewish *Yishuv* in Palestine sent us teachers, so we learned Hebrew and waited for aliya. Singer Shoshana Damari was there. But the *Yishuv* leadership didn't help us leave Cyprus. They said we would be let into Israel eventually anyway, and in the meantime, they applied for certificates for other immigrants. Then we went on a strike against this policy. We didn't let them bring us food. The British wanted to work, install electricity. We didn't let them do anything; we said we were fine as we were.

It took until 1949, after the State of Israel was declared, that we were allowed to leave Cyprus and enter Israel. First, we stayed in *beit olim* [temporary quarters for immigrants] in Pardess Hana. Needless to say, there too we lived with some forty people in one barrack. You had to wait with your plate for hours until you received some food. By then I was already married. I told my husband, "I can't stand being crowded with so many people again, I can't take it anymore. Whatever happens, I have to leave this place." Where did we go? I had a brother in Tel Hanan. We were barely out of Cyprus, and now we came to Tel Hanan, to a shelter located on a mountain, without windows, and you couldn't even close the door. We had nothing on Earth, not even underwear, only the things we made from rags.

We moved to this nowhere; we didn't have to worry about thieves, so we went to the *Sochnut* to ask for a job and better housing. My husband became a mechanic. He got a job in Haifa. I went to the *Sochnut* to look for an apartment. They told me to look for a place and then they would help me. But there were no apartments at all. Well, it is such a long story to be a new immigrant, you can't tell it all. This is in short, because it is all mixed up. In the end we found an apartment in which the water was pouring out from the wall. The apartment had one room and a common kitchen with the neighbors. We moved into this apartment. My sister wrote me from Rumania and asked how we were doing with water, because they knew about the water shortage here. I wrote her that I was living in a "hole-y" place. Moses must have hit our wall too, because water was pouring from it! Toward Yom Kippur my sister wrote and asked how we were doing. I wrote, we have a minister in charge of our meager supplies. Since there aren't enough chickens to give to everyone, the minister boards an airplane with a chicken in his arms and together they turn in circles over us all [to fulfill the tradition of *kapparot* on Yom Kippur] . . . You see, we still had a sense of humor even when we had nothing else.

Then we found this other apartment. But we only had twenty-four liras. Of these, I spent four and had only twenty left. To purchase the apartment, I had to go to a stepuncle of mine to ask him for a loan. He said he would only give me the money if a bank would guarantee for it. I left him, hopeless. He then called me back, saying he would give me something. He was working in the *Nesher* [cement] factory. He said he would give me a loan from the factory's account, and I would pay it back monthly. And so it was. He gave me sixty liras. Now I had eighty. I asked my aunt to lend me twenty more liras, so that now I had a hundred. Then I went to my friend Éva and told her, "Get me ten liras, no matter how, just get them." It was a fortune then. From my brother I asked the remaining ten, and now I had the money for the apartment. We went to the *Sochnut*. They asked us if we had paid any "key-money" before. No, we hadn't. Finally we received that apartment.

In 1951 my older daughter was born in that damp house. There was no illness that she didn't contract. She was feeble and didn't put on enough weight. I wasn't too healthy either. We had many *tzures*. In 1953 there was this campaign, "From the City to the Country," in which we were encouraged to move to the countryside. We left to the Galilee, to Rosh Pinah. There, we had to find a new apartment and settle in again. We lived there through all the wars. In the Six Days' War we sat in an air-raid shelter the whole time; the children also were stuck there all day. I suffered much from the tension during the war, and my hearing was ruined. All we wanted was to come out safely.

My son was born there in Rosh Pinah, and it was a good place as long as the children were small. Once they grew up, it wasn't good for us anymore. My daughter enlisted in the army, and she said, "On my vacations I shall not travel home but rent an apartment in Haifa and go there. I have nothing to do in Rosh Pinah." Well, that was all I needed to hear. I knew we had to leave, but I said, "Where shall we go? How do we get the money?" What did the good God give us? My husband worked in the Hulah nature reserve. At that time the company offered its workers very good conditions for earlier retirement, twice the usual sum. We took advantage of the opportunity—luckily we received that money just then—and we came to live here in Petach Tikva.

We endured all the wars. At times I thought that psychologically, I couldn't stand it. Now this thing came [the Gulf War]. In this war we sit in this sealed or silly [Hebrew: *atum, tumtum*] room and await our good luck. Now I only worry about the children, the grandchildren, the small kids. I don't worry about ourselves; I say, we aren't going to die young. We did our part. ·

That's in short. I did not tell it all, though—the great suffering. I don't know how to tell it in order, everything, all that happened. The main thing is that in the camps they tortured us, and we weren't considered human beings. Once we came back from disinfection and by mistake I turned my head the other direction. I received such a blow on my head that I thought that would be the end of me. Why, what have I done? That I looked the other way? You see, it's these small things that I can't tell all of. I forget and then remember them. At night, when we went out to the toilets, we tripped over the dead and dying women. Even when we moved to Petach Tikva in 1969, I still couldn't go out at night, because I was still afraid of tripping over the dead bodies. It is only since recently that I started convincing myself that it's irrational, that I should try to overcome my fear, force myself. But even now, when I walk the street in the dark, I am still afraid of tripping over the dead. You see, many of those dead or dying women in the camp were my friends and relatives.

Once, a pregnant woman was brought in. She came there already pregnant and now it was her time to give birth. They took the child from her, the Blockälteste, and killed it. She, the poor woman, immediately had to stand up for roll call. This woman survived, came back, found her husband and they now have other children. Her son is a physician, she has everything. She lives here and we get together at times. Still, she did go through this terrible experience of seeing her child killed so that she could be saved.

I have two children, I have grandchildren. There were times I didn't want to live, I was sure I wouldn't survive, but fate had its own way, and so it was destined for us. We survived. But I would be lying if I said I am not afraid. Now we relive the terrible experiences over and over. When the siren starts, my heart beats so fast with fear I can hardly breathe. But what can one do? Life goes on and that's that.

I.R.: I would like to ask if you noticed a growth in anti-Semitism before 1944?

Mrs. Markowitz: There was anti-Semitism, but the thing was that they were able to hide their intentions from us. They told us we would be sent to a place called Kenyérmező, to work there. So my father said, "That's not so bad, we will work and have everything again." They hid the truth from us, the Arrow Cross Fascist militia with the cock feather sign. The Hungarians themselves were bad to us, unbelievably bad. The Rumanians were better in that regard. When we were still in the ghetto, in a camp by the local brick factory, some people were smart and escaped from there. Two brothers escaped to Rumania, where they were caught and tried. The court wanted to assign them a lawyer, but this man, one of the two whose father was a lawyer himself, said, "We don't need a lawyer. I will be our lawyer." He stood up and spoke out. He said, "How have we sinned? All we wanted was to save our lives. Do we deserve to be punished for that?" The audience wept with them, and they weren't punished. One of them later came here to Israel. He lives here, he has a good job. So you see, you never know what is in store for you, you never know what the future holds.

Ruth Matias. Originally from Sziget, Hungary/Rumania. Interviewed in Kfar Sava, Israel, January 1991

(Translated from Hebrew and Hungarian)

Ruth Matias: My name is Ruth Matias. I was born in Marmarossziget seventy-one years ago. Later, in 1939, this region was returned to Hungary. My parents were wealthy people. I grew up in a family that had everything. When I had to go to school, I first learned with nuns, and then did the matriculation in my hometown. My mother died when I was fourteen, and in 1944 the Holocaust came. My brothers were taken to the labor battalions while my father and I were taken to Auschwitz. None of the men ever returned and I never heard from any of them. I still have a sister eleven years my senior; she lives near Haifa, in Kiriat Haim.

I arrived at Auschwitz with my father. I was led to the right and he was led to the left. From then on, our real troubles started. I stayed in Auschwitz for six weeks and then was taken to Gelsenkirchen, to a labor camp. After three weeks I was sent to Essen, where I worked too. When the British soldiers approached, the Germans moved us to Bergen-Belsen, where I was liberated by the Seventh Army of General Montgomery. I stayed in the Bergen-Belsen D.P. [Displaced Persons] camp for almost a year. I did not know about anyone of the family worth coming back to. Already then, I wanted to come to Israel. Then suddenly I heard that my sister survived and had gone home. I then went back home too and tried to convince her that we had nothing to look for in Rumania, that she should come with me to Germany and from there to Israel. I left Bergen-Belsen a month before the time that they registered all the remaining survivors of the camp. Because I had already left, I get no pension. Then I got married—

I.R.: Where?

Mrs. Matias: In Rumania. After returning home, I couldn't convince my sister to leave with me, so I stayed there too. I got married and had two sons; we came on aliya to Israel in 1961. My two sons now live close by in Kfar Sava. They have their own families, my grandchildren. I became a widow two years ago, and I too am ill. I hope to go on as best possible with my life. Now, what more shall I tell you?

I.R.: Unless you want to talk about anything in greater detail, I would like to ask some questions.

Mrs. Matias: Then ask me.

I.R.: I wanted to ask you about your religious background. What kind of home was it, what community did you belong to?

Mrs. Matias: We were a traditional family.

I.R.: Were you Orthodox?

Mrs. Matias: Yes, we were Orthodox. My father wore a *shtreimel* and a *kaftan* [Hasidic hat and coat]. My mother wore a wig, but she did not like wearing it; she preferred wearing hats instead. My father inherited the *gabai* [synagogue sexton] post from his grandfather and father. He was the *Talmud-Torah gabai*. So he had to wear a *shtreimel* and a *kaftan* on Shabbat in the synagogue. It was passed on from father to son.

I.R.: The position?

Mrs. Matias: This position, it was a duty of honor. The Talmud Torah was in front of our house. He went to the synagogue but then would not go out anywhere else on Shabbat so as not to go out with this costume. He was a fur merchant, rich, well known. On the one hand he was a scholar of Jewish wisdom, and on the other hand he also had a general education. In the nineteenth century he had a commercial matriculation, which he earned through correspondence courses. I remember that in our home we had a bookcase with Gemara and other sacred books on one side and all the great writers of German culture on the other side. Schiller, Goethe, Heine, Nietzsche, and all of them. We all received an education. I went to a rabbi to learn Hebrew, to read and pray, and I also studied German. In school I studied the languages then taught in foreign schools. But my home was certainly traditional, even more than that.

I.R.: Did you feel the escalation of anti-Semitism in the years preceding the Holocaust and deportations to Auschwitz?

Mrs. Matias: You see, anti-Semitism already existed even at the time when I went to school, when I studied in high school. Once we had an exam about the anatomy of fish, among them the carp. As a Jewish pupil, I got a grade of ten, which was the maximum. Now, when the teacher returned the exams, she called my name, Schwartz, and said, "She has the best exam, but that is no wonder, because Jews eat a lot of fish. They eat fish every Friday evening, they eat gefilte fish. That is why Schwartz knows everything." On another occasion, I was told, "Who do you think you are? You Jews are just barely tolerated here. You don't count." When the Hungarians were in power, we sometimes feared to go out to the street. At one point, Germans passed through our town, retreating after the Stalingrad battle, since we were close to the Polish border. By then we had to wear the yellow badge, so we were afraid to go out, we stayed at home. There was a shortage of food and we did not have enough to eat. We couldn't have non-Jewish servants anymore.

I.R.: And did the deterioration in the situation make you anticipate the events of 1944?

Mrs. Matias: Look, my father always said, "Whoever can, should escape. Run away, children," he said. We had a friend of the family who used to bring us furs and other materials every winter. He invited us to join him in his house in the woods. Although the woods officially belonged to the government, this man was in charge of the place. He offered to bring farmer clothes to my father and myself and said that he would hide us there. My father refused to go himself but urged me to go. I didn't want to go without him, so we both ended up in Auschwitz, like the whole family. We had a big family. My mother had died earlier, but we had two married sisters and two married brothers, all with children. All these were sent to Auschwitz, just like us.

I.R.: Before we started recording, we talked about how strong you were and are. Do you feel you already had it then?

Mrs. Matias: Yes I did.

I.R.: What helped you in the hard times?

Mrs. Matias: In the hard times, do you know what helped me? For one, the fact that I speak and write German and French. I can write German with Gothic letters. One day, when I was working in Bergstadt, doing welding work, there were these iron pieces that we had to weld, arrange in boxes, and put on a carriage. One of us had to take these to the warehouse and a German woman filled in the form to go with them, the delivery note. I stood next to this woman and made sure there were no defective parts, and then I packed them. At noon this woman said to me, "Let's go eat lunch." I said, "I am not allowed to eat with you, I can only eat in the camp in the evening." She went and brought me back something, some biscuits, some water. Someone among the German workers saw that she gave me some food. The German workers weren't allowed to make any contact with us, talk with us, ask us anything. So they took her away and she never returned.

In the afternoon we had to start working again; we started making packages, and there was no one to fill in the forms. So I wrote them myself. Suddenly, some SS men looked at me and asked, "Who wrote these?" I thought, If I deny it, they are going to find out anyway. I decided to step forward and say it was I. "Ja? Wie kommt es, dass Du Deutsch schreiben kanst, noch dazu gotische Schulshcrift [German: Really? How come you can write German and even with Gothic letters]?" I said, "I learned it at home." So the manager told me to continue filling out the forms and also to clean their office. In the office he always left me a package, which I shared with the girls I was working with. Knowing German and French certainly helped me survive.

Besides, I always came back to the girls I worked with, and they would say, "Tell us, tell us something," and I always told them encouraging stories, even if they weren't true, just to keep up their spirits. The work supervisor wanted to hide me when they came to take us away from Bergen-Belsen. I said, "No way. Whatever happens to the others will happen to me as well, I shall not part from them."

I had a very nice coat. Because my coat was very colorful, you couldn't see the swastika on it or the number. Once a girl took my coat and went out to town with it. There was a family there she once had worked for, and now they gave her food, which she shared with us. One Russian prisoner saw her, he noticed my coat, and came to inform the SS that this girl left and went out to town, to Essen. They came for roll call. Now, this girl had a twin sister. When they called out her number, her sister said, "Present," so it worked. But when we stood in rows just before going back to our camp, the Russian soldier came and pointed at my coat. The SS man came over and said, "Where were you, from eight in the morning until two at noon?" I said, "I didn't go anywhere, I was by your side, we had roll call, I counted the girls, and I was next to you." "No, Sage mir die Wahrheit, wo warst Du heute früh von acht bis zwei Uhr? Wenn Du mir nicht die Wahrheit sagst, erschiesse ich Dich [German: Tell me the truth, where were you today between eight in the morning and two in the afternoon? If you don't tell the truth, I will shoot you]." I thought to myself then, Well, they can do me a favor, at least I won't have to suffer anymore. They are going to shoot us all anyway, they won't let us out alive. The SS man started to beat me with his gun while the others behind me were yelling at the twin who took the coat—Raho, that was her name—Raho, don't let Ruth be killed, step forward, or else they are going to kill Ruth.

Suddenly there was a big bombing, we had no shelters and bunkers, so we just scattered everywhere. That air raid saved my life. Then we gathered again to be counted and go back to camp. The SS man told me, "So it wasn't you, but these twins are going to pay for it." It turned out that in the meantime, one girl asked another German worker to go to the SS and tell him not to beat me, because it was not I who had taken the coat but one of the twins who worked with the electrodes. Because, she said, I would rather be beaten to death than tell the truth about the twins. The German worker told this to the SS, and when they gathered us again they called out, "Die beiden Schwestern die mit den Elektroden arbeiten [German: The pair working with the electrodes]." When the sisters came up, they started checking their basket, and found in it civilian clothing, food tickets, and food that wasn't from the camp.

We had another air raid soon after, the whole town was bombed. When we returned to the camp after the air raid, the streetcar we were supposed to ride was gone because it had been bombed. People working in the TODT organization [organization responsible for the roads and transportation in Germany] came toward us, and children were shouting, "The camp is finished, kaput." And there was no camp anymore. Soldiers, SS men, no one was there. So we went in and lay down.

The next day the SS returned and took us back to work. The one who used to take care of me told me he had heard they were going to take us away from there and offered me to stay. I said, "Whatever happens to the other four hundred and ninety nine girls will happen to me too." Then they took us to Bergen-Belsen for five weeks and afterward we were released. In fact, the real troubles began just when we came to Bergen-Belsen; those last five weeks were the worst.

I.R.: In what way?

Mrs. Matias: Because we did not get any food, and there was typhus all over.

I.R.: Was this after liberation?

Mrs. Matias: No, these were the last five weeks *before* liberation. After that, the English soldiers came and took us to hospitals, washed us, for we were full of lice. Every one of us had such bad diarrhea that, pardon me, we couldn't reach the toilets no matter how hard we tried. We were lying there, and as one person tried to climb over the other to get to the toilet, she soiled her. I too contracted typhus and lost weight until I weighed twenty-seven kilograms. When I was able to stand on my feet and they weighed me, I weighed twenty-seven kilograms, and in addition I had an eye disease. I didn't realize it at the time, but we had been working in welding and they gave us no protective glasses, so my eyes became inflamed and I started going blind. Then I said,

"Now that I have been liberated, I don't want to live as a blind person, I'd rather jump off the upper floor and die." So they watched over me to make sure that I wouldn't jump. A young Belgian doctor came up to me and asked where I had worked. I thought he meant at home and replied that at home I was still too young and did not work. So he said, "No, in the camps." I said, "Oh, I welded with welding sticks." Then he realized that the nerves in both my eyes got hurt because of the strong light.

I.R.: And then were they able to help you?

Mrs. Matias: Yes, they helped but now the situation is bad again, my eyes are bad again. Now, how do I know if this is a result of the welding or is it my age? I am seventy-one years old already.

I.R.: I wish you good health.

Mrs. Matias: Healthy I shall not be, but I still have a strong will, to the point of . . . For example, I tell my children, "Whatever others can do, you can too. Let that be the motto of your lives." For example, my son won the Ackerman prize in school for a paper he wrote about the Holocaust. As for myself, I let no obstacle stand in my way. Whenever I had a goal, I reached it.

I.R.: Was that since your experiences in the Holocaust or even before?

Mrs. Matias: I always had a strong will.

I.R.: After the war, what did you think and feel about the Holocaust?

Mrs. Matias: Listen, I'll tell you what I thought and felt. When I lived with my husband in Rumania after the war, there was a period when we were well off in Temesvár. We had our own small house. It was a big thing to have a house all to ourselves. Temesvár was the second important city after Bucharest. It was like having a house in Jerusalem. I had everything, I didn't lack for anything, and still I wanted to come here. I told my husband, "I want to do it, I want to take the two boys out of here. Let everything stay here, I don't care."

I.R.: Did you have to persuade him?

Mrs. Matias: He was Zionist. And I did not want to be a "Jew," a "dirty Jew." I wanted to go to my own country, where I would be like everyone else. Then we came here and we became "Hungarian," "Igen, migen." And there were Polish, Russian, Yemenite, and Moroccan Jews.

I.R.: Did your children show interest in your past?

Mrs. Matias: No. I cannot say it wasn't difficult at the beginning and that I didn't regret coming here and leaving everything there. There I had everything, and here I came and became a housemaid. I couldn't do anything else because I didn't know the language. They wanted to send me to *ulpan* [Hebrew course]. A very nice official, originally from Rumania, tried to help me out. His name was Dejő Son, he wanted me to learn Hebrew. He said that I should learn Hebrew and then his wife Nehama would find me a job at a school as a housemother, or a clerk at a hospital, or in a warehouse, but first—I needed to know the language. But I said, "What shall I do with the two children? I cannot throw them out to the street so that I can go to *ulpan*." Then my husband started working in the Ma'agan factory and I had no other choice but to be a housemaid. I was always a very good housewife, and I had maids in Rumania. So now I became a maid myself, so that my children should not lack for anything, so they shouldn't look at their friends who eat yellow cheese, for example, and feel sorry that we cannot afford it.

I.R.: Didn't they ask about your past?

Mrs. Matias: Not so much. After we came here and things were difficult, I once said that if I could get my house back in Rumania, I'd go back. To that both my sons said, "Without us, *we're* not going back!" My older son went on a trip with school when we first came here; we arrived in May and he went on the trip in June. He went to the Galilee to Trumpeldor's grave. When he returned, he told me in Rumanian, "Mom, do you know what a beautiful country we have? And every leaf of grass is saturated with the blood of the Jewish boys who fought to win the country." Both my sons became patriotic immediately. In the Six Days' War it was I who said that we had no choice, this is our home and here we shall live or die, as the Hungarian anthem goes.

But in this war [the Gulf War], I told them, "We are old, don't pay any attention to us. You are young, save yourselves, leave." Then my younger son said, "Mom, you talk like that, the big patriot? And who will stay, the old? Shall we leave the country we fought so hard for; shall we leave it behind us as easy loot for our enemies? That is impossible. And *you*, who was such a big patriot, *you* can say this?" I say, "Children, you should leave this country; here will be wars every two or three years." The other night I was talking with my son and asked him, "Moshe, what will be with us, what will be?" He said, "Whatever happens to everyone else will happen to us too. Nothing will happen."

I.R.: Let us hope so.

Mrs. Matias: Hope, that is what sustains us.

I.R.: Now a more general question. It is difficult to understand the Holocaust. Even historians find it hard to explain how the Holocaust could happen. Did you ever think about it, look for an answer?

Mrs. Matias: I thought about it. It happened because we didn't stand up for ourselves. First of all, the Jews themselves weren't united. Besides, we did not behave like the Arabs here. If we got on a streetcar, we shrank so as not to be noticed, not to disturb anyone.

I.R.: Even before the war?

Mrs. Matias: Even before the war. This is why the Holocaust occurred. If we had more courage, we would have obtained weapons, at least tried to . . . Then, we had no weapons, they stuffed us in cattle cars, eighty people, old, young, children in one cattle car. First they sent the young to labor camps. What did it matter? Either way they gassed us. We should have rebelled, with knives, to pick out the eyes of the Hungarian supervisors or the Nazi SS men.

I.R.: Did you think so then as well?

Mrs. Matias: Yes, I thought so then too, but there was no one to guide me. In vain did my father say, "Children, run away." Where could we go?

I.R.: Did your beliefs change?

Mrs. Matias: I became an atheist immediately after deportation because of all the terrible things I saw. For example, my father was a well-known man in Sziget for his good deeds. If someone came begging for money, he would say, "Surely this person is in need." If they had to marry off a girl, to give a dowry for the wedding, immediately they turned to Gershon Schwartz. If a preacher came to the synagogue, he would stay at our house for the Sabbath. It was always the same: My father never wronged a soul. And not only was he wronged, but also so many small innocent children. I saw it with my own eyes, they caught them by their feet, banged them against the wall and their brains split open. What did they do, how did they sin? I became faithless. Now I am fatalist. Whatever has to happen shall happen, and nothing in the world, no force is able to prevent it. Whatever is fated for someone, be it by God or fate, shall come true, shall haunt you and get you in the end.

I.R.: And what can a person do?

Mrs. Matias: Nothing.

I.R.: Do one's best?

Mrs. Matias: Do one's best. I like people and love to help. I pity them, but I rebel against a superior Will. How can a person deserve so much suffering? I cannot look into the souls of others, cannot see their sufferings, but I see myself, what I went through, why do I deserve it? Do you know that in the camps I always helped others? Did you know? I was with a girl who was not a hundred percent sane. People like this have a big appetite, and for nights she cried that she was hungry. I did not want to go and ask, especially not from this supervisor. But someone intervened and told the supervisor, "See Ruthy Schwartz, how she suffers, how hungry she is? Give her a bowl of soup." So the supervisor says, "Do you think that you are still the daughter of Gershon Schwartz, who saunters through the corridors with her new stockings and suits ordered from Budapest? Let her come and ask." I did not want to go and ask. But when I saw how this girl suffered, I did go and told her, "Rozsie, I'm hungry, give me a bowl of food, of potatoes." She said, "I'll give it to you, but you must gobble it up here in front of me."

I.R.: Couldn't you say that it was meant for another girl?

Mrs. Matias: No. She said, "Eat it up right here, in front of me." I said, "No, Rozsy. I cannot eat so much at once. I'll eat some today and some tomorrow," and I took it to that girl. I woke her up, she was sleeping and sobbing, and I told her, "Rozsie,"—for her name too was Rozsie—"Take it, eat." Now, she had a sister called Lucy who now lives in America and we correspond to this day. Once I got a loaf of bread from a French soldier who told us to share it among the girls who worked in welding. The three of us were working there, these two sisters and I. I wanted to cut the bread into three pieces, but the sister with whom I correspond said, "No, Rozsie shouldn't have any, because she isn't here." I said, "So how do you want us to divide it, into two?" She said, "Yes." And I swear—so help me God if God exists, as I always say—I gave her half and shared my half with Rozsie, her sister. She didn't want to share with her own sister. "Rozsie isn't here, she doesn't deserve any."

I.R.: Did you witness incidents of inhuman behavior, among you?

Mrs. Matias: Yes, I saw a girl hitting her mother. The mother would not eat anything but gave her entire ration to her daughter, and still, if the mother took as much as one spoon of food for herself, the daughter hit her. How come she did not give her mother all of it?

I.R.: And how did other women respond, did anyone try to interfere, say something?

Mrs. Matias: No, they didn't, and even if they did, it didn't help. The mother would defend her daughter, be angry at our interference, "Don't mix in, I'm not hungry."

I.R.: Did your feelings change after you came here, to Israel?

Mrs. Matias: Not at the beginning. For example, consider this incident. I wanted my son to go to a boarding school, to learn Hebrew. The family advised me to do this. I asked for a school near Kfar Sava belonging to the Mizrahi youth movement, because I wanted him to have a traditional education, I wanted him to learn about Judaism. Well, they sent him far away up north. It seemed too far to me, so I spoke with the clerk at Youth Aliya. I said the boy had never been so far away from home, how come you sent him there? He may even run away. She replied, "If he runs away, we shall bring him back, and besides, Nous n'avons pas besoin de jeunes demoiselles [French:] we don't need spoiled young kids but youth who are ready for anything."

So I found the Kfar Avraham Institute for him. He later wanted to become an airplane engineer, even in Rumania he had talked about it, but here I needed the means for that, and Kfar Avraham could not equip him with the suitable education to become an engineer. So in 1965 he transferred to the Air Force Technical School. In the Six Days' War he was such a good technician and so full of motivation that he was sent almost everywhere. He once was called to take apart a Russian airplane that was later sent to the States to be checked up. He got compliments for his work. He has been working in the Bedek Aviation Group for twenty-three years. He was among the first to work on jet-commanders, although later they had to close this department for lack of orders and he had to move to another department. This is it, and now we can have some coffee.

Yoseph and Leah Heiman. Originally from Szolnok, Hungary. Interviewed in Netanya, Israel, October 1989 (The couple lives in Jerusalem, Israel)

(Translated from Hebrew and Hungarian)

Yoseph Haiman: I was born in 1922 in Szolnok, one hundred kilometers east of Budapest. The Jewish population in town consisted of about two thousand people. There was a Jewish school for grades one to four. Then you went on in the regular junior high or high school. Some people went to university. The Jews had their typical occupations. Most of them were merchants. Some were intellectuals, lawyers, doctors, officials. We spoke Hungarian. Although some also spoke Yiddish or German, usually all our education and culture were in Hungarian. People were active in educational organizations. They liked to go to the movies and the theater. There were concerts and even a town orchestra in which many Jews took part. Children, depending on the financial situation of their families, went to music schools. In general, though, we didn't have any artists or exceptional people in our community.

Before the war, there was a lot of assimilation. Jewish young men married Christian girls, and Jewish girls married Christian men. Some left the Jewish religion too. There were two main groups in the Jewish community. One was of modern Jews, called Neologists. They had a huge modern synagogue, with a chorus and an organ. They also had a rabbi—and the rabbi objected to Zionism. Then you had the Orthodox synagogue for the "Keepers of Religion." But this religious group was very small, it only consisted of about thirty or forty people. They had only one person to carry out the functions of cantor, rabbi, and *shochet* [ritual slaughterer].

Ilana Rosen: Which rabbi was anti-Zionist?

Mr. Heiman: The Conservative. The Neologists were against Zionism. I remember well that in the early thirties, an organization called "the Szolnok Jewish Youth" organized lectures once a month. It was an opportunity for the young people to meet and listen to lectures. At the beginning of the thirties just a few of us were Zionist. Once there was a lecture about *Eretz Israel* [the Land of Israel]. Many young people came to listen.

I.R.: Meaning, you too among them?

Mrs. Heiman: I too was there. The speaker started to speak about the Land of Israel, about its future. The rabbi was present and so was the man in charge of education and culture in our community. And they did not want to listen to this lecture. The rabbi stood up and asked the chairman to stop the lecture.

I.R.: The Conservative rabbi?

Mr. Heiman: Yes, the Conservative rabbi. The atmosphere became really tense. Otherwise it was democratic, usually anyone could speak about whatever subject they wanted. But in this incident, to honor the rabbi, they stopped the lecture about *Eretz Israel*. This is the general picture of the Jews of Szolnok until World War II.

Myself, I was born into a poor family. I was the fifth child [laughs] and the worst of them. I gave my mother a lot of grief, because I was the youngest and received too much attention. So I was spoiled and not very well behaved. I went to the Jewish school. I wasn't such a good pupil but was always interested in religious studies. In religion, my grades were good. All the rest was bad [laughs].

Mrs. Heiman: He was bad in mathematics.

Mr. Heiman: Right, but that's not relevant now. Then I went to junior high school and finished my studies there. In the Jewish elementary school we studied religion every day, but in the junior high we only had religious studies twice a week, when I studied in a *Talmud Torah* learning institute after regular school. The *Talmud Torah* wasn't compulsory, of course, but my parents insisted that I go. When I finished junior high school, I went to learn a profession, and I've worked in it ever since.

By 1943, we already had all the new laws and regulations against the Jews. Young Jewish men couldn't enroll in the army, but only in the labor battalions. I, too, went to a labor battalion from July 1943 until they released us in 1945. We were in Austria near Wels. I was also in a labor battalion in Transylvania near Szászregen. There was a German headquarters near us and we worked in the airport. What next?

I.R.: What happened after that?

Mr. Heiman: In September 1944 the Russian army approached our camp, which was in Transylvania. The Hungarians then marched us away from there on a route of retreat from September until December 1944. We were in several places in Hungary. We went through Körmend, which is in trans-Danube [westward of the Danube]. This was close to the Austrian border. Shall I continue to our passage through Austria?

I.R.: And all this time you were still single? Meaning, since when are you two together?

Mr. Heiman: Now I'll talk about our shared history. In September 1945 I met my future wife and we married. We lived in Szolnok and had two children, a son in 1948 and a daughter in 1954. Then we came to Israel. This was because I had gone through so much torture and trouble that after the war, after my release, I didn't want to stay in Hungary anymore.

I.R.: What do you mean by torture?

Mr. Heiman: The labor battalions. We didn't want to live there anymore, and we wanted to come to Israel. Now in 1948 we had our son, and he was ill since birth. We wanted to move to Israel, but because of our son's medical condition we couldn't do it. We couldn't fulfill our dream. So we stayed in Hungary but never gave up the idea to come when it became possible. The Hungarian policy was against emigration. They closed the borders and we couldn't leave, couldn't have a passport, couldn't even ask for it in the Communist regime. We had no other choice. I was working in a governmental factory. In 1954 our first daughter was born, and all this time I was looking for ways to leave the country. For example, because my father was not born in Hungary but in Poland, I thought I could receive a foreign passport. I looked for a way. But the Hungarian authorities said that since that part of Poland where my father was born belonged at the time to the Austro-Hungarian Empire, then it is considered Hungary, no matter where it belongs to now. Still, I did not lose hope.

At last the Hungarian Revolution came in October 1956, on the 23rd of

October. There was a revolt against the Communist regime. Then I felt that the time was ripe for moving. But everything was a mess then. I couldn't travel from my town to Budapest; there was no transportation, and there were other problems. But deep down, in my heart and soul, I felt and believed that one more day, one more week, one more month, and we'll be able to leave. At the end of 1956, in December, there was an opportunity to travel to Budapest. I then consulted Jewish friends and asked about the possibilities of leaving to Israel, and they told me that at that time there was a possibility to get a passport. I grasped the opportunity; we got the passports and came to Israel in 1957, right after Passover. We are here since then, and we feel part of the Jewish Israeli people. We even received a welcome gift, another daughter, in 1959. [The couple giggle.]

Mrs. Heiman: But she went far away from us.

I.R.: Jewish fate.

Mr. Heiman: We are a people scattered in the diaspora. What next?

I.R.: Why was it difficult to leave until 1956 and why did it become easier then?

Mr. Heiman: In 1948 the Communists came to power. There was a Communist regime. They did not acknowledge a Jewish people or religion. In the Communist regime, there were no such things. Naturally, if you wanted to leave, you had to ask for a legal passport, but they simply refused to give me a passport. First, they said I was still young, and second, there is no reason to leave because there is no anti-Semitism.

I.R.: So they said.

Mr. Heiman: So they said formally.

Mrs. Heiman: But there was anti-Semitism.

Mr. Heiman: There were young people who escaped.

I.R.: Jews?

Mr. Heiman: Jews, yes. You could escape through Czechoslovakia. But since we had two small children and a coward wife, it couldn't be done. With small children it was almost impossible. There were some people who left with small children, gave them sleeping pills.

Mrs. Heiman: And some children never woke up.

Mr. Heiman: And thus they passed the Czechoslovak border. It sometimes happened that a child woke up when they were almost there. The child would start to cry and they were noticed and caught.

I.R.: And then, what happened to those who were caught?

Mr. Heiman: Those who were caught by the Hungarian guards, at first they weren't punished severely, because they had small children. So they were sent home. They weren't tried or imprisoned. But there were others—for example our neighbors, whose daughter escaped too. She went another way, the wrong way, and she tried to escape via the Austrian border. It was very dangerous to escape through there, so she got three months in prison. It was better to escape in the direction of Czechoslovakia, because the guards there weren't so strict. Through Austria not just Jews escaped, but also Christians who opposed the regime, and the watch on that border was very strong.

Now in 1948, after they closed the border and created the "iron curtain," there was still an immigration movement called *aliyat Haggana*. Those were all young people. In 1948, you know, they needed young people here in Israel. There weren't enough young people. Those young men, who were already in the army, knew how to escape through the Austrian border, they were people who could manage—they could say they were *Haggana* people. Many young people, men and women, passed through that route, through the Austrian border. Then later, they closed the "iron curtain" hermetically, but you could still escape through Czechoslovakia.

I.R.: Were you in touch with anyone in Israel throughout that period?

Mr. Heiman: Yes, we were in touch with Israel all the time. We had family, meaning an aunt, who came to Israel through an agreement that included two thousand souls. Two thousand people were allowed to leave Hungary to Israel. For example, people who had close relatives in Israel. If a son or daughter were living here, then they could send affidavits to their parents. But brothers and sisters, for example, couldn't. Parents could send for their children, or children for their parents. Thus, some two thousand souls left Hungary in the years 1952, 1953. Our aunt left too, because her son was here since 1949. He also escaped through Czechoslovakia. If you want, I can tell you which way.

I.R.: Yes, please do.

Mr. Heiman: This aunt was still living here, and we were corresponding constantly. We were in constant touch and knew what was going on. This aunt's son, he was a young man in his twenties. There was an agricultural *hachshara* course in Györ, a place close to the Danube, and the Danube there was on the border with Czechoslovakia. Of these *hachshara* people, naturally all the participants wanted to come to Israel. But there was the "iron curtain," there were no possibilities. Still, he was in touch with the *Sochnut*, and in 1949, on the first Seder, all the participants of the *Hachshara* group took a boat and crossed the Danube to Czechoslovakia. They stayed in Czechoslovakia for a few days, after the first Seder. They stayed in Pozsony. My cousin came here this way. I could tell you more about it. After the revolution in 1956, not everyone who came had a passport, because the Hungarians limited them. They only gave passports to those older than thirty-five. Those who were younger couldn't receive a passport. These could only escape illegally. At that time, it was somewhat easier to escape because the "iron curtain" was temporarily raised and you could leave. The guard-patrols weren't serious, and there were guides from the villages on the border who knew the way.

I.R.: And this aunt's son?

Mr. Heiman: He came in 1949 and she in 1954.

I.R.: So they were your Israeli contact.

Mr. Heiman: Yes, throughout. What else would you like to know?

I.R.: Now it depends on how you wish to proceed, but I am also interested in Julishka's [Leah Heiman's] life history, and then hear what happened next to both of you.

Mr. Heiman: Well, you can now tell about our life after 1956.

I.R.: This is when you were together already, but I'd like to know about Julishka's life during the time she wasn't yet married to you.

Leah Heiman: Well, my family was just as poor as his family.

Mr. Heiman: The Hungarian saying goes: For two poor people to have a third and a fourth [child] is success. You needn't dwell on the poverty. Talk about school, you studied too.

Mrs. Heiman: I went to school in Szolnok and studied eight years.

Mr. Heiman: You finished school and then had a job at my aunt's. You should talk into the microphone.

Mrs. Heiman: I know. We were nine brothers and sisters and we received a good education. I went to school, studied eight grades. There, if you studied for eight years, you needed to study two more to get a certificate, but I wasn't able to study further. By then I was thirteen and went to work at his aunt's shop, instead of finishing the last two years of school. She had a crafts shop. I did some of the housework and helped at the shop. Then, what can I say, the years passed. I worked there for two years and then got married, but the marriage didn't work out. So after two, two and a half years, I divorced him. I had a daughter who is a grandmother today. Then war broke out, it was terrifying. Then I met—

Mr. Heiman: But wait, why don't you talk about the war in Budapest?

Mrs. Heiman: During the war, in 1944, we hid in Budapest with my sister.

I.R.: Who is "we"?

Mrs. Heiman: My daughter and I.

Mr. Heiman: Her daughter.

Mrs. Heiman: This went on until the Russians came. When the Russians liberated us, we were very happy. After a few months my future husband returned and we got to know each other. It turned out we lived close to each other and I knew his parents, and like Jews, we all belonged to the same community. We married in 1945 just before Rosh Hashanah. After the war, at first I worked for the Joint, we cooked for those who returned by themselves and didn't have any relatives. I worked there and lived at my sister's with my daughter of my first marriage. Then, my future husband returned and we married in 1945. Then our children were born. First we had a son and then a daughter. And just as my husband said, we went on with our lives.

I.R.: Meaning that you agree with everything he said?

Mrs. Heiman: Yes, all of it. I am not a good interviewee.

I.R.: Everyone can be a good interviewee.

Mr. Heiman: After the ending of the Second World War, in 1945, emissaries from Israel came to our town and community. We had a few Communist Parties, and some other parties. The Jewish youth received a Jewish education and we learned the history of the land and the people. I can say that this was a very important education. We also had an *ulpan*. The young people arranged courses and meetings, and everyone without exception was in some Zionist framework or activity. I had my roots in religion and Jewish history, and after hearing these lectures my roots went even deeper and I missed living in Israel. Most of the youth of our community did emigrate to Israel. They participated in the wars, as early as 1956, and today their own children serve in the army.

I.R.: When you were about to come to Israel, what did you expect, what did you feel? And did your attitude change after you arrived?

Mrs. Heiman: We had great expectations.

Mr. Heiman: Before we came, we didn't have many expectations. I lived through great difficulties in the Holocaust so that when I came here to Israel, whatever I had was good and there were no disappointments. I worked hard and what I imagined did come true. After our aliya, we received an apartment in Beit-Shemesh. It was a very small place then. So with the help of an acquaintance I came to work in Jerusalem. In this place I met the Rosberger family [the author's family]. They too were of Hungarian origins. I could say that we received much help and attention from them, which helped our absorption.

I.R.: Did you know other people? How did they help you?

Mr. Heiman: Because we knew very little Hebrew, it was difficult for us to make official arrangements, and there were many official arrangements to make for our future. We had to change our housing, ask for loans, etc. Mrs. Rosberger did not mind spending hours and days with us. She went to all these places with us, translated for us, and helped us so much that we will never forget her. When our Malka was born, your father [to I.R.] was working in that shift at the hospital. My wife didn't know a word of Hebrew besides *Shalom*. Your father came and was ready to help us with whatever was needed. We will never forget that. By chance, there was no Hungarian speaker at the hospital at the time, only your father.

I.R.: Did you want to leave Beit-Shemesh?

Mr. Heiman: Yes, of course. We came to Beit-Shemesh straight from the ship. Beit-Shemesh was an entirely new place. There was nothing there. We saw that the situation was difficult, with four souls in the family and nothing to do, so we had to leave. I already knew a certain place for work in Jerusalem, so I went there and got the job. This was in April 1957. After a few months we moved to Jerusalem, and since then we are Jerusalemites. There was nothing to miss in Beit-Shemesh, because there was nothing to do there. People actually ran away from there. There was one family that arrived just before us. They arrived on Thursday afternoon, and by Friday morning they were gone and we never saw them again.

Mrs. Heiman: Everyone had someone to go to.

Mr. Heiman: They went to Holon, Netanya, Haifa, Beer-Sheva. The officials on the ship called each family and inquired about their situation. Because we had two children, they recommended that we go to a kibbutz. I could accept anything, except for living on a kibbutz. No way. My nature is such that I hate crowds, I can't be around more than three people in my close environment without getting nervous. It is a nice place, the kibbutz, no problems, nothing to worry about. But everything is always the same, the same people, all is the same. For me it is like a labor camp, everything is always the same. It is good to visit the kibbutz, stay for two, three, four, or five hours, and that's it. It's a psychological thing I have since the Holocaust. I don't like to live in a cooperative framework, and I don't want to live in such a small community. Tell me what else you need.

I.R.: Once here, what did you lack, what was difficult?

Mr. Heiman: The situation is such that we are here since 1957, and we never missed Hungary, never dreamed of going back there, nor do we have plans of going to any other country. Of course, life has its ups and downs, but we wish to go on living just here.

I.R.: Do you have any family abroad?

Mr. Heiman: There is a cousin in Canada. None of my brothers returned from the Holocaust. One sister moved to the States, she already died. There are a few nephews, but they are not young. They have no intentions of coming here.

I.R.: How did you raise your children here?

Mr. Heiman: In fact, the children helped us [the couple laugh]. We had limitations, because we never went to *ulpan* intensively and couldn't help our children in Hebrew. I had to explain to them that my Hebrew was poor. But we did teach them about how a person should behave, the difference between right and wrong. Thank God, all three children are fine people. My son and my older daughter served in the army. My son has three children. He stayed in the army. Our older daughter married too, went to live on a kibbutz and has three children. Religion is very important to us. We are both Sabbath observers. Our son and older daughter are not religiously observant, but they know about tradition and religion. Of our three children only our younger daughter follows our religious practices. Our parents were more religious than us, we are less than them. Still, we are Sabbath observers and adhere to *mitzvot* [religious dictates].

I.R.: How would you sum up your life?

Mr. Heiman: Well, thank God we have three children. The most important thing for us is that we were able to bring them up. Also, I passed on to my children things I learned myself, like honesty, and the love for Israel. Thank God, even those two of my children who are not religious still know what it means to be Jewish, even though they are not observant Jews. Their lives went other ways, and we cannot force our way on them.

Dr. Ernő, Anna, and Mrs. Bihari. Originally from Szombathely, Hungary. Interviewed in Budapest, September 1991

(Translated from Hungarian)

Dr. Ernő Bihari: I was born in Szombathely, a provincial Hungarian town which then had about fifty thousand citizens. Now there are much more. In my family there were three brothers and a sister. I also had another brother, who died before I was born. There was a typhus epidemic in Szombathely, which killed many of the people in town. Two of my brothers contracted the disease and one of them died of it. The other survived the disease, became stronger and lived on. Of the four children born before me, three survived, and I was born in 1910. So there were four of us children until the Holocaust. We didn't stay together, because they got married, had children; the family grew, spread around. I will later say where to.

Now, since I concentrate on myself, I was born in 1910, before World War I. My parents had a grocery shop. Our parents worked in the shop and we children were asked to help in the shop at rather early ages. Personally, I think it was too early for us. Our parents were middle class, small bourgeoisie, not real bourgeoisie, and they worked hard. Then, in pre- and postwar Hungary, people were poor, just as now. Problems started with the breaking out of World War I. World War I broke out in 1914, and Hungary became involved in the war. [Dr. Bihari gives a historical survey of the reasons for the war and goes beyond his own personal history.] I was then four years old. I did not go to kindergarten, I don't know why. But my parents did take care of me. We had a housekeeper. We weren't, I say, rich, but we could afford this, because my parents had a shop. The housekeeper looked after the house, looked after my brothers and sister and myself; we weren't neglected.

After 1914, my brothers went to school, because they were older. My older brother was born in 1901, the second in 1903. My sister was born in 1905, and I in 1910. With our parents, this was the family. We had relatives on my mother's side across the Danube. My father came from a place called Sümeg. They met in 1898, got married, and started the shop. They worked hard, as I said. We went to school and grew up. My older brother, I think, when did he start school? I think in 1906, my second brother in 1908. I am not sure that these are the exact dates, I should have prepared better, but these are the years, approximately. Then my sister started school, and finally I too started school in 1916, in the midst of the war.

In those days, Szombathely was a complete reflection of the war atmosphere. When soldiers were drafted, they had to report to a base near town. Then, when they were given short vacations, they also came into town. So we saw a lot of soldiers. All of my uncles were soldiers who served in World War I and then came back and started their lives anew. Life started in Hungary again after the war, and there was this peace treaty that had severe implications for

Hungary. Hungary, which before the war had 300,000 square kilometers, shrunk into a country of 90,000 square kilometers. This was imposed by a terrible Parisian peace treaty, dictated by whom?

Mrs. Bihari: Clemenceau?

Dr. Bihari: Clemenceau, the French president, the Austro-Hungarian Empire's big enemy. They divided Hungary up. Yugoslavia was born as a result of this peace treaty. [Dr. Bihari again discusses history, this time the creation of Yugoslavia. This concerns him, as the interview is conducted during the civil war in Yugoslavia and the events in this war affect Hungary and are widely discussed in the country. At some point I remind Dr. Bihari that the subject of the interview is supposed to be his own life and not Hungarian history.] Yes, I was just showing you the framework of my life. So, as I said, I was born in 1910 and went to school in 1916. At that time in Szombathely the main subjects in high school were Latin, Hungarian, German, Greek. I do not count the secondary subjects.

After high school, I enrolled in university to study medicine. This was quite complicated, because in order to be accepted, it was not enough just to pass admittance exams. You needed "influence" or connections, and I had none, because in Hungary, which had just lost World War I, there were anti-Semitism and persecution of Jews. This subsided slowly, with the years. Since I wasn't accepted in Hungary, I started university in Vienna, in the University of Vienna. I finished one year in Vienna, took my exams, and then was able to transfer, because of some connections, to a Hungarian university. After finishing my university studies, I chose to become a dentist, which needed further studies. I opened a clinic, a private clinic in Szombathely, in my parents' town. Still, I couldn't ensure a stable and consistent living in that community. So I moved from Szombathely to Budapest after World War II, and here I worked in a government clinic [under the Communist regime]. Eventually, I retired and now [after the fall of the Communists], I opened a private clinic at age eighty-one, an age at which most people don't work anymore.

I met my wife in 1947. We got married. My wife was born in Budapest. She finished school in Budapest. She lived there with her parents and a sister close to her age, so that they grew up together more or less. Thus they lived and grew up like friends. Now, we met and got married. During our marriage we had two sons. They are adults by now. They are married too. One of them is a doctor too, a surgeon. He started his work as a physician in quite good conditions, since he got his job immediately after receiving his diploma, and has practiced surgery ever since then. He got a job in the Jewish hospital, which is a sectarian, private hospital. He was lucky. He was trained by very good professors, some of them are already dead by now. But he received a good training and he is a well-known surgeon here in Budapest. He goes to conferences. [Throughout this part Mrs. Bihari helps him out in details he seems to forget.] Is this disturbing you, that my wife helps me with some of the details?

I.R.: No, it's natural.

Dr. Bihari: And my son has been to Europe, America, West Germany, where he gives lectures and is known because his articles appear in professional journals abroad. People who have read him look him up in the hospital here and want to come and learn from him. He too has a family, he has . . .

Mrs. Bihari: Two sons and a daughter.

Dr. Bihari: Two sons and a daughter, who are teenagers at present, go to high school, growing up.

Mrs. Bihari: His wife is a physician too.

Dr. Bihari: My second son is a translator working with many languages. He wanted to be a painter. My waiting room is full of his paintings. He has been painting since a very early age. Now his occupation is translation. He works for a company, with many languages, English, German, Russian. Russian was in those years a first foreign language, which isn't the case anymore. Unfortunately, he does not know any Hebrew. I have grandchildren from him as well. I hope they study well, because I was a very good pupil. My surgeon son, when he started to operate in medical school, the professor who supervised him said, "I hope you follow in the footsteps of your father."

Hungarian life goes on as in the rest of the world. Thank God, there are no upheavals or revolutions in our country, except that our border is hectic from the civil war in nearby Yugoslavia. Anti-Semitism, which does exist here and in Europe, is at least of the latent kind, which has not developed into overt persecution of Jews. But it is enough that the Jewish "issue" is brought up in the work environment, and the entire day is ruined for you. Sometimes someone cannot get a job they are qualified for, only because they are Jewish. But this is the way things seem to be now. Maybe we are not actively persecuted thanks to leaders abroad, maybe thanks to the existence of Israel, which we feel is ours even though we don't live there. But we are proud and will continue to be proud to see the progress over the years in Israel. I haven't been there yet, but many friends and acquaintances have, and they came back with awe. I don't want you to think this is just flattery, it's a well-known thing. Here anti-Semitism seems to have shrunk. Israelis have a hard time, and Israeli leaders work hard. America, on the other hand, changes its tune frequently—sometimes pro-Israel, sometimes not.

I.R.: Don't you want to talk about the war years and the labor battalions?

Dr. Bihari: Oh, yes, I forgot.

I.R.: I don't want to pressure you.

Dr. Bihari: No, I forgot it, thank you for reminding me. I already reached the point when I opened a clinic, like this one in Pest, and I worked mornings and afternoons, which was allowed, the same as now, until suddenly the world went mad and World War I, I mean II, broke out. This ignited anti-Semitism to the point that they recruited everyone to the army, all those of suitable age, but the Jews were recruited differently; they built separate camps for them. Those were labor camps, and their service was in labor battalions. I was there too. Imagine: from the dentist's clinic, from the dentist's chair and the dentist's tools, right into the war, in one day. I was called to a place in this area in a camp with very bad conditions. Then I was lucky not to be alone, because the Jews were separated from the others. Luckily for us we were in another part of the camp; the Christians were separated from us, and eventually they were sent to the front quite early. There, too, there were many casualties. But to return to our point of view, it was quite horrible, because we lay on the earth and in the dirt, and who knows what. It was the same for all those from a similar background: doctors, lawyers, teachers. It was good that we were of the same occupations and mentality. The women stayed at home. The women were at home, and I served for three years.

Suddenly, it all ended and we came back home. In Szombathely, after I just arrived, I contracted typhus. I spent about six weeks in the hospital. When I left the hospital, not only did I not have any clothes, I didn't have food either. The Jewish organizations and the Joint were active, but not for the "rich" dentist, for they considered me to be rich, although by then I wasn't rich but broke. I couldn't get anything, because others were in greater need. When I was released from the hospital, I looked for my dental clinic. I could only find the place where it had stood, because the house had split into two in a bombing. It turned out that the Germans had broken into the place, turned it into a military dental clinic. They took all the tools, stole them. They also stole everything from the apartment, and so did the Hungarians. But luckily there were still some tools left; I found a few things and I started again, and at first I used the apartment. At first there were also some refugees there, but they left and the house became empty. Friends helped me gather up things, put them together, and I started to work in my profession again. I succeeded immediately. That was in 1945, at the end of the war. Until then I was by myself, but at that time, the war's ending, I met my future wife and we got married.

I started all on my own, because it's a good occupation, working as a dentist. Patients come to you, and if you can work and you have the skill, then you are successful. Well, within a few years I reached a state which enabled me to marry and support my wife. Her family lived here, together with Zsuzsiká's [Hungarian folklorist Zsuzsánna Tátrai, our contact] parents. Then they were in the shelter, suffered the bombing, she may have told you already.

We got married and the children were born. My wife suddenly said, "Are we going to stay here, in this town?" She was born in [Buda]Pest and all her acquaintances were there. Whereas I, of all my childhood family, I was the only one left, only me. All the men in my family were drafted to the labor battalions, and those labor battalion camps were bombed, all of them. I'm sure that much was written about this in Israel too, and you should know that whatever they wrote, the reality was much worse. Terrible things were done by the Nazis and their partners, which included the Hungarians. All my brothers were killed in

Hungary. Of my parents, my father died already in 1927. My mother was taken to Auschwitz. There in Auschwitz, she was killed by the gas. I had a sister as I mentioned. She in the meantime got married, had a nice family, three, four daughters at the ages of four, five, at the time of the war. My brother-in-law arrived at Auschwitz. The children to Auschwitz. All of them were taken immediately to the gas chambers. They took my mother immediately, from the train to the gas chambers. Meaning, this is how the family was wiped out and this is how I came home. Completely alone.

My brother-in-law survived. He was a doctor too, and as a doctor, he was exempt from the hard work. He worked in first aid and wasn't put to do hard physical work. At the end of the war, these survivors were found hungry, sick with typhus, and in rags. They rehabilitated these survivors, my brother-in law included, in Sweden. I corresponded with him. He wrote me his first letter when I was still in Szombathely; he mailed the letter to me and my brothers and those who survived of the family. I received his letter. He wrote that he was alive, but to his sorrow his wife was dead, exterminated in the gas chambers [crying]. Imagine, we had once been a real extended family, and then they murdered most of us. Many people had brothers, parents, at least one parent who survived. Brothers and sisters can visit each other. I had nobody. I kept saying that I was going home to Szombathely, but where did I really go? I had no home in Szombathely to go to. That is how I lived since the time I came back alone after the war. I reached a sad part.

I.R.: It's true.

Dr. Bihari: And to talk about it, honestly, makes you cry. Well, now you can ask me questions.

I.R.: Why do you think the Holocaust happened?

Dr. Bihari: I thought a lot about it. But the situation is the following. In the previous century, Hungary was part of the Austro-Hungarian Empire. There weren't many Jews in the Empire in the nineteenth century, and the country developed. Eastward in Russia there were pogroms and killing. Jews tried to leave those places. I believe many of those now living in Israel came from there. The word spread that in Hungary, no one hurts the Jews. The Jews really were safe. The court loved them, the prince, his wife the queen Erzsébet [Hungarian: Elizabeth]. Here there was no anti-Semitism but philo-Semitism instead. Jews tried to integrate quickly, and not only did they learn the language, but they even learned it fast. They were energetic. They had a sense for crafts, for commerce. They became teachers. The others couldn't compete with the industriousness of the Jews, with their ability, so they became jealous. Already by the end of the nineteenth century there were terrible anti-Semitic incidents. There was a blood libel.

I.R.: I know about this.

Dr. Bihari: It was terrible. The Jews fought in World War I and were better than the other soldiers. They received many award and praises from Franz

Jozsef. Financially, they weren't as badly hurt by the war; they weren't as impoverished as were other parts of the population. Meanwhile, the war ended and hatred came. They said, "We lost the war because of the Jews, the Jews are guilty of everything." Clemenceau himself wasn't anti-Semitic, but his terrible peace treaty created new nations—Rumania, Yugoslavia—that were cut off from Hungary—

Mrs. Bihari: This is off the topic.

I.R.: Never mind, he is trying to make a point.

Dr. Bihari: I want to explain the political situation in order to relate to how anti-Semitism was created. Here you had Lajos Kossuth, here you had Széchényi, the new Hungarian leaders. And the war prisoners came back from the front and brought with them the hatred for Jews. Then there was Béla Kun. Then came Lenin. Then came this gang [Communists, many of them Jews, who tried to seize power in 1919, but were eventually defeated].

Mrs. Bihari: And Stalin.

Dr. Bihari: Stalin came later on. It reached the point when they said, first of all, that they lost the war because of the Jews. Then they said that the Jews were Communists. "It all happened because of the Jews. It all happened because of the Communists." Unfortunately, the Jews were the ones who hurried to endorse Communism. "You, the Communists and Jews, are to blame for our defeat!" And it went on this way step by step. They created brigades, gangs of retired soldiers. They went to the small, outlying towns and caught the Jews. Gathered them together, and murder, and murder. This lasted more or less until 1920, 1923, 1924.

Then things relaxed. Slowly. Then there came a more stable phase, which wasn't philo-Semitic either. But it got better; they didn't hurt the Jews anymore and were ready to accept them into the universities. They decided on a "Numerus Clausus" [quota] system. I left for Vienna, but my parents stayed here and looked for connections to help me, so they helped me become a protégé of a Catholic priest. They were able to do that because earlier on, they had enrolled me to study in a Catholic school, but there were no Catholic prayers there, nothing. My family was a religious family and would never have allowed me to go to a school where I had to say Catholic prayers. They sent me to the Catholic school because the teachers had a liberal way of thinking, so that there was no anti-Semitism there. I was a good pupil, and my life until graduation from school had no hindrances. Moreover, now school gave me a letter of recommendation, which helped me be admitted to university.

I.R.: How were you able to continue your lives while surrounded by those who hated you, how was it possible to return to life among them?

Dr. Bihari: Because those who had hated and beaten us now said, "We're glad that you came back, glad that you're here. We missed you." The flatterers came.

I.R.: But it was artificial.

Dr. Bihari: Meaning, they helped us to start our lives again. Those who had been our enemies now came to me as patients. The doctors who had been enemies, who didn't say hello, now they looked me up at the clinic and said, "We missed you." When I was sick with typhus, they said, "We're glad that you're back." Then everything quieted down and my wife suggested that we come to Budapest. Our sister-in-law found a house for us; there were many empty houses. She found this house. I brought my tools over and started working, fixing, and adding to the house. The house was a beautiful house even then, when it wasn't in as good a state as it is now. And so we lived there pleasantly. There was one more problem. This country went mad in 1956 in what came to be called a revolution. Meaning, whatever you call it, say a revolution. Here too anti-Semitism played a central role. They hanged Jews and claimed they were against the revolution. Many people escaped the country and went abroad. It did not last long, though. Soon it all quieted down, and again you could continue work and everything.

I.R.: Thank you very much. And now, Mrs. Bihari, can you tell me your own life history?

Anna Bihari: I was born in 1920. My parents were wealthy. Later, to my sorrow, my father became very ill. He contracted an illness when he fought in World War I, when he served as a regular soldier for fifty-nine days. He had a kidney disease and had to be in the hospital for a year when I was about twelve, thirteen years old. Our life went into a crisis then, but luckily, our mother knew how to run the house, and we did not lack anything. My sister was able to complete her high school studies, whereas I, to my sorrow, only finished the four grades of junior high. This became an unpleasant memory in my life. I always think with sorrow about not having studied further. I had talent. On the other hand, I excelled in sports and was a champion swimmer at the age of sixteen, which was a big compensation. Then I worked, first as a salesperson and then as a clerk in the same company. I worked regularly until the age of nineteen. I was nineteen in 1939, when Jews could no longer work in offices, that is, only a certain number of them were allowed to work. They left the older Jews at work and they sent me, as a younger person, to work in a factory. I worked for three years; I was outstanding there too and had accomplishments. Whatever they asked me to do, I immediately did well because I had the capabilities. I worked there until 1942. Then Jews couldn't work there either.

I had a Christian brother-in-law, so my uncle had him register the store in his name, and I worked there with my sister until 1944, while it was still possible. Then I made a living from knitting, and the clients liked my work. In 1943 I married my first husband. I lived with him for ten months, after which he never came back from the labor battalions. In 1947 I remarried. In the meantime, between 1944 and 1947, I was sometimes employed and sometimes unemployed. It all depended on whether we were allowed to go out to the street or not, and upon the circumstances. I married my present husband in 1947. In

1948 we had our first son, and in 1949 the younger one. In 1950 we moved from Szombathely to Budapest and since then I [unclear].

This is my life. Housework, child rearing. Meaning, there were no big upheavals in my life. In 1944 we spent months in the shelter, during the war. We suffered great scarcity because we did not imagine that the war would last that long. We were all together in the shelter: my older sister, my brother-in-law, my mother, and I. My father was away; he was sent to the labor battalions. They took him at the age of fifty-two, and to our sorrow we never saw him again. My first husband too, he was twenty-six or twenty-seven when they took him away, and he, too, never returned. Of all my relatives, only one or two survived. They all used to live in the provincial towns, from where more people were deported than from Budapest. In fact, from Szombathely, for example, out of about four thousand people only about two hundred survived, which is only 5 percent. But in Budapest you could hide. Jews hid and thus survived. Now I am a grandmother [laughs] and have three grandchildren.

I.R.: Didn't you find it difficult to pick up the pieces and continue with your life at the same place where you were rejected?

Mrs. Bihari: As a rule, no, there was no hatred. No one ever hurt me personally. Now, in such a big city you could more easily get lost, disappear. So that I never met people who hurt me personally, or called me a Jew, a Jewess. Moreover, in the factory in which I worked before the German invasion, there were no Jews besides the three of us. And they very much respected me and appreciated my work. I was a good worker and it showed, and I had good colleagues. When I had a throat operation, half the factory came to visit me. I personally was hurt only, well not *only*, by the loss of my father and my first husband. It is a loss that hurts me to this day.

Berta Wazner, Originally from Somorja, Hungary/Czechoslovakia. Interviewed in Bazera, Israel, January 1990

(Translated from Hungarian)

Berta Wazner: I was born in 1922 in Somorja, a small town on the bank of the Danube. My parents were merchants, and there were four brothers and sisters. There were ninety Jewish families in town, and we had a separate Jewish school. We met with Christian children only in elementary school. Except for our neighbors' children, we usually had contact with the Christian society only later on. I belonged to an average religious family. We only had an Orthodox community in town. My father wasn't a Jewish scholar or anything like that, but he did lead an Orthodox way of life at home. My older brother was two years my senior, and I had a brother and sister younger than I. I was in the camps together with my sister. My brother was drafted in the city of Pápa, where he had been working at my relatives' glass shop.

I don't know why, but I don't have many memories from the town, except that my mother had two brothers so we had a large family circle. Besides, in school, I always had friends. But mainly I remember that in those times, the family governed one's life. I went to a Jewish elementary school as well as to a Christian one, but even then we lived in a Jewish environment. In 1936 I enrolled in a commercial school in Pozsony. The Jews of Pozsony lived in a separate world, so to speak, from the Christians, especially in the sense of close relations with them.

I.R.: When was that?

Mrs. Wazner: That was in 1936.

I.R.: And how old were you then?

Mrs. Wazner: I was fourteen, fifteen.

I.R.: And you were in high school.

Mrs. Wazner: Yes, in a commercial high school. I lived at my aunt's, where I had mainly Jewish friends. In 1938 the Hungarians entered the country. Already in 1938 there were harsh events. I had relatives from Austria who had fled from there. One aunt and her family stayed with us for a few months, and then they continued to America, so that the atmosphere in Slovakia was already very tense. In 1938 the Hungarians came in; they closed many Jewish shops and caused many problems. My father, though, was able to keep his shop until the last moment. By 1941 the situation was really tense and problematic. My brother was drafted to the army, they took him to Russia. My mother became ill and died in the hospital. For me it was very traumatic. One aunt came to the ghetto with us. We lived in the ghetto for a while in 1944, and then they took us to the camps, with my father. And in 1945, when we returned from the camps, my sister and I were all alone. We were informed that my father and my two brothers had died.

My sister and I tried to start a new life. We had cousins, three girls who returned together, and we lived with them, wherever we could. At that time most Jews had the same problem: only a few family members survived the camps, and then those survivors had great difficulty in becoming reintegrated into life in Czechoslovakia. I then went to work in Pozsony. My sister got married. For half a year I lived in the same neighborhood as a cousin of mine who came home very sick, and I stayed with him. In fact, Jews did not know how to start their lives again. In 1945, 1946, 1947, people started to talk about Zionism and emigration to Israel. Of the whole Somorjan community there were only a few who went back to Slovakia. Everyone prepared to leave, mainly to Israel. My sister and I also wanted to leave, but after my sister got married she remained in Somorja until our cousin recovered. Then he, our cousin, left to Israel before us with a group of men. Finally, in 1949, I moved to Israel together with my sister and her husband, who by then had two children already. We came to *beit olim* in Beer-Yaacov.

At that time I was still alone. I headed to Tel Aviv and continued with the job I had learned in Pozsony, doing tapestry work for a year. My future husband came later; he only arrived in October. We met and in 1950, we married and moved to Haifa. He had a laundry in Haifa, a family business. Both of us worked there for two years, and then my husband's family settled here in Bazera. At that time my sister's family settled in Kfar Achim, and we remained here in Bazera with my husband's family. We always lived very close to each other.

I.R.: Who was included in the family?

Mrs. Wazner: My husband's father. Of my husband's family everybody returned except for his mother. All three sons returned and all three of them live in Bazera. We too remained in Bazera. First my husband worked in the grocery store as a helper and then in accounting [unclear]. In 1952 my daughter was born, and in 1958 my son. I now have six grandchildren, three and three. The children live close by with their families. In 1962 my husband started to work in Netanya and so did I for two, three years. Then he joined a company in Tel Aviv and worked there until retirement. Now he is retired and runs the gas station in Bazera. We did not have any special problems with our absorption in Israel. We did not expect much and we did our best.

I.R.: You can't say you weren't prepared for a hard life.

Mrs. Wazner: We did not expect a very easy life. But I can say that thank God we always had what we needed. We both worked and we were satisfied. First we lived in a shack. Then we built this small house. Then we enlarged and added another section to it. And we were very happy, both of us and the children too. This is it.

I.R.: Can I ask you some questions?

Mrs. Wazner: Yes.

I.R.: When you said there was tension in the early years of the war, 1939–44, before the deportations—what did you mean exactly, and how was it different compared to the period before that?

Mrs. Wazner: The Christians broke the windows of Jewish houses, they robbed the stores, the same Christians who had said before they were our friends. Now they seized our houses. My father was a beekeeper, he had a store and a beehive. Six families kept their beehives at the same place and my father, who was one of them, was the only Jew. After he sold his beehive, only one of the six families remained his friend, whereas before, all six families had been friends. They were not anti-Semitic people, but they were afraid of the war. Also, we had relatives in Vienna who were arrested. And we stopped going to the theater, to the movies.

I.R.: Before the war?

Mrs. Wazner: Before the war. When the war first broke out, there was no war yet in Czechoslovakia, they didn't conquer Czechoslovakia yet. Life was bearable until the Hungarians invaded, in 1944. My poor mother died. Once the Hungarians were here, we didn't dare go out to the street. They beat the Jewish children when they came home from the synagogue.

I.R.: Even the Christians you knew hurt you now?

Mrs. Wazner: Yes, those same Christians we knew. It was a small town. We used to be friends. We went to elementary school together with the Christian children.

I.R.: Until things changed.

Mrs. Wazner: It all changed. The newspapers were full of anti-Semitic propaganda. When the Germans came to Hungary, they first conquered Sopron. It used to belong to the Austro-Hungarian Empire. Now they annexed it to Hungary. That was in 1938. They annexed the parts in which we lived. They forbade us to go to school, took away our sources of living, closed down Jewish shops, put all kinds of limitations on our lives. Then Jews started to flee from Slovakia, and the Hungarian regime started to persecute the remaining Jews. Everyone tried to hide with their relatives. Then they started to catch Jews, and arrest them.

I.R.: Did you try to hide, or escape?

Mrs. Wazner: Traveling was dangerous. From March 1944 the war was at its peak in Hungary, and then they took everyone to camps. My sister and I were together in the camps throughout.

I.R.: Where did they take you?

Mrs. Wazner: First of all to Auschwitz. From June until the beginning of August. Then they took us to another camp until the Germans took us back to Auschwitz. This was in November. And in March they took us to [unclear] and we worked there. There were air raids already, and we were liberated there.

I.R.: I also wanted to ask you about religion. Did your attitude change? Are you religious today?

Mrs. Wazner: At present I am not religious. I don't observe the Sabbath. I think that immediately after the war, people lost their faith. If such terrible things could happen, then one cannot believe anymore. When we came back from the camps, there was no family support. Everyone was alone. Everyone was in a bad psychological state. Everyone was young, still unmarried. Many young people returned and did not know how to rebuild their lives. We returned from the camps and we had no means of support, no way to make a living. The men . . . My husband was a wheat dealer. He found a company that the government had nationalized and became a manager. He used to have many Christian friends. At work, he had very good relations with them, but he did not socialize with them outside of work. His father returned and he too joined the company. There was another older couple from Somorja that came back. But they were the exceptions; except for them, almost all of those who returned were young people, all by themselves, at the ages of twenty, twenty-two, and they had no idea how to go on with their lives. If someone had a father who had been a merchant, and he knew something about the profession, like my cousin who returned very ill, then he reopened the business. My cousin and I ran his father's business for a year, in a small village.

At that time, my sister married in Somorja, and they had a shoe shop. Those who returned and had their parents' shops and could manage them, worked in that. I think most of them went back to their parents' occupations. Women tried to get married, often with older men. I worked there for a year. Then I moved to Pozsony and learned the profession of tapestry. The Joint had a workshop where single women like me worked. There was very little merchandise in Czechoslovakia. Then I married a shoe merchant, one year older than I. We left for Israel in March, my husband and I, and then his family joined us.

I.R.: When was that?

Mrs. Wazner: Already in 1949.

I.R.: When Mrs. E.K. [also interviewed for my doctoral thesis] told you about her meeting with me, did you think about what you were going to tell me?

Mrs. Wazner: No I did not. I realized it is a research project and that you were going to ask me questions. My friend and neighbor said she would come too, although she has very bad memories, so in the end she didn't join us. I'll tell you frankly, ever since we came to Israel, I think of the past only very rarely. I don't miss Slovakia. I don't want to go back there. My poor father was a born Zionist; we often talked about why we weren't coming to Israel. He worked in construction, windows and glass for construction. He always said that surely he could integrate in a young country. But then his son went into the army, and you could only come illegally. By then he was fifty, so he couldn't leave. But we always talked about it, said that when the war would be over, he would go to Israel with his family. I became part of life in Israel very quickly and thought very little about life there. We left Slovakia with almost nothing, and in Israel we had to work for everything by ourselves. We worked very hard, and we were very busy. Those were times of scarcity and austerity. You couldn't get many things.

When I married in 1952, we rented a room and our kitchen was on the balcony. We lived there in Haifa for four years. Then my husband's family moved to Bazera, and at the first opportunity to get a simple shack there, we moved too. Our house was built after a year. We had one room and a kitchen and we added another room. My daughter was born in 1952 when we still lived in Haifa, and in 1953, we moved here to Bazera.

I.R.: When did you decide to come to Israel?

Mrs. Wazner: When the war ended we knew we weren't going to stay in Slovakia. Even though my husband integrated well there, we knew we wouldn't stay for long. After Hitlerism the life of the Jews in Europe was very hard. In Poland, as in Slovakia, Hitlerism went so deep into the people's consciousness that even though many people suffered during the war, Christians as well, the Jews were still the scapegoats for all the problems in Europe. And when Jews returned alive, they said that even though Hitler exterminated many of the Jews, he didn't exterminate enough of them. Since some Jews survived from almost every family, they wanted to get their houses back, and the Christians who had taken over those houses now had to leave. So Jews were resented, Jews were blamed again for everything. Even survivors who set themselves up well in business, who were more secure financially, they still felt they couldn't remain there in that society with their memories. Everyone was very happy once they had an opportunity to leave to the West.

I.R.: And now, forty years later, are the memories from there still strong?

Mrs. Wazner: No, not at all. In the first years here we had to cope with wars: the 1956 War, the Six Days' War, the Yom Kippur War—all of them.

I.R.: New troubles?

Mrs. Wazner: Yes, new troubles. My husband was not a combat soldier, but he was called to reserve service every year. Then we had the Fadayeen attacks [terrorist incursions from Jordan]. Meaning, life was difficult. Then my first child was born, and I used to think, now in Europe there's peace, and here there's always danger and fighting. But in the end we realized we couldn't have stayed there. I didn't really want to go back to visit, but when we did finally return for a visit I was very critical. I'll always remember the suffering of the Jews in our town. My husband always said that in Slovakia things were difficult for everyone, not just for the Jews. For him this was a kind of revenge, that things were bad for the Slovakians now and this is how they were getting paid back for what they did to the Jews. I don't exactly feel revenge, but I did feel a strong resentment toward my past town and its people. We only stayed there for three days, because I felt very upset and distressed there.

I.R.: Do you have any family, acquaintances, or friends there?

Mrs. Wazner: We have very good friends, and in Budapest I have a cousin. And my mother, I was able to locate my mother's grave. My mother died one year before the camps, so she was buried in Somorja. It was very painful to visit the cemetery and the town where I was born. The way the cemetery looked, the whole town, the synagogue—somehow it affected me very strongly. I mean, the Jewish houses were very neglected, although they built some new buildings, many blocks of bad quality, close to town. Many people come there to work. In fact, I did not find what I had left behind me. The town is entirely changed. One or two houses remained, and they look like terrible ruins, without any windows, like bunkers. One sees how much was destroyed.

I.R.: The past is dead?

Mrs. Wazner: Yes, the past is dead, just as you say. I always feared this encounter with my past: the cemetery, the whole town. I don't know, I didn't want to go at all, it was my husband who pushed me to go. I didn't want to visit the old community, I didn't want to see where my past is dead and buried, where my terrible memories are from. It's true that I have good memories from my childhood, but those years are gone, and only the bad years remained.

I.R.: And you don't miss those.

Mrs. Wazner: Those I don't miss.

I.R.: And why did you go there?

Mrs. Wazner: My husband wanted to go there and I did not want to. When we visited the cemetery, we stayed at our friends' house. They wanted to take us out and show us around, to see things, and I just didn't feel like it.

I.R.: So, didn't you go?

Mrs. Wazner: We went out to town a bit, but I only became more tense as time went on. Finally we left to Pest, which was an enjoyable trip for me because I did not know the city so well, so I had no bad memories. But returning to Slovakia, to the place where I had once lived—that was very hard for me.

I.R.: That gave you bad memories.

Mrs. Wazner: Here in Israel, I have my children and grandchildren, and my bad memories have somehow quieted down. But going back there seems to have stirred up the memories again. Sometimes at night I have terrible nightmares about the visit to the cemetery, to my poor mother's grave. I dream I cannot find her grave. In reality I did find it, only the tombstone was gone. That's because I knew that my grandparents were also buried there, side by side, and my mother was buried next to my grandmother. Once I found my grandmother's tombstone was still there, I knew that my mother's grave must be there too, but the stone was missing. Only about ten stones were still there, out of a total of about fifty or sixty graves.

Jews started to settle in Somorja only as late as about 1900. Even after they started to settle there, and many more Jews moved there too, the cemetery and the synagogue that served them remained in the village nearby. That's why the cemetery in Somorja didn't have many graves, only some fifty or sixty. Once there was a flood in the village, and the old graves were ruined. So that now, my friend writes me, the Jewish community wants to rehabilitate the Somorja cemetery for the entire Pozsony county and bring over the bones left in the village cemetery. One part of the cemetery had a fence around it, and that part is still there.

I.R.: Of the Jewish cemetery?

Mrs. Wazner: Yes, all the graves there are of Jews. But next to that place there is a Christian cemetery. There are many places in Czechoslovakia where the Jewish cemeteries are outside the Christian ones, and often the Christians took apart the Jewish cemeteries and built houses instead.

I.R.: Do you talk about your previous life with your children, do they ask questions?

Mrs. Wazner: That is a very interesting issue. On the one hand you want to forget the past, although some people say that we should pass it down to our children, so that no one ever forgets what happened to the Jews of Europe. We raised our children to be Zionists, but we did not tell them much about the past. Once our teacher from Somorja, who had moved to Brazil, came to visit us here in Israel. He met our children and saw they didn't know anything about their grandparents and about our life in Slovakia. He asked us why we hadn't told them anything. We never tell the children, we said. Sometimes the adults meet, guests come to visit and we talk. My son did ask me why we never talk about it with the children. Now in recent years they talk a lot about the Holocaust at school. They ask, show interest. But when they were small they didn't.

I.R.: They didn't ask?

Mrs. Wazner: They didn't ask because they were born here, and until they went to school they didn't know. Meaning, they knew we weren't from here originally, because the Hebrew we spoke was very poor, but only later did they ask about why and how we came here. We didn't discuss these things with the children. If friends came over we talked, and our conversation always ended up in those years, what happened to this person or that. We often talked about these things among ourselves. But then the children heard us and started to ask questions. In fact, as they grew up and saw that other children had grandparents, they wanted to know how come they didn't have any grandparents. Where were they? Even my own grandchildren ask me that. My friend was here for a visit, together with her mother, who died about a year ago. Everyone loved her. She was everyone's grandmother. Our small grandchildren already have grandparents, and in our extended family everyone is from Slovakia. The parents of my son-in-law are from Slovakia. The mother of my daughter-in-law escaped from Germany. Somehow we told the children more about the difficulties of starting a new life here than we did about our experiences in Europe.

I.R.: That was easier to talk about?

Mrs. Wazner: I think it was easier to talk about our new life here than to tell about how we came home to Slovakia, after the war, and there was nothing. That we lived in Slovakia for a few years, but there was no reason to be happy. When we came here to Israel and had the children, that's when we started our new lives. I don't think we could have had a new life in Slovakia. I see our friends there in Slovakia, still suffering, still having a hard time psychologically. There is no real release there.

Esther Israel. Originally from Dunaszerdahely, Hungary/Czechoslovakia. Interviewed in Hod-Hasharon, Israel, February 1990

(Translated from Hebrew)

Esther Israel: I was born in Czechoslovakia, almost twenty years before the Holocaust, when the place was still Czech. My mother was a widow and hard-pressed to support the family, so we children had to start working as early as the age of twelve. Already then, we went through hard times. Then the Hungarian regime started in 1938, 1939. We had trouble, problems. My brother was drafted to the labor battalions in 1940. They took the Jewish men to the Ukraine, where they suffered terribly and none of them survived. My brother also never came back. Then came 1944, and when I was seventeen I was sent to the camps. I was there for a year, until 1945. I was in several camps: I was in Auschwitz twice, I was in Poland, in Krakow, in Dachau, and I was released in Bergen-Belsen. I then stayed there for four more months. The situation was very difficult. We were three sisters who survived and we stayed together. Our mother had gone to Auschwitz with us, and she remained there, she died there. We, the three sisters, came back after the war. Again we started to work hard to make a living again.

I.R.: Did you go back to your home?

Mrs. Israel: Yes, and then I came here to Israel in 1949. Here too I worked hard. I got married. I have three children. Before I had the children I worked very hard. My husband died almost a year ago. We both worked very hard. What can I tell you, I don't have much of a story. We lived in the same street as Dora [Ashkenazi]. We both belonged to the same extended family.

I.R.: The two families knew each other well?

Mrs. Israel: Of course. We lived close to each other, on the same street. Then they moved a bit further away, but they were still within walking distance. I cannot tell you much. I don't have much to tell.

I.R.: I see. Can I ask you questions then?

Mrs. Israel: Please do.

I.R.: Before the war you lived amongst Gentiles. Were there any signs of anti-Semitism?

Mrs. Israel: Sure. Until . . . We were part of Czechoslovakia for twenty years; you probably heard of President Masaryk. For as long as we were under the Czechoslovakian regime, we had no problems at all. Then the Hungarians took over and it all started. They broke our windows. They caught yeshiva students and cut off their beards. They broke windows, came in, broke into shops. Then they took us away.

I.R.: All this happened after the Hungarians came in?

Mrs. Israel: Immediately as the Hungarians came in, in 1938, all our troubles began. They took the men first to army service in the labor battalions. Then they took mothers, old women, old men, and children to the concentration camps, the death camps. They all stayed there, perished. Then they took us, the single healthy women to the work camps and factories. We came back alone. Tried to rebuild our lives again, started working again. That's it.

I.R.: During the years after that, from 1945 to 1949, what was the attitude toward Jews?

Mrs. Israel: It depends where. We were fine, but there were places where there were pogroms.

I.R.: After the war?

Mrs. Israel: It was terrible. You know, I remember that I had worked in this town called Bratislava [Hungarian: Pozsony], by the border. This was already after the war. The place was all black, burnt, ruined. We were so afraid. We went there, you know, after the war. Many people didn't have any family left, and there was this place where they fed all the survivors. Then one day hooligans attacked the dining room where the Jews ate, spilt everything, broke everything. The Jews went down to the shelter. Had they not hidden themselves, the hooligans would have killed them all.

I.R.: They hid.

Mrs. Israel: Yes.

I.R.: Was this the reason that you decided to leave for Israel?

Mrs. Israel: No. I was in the Czech Brigade of the *Haggana* organization with my older sister; I came to Israel in 1949 with the *Haggana*. We had weapons, we had everything just like here in Israel. I stayed in a *ma'abara* [temporary lodging] in Israel for four months. The third sister remained in Europe.

I.R.: Where was that?

Mrs. Israel: It was then called Agrobank, just before Haifa. Now it's Hadera. We were sent to work in the orchards there. Then I got married, had children, and that's it. I worked hard all my life and that's all. What else can I tell you?

I.R.: Did you ever tell your children about your Holocaust experiences?

Mrs. Israel: I told them. On Holocaust Memorial Day they always asked me.

I.R.: Who did?

Mrs. Israel: The children, the children. You know, some of my stories are quite scary, maybe. The children always said, "Why don't you want to tell us?" So I told them the names of the camps where I had been, what and how it was. You know, they didn't bury the dead people there, so there were corpses all over the place. That caused typhus, and I became very sick. If it weren't for the British army, we would have all perished.

I.R.: You were liberated by the British?

Mrs. Israel: Yes, by the British. The corpses were piled up like a mountain, they weren't buried at all. It was horrible. You can ask me questions, maybe you know what to ask me. I don't know what to say, otherwise.

I.R.: I would like to ask more about—

Mrs. Israel: About what you are interested in.

I.R.: I'd like to ask you about the prewar period. Did you belong to a religious family and did anything change later on in this regard?

Mrs. Israel: Yes, yes, in fact our area in Czechoslovakia was called the "small Palestine." There were many Jewish families there, and I tell you, as long as the Czech president was in charge, it was good for the Jews.

I.R.: Were the Jews religious people, were they Orthodox?

Mrs. Israel: There were only Orthodox Jews there. There were no Neologist Jews. Actually there were some, but very few.

I.R.: And your own family?

Mrs. Israel: We were a religious family. Not fanatic but definitely religious.

I.R.: And at present?

Mrs. Israel: Today I am traditional. I eat kosher food, I don't work on Shabbat, but I watch television, things like that.

I.R.: Were you familiar with Zionism at that time?

Mrs. Israel: A bit maybe. There were people who belonged to *Hashomer Hatzair*. But our parents objected, didn't let us go there, because they were not religious. Now, after the war we did join a movement, it was the *Betar* movement this time. Then in 1949 I came here, to Israel. I didn't stay in Czechoslovakia for long, I didn't want to stay.

I.R.: This is it, more or less.

Mrs. Israel: I told you, whatever Dora said, I cannot add much to it.

I.R.: Each person has his or her own story.

Mrs. Israel: I told you what I know. I cannot know about other things.

Piri Meister. Originally from Gyergyóvárhegy, Hungary/Rumania. Interviewed in Ra'anana, Israel, July 1991

(Translated from Hungarian)

Piri Meister: I was born in Gyergyóvárhegy in 1916. At that time, it was part of the Csikmegye county. We lived there until I was five years old. Then we moved to Marosheviz, where I started school not long afterward. I started to go to school at an early age; there was no kindergarten there. My family was religious but not ultra-Orthodox. My father worked in the wood industry, my mother was a housewife, and I had five sisters.

After I finished six years of elementary school, they founded a commercial school in Marosheviz. Because I very much wanted to study further, I enrolled in this school. However, I was able to finish only three years in the commercial school before they closed it down. Although you could continue your studies either in Bucharest or in Gyulafehérvár, my parents refused to let me study there. In the old days, many parents didn't want to send a young girl out into the big world. So I continued to study on my own. For a short time I studied French and German. Earlier on I had a German nanny who had taught me German. This was a poor girl who dined at our house on certain days each week. We had a big house, with six daughters. My father could afford it with a clerk's salary. So this woman taught me German and also had a sort of a kindergarten for a few children. After I finished school, I started learning sewing. I didn't like it, though, and therefore became a clerk.

I.R.: Did you study it or did you learn it on the job?

Mrs. Meister: I learned it at the commercial school. Then I worked until the deportation.

I.R.: Once the Germans invaded?

Mrs. Meister: Yes, after the invasion. My mother was born in Hungary, so at first when the Hungarian regime took over, she was very happy. But she was soon disillusioned. First they sent our men to army service in the labor battalions in Russia, then they gathered us all in the Szászregen ghetto, and then— they deported us. At first, there were still Zionist organizations, there were *Halutz* settlements in [Maros]Heviz. Pioneers worked in farms and factories. I also belonged to a Zionist organization. I was member in the *Aviva* section for girls. I wanted to emigrate with the *Halutz* movement, but my parents didn't let me. So I stayed at home and was deported like everyone else. That is the general story of the deportations.

I.R.: Did you work in a factory?

Mrs. Meister: Yes we did. First we were put in the so-called Gypsy camp. There they made constant "selections," either for the crematorium or to work. After six weeks they sent us to work in a field, sowing and picking vegetables, cabbage, and I don't know what. In the fall they took us to work in an ammunitions factory, where we worked until liberation.

After liberation, we wandered some six weeks in Germany, this way, that way, but at first we couldn't go back home. I stayed in Dresden and couldn't leave—once there was a contagious disease, another time they had to bomb a bridge. Eventually we came home in gas or petroleum tanks. First we reached Budapest. We spent one night in Pest, and the next night we reached Nagyvárad. There we stayed a day or two. We were released on the 9th of May and I arrived at Vásárhely on the 20th of June, after six weeks of travel. There, in Vásárhely, I was so weak that I was hospitalized in a sanatorium for six weeks. Of my entire family, which had consisted of six sisters, four brothers-in-law, six grandchildren and two grandparents, of all these only my younger sister and I survived.

I.R.: Which sister were you?

Mrs. Meister: I was the fourth.

I.R.: Which means that only the younger ones survived.

Mrs. Meister: Right, because the others had children. The two of us weren't married, and so we returned home.

I.R.: What kind of a world was it after the war?

Mrs. Meister: We returned in July, and as of August or September the region again belonged to Rumania. So we went back. At first I didn't want to go to Heviz because I said I couldn't stand the people there. But in the meantime I got married and we did go back to Heviz. I didn't look for a job, because my husband worked as a photographer and I helped him. I also had our daughter to raise, and soon after that we also had a son. Still, I wanted to do something else in addition to housework. My husband became a party member, like many of our colleagues, and I joined too. We had a women's organization.

Then in 1958 we decided to come to Israel, because our relatives had all emigrated. Only our immediate family was still in Rumania. We said, "Let's register, let's leave." It didn't work, though. They didn't let us. They forced my husband to leave the studio where he worked and become a party activist, first as a volunteer, and then as a job. The children weren't allowed to study further. They started to transfer my husband from one job to another, until he again became a newspaper photographer, although not as a manager and education board member, as he used to be beforehand. I too had been the representative of our region to the national party section. Despite all this, we applied for permission to make aliya time and again. They told us, "Why leave? Give it up." We replied, "Only because all our family is gone, we have no parents, nobody in the entire world here." They turned us down. At that time my daughter had to graduate but wasn't allowed to take her final matriculation exams, because we had applied for aliya. Then they said, "Give up your attempts to leave the country, and you may still get the approval when your turn comes." So after two years of trying, we gave up trying to emigrate, and our daughter was admitted to school. She passed her matriculation exams but wasn't accepted to university, and our son couldn't join the youth movement. That was unpleasant; everyone else was in and he was out. We kept on waiting, but nothing came out of it. Eventually our daughter got married and came to live in Israel. We came to visit them several times. We, too, struggled to leave the country. Then our son finished university and also came to live in Israel.

I.R.: When was that?

Mrs. Meister: My son came here, to Israel, ten years ago, in 1981. Once both our children were here, there was no reason for us to stay in Rumania. We just waited for an opportunity to leave and finally, it happened. Ever since we came to Israel, we live here in Ra'anana. As long as we lived in Rumania, we worked; once here, we have become pensioners and couldn't work much. Still, my husband worked a few hours a day until he fell ill.

I.R.: So you see, it wasn't so hard to tell it all.

Mrs. Meister: No. It's not hard to tell, as long as I don't tell about *all* we went through. That is why I say that it's no use to tell people how much we suffered. In the camps, my sister had a high fever and they took her away to this so-called hospital. She stayed there for a couple of weeks. During that time, my friend and I sneaked out of our barracks every morning and brought my sister something to eat. What could we bring her, with our poor nutrition? Still, of our meager portions, we gave her something. As a result I became so feeble that by the time she was released from the hospital, I weighed thirty kilograms. That remained my weight until liberation, thirty kilograms! Then I spent six weeks in a sanatorium in Vásárhely, until I recovered.

I.R.: In what ways did you face anti-Semitism throughout this time?

Mrs. Meister: Before the Hungarians came in, in the Rumanian regime, I had no complaints. You could manage things with them more easily. With the Hungarians, once we saw the Arrow Cross militia men, we started to be afraid. We could see how they took people away, this one at one time, and that one at another time. At one time, they gathered people in order to take their gold and valuables away from them. We weren't rich, so we weren't taken away for that. We didn't have any brothers sent to the labor battalions, but our brothers-in-law were sent there. Of course it hurt us that they left and never came back. One of them was sent to the Ukraine. The second, we don't know what happened to him. And the third one was also sent to the Ukraine. Two of my nephews, who were old enough, were also taken to the labor battalions. One niece was sent to the camps. We met her once, by chance, and asked her to move to our group. She said she was afraid to leave her group because if someone was missing, she might be shot. I didn't have the courage to be responsible for her moving. She, too, never returned. Out of eighteen souls in the family, my sisters and their families, just two of us—my sister and I—survived. My sister and her family came here, to Israel, in 1948. My husband's relatives came here as well. My husband and I were left in Rumania, alone by ourselves in the big world. There was a period of years during which you couldn't even receive any letters. Then, in 1969, we were allowed to correspond and leave the country for short visits abroad. My husband and my daughter came to Israel for a visit. My daughter wanted to stay here, became fond of the place. But my husband wouldn't let her stay here by herself. She returned home, got married, and after a while came back to Israel. My son also came once he finished his studies.

I.R.: Were there any incidents in which Hungarians treated you badly after the war?

Mrs. Meister: In general we were well liked. But there were incidents, I remember now. For example, when they came to take us to the ghetto, many of the people with whom we had been on good terms now looked at us with malicious joy as we boarded the carriages with our belongings. On the other hand, there were a few neighbors who broke the fence around the ghetto to pass us some bread. In that regard, our Rumanian neighbors were more sympathetic toward us than the Hungarians.

Notes

Chapter 1

1. On "memorial candle" names, see Vardi, *Memorial Candles*. On the "second generation," see Hass, *In the Shadow of the Holocaust*.
2. Rosen, "Holocaust at the Center of Life."
3. Braham, *Hungarian Labor Service System*. I will henceforth use the terms *Labor Service* and *Labor Battalions* interchangeably, as do the survivors in their accounts.
4. For the phenomenon in world literature, see, for example, the case of Du Maurier's *Rebecca*. The sense of a "shadow" whose existence is keenly felt by its "analogous" family member is expressed in contemporary Israeli "second generation" literature such as Govrin's *The Name* and Semel's *Glass Cap*.
5. In the field of the personal narrative, a relatively new genre among the more traditional folklore genres, the scholar Sandra K. Dolby Stahl presents an analytic model based on the study of written as well as oral literature. Stahl analyzes, among other narratives, her own family's stories, which she therefore terms *family folklore*, thus illustrating the inevitable ties between individual, family, and community. See Stahl, *Literary Folkloristics*.
6. A *proairetic ploy* is a narrative technique stressing the tension between statements about action and their actual carrying out. See Rimmon-Kenan, *Narrative Fiction*, 13, 124, 125; Barthes, *S/Z*, 19.
7. About the dialogue of shadows, see Ben-Amos, "Elusive Audience of Benin Narrators"; and Crapanzano, *Hermes' Dilemma and Hamlet's Desire*, 213.
8. In my later work, about the oral tradition of the Jews of Carpatho-Russia, I discerned an opposite phenomenon. There, I noted that men related more to religion and ethos, whereas women were more personal and less dominant as upholders of tradition. See Rosen, *There Once Was . . .*, 17, 128.
9. Barthes, *S/Z*, 18–22.
10. The original thesis deals with Jews from Imperial Hungary, or "Great" Hungary as it was once called, defining them as such even if they currently resided in Hungary's neighboring countries, or if some of them chose to tell their life history in poor Hebrew instead of proper Hungarian.

11. For an overview of studies of children and families in the Holocaust, see Baumel, "Gender and Family Studies of the Holocaust," in *Double Jeopardy*, 39–52.
12. Smith, "Women and Genocide."
13. Jackson, *Elli*; Lengyel, *Five Chimneys*; Karmel, *Estate of Memory*.
14. Goldenberg, "Testimony, Narrative, and Nightmare"; Kremer, "Estate of Memory," 101.
15. Baumel, "Gender and Family Studies of the Holocaust," in *Double Jeopardy*, 39–52.
16. Baumel, "Social Interaction among Jewish Women in Crisis during the Holocaust."
17. Schiffrin, "Mother-Daughter Discourse in a Holocaust Oral History."
18. Mintz, *Ḥurban*, 37; Roskies, *Against the Apocalypse*; de Koven-Ezrahi, *By Words Alone*, 97.
19. Langer, *Versions of Survival*, 9.
20. Langer, *Versions of Survival*, 68–69; de Koven-Ezrahi, *By Words Alone*, 10.
21. Primo Levi for one calls against the use of rhetoric in writing about the Holocaust. See Levi, *Drowned and the Saved*, 53.
22. Foley, "Fact, Fiction, Fascism," 332.
23. Felman and Laub, *Testimony*.
24. Langer, *Holocaust Testimonies*, 61.
25. Ibid., xi.
26. For the Langer references in this paragraph, see ibid., 16–17, 56–57, 128–29.
27. Rosen, *Hungarian Jewish Women Survivors*, 91.
28. Gutman, *Encyclopedia of the Holocaust*, vol. B, 695.
29. Szalai, "Will the Past Protect Hungarian Jewry?"
30. These strains roughly parallel the Orthodox, Conservative, and Reform movements in the United States, as both derived from divisions that took place among German Jewry in previous centuries.
31. Rothkirchen, "Jews of Hungary in the Holocaust," 62.
32. Cohen, *Halutz Resistance in Hungary*.
33. Weitz, *Man Who Was Murdered Twice*.
34. Gutman, *Encyclopedia of the Holocaust*, vol. B, 698–703; Braham, *Politics of Genocide*.
35. The title of this section is inspired by the following: "I think there are as many ways to survive survival as there have been to survive," testimony of Philip K. (t-1300), the Fortunoff Video Archives for Holocaust Testimonies at Yale University, quoted in Langer, *Holocaust Testimonies*, 205.
36. Kirshenblatt-Gimblett, "Culture Shock and Narrative Creativity," 114; Voigt, "Why Do People Lie?" 216.
37. McCann and Pearlman, *Psychological Trauma and the Adult Survivor*; Yehuda, ed., *Psychological Trauma*; Rogers, Leydesdorff, and Dawson, eds., *Trauma and Life Stories*.

38. Mintz, *Ḥurban*, 239–41.
39. Ibid., 245–63.
40. Eschenazi and Nissim, *Invisible Jews*, 31–108.
41. Rosen, "Memory of the Holocaust as Lament," 102–4.
42. Langer, "Gendered Suffering?" 355.
43. Stahl, *Literary Folkloristics*; Langllier, "Personal Narratives."
44. A relatively recent school in folklore views the storytelling event as a performance that includes many more aspects than the literary one. See Georges, "Toward an Understanding of Storytelling Events"; Ben-Amos, "Toward a Definition of Folklore in Context"; Kirshenblatt-Gimblett, "Parable in Context"; Alexander and Govrin, "Story Telling as a Performing Art."
45. Des Pres, *The Survivor*, 30.
46. Holocaust testimony research acknowledges the need to present the actual voices of survivors, apart from analyzing and interpreting them. See Horowitz, "Memory and Testimony of Women Survivors of Nazi Genocide."

Chapter 2

1. In Hungarian, married women (as well as widows and divorced women) are called by their husbands' names with the suffix *né*, which stands for "Mrs." In this work, though, I decided to call these Hungarian women by their names to match Israeli and American English naming conventions.
2. About autobiographical narration within the framework of intergenerational family communication, and methods of understanding this communication, see Noy, "Folktales in a Jewish Tunisian Family," 181–88; Alexander and Hasan-Rokem, "Proverbs of a Sephardic Woman"; Stahl, "Literary Folkloristic Methodology."
3. Nelson, "Psychoanalysis as an Intervention," 16.
4. On parallels between folkloric phenomena and mental processes, see E. Jones, "Psychoanalysis and Folklore," 92–94. On ontogenetic and phylogenetic analogies about the development of the human race, see Freud, *General Introduction*, 209, 375; Jung, *Psychology of the Unconscious*, 157–90, and *Undiscovered Self*, 3–18, 43–70.
5. Bettelheim, *Uses of Enchantment*.
6. Dundes is the main advocate of this approach in folkloristics, as exemplified in his works *Interpreting Folklore* and the edited collection *Blood Libel Legend*.
7. Murray M. Schwartz, "Critic, Define Thyself," 3; Gunn, *Psychoanalysis and Fiction*, 191.
8. On the dream and the artistic work or text, see Crews, ed., *Psychoanalysis and the Literary Process*, 13. On the creative process and psychoanalytic analysis, see Gunn, *Psychoanalysis and Fiction*, 1–7. On the relationship between the patient and the therapist, the author and the reader or the

literary critic, see Gunn, ibid., as well as Murray M. Schwartz, "Critic, Define Thyself," 11; and Derrida, "Coming Into One's Own," 121. On the text itself and the literary criticism written in its wake, see Nelson, "Psychology of Criticism," 46.

9. Barthes, "Structural Activity." In this case, the focus is on the creative activity of the reader of the text. See also Hawkes, *Structuralism and Semiotics*, 117–18.

10. Herman, *Trauma and Recovery*.

11. Ibid., chap. 1.

12. Murray M. Schwartz, "Critic, Define Thyself," 7. See also Freud's treatment of his own dreams—their analysis and categorization according to topic—in *The Interpretation of Dreams*, and Derrida's analysis of Freud's description of watching his grandson Ernst playing, shortly after the death of his mother, Sophia, Freud's daughter (Freud, *Beyond the Pleasure Principle*, 8–11; Derrida, "Coming Into One's Own," 7). These analyses demonstrate that Freud was not concerned with his own pathology, since he felt that a person studies psychoanalysis, first and foremost, of himself (Freud, *General Introduction*, 23–24). However, this instruction did not entail viewing himself as patient; rather, he seems to view two separate types of pathology, that of the patient and that of the therapist. It is in this context that we may see the criticism of Donald P. Spence regarding Freud's view of the therapist, whom he compares to an archeologist or a traveler gazing outside the window of a train (Spence, *Narrative Truth and Historical Truth*, 11).

13. Nelson, "Psychoanalysis as an Intervention," 12–13.

14. Georges and M. Jones, *People Studying People*, 65.

15. Nash and Wintrob, "Emergence of Self-Consciousness in Ethnography."

16. See the discussion regarding the ethnicity of Jewish east European communities in the concluding chapter of my book *There Once Was . . .*, 153–56.

17. On "writerly" reading, see Barthes, *S/Z*, 4.

18. Lacan, "Agency of the Letter in the Unconscious," in *Écrits*, 78–146.

19. Murray M. Schwartz, "Critic, Define Thyself," 6.

20. Freud, *General Introduction*, 291, 294, 443, 445.

21. Caruth, introduction to "Psychoanalysis, Culture, and Trauma," a special issue of *American Imago*, edited by Caruth, 2–3; Caruth, *Unclaimed Experience*; Lifton, *Broken Connection*, 170–73; Tedeschi and Calhoun, *Trauma and Transformation*, 17–18.

22. Brown, "Not Outside the Range."

23. Hartman, "On Traumatic Knowledge and Literary Studies."

24. These trends are characteristic of French feminist writers and their works, such as Irigaray, *Speculum of the Other Woman* and *This Sex Which Isn't One*; Cixous, *Coming to Writing and Other Essays*; and Kristeva, *Revolution in Poetic Language*.

25. This refers to the Transylvania region, where the narrator lived. This region belonged in the past to the Austro-Hungarian Empire and was ceded to Rumania after World War I in the Trianon Treaty. The reannexation of Transylvania by Hungary took place in the summer of 1940. See Gutman, *Encyclopedia of the Holocaust,* vol. B, 694–96.

26. For a discussion of proairetics, see Rimmon-Kenan, *Narrative Fiction,* 13, 124–25; and Barthes, *S/Z,* 19.

27. For information on the role of color in creating racist stereotypes and prejudices, see E. Jones, "Psychology of the Jewish Question," 285.

28. These processes of disinfection and shaving of intimate organs are described in female Holocaust literature with various levels of explicitness. Some use more general descriptions, such as "body" and "skin," while others are more direct and cite "nakedness" and "genitals." For comparison and contrast, see the stories of two Munkács survivors, Beinhorn (Klein) and Golan, *Leaves That Arose from the Ashes,* 117; and Bernheim (Friedmann), *Earrings in the Cellar,* 79.

29. Levi, *Is This Man?* (99–115) and *Drowned and the Saved.*

30. See, in a similar context, Karay's story "Apples for 'Whores'" in her book *Rockets and Rhymes,* 102–11.

31. Milton, "Women and the Holocaust," 315.

32. Ringelheim, "The Split between Gender and the Holocaust," 343.

33. Horowitz, "Women in Holocaust Literature," 366; Ringelheim, "Women and the Holocaust," 743; Heinemann, *Gender and Destiny,* 19–27.

34. Cixous, "Feminine Writing."

35. Goldenberg, "Testimony, Narrative, and Nightmare" and "Memories of Auschwitz Survivors," 327; Heinemann, *Gender and Destiny,* 109–13.

36. Contrasting stagnation and movement is common in psychoanalytic analyses of texts. See Gunn, *Psychoanalysis and Fiction,* 12; Weber, "Psychoanalysis, Literary Criticism, and the Problem of Authority," 30.

37. Wiesel, *Night,* 107.

38. Bettelheim, *Uses of Enchantment,* 159–62, 188–90, 207–8, 214.

39. Darnton, "The Meaning of Mother Goose," in *The Great Cat Massacre,* 9–72.

40. Gutman, *Encyclopedia of the Holocaust,* vol. B, 699–700; Braham, *Hungarian Labor Service System* and *Wartime System of Labor Service in Hungary.*

41. Psychotherapy directs much attention to the connection between sexual abuse and eating disorders. In this case, however, as well as in the general context of the Holocaust experience, the opposite seems to be just as relevant; namely, that the nutritional deprivation she had experienced made the woman survivor more daring, considering her upbringing and psychological setup, in contacting men. See Mark F. Schwartz and Cohn, eds., *Sexual Abuse and Eating Disorders;* Zerba, *The Body Betrayed.*

42. Des Pres, *The Survivor,* 63. In Des Pres's book, the filth, lack of privacy in

mass toilets, and, later on, intestinal diseases are all seen as part of the Nazi-German system and aim of annihilation.

43. Wiesel, *Night*, 22–24.

44. Rosen, "Holocaust at the Center of Life," 86, 171, 175, 179, 180. For Rika's account, see also Rosen, *Hungarian Jewish Women Survivors*, 81–86. Since *Hungarian Jewish Women Survivors* was prepared for the general public, it may not include the exact full text as presented in "Holocaust at the Center of Life," which is as faithful as possible to the texts of the narrators.

45. For the function of objects and "signs" in the concentration camps, see Bettelheim, *Surviving*, 107.

46. Blumental, "Magical Thinking among the Jews."

47. About defense mechanisms, see Freud, *General Introduction*, 114–18; Slander and A. Freud, *Analysis of Defense;* Cramer, *Development of Defense Mechanisms.*

48. Rosen, "Holocaust at the Center of Life," 291–97, and *Hungarian Jewish Women Survivors*, 15–20.

49. Rosen, "Holocaust at the Center of Life," 258, and *Hungarian Jewish Women Survivors*, 7–10.

50. Ben-Amos, "Context in Context," 213–14.

51. Dégh and Vázsonyi, "Hypothesis of Multi-Conduit Transmission"; Shenhar-Alroy, "Rumor Stories" [in Hebrew] in *The Story, the Storyteller, and the Audience*, 105–34.

52. On Freud's notion that opposites do not necessarily mean contradiction, see Freud, *General Introduction*, 186–87, 230. For the notion that dialectic choices best reflect the reality of our lives, see Gunn, "Psychoanalysis and Fiction," 3.

53. Weber, "Psychoanalysis, Literary Criticism, and the Problem of Authority," 30; Gunn, *Psychoanalysis and Fiction*, 12.

54. In this respect, Mrs. Faludi is an example of the "negative identification type" who defines himself or herself in terms of negation as "not Hungarian," etc. See Erős and Kovács, "Biographical Method," 352.

55. Katz, "The Holocaust."

56. Görög-Karady, "Ethnic Stereotypes and Folklore," 120; Zenner, "Folklore of Jewish-Gentile Relations," 2–4; Huseby-Darvas, "Remembering Our Jews."

57. Rosen, "Holocaust at the Center of Life," 222.

58. This subject was brought up even more powerfully in the interviews I conducted with Carpatho-Russian Jews. There, the Hungarian army is described as actively involved in their deportation to the east and in their murder as early as 1941, in the so-called Kamenetz-Podolski events. See the stories of the "Benedek group" in Rosen, *There Once Was. . .*, 75–87.

59. Rosen, "Holocaust at the Center of Life," 82–166.

60. Rosen, "Holocaust at the Center of Life," 297–307.

61. Gutman, *Encyclopedia of the Holocaust,* vol. B, 703.
62. According to William Labov's work, *orientation* is the second-in-order component of short personal narratives that describe dangerous experiences. See Labov, *Language in the Inner City,* 354–96. Orientation is explained on pages 364–65. See also Labov and Waletzki, "Narrative Analysis."
63. Rosen, "Holocaust at the Center of Life," 189–97, 228; Rosen, *Hungarian Jewish Women Survivors,* 75–80, 41.
64. In the "Seventh Eclogue," written by Radnóti when he served in the Hungarian army's labor battalions in the summer of 1944, he mentions the sufferings of the Jews in the same breath as the sufferings of people of other nations, such as "Frenchman or Polish / Loud-voiced Italian, partisan Serb, sad Jew," who were all sentenced to a life "among rumors and lice." See Radnóti, *Complete Poetry,* 269. Interestingly, the phenomenon of playing down one's Jewish identity and ensuing suffering in the labor battalions is also noted in Andrew Vázsonyi's work (in collaboration with Dégh) concerning the dynamics of rumor stories.
65. Nancy Friday writes that daughters often create an identity different from that of their mothers in terms of profession, lifestyle, and external appearance. However, these changes only serve to camouflage the fact that these daughters resemble their mothers in certain innate traits such as conduct and emotional makeup, and that the daughters are well aware of this inevitable similarity. See Friday, *My Mother/My Self,* 45–46.

Chapter 3

1. Dilthey, "Rise of Hermeneutics"; Z. Levy, *Hermeneutics in Modern Jewish Thought,* 95–100.
2. On hermeneutics as a scientific process, see Dilthey, "Rise of Hermeneutics," 232. On its ability to predict, see Habermas, *Knowledge and Human Interest,* 259.
3. Gadamer, *Truth and Method,* 91, 99; Warnke, *Gadamer,* 49–51.
4. Dilthey, "Rise of Hermeneutics," 233.
5. Warnke, *Gadamer,* 42; Iser, "Interaction between Text and Reader," 108.
6. Gadamer, *Truth and Method,* 147; Palmer, *Hermeneutics,* 13.
7. Poulet, "Phenomenology of Reading," 1214; Warnke, *Gadamer,* 48.
8. Habermas, *Knowledge and Human Interest,* 146; Ricoeur, *Hermeneutics and the Human Sciences,* 158. On Husserl and the life world, see Watson, "Understanding a Life History as a Subjective Document," 99. For Iser, see Iser, "Reading Process," 286, 287, and 298.
9. Frank, "Finding the Common Denominator," 89.
10. Todorov, "Reading as Construction," 67.
11. Fish, "Literature in the Reader," 83, 85; Maranda, "Dialectic of Metaphor," 188, 189; Hasan-Rokem, *Web of Life,* 16–38.

12. Rosen, "Holocaust at the Center of Life," 350.
13. It is interesting to note that Ricoeur also emphasizes the importance of context not for folkloristic considerations, but because of his view of language as made of many layers, or in his parlance, *polysemic.* See Ricoeur, *Hermeneutics and the Human Sciences,* 44.
14. Fish, "Literature in the Reader," 72, 88.
15. Fish, "Literature in the Reader," 78; Iser, "Reading Process," 285, 286; Todorov, "Reading as Construction," 69.
16. Eco, *Role of the Reader,* 256.
17. Brooke-Rose, "Readerhood of Man," 120–48.
18. Eco, *Role of the Reader,* 204.
19. On the need to maintain open vistas, see Iser, "Reading Process," 288, and *Implied Reader,* 281–83. On handling consistency and inconsistency, see "Reading Process," 288. On blockages, see *Implied Reader,* 279.
20. Iser, "Reading Process," 279.
21. Eco, *Role of the Reader,* 229; Iser, *Implied Reader,* 288.
22. Iser, *Fictive and the Imaginary,* and *Prospecting.*
23. Colebrook, *New Literary Histories,* 1; Cox and Reynolds, eds., *New Historical Literary Study,* 3–38.
24. See, for example, the following literary, historical, or general cultural "anthropologies": Livingston, *An Anthropology of Reading;* Hirsch and O'Hanlon, eds., *Anthropology of Landscape;* R. Levy, *Antisemitism in the Modern World;* C. Robinson, *An Anthropology of Marxism.*
25. On qualitative methods in anthropology, sociology, and psychology, see Alasuutari, *Researching Culture;* Weiss, *Learning from Strangers;* Hollway and Jefferson, *Doing Qualitative Research Differently.* On literary cultural studies, see Grossberg, Nelson, and Treichler, eds., *Cultural Studies;* During, ed., *Cultural Studies Reader;* Campbell, *American Cultural Studies;* Turner, *British Cultural Studies.* On interdisciplinarity, see Easterlin, ed., *After Poststructuralism;* Sell and Verdonk, eds., *Literature and the New Interdisciplinarity.*
26. See, for example, the special attention paid to the level of sounds and its significance in the explanation of the narrative's psychological and ideological levels in Hasan-Rokem, *Web of Life,* 20, 32–38.
27. For the unique meaning of the term *responsibility* in the context of testimonies and memories of Holocaust survivors, see Felman and Laub, *Testimony.*
28. About rumors as a folkloristic genre and aspects of their analysis, see Dégh and Vázsonyi, "Hypothesis of Multi-Conduit Transmission in Folklore"; and Shenhar-Alroy, "Rumor Stories," in *The Story, the Storyteller, and the Audience,* 105–34.
29. Kertész, *Sorstalanság.*
30. The Hungarian word used by the narrator to refer to the boy is *kölyök.*

Literally, the word means "puppy," but it is also used as a derogatory term, like *brat* in English.

31. Iser, *Implied Reader*, 281–83.
32. Austin, *How to Do Things with Words*, 14–15.
33. Rosen, "Holocaust at the Center of Life," 84–85.
34. Regarding the principle that "the abnormal becomes normal" or "everything is upside down," see Gerson, "Silent Tales," 108.
35. Derrida, *Margins of Philosophy*, 3–27; Norris, *Deconstruction*, 46–48.
36. On the Babel of languages in the context of social or cultural chaos, see Roskies, *Against the Apocalypse*, 167.
37. Görög-Karady, "Ethnic Stereotypes and Folklore"; Huseby-Darvas, "Remembering Our Jews."
38. Rosen, "Holocaust at the Center of Life," 174, and *Hungarian Jewish Women Survivors*, 83. Since *Hungarian Jewish Women Survivors* was prepared for the general public, it may not include the exact full text as presented in "Holocaust at the Center of Life," which is as faithful as possible to the texts of the narrators.
39. See, for example, the references to this issue in the life histories of Klára Nagy and Roselia Jozsef in Rosen, "Holocaust at the Center of Life," 265, 294, and *Hungarian Jewish Women Survivors*, 16–17, 65.
40. In folkloristics of the recent decades, the concept of storytelling as dramatic and live performance rooted in its immediate as well as a wider context is heavily stressed; this seems to replace the emphasis placed in previous decades on the content of the (written) narrative. See Georges, "Toward an Understanding of Storytelling Events"; Ben-Amos, "Toward a Definition of Folklore in Context"; Kirshenblatt-Gimblett, "A Parable in Context"; Alexander and Govrin, "Story Telling as a Performing Art."
41. Charles L. Briggs objects to the structuralist view that the creators of oral texts are not aware of their hidden or subtle meanings. Briggs claims that they are indeed aware of the text's meaning and that they even feel responsibility for the meaning and the mission of transmitting it. See Briggs, *Competence in Performance*, 18–19.
42. Levi, *The Truce*, 71.
43. Bakhtin, *Problems in Dostoevsky's Poetics*, 5–6.
44. For the metaphor of voyeurism as an action or interaction in the context of the world of concentration camps, see Langer, *Holocaust Testimonies*, 31, 55.
45. In fact, the couples engage in folkloric family discourse similar to that described in Dégh's essay "Symbiosis of Joke and Legend."
46. Rosen, "Holocaust at the Center of Life," 345–49, 350–55.
47. About the interview as a "transaction," see Kenny, "Patron-Client Relationship in Interviewing."
48. See, in this context, Gideon Greif's book *"We Wept without Tears . . . ,"*

which documents the experiences of the Sonderkommando men in their own words.

49. Austin, *How to Do Things with Words,* 14–15.
50. Gutman, *Encyclopedia of the Holocaust,* vol. A, 241.
51. Langer, "Gendered Suffering?"

Chapter 4

1. Langer, *Holocaust Testimonies,* xi.
2. Szalai, "Will the Past Protect Hungarian Jewry?"
3. Rosen, *Hungarian Jewish Women Survivors,* 71–72.
4. Colebrook, *New Literary Histories,* 26.
5. Des Pres, *The Survivor,* 30.

Appendix

1. Where the place of origin has changed regimes during the lifetime of the narrator, the names of both countries/regimes will be given.
2. In Hungarian, married women (as well as widows and divorced women) are called by their husbands' names with the suffix *né,* which stands for "Mrs." In this work, though, I decided to call these Hungarian women by their names to match Israeli and American English naming conventions.

Bibliography

Adams, Hazard, ed. *Critical Theory since Plato*. New York: Harcourt, Brace, Jovanovich, 1971.

Alasuutari, Pertti. *Researching Culture: Qualitative Method and Cultural Studies*. London: Sage, 1995.

Albee, Edward. *Who's Afraid of Virginia Woolf?* Harmondsworth: Penguin, 1965.

Alexander, Tamar, and Michal Govrin. "Storytelling as a Performing Art." *Assaph-Studies in Theatre* 5 (1990): 1–35.

Alexander, Tamar, and Galit Hasan-Rokem. "The Multivalent Construction of Ethos in the Proverbs of a Sephardic Woman." [In Hebrew.] *Jerusalem Studies in Jewish Folklore* 17 (1995): 63–87.

Angronsino, Michael V. "The Use of Autobiography as 'Life History': The Case of Albert Gomes." *Ethos* 4 (1976): 133–54.

Austin, John Langshaw. *How to Do Things with Words*. London: Oxford University Press, 1962.

Babcock, Barbara A. "Shaping Selves, Reshaping Lives: The Art and Experience of Helen Cordero." In Hofer and Niedermüller, *Life History*, 281–309.

Bakhtin, Mikhail. *Problems in Dostoevsky's Poetics*. Minneapolis: University of Minnesota Press, 1983.

Banks, Ann, ed. *First-person America*. New York: Knopf, 1980.

Barthes, Roland. "The Structural Activity." In *Critical Theory since Plato*, edited by Hazard Adams, 1196–99. New York: Harcourt, Brace, Jovanovich, 1971.

———. *Writing Degree Zero*. New York: Hill and Wang, 1977.

———. *S/Z: An Essay*. New York: Hill and Wang, 1985.

Bascomb, William. "Verbal Art." *Journal of American Folklore* 68 (1955): 245–52.

———. "The Forms of Folklore: Prose Narrative." *Journal of American Folklore* 78 (1965): 3–21.

Baskin, Judith R., ed. *Women of the World: Jewish Women and Jewish Writing*. Detroit: Wayne State University Press, 1994.

Bauman, Richard R. *Verbal Art as Performance*. Rowley, MA: Newbury House, 1979.

———. *Story, Performance, and Event: Contextual Studies of Oral Narrative*. Cambridge: Cambridge University Press, 1986.

———. "Ed Bell, Texas Storyteller: The Framing and Re-framing of Life Experience." In Hofer and Niedermüller, *Life History*, 247–78.

Bauman, Richard R., and Joel Sherzer, eds. *Explorations in the Ethnography of Speaking*. Cambridge: Cambridge University Press, 1974.

Baumel, [Esther] Judith Tydor. *Double Jeopardy: Gender and the Holocaust*. London: Vallentine Mitchell, 1988.

———. "Social Interaction among Jewish Women in Crisis during the Holocaust: A Case Study." *Gender and History* 7 (April 1995): 64–84.

Bausinger, Hermann. "Constructions of Life." In Hofer and Niedermüller, *Life History*, 477–90.

Beinhorn (Klein), Sarah, and Yehudit Golan. *Leaves That Arose from the Ashes*. [In Hebrew.] Jerusalem: Yad Vashem, the A.M.O.S. Fund, 1999.

Ben-Amos, Dan. "Toward a Definition of Folklore in Context." *Journal of American Folklore* 84 (1971): 3–15.

———. "The Concept of Motif in Folklore." In *Folklore Studies in the Twentieth Century: Proceedings of the Centenary Conference of the Folklore Society*, edited by Venitia J. Newall, 17–36. Totowa, NJ: Rowman and Littlefield, 1980.

———. "The Elusive Audience of Benin Narrators." In *Folklore in Context*, 169–76. New Delhi, Madras: South Asian Publishers, 1982.

———. " 'Context' in Context." *Western Folklore* 52 (1993): 209–26.

Ben-Amos, Dan, and Kenneth Goldstein, eds. *Folklore: Performance and Communication*. The Hague: Mouton, 1975.

Bendremer, Jutta T. *Women Surviving the Holocaust in Spite of the Horror*. New York: Edwin Mellen Press, 1997.

Benedek, István Gábor és Vámost György. *Tépd le a sárga csillagot* (Tear off the yellow star). Budapest: Pallas Lap és Könyvkiado, 1990.

Bennett, Gillian. "Narrative as Expository Discourse." *Journal of American Folklore* 99 (1986): 415–34.

Bernheim (Friedmann), Rachel. *Earrings in the Cellar: To Spring from Destroyed Worlds: A Personal Story*. [In Hebrew.] Tel Aviv: Moreshet, 1999.

Bertaux, Daniel, ed. *Biography and Society: The Life History Approach in the Social Sciences*. Thousand Oaks, CA: Sage, 1981.

Bettelheim, Bruno. *The Uses of Enchantment: The Meaning and Importance of Fairy Tales*. London: Thames and Hudson, 1976.

———. *Surviving, and Other Essays*. New York: Vintage, 1980.

Bilu, Yoram, and Galit Hasan-Rokem. "Cinderella and the Saint: The Life Story of a Jewish Moroccan Female Healer in Israel." *The Psychoanalytical Study of Society* 15 (1989): 227–60.

Biró, Imre. "Adatok a magyar kultura zsidó mártirjainak történetéhez" (Facts about the history of the martyrs of Hungarian Jewish Culture). *Miok: State Center of Hungarian Israelites* (Magyar Izraeliták Országos Központja) (1973–74): 130–45.

———. "Váradi emlékek" (Memories of Várad). *Miok: State Center of Hungarian Israelites* (1981–82): 84–97.

Blumental, Nachman. "Magical Thinking among the Jews during the Nazi Occupation." *Yad Vashem Studies* 5 (1963): 22–36.

Borowski, Tadeusz. *This Way for the Gas, Ladies and Gentlemen.* Middlesex, England: Penguin, 1976.

Braham, Randolph L. *The Hungarian Labor Service System, 1939–1945.* New York: Columbia University Press, 1977.

———. *The Politics of Genocide: The Holocaust in Hungary.* 2 vols. New York: Columbia University Press, 1981.

———. *The Wartime System of Labor Service in Hungary: Varieties of Experience.* New York: Columbia University Press, 1995.

Brainer, Shoshi. *Ariadna: A Novel.* [In Hebrew.] Tel Aviv: Hakibbutz Hameuchad, 1990.

Brámer, Frigyes. "A budapesti gettó utolsó két hete." (The Last Two Weeks of the Budapest Ghetto) *Miok: State Center of Hungarian Israelites* (1975–76): 9–17.

Bridenthal, Renata, Atina Grossman, and Marion Kaplan, eds. *When Biology Becomes Destiny: Women in Weimar and Nazi Germany.* New York: Monthly Review Press, 1988.

Briggs, Charles L. *Competence in Performance: The Creativity of Tradition in Mexicano Verbal Art.* Philadelphia: University of Pennsylvania Press, 1988.

Brink, T. L. "Oral History and Geriatric Mental Health: Distortions of Testimony Produced by Psychopathology." *Oral History Review* 13 (1985): 93–105.

Brooke-Rose, Christine. "The Readerhood of Man." In Suleiman and Crosman, *Reader in the Text,* 120–48.

Brown, Laura S. "Not Outside the Range: One Feminist Perspective on Psychic Trauma." In "Psychoanalysis, Culture, and Trauma," edited by Cathy Caruth. Special issue, *American Imago: Studies in Psychoanalysis and Culture* 48 (1991): 119–33.

Bruner, Jerome. "Life as Narrative." *Social Research* 54 (1987): 11–32.

Budick, Sanford, and Wolfgang Iser, eds. *Languages of the Unsayable.* New York: Columbia University Press, 1989.

Campbell, Neil. *American Cultural Studies: An Introduction.* London: Routledge, 1997.

Cantor, Aviva. *Jewish Women/Jewish Men: The Legacy of Patriarchy in Jewish Life.* San Francisco: Harper, 1995.

Carey, George, "The Storyteller's Art and the Collector's Intrusion." In Dégh, Glassie, and Oinas, *Folklore Today,* 81–91.

Carpenter, Inta Gail. "Exile as Life Career Model." In Hofer and Niedermüller, *Life History,* 329–44.

Caruth, Cathy, ed. "Psychoanalysis, Culture, and Trauma." Special issue, *American Imago: Studies in Psychoanalysis and Culture* 48 (1991).

———. *Unclaimed Experience: Trauma, Narrative, and History.* Baltimore: Johns Hopkins University Press, 1996.

Chodorow, Nancy. *The Reproduction of Mothering.* Berkeley: University of California Press, 1978.

Cixous, Hélène. *Coming to Writing and Other Essays.* Cambridge, MA: Harvard University Press, 1991.

———. " 'Feminine Writing' in 'Laugh of the Medusa.' " In *Feminist Literary Theory: A Reader,* edited by Mary Eagleton, 320–22. Oxford: Blackwell, 1996.

Clifford, James, and George E. Marcus, eds. *Writing Culture: The Poetics and Politics of Ethnography.* Berkeley: University of California Press, 1986.

Cohen, Asher. *The Halutz Resistance in Hungary, 1942–1944.* Boulder, CO: Social Science Monographs, 1986.

Colebrook, Claire. *New Literary Histories: New Historicism and Contemporary Criticism.* Manchester: Manchester University Press, 1997.

Cotharne, Kay. "The Truth as a Lie—The Lie as Truth." *Journal of the Folklore Society of Greater Washington* 3 (1972): 3–6.

Cox, Jeffery N., and Larry J. Reynolds, eds. *New Historical Literary Study: Essays on Reproducing Texts, Representing History.* Princeton: Princeton University Press, 1993.

Cramer, Phebe. *The Development of Defense Mechanisms: Theory, Research, and Assessment.* New York: Springer, 1991.

Crapanzano, Vincent. *Tuhami: Life of a Moroccan.* Chicago: University of Chicago Press, 1980.

———. *Hermes' Dilemma and Hamlet's Desire: On the Epistemology of Interpretation.* Cambridge, MA: Harvard University Press, 1992.

Crews, Frederick, ed. *Psychoanalysis and the Literary Process.* Cambridge, MA: Winthrop, 1970.

Crocker, John Christopher. "The Social Function of Rhetoric Forms." In *The Social Use of Metaphor: Essays on the Anthropology of Rhetoric,* edited by Davis Sapir and John Christopher Crocker, 33–66. Philadelphia: University of Pennsylvania Press, 1977.

Culler, Jonathan. "Prologomena to a Theory of Reading." In Suleiman and Crosman, *Reader in the Text,* 45–66.

Darnton, Robert. *The Great Cat Massacre and Other Episodes in French Cultural History.* New York: Vintage, 1985.

De Koven-Ezrahi, Sidra. *By Words Alone: The Holocaust in Literature.* Chicago: University of Chicago Press, 1980.

———. *Booking Passage: Homecoming in the Modern Jewish Imagination.* Berkeley: University of California Press, 2000.

Derrida, Jacques. *Margins of Philosophy.* Chicago: University of Chicago Press, 1982.

———. "Coming Into One's Own." In Hartman, *Psychoanalysis and the Question of the Text,* 114–48.

Des Pres, Terrence. *The Survivor: An Anatomy of Life in the Death Camps.* New York: Pocket Books, 1976.

Dégh, Linda. *Folklore and Society: Storytelling in a Hungarian Peasant Society.* Bloomington: Indiana University Press, 1969.

——. "Symbiosis of Joke and Legend: A Case of Conversational Folklore." In Dégh, Glassie, and Oinas, *Folklore Today*, 101–22.

——, ed. *Studies in East-European Folk Narrative.* Bloomington: Indiana University Folklore Monographs, American Folklore Society, 1978.

——. "Beauty, Wealth, and Power: Career Choices for Women in Folktales, Fairytales, and Modern Media." In Hofer and Niedermüller, *Life History*, 13–47.

Dégh, Linda, and Andrew Vázsonyi. "The Memorate and the Proto-Memorate." *Journal of American Folklore* 87 (1974): 225–38.

——. "The Hypothesis of Multi-Conduit Transmission in Folklore." In *Folklore: Performance and Communication,* edited by Dan Ben-Amos and Kenneth Goldstein, 207–52. The Hague: Mouton, 1975.

Dégh, Linda, Henry Glassie, and Felix J. Oinas, eds. *Folklore Today.* Bloomington: Indiana University Press, 1976.

Dilthey, Wilhelm. "The Rise of Hermeneutics." *New Literary History* 3 (1971–72): 229–44.

Dobos, Ilona. "True Stories." In *Studies in East-European Folk Narrative,* edited by Linda Dégh, 167–205. Bloomington: Indiana University Folklore Monographs, American Folklore Society, 1978.

Dorson, Richard M., ed. *Folklore in the Modern World.* The Hague: Mouton, 1978.

Du Maurier, Daphne. *Rebecca.* London: V. Gollancz, 1938.

Dundes, Alan, ed. *The Study of Folklore.* Englewood Cliffs, NJ: Prentice-Hall, 1965.

——. *Interpreting Folklore.* Bloomington: Indiana University Press, 1980.

——, ed. *The Blood Libel Legend: A Casebook in Anti-Semitic Folklore.* Madison: University of Wisconsin Press, 1991.

During, Simon, ed. *The Cultural Studies Reader.* London: Routledge, 1993.

Eagleton, Mary, ed. *Feminist Literary Theory: A Reader.* Cambridge, MA: Blackwell, 1996.

Easterlin, Nancy, ed. *After Poststructuralism: Interdisciplinarity and Literary Theory.* Evanston: Northwestern University Press, 1993.

Eco, Umberto. *The Role of the Reader.* Bloomington: Indiana University Press, 1979.

Eisen, György. *Árnyak játékai—gyermekek a Holocaustban* (Shade games—children in the Holocaust). Budapest: Akademiai Kiado, 1990.

Eliach, Jaffa, ed. *Hasidic Tales of the Holocaust.* New York: Vintage, 1988.

Ember, Mária. *Hajtűkanyar* (Hairpin Bend). Budapest: Szépiradalmi Könyvkiado, 1977.

Engel, Alfréd. *A Dunaszerdahelyi hitközség émlékkönyve* (The Dunaszerdahely community memorial book). Tel Aviv: Izráel, 1975.

Epstein, Julia, and Lori Hope Lefkovitz, eds. *Shaping Losses: Cultural Memory and the Holocaust.* Urbana: University of Illinois Press, 2001.

Erős, Ferenc, and Ándrás Kovács. "The Biographical Method in the Study of Jewish Identity in Present-Day Hungary." In Hofer and Niedermüller, *Life History,* 345–56.

Eschenazi, Gabriele, and Gabriele Nissim. *Invisible Jews.* [In Hebrew.] Tel Aviv: Dvir Publishing House, 1995.

Feldstein, Richard, and Henry Sussman, eds. *Psychoanalysis and . . .* London: Routledge, 1990.

Felman, Shoshana. *The Literary Speech Act.* Ithaca: Cornell University Press, 1983.

Felman, Shoshana, and Dori Laub. *Testimony: Crises of Witnessing in Literature, Psychoanalysis, and History.* New York: Routledge, 1992.

Fine, Elizabeth. *The Folklore Text.* Bloomington: Indiana University Press, 1984.

Fine, Ellen S. "Literature as Resistance: Survival in the Camps." *Holocaust and Genocide Studies* 1, no. 1 (1986): 79–89.

Fish, Stanley. "Literature in the Reader: Affective Stylistics." In *Reader-Response Criticism from Formalism to Post-Structuralism,* edited by Jane P. Tompkins, 70–100. Baltimore: Johns Hopkins University Press, 1981.

Foley, Barbara. "Fact, Fiction, Fascism: Testimony and Mimesis in Holocaust Narrative." *Comparative Literature* 34 (1982): 330–60.

Frank, Gelya. "Finding the Common Denominator: A Phenomenological Critique of the Life History Method." *Ethos* 7 (1979): 69–94.

Freud, Sigmund. *The Interpretation of Dreams: Freud's Seminal Exploration of Human Nature.* New York: Avon Books, 1965.

——. *A General Introduction to Psychoanalysis.* New York: Washington Square Press, 1968.

——. *Beyond the Pleasure Principle.* New York: Liveright, 1970.

Friday, Nancy. *My Mother/My Self: The Daughter's Search for Identity.* New York: Dell, 1982.

Fuchs, Esther, ed. *Women and the Holocaust: Narrative and Representation.* Lanham: University Press of America, 1999.

Gadamer, Hans Georg. *Truth and Method.* New York: Seabury Press, 1988.

Geiger, Susan. "Women's Life Histories: Method and Content." *Signs: Journal of Women in Culture and Society* 11 (1986): 334–51.

Georges, Robert A. "Toward an Understanding of Storytelling Events." *Journal of American Folklore* 82 (1969): 313–28.

Georges, Robert A., and Michael O. Jones. *People Studying People.* Berkeley: University of California Press, 1980.

Gerend, László. "Dachau." *Miok: State Center of Hungarian Israelites* (1979–80): 151–65.

Gerson, Stéphane. "Silent Tales: Survivors as Storytellers." *Response: A Contemporary Jewish Review* 68 (1997–98): 102–16.

Gilligan, Carol. *In a Different Voice: Psychological Theory and Women's Development.* Cambridge, MA: Harvard University Press, 1982.

Goldenberg, Myrna. "Testimony, Narrative, and Nightmare: The Experience of Jewish Women in the Holocaust." In *Active Voices: Women in Jewish Culture,* edited by Maurie Sacks, 94–106. Urbana: University of Illinois Press, 1995.

———. *Lessons Learned from Gentle Heroism: Women's Holocaust Narratives.* Thousand Oaks, CA: Sage, 1996.

———. "Memories of Auschwitz Survivors: The Burden of Gender." In Ofer and Weitzman, *Women in the Holocaust,* 327–39.

Govrin, Michal. *The Name.* [In Hebrew.] Tel Aviv: Hakibbutz Hameuchad, 1995.

Görög-Karady, Veronika. "Ethnic Stereotypes and Folklore—the Jew in Hungarian Oral Literature." In *Folklore Processed: In Honor of Lauri Honko on his 60th Birthday, 6th March 1992,* edited by Reimund Kvideland, 114–26. Helsinki: Suomalaisen Kirjallisuuden Seura (Finnish Literature Society), 1992.

Greif, Gideon. *"We Wept without Tears."* [In Hebrew.] Jerusalem and Tel Aviv: Yad Vashem and Yediot Achronot, 2000.

Gross, S. Y., and Y. Yosef Cohen, eds. *The Marmaros Book: In Memory of a Hundred and Sixty Jewish Communities.* [In Hebrew.] Tel Aviv: Beit Marmaros, 1983.

Grossberg, Lawrence, Cary Nelson, and Paula Treichler, eds. *Cultural Studies.* New York: Routledge, 1992.

Gunn, Daniel. *Psychoanalysis and Fiction: An Exploration of Literary and Psychoanalytic Borders.* New York: Cambridge University Press, 1988.

Gurewitch, Brana, ed. *Mothers, Sisters, Resisters: Oral History of Women who Survived the Holocaust.* Tuscaloosa: University of Alabama Press, 1998.

Gutman, Israel, editor in chief. *The Encyclopedia of the Holocaust.* 5 vols. London: Macmillan, 1990.

Gutman, Israel, Béla Vago, and Livia Rothkirchen, eds. *Hungarian Jewish Leadership in the Trial of the Holocaust.* [In Hebrew.] Jerusalem: Yad Vashem, 1976.

Habermas, Jurgen. *Knowledge and Human Interest.* London: Heinemann, 1972.

Hartman, Geoffrey H., ed. *Psychoanalysis and the Question of the Text.* Baltimore: Johns Hopkins University Press, 1985.

———. "On Traumatic Knowledge and Literary Studies." *New Literary History* 26 (1995): 537–63.

Hasan-Rokem, Galit. *Web of Life: Folklore and Midrash in Rabbinic Literature.* Stanford: Stanford University Press, 2000.

Hass, Aaron. *In the Shadow of the Holocaust: The Second Generation.* Ithaca: Cornell University Press, 1990.

Hawkes, Terence. *Structuralism and Semiotics.* London: Routledge, 1992.

Heinemann, Marlene E. *Gender and Destiny: Women Writers and the Holocaust.* New York: Greenwood Press, 1986.

Helm, June, ed. *Essays on the Verbal and Visual Arts: Proceedings of the 1966 Annual Spring Meeting of the American Ethnological Society.* Seattle: University of Washington Press, 1967.

Herman, Judith Lewis. *Trauma and Recovery.* New York: Basic Books, 1992.

Hirsch, Eric, and Michael O'Hanlon, eds. *The Anthropology of Landscape: Perspectives on Place and Space.* Oxford: Clarendon Press, 1995.

Hofer, Tamás, and Péter Niedermüller, eds. *Life History as Cultural Construction/Performance.* Budapest: Hungarian Academy of Sciences (M.T.A), 1989.

Holland, Norman, N. "Re-Covering 'The Purloined Letter': Reading as Personal Transaction." In Suleiman and Crosman, *Reader in the Text,* 350–70.

Hollway, Wendy, and Tony Jefferson. *Doing Qualitative Research Differently: Free Association, Narrative, and the Interview Method.* London: Sage, 2000.

Honko, Lauri. "Memorates and the Study of Folk Beliefs." *Journal of the Folklore Institute* 1 (1964): 5–19.

——. "Types of Comparison and Forms of Variation." *Journal of Folklore Research* 23, nos. 2–3 (1986): 110–24.

Horák, Madga. "Szinház a gettóban" (Theater in the Ghetto). *Miok: State Center of Hungarian Israelites* (1983–84): 167–93.

Horowitz, Sarah R. "Memory and Testimony of Women Survivors of Nazi Genocide." In *Women of the World: Jewish Women and Jewish Writing,* edited by Judith R. Baskin, 258–82. Detroit: Wayne State University Press, 1994.

——. "Women in Holocaust Literature: Engendering Trauma Memory." In Ofer and Weitzman, *Women in the Holocaust,* 364–77.

Huseby-Darvas, Éva V. "Migrating Inward and Out: Validating Life Course Transitions through Oral Autobiography." In Hofer and Niedermüller, *Life History,* 379–408.

——. " 'Remembering Our Jews': The Complexity of Village Relations in North Hungary." *Jewish Folklore and Ethnology Review* 13 (1991): 5–7.

Hymes, Dell H. "The Ethnography of Speaking." In *Anthropology and Human Behavior,* edited by Thomas Gladwin and William Strutevant, 13–53. Washington: Anthropological Society of Washington, 1971.

Irigaray, Luce. *Speculum of the Other Woman.* Ithaca: Cornell University Press, 1985.

——. *This Sex Which Isn't One.* Ithaca: Cornell University Press, 1985.

Iser, Wolfgang. "The Reading Process: A Phenomenological Approach." *New Literary History* 3 (1971–72): 279–99.

——. *The Implied Reader: Patterns of Communication in Prose Fiction from Bunyan to Beckett.* Baltimore: Johns Hopkins University Press, 1974.

———. "The Reality of Fiction: A Functionalist Approach to Literature." *New Literary History* 7 (1975): 7–38.

———. "Interaction between Text and Reader." In Suleiman and Crosman. *Reader in the Text,* 106–19.

———. *The Fictive and the Imaginary: Charting Literary Anthropology.* Baltimore: Johns Hopkins University Press, 1993.

———. *Prospecting: From Reader Response to Literary Anthropology.* New York: Columbia University Press, 2000.

Ives, Edward D. "Common-Man Biography: Some Notes by the Way." In Dégh, Glassie, and Oinas, *Folklore Today,* 251–64.

Jackson, Livia Bitton. *Elli: Coming of Age in the Holocaust.* New York: Time Books, 1980.

Jansen, Wm. Hugh. "Legend: Oral Tradition in the Modern Experience." In Dégh, Glassie, and Oinas, *Folklore Today,* 265–72.

Johnson, Barbara. "The Frame of Reference: Poe, Lacan, Derrida." In Hartman, *Psychoanalysis and the Question of the Text,* 149–71.

Jones, Ernest. "The Psychology of the Jewish Question." In *Essays in Applied Psychoanalysis,* 284–300. London: Hogarth Press, 1951.

———. "Psychoanalysis and Folklore." In *The Study of Folklore,* edited by Alan Dundes, 88–102. Englewood Cliffs, NJ: Prentice-Hall, 1965.

Jordan, Rosan A., and Susan Kalčik, eds. *Women's Folklore, Women's Culture.* Philadelphia: University of Pennsylvania Press, 1985.

Jólesz, Károly. *Kisvárda és környéke zsidósága: Emlékkönyv* (The Jewry of Kisvárda and its surroundings: a memorial book). Tel Aviv: Lahav Press, 1980.

Jung, Carl Gustav. *Psychology of the Unconscious: A Study of Transformation and Symbolism of the Libido: A Contribution to the History of the Evolution of Thought.* London: Kegan Paul, Trench, Tauber, 1919.

———. *The Undiscovered Self.* London: Little, Brown, 1958.

Kaivola-Bregenhøj, Annikki. "Factors Influencing the Formation of Narration." *Studia Fennica* 33 (1989): 73–89.

Karay, Felicja. *Rockets and Rhymes: The Hasag-Leipzig Women Labor Camp.* [In Hebrew.] Jerusalem: Yad Vashem, Moreshet, 1997.

Karmel, Ilona. *An Estate of Memory.* Boston: Houghton Mifflin, 1969.

Katona Ferenc. "Zsidó problemák a modern magyar iradalomban" (Jewish issues in modern Hungarian literature). *Miok: State Center of Hungarian Israelites* (1975–76): 218–27.

Katz, Yaacov. "The Holocaust: Could It Have Been Foreshadowed?" In *Jewish Nationalism: Essays and Studies,* 54–71. [In Hebrew.] Jerusalem: Zionist Library, 1979.

Kenny, Michael. "The Patron-Client Relationship in Interviewing." *Oral History Review* 15 (1987): 71–79.

Kertész, Imre. *Sortalanság* (Fatelessness). Budapest: Magvető, 1975.

Kielar, Wieslaw. *Anus Mundi—Fünf Jahre Auschwitz.* Frankfurt: S. Fischer, 1979.

Kirshenblatt-Gimblett, Barbara. "A Parable in Context: A Social Interactional Analysis of Storytelling Performance." In *Folklore: Performance and Communication,* edited by Dan Ben-Amos and Kenneth Goldstein, 105–30. The Hague: Mouton, 1975.

———. "Culture Shock and Narrative Creativity." In *Folklore in the Modern World,* edited by Richard M. Dorson, 109–22. The Hague: Mouton, 1978.

———. "Authoring Lives." In Hofer and Niedermüller, *Life History,* 133–78.

Koontz, Claudia. *Mothers in the Fatherland: Women, the Family, and Nazi Politics.* New York: St. Martin's Press, 1987.

Kremer, Lillian. "An Estate of Memory: Women in the Holocaust." *Holocaust Studies Annual* (1991): 99–110.

Kristeva, Julia. *Revolution in Poetic Language.* New York: Columbia University Press, 1993.

Kriza, Ildikó, ed. *A hagyomány kötelékében—tanulmányok a magyarországi zsidó folklor köréből* (In the bonds of tradition—studies in Hungarian Jewish folklore). Budapest: Akadémiai Kiado, 1990.

Kugelmass, Jack, and Jonathan Boyarin, eds. *From a Ruined Garden: The Memorial Books of Polish Jewry.* New York: Schocken Books, 1983.

Kvideland, Reimund, ed. *Folklore Processed—in Honor of Lauri Honko on his 60th Birthday, 6th March 1992.* Helsinki: Suomalaisen Kirjallisuuden Seura (Finnish Literature Society), 1992.

Labov, William. *Language in the Inner City: Studies in the Black English Vernacular.* Philadelphia: University of Pennsylvania Press, 1972.

Labov, William, and Joshua Waletzki. "Narrative Analysis: Verbal Versions of Personal Experience." In *Essays on the Verbal and Visual Arts: Proceedings of the 1966 Annual Spring Meeting of the American Ethnological Society,* edited by June Helm, 12–44. Seattle: University of Washington Press, 1967.

Lacan, Jacques. *Écrits: A Selection.* New York: Norton, 1977.

Langer, Lawrence. *Versions of Survival: The Holocaust and the Human Spirit.* Albany: State University of New York Press, 1982.

———. *Holocaust Testimonies: The Ruins of Memory.* New Haven: Yale University Press, 1990.

———. "Gendered Suffering? Women in Holocaust Testimonies." In Ofer and Weitzman, *Women in the Holocaust,* 352–63.

Langllier, Kristin M. "Personal Narratives: Perspectives on Theory and Research. *Text and Performance Quarterly* 9, no. 4 (1989): 243–76.

Langness, Lewis L. *The Life History in Anthropological Science.* New York: Holt, Rinehart, and Winston, 1965.

Langness, Lewis L., and Gelya Frank. *Lives: An Anthropological Approach to Biography.* California: Chandler and Sharp, 1988.

Lawless, Elaine. "Women's Life Stories and Reciprocal Ethnography as Feminist and Emergent." *Journal of Folklore Research* 28 (1991): 35–60.

Láng, Éva. *Kifogia elbeszélni?* (Who will tell of it?) Budapest: Pallas Lap és Könyvkiado Vállalat, 1990.

Lengyel, Olga. *Five Chimneys.* New York: Granada, 1959.

Levai, Jenő. *Eichmann in Hungary: Documents.* Budapest: Pannonia Press, 1961.

Levi, Primo. *Is This Man?* London: Orion, 1960.

———. *The Truce: A Survivor's Journey Home from Auschwitz.* London: Bodley Heard, 1965.

———. *The Drowned and the Saved.* London: Michael Joseph, 1988.

Levy, Richard S. *Antisemitism in the Modern World: An Anthropology of Texts.* Lexington: D.C. Heath, 1991.

Levy, Ze'ev. *Hermeneutics.* [In Hebrew.] Tel Aviv: Sifriat Poalim, Hakibbutz Hameuchad, 1989.

Lewis, Oscar. *La Vida; A Puerto Rican Family in the Culture of Poverty—San Juan and New York.* New York: Random House, 1966.

Lifton, Robert J. *The Broken Connection: On Death and the Continuity of Life.* New York: Simon and Schuster, 1979.

Linde, Charlotte. "Private Stories in Public Discourse: Narrative Analysis in the Social Sciences." *Poetics* 15 (1986): 183–202.

Linden, Ruth R. *Making Stories, Making Selves: Feminist Reflections on the Holocaust.* Columbus: Ohio State University Press, 1992.

Livingston, Eric. *An Anthropology of Reading.* Bloomington: Indiana University Press, 1995.

Luborsky, Mark R. "Analysis of Multiple Life History Narratives." *Ethos* 15 (1987): 366–81.

Luchterhand, Elmer, and Norbert Wieland. "The Focused Life History in Studying Involvement in a Genocidal Situation in Nazi Germany." In *Biography and Society: The Life History Approach in the Social Sciences,* edited by Daniel Bertaux, 267–87. Thousand Oaks, CA: Sage, 1981.

Luel, Steven, and Paul Marcus, eds. *Psychoanalytical Reflections on the Holocaust: Selected Essays.* New York: Holocaust Awareness Institute, Ktav, 1984.

Maier, Charles S. "A Surfeit of Memory? Reflections on History, Memory, and Denial." *History and Memory—Studies in Representation of the Past* 5, no. 2 (1993): 136–52.

Mancuso, James C., and Theodore R. Sarbin. "The Self-Narrative in the Enactment of Roles." In *Studies in Social Identity,* edited by Theodore R. Sarbin and Karl E. Scheibe, 233–53. New York: Praeger Special Studies, 1983.

Maranda, Pierre. "The Dialectic of Metaphor: An Anthropological Essay on Hermeneutics." In Suleiman and Crosman, *Reader in the Text,* 183–204.

Matejka, Ladislav, and Kristina Pomorska, eds. *Readings in Russian Poetics: Formalist and Structuralist Views.* Ann Arbor: University of Michigan Press, 1978.

McAdams, Dan P. *Power, Intimacy, and the Life History.* New York: Guilford Press, 1988.

McCann, Lisa, and Laurie Ann Pearlman. *Psychological Trauma and the Adult Survivor*. New York: Brunner and Mazel, 1990.

Meyerhoff, Barbara. *Number Our Days*. New York: E. P. Dutton, 1979.

———. "Telling One's Story." *The Center Magazine* 13 (1980): 22–40.

Milton, Sybil. "Women and the Holocaust: The Case of German and German-Jewish Women." In *When Biology Becomes Destiny: Women in Weimar and Nazi Germany,* edited by Renata Bridenthal, Atina Grossman, and Marion Kaplan, 297–323. New York: Monthly Review Press, 1984.

———. "Images of the Holocaust." *Holocaust and Genocide Studies* 1, nos. 1, 2 (1986): 27–61, 193–216.

Mintz, Alan. *Ḥurban: Responses to Catastrophe in Hebrew Literature*. New York: Columbia University Press, 1984.

Mintz, Sydney W. "The Anthropological Interview and the Life History." *Oral History Review* (1979): 18–26.

Morrison, Jack G. *Ravensbrück: Everyday Life in a Women's Concentration Camp, 1939–45*. Princeton: Markus Wiener, 2000.

Mozes, Teréz. *Bevérzett Kőtáblák* (Blood-smeared stone tablets [gravestones]). Nagyvárad: Literator Könyvkiado, 1993.

Murphy, William P. "Oral Literature." *Annual Review of Anthropology* 7 (1978): 113–36.

Nash, Dennison, and Ronald Wintrob. "The Emergence of Self-Consciousness in Ethnography." *Current Anthropology* 13, no. 5 (1972): 527–42.

Nelson, Cary. "The Psychology of Criticism, or What Can Be Said." In Hartman, *Psychoanalysis and the Question of the Text,* 45–61.

———. "Psychoanalysis as an Intervention in Contemporary Theory." In Feldstein and Sussman, *Psychoanalysis and . . .,* 11–20.

Nemiroff, Robert M. *Adult Development*. New York: Plenum Press, 1981.

Neugarten, Bernice L. "Adult Personality: Toward a Psychology of the Life Cycle." In Neugarten, *Middle Age and Aging,* 137–47.

———, ed. *Middle Age and Aging: A Reader in Social Psychology*. Chicago: University of Chicago Press, 1968.

Neugarten, Bernice L., Robert J. Havighurst, and Sheldon S. Tobin. "Personality and Patterns of Aging." In Neugarten, *Middle Age and Aging,* 173–77.

Newton, Judith, and Deborah Rosenfelt, eds. *Feminist Criticism and Social Change: Sex, Class, and Race in Literature and Culture*. New York: Methuen, 1985.

Niedermüler, Péter. "From the Stories of Life to the Life History: Historic Context, Social Processes, and the Biographical Method." In Hofer and Niedermüller, *Life History,* 451–74.

Norris, Christopher. *Deconstruction: Theory and Practice*. London: Methuen, 1982.

Noy, Dov. "Folktales in a Jewish Tunisian Family." In *Hagut Ivrit Be'Artzot Ha'Islam—Studies in Jewish Themes by Contemporary Jewish Scholars from Islamic Countries*, edited by Menachem Zohori et al., 181–88. Jerusalem: World Hebrew Union and World Jewish Congress Cultural Department, 1981.

Nyiszli, Miklós. *Auschwitz*. London: Grafton Books, 1973.

Ofer, Dalia, and Lenore J. Weitzman. *Women in the Holocaust*. New Haven: Yale University Press, 1998.

Olney, James. *Metaphors of Self: The Meaning of Autobiography*. Princeton: Princeton University Press, 1981.

Oring, Elliott. "Generating Lives: The Construction of an Autobiography." In Hofer and Niedermüller, *Life History*, 179–211.

Palmer, Richard E. *Hermeneutics*. Evanston: Northwestern University Press, 1969.

Pataki, Ferenc. "Identity Models and Identity Construction." In Hofer and Niedermüller, *Life History*, 358–78.

Pentikainen, Juha. *Oral Repertoire and World View: An Anthropological Study of Marina Takalo's Life History*. Helsinki: Academia Scientiarum Fennica, 1987.

Pingel, Falk. "The Destruction of Human Identity in Concentration Camps: The Contribution of the Social Sciences to an Analysis of Behavior under Extreme Conditions." *Holocaust and Genocide Studies* 6, no. 2 (1991): 167–84.

Poulet, Georges. "Phenomenology of Reading." In *Critical Theory since Plato*, edited by Hazard Adams, 1213–22. New York: Harcourt, Brace, Jovanovich, 1971.

Pratt, Mary Louise. *Toward a Speech Act Theory of Literary Discourse*. Bloomington: Indiana University Press, 1977.

Propp, Vladimir. *Morphology of the Folktale*. Austin: University of Texas Press, 1968.

Radnóti, Miklós. *Összes versei és műfordításai*. Budapest: Szépiradalmi Könyvkiado, 1959. Edited and translated by Emery George as *The Complete Poetry*. Michigan: Ann Arbor, 1980.

Resenfeld Vago, Lidia. "One Year in the Black Hole of Our Planet Earth." In Ofer and Weitzman, *Women in the Holocaust*, 273–84.

Ricoeur, Paul. "Metaphor and the Main Problem of Hermeneutics." *New Literary History* 6 (1974–75): 95–110.

——. *Hermeneutics and the Human Sciences*. Cambridge: Cambridge University Press, 1982.

Rimmon-Kenan, Shlomith. *Narrative Fiction: Contemporary Poetics*. London: Methuen, 1983.

——. *Discourse in Psychoanalysis and Literature*. London: Methuen, 1987.

Ringelheim, Joan. *The Unethical and the Unspeakable: Women and the Holocaust*. New York: Institute for Research in History, 1983.

——. "Women and the Holocaust: A Reconsideration of Research." *Signs: Journal of Women in Culture and Society* 10, no. 4 (1985): 741–61.

——. "The Split between Gender and the Holocaust." In Ofer and Weitzman, *Women in the Holocaust,* 34–50.

Ritvo, Roger. *Sisters in Sorrow: Voices of Care in the Holocaust.* College Station: Texas A&M. University Press, 1998.

Robinson, Cedric J. *An Anthropology of Marxism.* Aldershot, Hampshire: Ashgate, 2001.

Robinson, John A. "Personal Narratives Reconsidered." *Journal of American Folklore* 94 (1981): 58–85.

Rogers, Kim Lacy, Selma Leydesdorff, and Graham Dawson, eds. *Trauma and Life Stories: International Perspectives.* London: Routledge, 1999.

Rosen, Ilana. "The Holocaust at the Center of Life: A Folkloristic Analysis of Life Histories Told by Hungarian-Speaking Holocaust Survivors." [In Hebrew.] PhD diss., Hebrew University, 1994.

——. "The Memory of the Holocaust as Lament: The Life Histories of Two Holocaust Survivors Mourning their Fate." [In Hebrew.] *Jerusalem Studies in Jewish Folklore* 16 (1994): 97–111.

——. *There Once Was . . . : The Oral Tradition of the Jews of Carpatho-Russia.* [In Hebrew.] Tel-Aviv: Diaspora Research Institute at Tel Aviv University, 1999.

——. *Sister in Sorrow: A Journey to the Life Histories of Female Holocaust Survivors from Hungary.* [In Hebrew.] Beer Sheva: Ben Gurion University of the Negev Publishers, 2003.

——. *Hungarian Jewish Women Survivors Remember the Holocaust: An Anthology of Life Histories.* Lanham: University Press of America, 2004.

——. *In Auschwitz We Blew the Shofar: Carpatho-Russian Jews Remember the Holocaust.* [In Hebrew.] Jerusalem: Yad Vashem and the Hebrew University at Jerusalem, 2004.

Rosenblatt, Paul C., Patricia Walsh, and Douglas A. Jackson, eds. *Grief and Mourning in Cross-Cultural Perspective.* New Haven, CT: Human Relations Area Files, 1976.

Rosenfeld, Alvin H. "Holocaust Fictions and the Transformation of Historical Memory." *Holocaust and Genocide Studies* 3, no. 3 (1988): 323–36.

Roskies, David G. *Against the Apocalypse: Responses to Catastrophe in Modern Jewish Culture.* Cambridge, MA: Harvard University Press, 1984.

Ross, Andrew. "The Politics of Impossibility." In Feldstein and Sussman, *Psychoanalysis and . . . ,* 113–25.

Rotenberg, Mordechai. "The Horizontal and Vertical Structure of Social Identity: Applications to the Hasidic Revolution." In *Studies in Social Identity,* edited by Theodore R. Sarbin and Karl E. Scheibe, 165–83. New York: Praeger Special Studies, 1983.

Rothkirchen, Livia. "The Jews of Hungary in the Holocaust: A General Survey." In *Hungarian Jewish Leadership in the Trial of the Holocaust,* edited by Israel Gutman, Béla Vago, and Livia Rothkirchen, 25–59. [In Hebrew.] Jerusalem: Yad Vashem, 1976.

Runyan, William McKinley. *Life Histories and Psychobiography: Explorations in Theory and Method.* Oxford: Oxford University Press, 1984.

Sacks, Maurie, ed. *Active Voices: Women in Jewish Culture.* Urbana: University of Illinois Press, 1995.

Salvagio, Ruth. "Psychoanalysis and Deconstruction and Woman." In Feldstein and Sussman, *Psychoanalysis and . . .* , 151–60.

Sapir, David, and John Christopher Crocker, eds. *The Social Use of Metaphor: Essays on the Anthropology of Rhetoric.* Philadelphia: University of Pennsylvania Press, 1977.

Sarbin, Theodore R., and Karl E. Scheibe, eds. *Studies in Social Identity.* New York: Praeger Special Studies, 1983.

Schiffrin, Deborah. "Mother-Daughter Discourse in a Holocaust Oral History: Because Then You Admit That You Are Guilty.' " *Narrative Inquiry* 10, no. 1 (2000): 1–44.

Schrager, Samuel. "What Is Social in Oral History?" *Indiana Journal of Oral History* 4 (1983): 76–95.

Schwartz, Mark F., and Leigh Cohn, eds. *Sexual Abuse and Eating Disorders.* New York: Brunner/Mazel, 1996.

Schwartz, Murray M. "Critic, Define Thyself." In Hartman, *Psychoanalysis and the Question of the Text,* 1–17.

Searle, John. *Speech Acts: An Essay in the Philosophy of Language.* Cambridge: Cambridge University Press, 1968.

Sell, Roger D., and Peter Verdonk, eds. *Literature and the New Interdisciplinarity: Poetics, Linguistics, History.* Amsterdam: Rodopi, 1994.

Semel, Nava. *Glass Cap.* [In Hebrew.] Tel Aviv: Sifriat Poalim, 1988.

Shenhar-Alroy, Aliza. *The Story, the Storyteller, and the Audience.* [In Hebrew.] Tel Aviv: Hakibbutz Hameuchad, 1994.

Shostak, Marjorie. *Nisa: The Life and Worlds of a !Kung Woman.* Cambridge, MA: Harvard University Press, 1981.

Sicher, Efraim. "Writing After: Literature and Moral Reflections of the Holocaust." *Holocaust Studies Annual* (1991): 147–68.

Skevington, Suzanne, and Deborah Baker, eds. *The Social Identity of Women.* London: Sage, 1989.

Slander, Joseph, and Anna Freud. *The Analysis of Defense: The Ego and the Mechanisms of Defense Revisited.* New York: International Universities Press, 1985.

Smith, Roger W. "Women and Genocide: Notes on an Unwritten History." *Holocaust and Genocide Studies* 8, no. 3 (1994): 315–34.

Spence, Donald P. *Narrative Truth and Historical Truth: Meaning and Interpretation in Psychoanalysis.* London: Norton, 1982.

Stahl, Sandra K. Dolby. "The Oral Personal Narrative in Its Generic Context." *Fabula: Journal of Folktale Studies* 18 (1977): 18–39.

———. "The Personal Narrative as Folklore." *Journal of the Folklore Institute* 14 (1977): 9–30.

——. "A Literary Folkloristic Methodology for the Study of Meaning in Personal Narrative." *Journal of Folklore Research* 22 (1985): 45–70.

——. "Family Settlement Stories and Personal Values." In *The Old Traditional Way of Life: Essays in Honor of Warren F. Roberts*, edited by Robert Walls et al., 362–66. Bloomington: Indiana University Press, 1989.

——. *Literary Folkloristics and the Personal Narrative*. Bloomington: Indiana University Press, 1989.

Steiner, George. *In Bluebeard's Castle: Some Notes toward the Redefinition of Culture*. New Haven: Yale University Press, 1979.

Suleiman, Susan, and Inge Crosman, eds. *The Reader in the Text: Essays on Audience and Interpretation*. Princeton: Princeton University Press, 1980.

Szalai, Anna. "Will the Past Protect Hungarian Jewry? Responses of Jewish Intellectuals to Anti-Jewish Legislation." *Yad Vashem Studies* 32 (2004): 171–208.

Tabory, Ephraim, and Leonard Weller. "The Impact of Cultural Context on the Mental Health of Jewish Holocaust and Concentration Camps Survivors." *Holocaust and Genocide Studies* 2, no. 2 (1987): 299–305.

Tedeschi, Richard G., and Lawrence G. Calhoun. *Trauma and Transformation: Growing in the Aftermath of Suffering*. Thousand Oaks, CA: Sage, 1995.

Thompson, Paul. "Life Histories and the Analysis of Social Change." In *Biography and Society: The Life History Approach in the Social Sciences*, edited by Daniel Bertaux, 289–306. Thousand Oaks, CA: Sage, 1981.

Titon, Jeff Todd. "The Life Story." *Journal of American Folklore* 93 (1980): 276–92.

Todorov, Tzevetan. "Reading as Construction." In Suleiman and Crosman, *Reader in the Text*, 67–82.

Tomashevskii, Borris. "Literature and Biography." In *Readings in Russian Poetics: Formalist and Structuralist Views*, edited by Ladislav Matejka and Kristina Pomorska, 47–55. Ann Arbor: University of Michigan Press, 1978.

Tompkins, Jane P., ed. *Reader-Response Criticism from Formalism to Post-Structuralism*. Baltimore: Johns Hopkins University Press, 1981.

Turner, Graeme. *British Cultural Studies: An Introduction*. London: Routledge, 1996.

Turner, Victor. *The Forest of Symbols*. Ithaca: Cornell University Press, 1967.

Urban, Greg. "Speech about Speech in Speech about Action." *Journal of American Folklore* 97 (1984): 310–28.

Van Gennep, Arnold. *The Rites of Passage*. London: Routledge and Kegan Paul, 1960.

Vansina, Jan. *Oral Tradition as History*. Madison: University of Wisconsin Press, 1985.

Vardi, Dina. *Memorial Candles: Children of the Holocaust*. London: Tavistock/Routledge, 1992.

Voigt, Vilmos. "Why Do People Lie? Origins of Biographical Legend Pattern." In Hofer and Niedermüller, *Life History*, 212–46.

Walls, Robert, et al., eds. *The Old Traditional Way of Life: Essays in Honor of Warren F. Roberts*. Bloomington: Indiana University Press, 1989.

Warnke, Georgia. *Gadamer: Hermeneutics, Tradition, and Reason*. Stanford, CA: Stanford University Press, 1987.

Watson, Lawrence C. "Understanding a Life History as a Subjective Document: Hermeneutical and Phenomenological Perspectives." *Ethos* 4 (1976): 95–131.

Weber, Samuel. "Psychoanalysis, Literary Criticism, and the Problem of Authority." In Feldstein and Sussman, *Psychoanalysis and . . .* , 21–32.

Weinreich, Uriel. "Culture Geography at a Distance: Some Problems in the Study of East European Jewry." In *Symposium on Language and Culture*, edited by Viola Edmundson Garfield et al., 29–39. Seattle: University of Washington, American Ethnological Society, 1963.

Weiss, Robert Stuart. *Learning from Strangers: The Art and Method of Qualitative Interview Studies*. New York: Free Press, 1995.

Weitz, Yehiam. *The Man Who Was Murdered Twice*. [In Hebrew.] Jerusalem: Keter, 1995.

Wiesel, Elie. *Night*. New York: Bantam, 1982.

Woolf, Virginia. *Mrs. Dalloway*. London: Granada, 1983.

Yehuda, Ruth, ed. *Psychological Trauma*. Washington, DC: American Psychiatric Press, 1998.

Young, James Edward. *Writing and Rewriting the Holocaust*. Bloomington: Indiana University Press, 1988.

Zenner, Walter P. "The Folklore of Jewish-Gentile Relations." *Jewish Folklore and Ethnology Review* 13 (1991): 2–4.

Zerba, Kathryn. *The Body Betrayed: Women, Eating Disorders, and Treatment*. Washington, DC: American Psychiatric Press, 1993.

Zohori, Menachem et al., eds. *Hagut Ivrit Be'Artzot Ha'Islam—Studies in Jewish Themes by Contemporary Jewish Scholars from Islamic Countries*. Jerusalem: World Hebrew Union and World Jewish Congress Cultural Department, 1981.

Zsolt, Béla. *Kilenc koffer* (Nine suitcases). Budapest: Magvető, 1980.

Term Index

abortion 53–54, 132, 141
absurd 36, 130
abuse 19, 36
achtung (German: attention) 104, 106, 161
activation 88
active person 43, 56, 78; member 55; memory 117
activity 26, 27, 42, 85; analytical 91, 99; hermeneutic 84, 86
adolescence 2, 49, 67
aesthetics 88
afraid 154, 157, 160, 164, 167, 179, 180, 184, 185, 187 210, 217, 220, 221; of dreams 140; of the future 62, 147; of Jews 107, 165; of Russians 107, 154, 165
agency 7; agent 34, 68
agents provocateurs 155
Air Force Technical School 193
air raid 73, 145, 149, 152, 163, 178, 189
aliya 4, 24, 63, 112, 113, 123, 182, 183, 219
aliyat Haggana (immigration movement) 197
allusion 46, 92, 111
ambiguous 49, 74, 114
American culture 70; troops 162, 165
American Psychoanalytic Association 29
amnesia 30
Amnesty International 155
analytical 7, 9, 20; process/path 27, 41; method 90; activity of audience 91–99; activity of narrators 99–111; units 31
anger 65, 66, 76, 97, 133, 181; unconscious 72
anonymity 79; anonymous 17, 39, 76, 79
anthropology 3, 27; anthropological 89, 90
anticlimax 10

anti-Semitism 4, 7, 11, 45, 70, 113, 129, 139, 202, 203; attitude toward 120; during Hungarian Communist regime 151, 196, 207; escalation of 185, 187, 220; horrors of 62; prior to Holocaust 13, 18, 69, 71, 105, 125, 139, 148, 187, 206, 211, 216
anxiety 62, 74
appell 8, 91, 106. *See also* roll call
appendix, reference to 20, 128
Arrow Cross Party (Nyilas) 68, 73, 74, 75, 145, 149, 153, 154, 185, 220
art 17, 25, 40, 84
arthritis 149
artifact 25
artificiality 5, 25
assimilation 194
asylum 160
atrocity 129; atrocities 30, 32, 40, 121
audience 11–12, 37, 86, 87, 108, 115–16, 124, 126; analytical activity of 28, 91–99; involvement 9, 26, 28, 29, 33–34, 54, 61, 90, 105, 114, 122, 133; responsibility to 111
aunt 58, 63, 111, 112, 129, 197, 209
Austro-Hungarian culture 103, 128; Austro-Hungarian Empire 12, 123, 130, 205, 211
author 26, 76, 87, 89
Aviva (section in *Halutz* movement) 219
Axis 12

babies 156–57, 160, 172; in Auschwitz 93, 156; handing over 75, 91, 93
bargain/bargaining 9, 57, 58, 118
barishna (Russian: woman) 39, 137, 138, 180
barn 142
barracks 158, 176, 177, 183, 220

beating 148, 211
Bedek Aviation Group 193
beit olim (immigrant house) 210
belief 63, 65, 66
Betar (Zionist movement) 174, 218
biography 86; biographically 18
biological 49
birth 17, 40, 77, 110, 116, 123, 185; rate 129;
    Dora Ashkenazi 156; Ernő Bihari 116;
    Zsuzsa Faludi 150; Rozsi Háger 44–45,
    139; Leah Heiman 113, 115
"blockage" 89
Blockälteste (block commander) 100, 159,
    160, 176, 177, 185
block in camp 124, 136, 140, 176
blood libel 205
blood sausage 174
blueberries 39, 138
bombs 160, 162, 189
bread 101, 140, 142, 165, 221; getting sup-
    plies 104, 135, 161; hiding 49, 100, 159; in
    camps 157, 158, 159, 161, 164, 174, 178,
    182, 192
bribes 13
British authorities 182; ships 182; soldiers
    186, 189, 217
bromide 140, 182
brother 1, 2, 66, 68, 129, 138; Dora Ash-
    kenazi 156, 159, 163, 166, 168, 169, 170,
    171, 172, 173, Anna Bihari 18, 201, 204,
    205; Zsusza Faludi 66, 74, 149; Aranka
    Friedmann 48, 53, 57, 58, 140, 141, 142;
    Irma Fischer 59, 69, 144, 145, 146, 147;
    Rozsi Háger 138; Leah Heiman 197, 198,
    200; Esther Israel: 215, 216, 221; Rachel
    Markowitz 98, 174, 181, 182, 183, 184, 185;
    Ruth Matias 186, 187; Piri Meister 219;
    Berta Wazner 208–9
bunk bed 160, 175, 177
bunkers 141

cabbage 219
cake 170
camouflage 61, 62, 229
camp doctor 178, 229n65
"camp-mate" 129

"camp sister" 182
Capo 8, 140
catharsis 10, 28, 29
Catholic 154, 206
cattle car 8, 33, 99, 101, 102, 136, 140, 158,
    163, 175, 179, 191
cellar 69, 144
cemetery 123, 124, 140, 213, 214
certificate 14, 137, 183
challa (bread for blessing) 174
chaos 110, 231n36
character 20, 24, 42, 46, 47, 49, 50, 59–60,
    62, 87, 117
cheese 142, 167, 191
cherries 181
chicken pox 157
child 7, 24, 53, 57, 62, 63, 67, 69, 71, 139,
    144, 145, 150, 153, 170, 181, 185; behavior
    of 1, 5, 25, 37, 42, 43, 45, 47, 69, 72, 98,
    139, 147, 148, 181, 196, 189, 200, 211, 201,
    230n30; children 2, 14, 26, 31, 44, 52, 53,
    58, 59, 60, 68, 73, 104, 113, 118, 119, 123,
    129, 132, 141, 144, 145, 146, 149, 151, 161,
    184, 185, 187, 191, 192, 195, 196, 214, 216,
    220, 224n11; communication with 11, 15,
    32, 61, 123, 124, 125, 190, 214–15, 217; sep-
    aration of 75, 91, 92, 93, 95, 156–57,
    175, 205
childhood 3, 18, 25, 26, 49, 50, 51, 59, 62,
    64, 81, 112, 114, 132, 147, 156, 204; happy
    31–32, 63, 80, 135, 147, 156; memories 37,
    45, 65, 67, 123, 213; childish 31, 33, 34, 37,
    54, 66; childlike 24, 26, 42, 47, 48, 64
Christians 3, 14, 33, 136, 139, 150, 153, 154,
    194, 197, 204, 208, 209, 210, 211, 212, 214
circularity 45
civil war in Yugoslavia 87, 202, 203
clairvoyance 46
classification by Nazis 93
clinic, dental 117, 143, 202, 203, 204, 207
clogs, Dutch wooden 177
closure 9, 45
clothing 93, 136, 138, 148, 149, 158–59, 160,
    175, 176, 181, 182, 189; warehouse 159,
    179, 188, 190
coal (tablet) 140, 164; for heating 160, 170

code 8, 95, 117

cognitive 28, 99

cold 8, 14, 51, 54, 130, 142, 158, 177, 179

collaboration with Germans 96, 97

collective 38, 119

colorful 48, 49, 50, 144, 188

Communism 62, 128, 206

Communist Party 54–55, 80, 143, 154, 155, 182, 199, 219, 220

Communist regime 4, 11, 15, 68, 69, 78, 132, 148, 151, 153, 195–96, 202, 206

concealing 35, 83, 84, 90, 110–11, 112, 113, 116, 118, 121, 128

concentration 61, 94

concentration camp 6, 7, 38, 70, 106, 108, 122, 137, 179, 208–9, 211, 228n45; deportation to 32, 46, 120, 141, 154, 216, 231n44; experience of 9, 10, 14, 21, 30, 35, 36, 37, 39, 40, 41, 42, 49, 51, 52, 60, 71, 93, 102, 128, 129, 130, 138, 165, 178, 182, 188, 220, 221; horrors of 23, 99, 109, 120, 126, 138, 162, 176, 182, 217; liberation from 50, 53, 96, 140, 163, 172, 177

conflict 9, 10, 38, 67, 127

conscience 92

consciousness 2, 6, 8, 21, 47, 61, 64, 70, 85, 86, 88, 89, 99, 175, 212; of narrator 28, 34, 111, 118, 123

construct (noun) 21, 31, 224

content 10, 15, 33, 34, 47, 48, 64, 85, 92, 109, 112, 114, 118, 231n40

context 5, 15, 27, 41, 47, 50, 54, 61, 62, 67, 87, 88, 90, 92, 95, 99, 102, 113, 131, 226n12, 230n13, 231n40

contextualization 87

contract 12

control 8, 49, 55, 61, 64, 153; of memories 50, 121, 123, 125

convent 154

conventions 21, 54, 225n1, 232n2

convert 8

corpses, 125, 127, 136, 183–84, 217

coordinate (grammatical phrases) 26, 48

couple 5, 57, 69, 83, 111, 113, 116, 118, 122, 170, 211, 231n45

coupons 135

courtship 41–42, 43, 44

cousins 129, 136, 155, 158, 163, 166, 167, 168, 170, 171, 172, 181, 197, 209, 212, 213

crazy 35, 37, 136

crematorium 45, 53, 91, 95, 100, 158, 176, 219

criticism 13, 14, 24, 26, 38, 57, 59, 60, 61, 63, 65, 76, 86, 109, 129, 226n8

cross-reference 28

cultural context 3, 12, 14, 15, 25, 30, 44, 87, 88, 102, 104, 105 atmosphere 16, 17; implications 25, 89, 128; pluralism 103

curfew 152, 176

Czechs 140, 166; army 168, 169, 181, 215; brigade 169, 217; language 100, 159; partisans 137; village 98, 180; women 96, 97, 98, 180

"darker text" 19, 126

daughter 42, 44, 45, 72, 145, 147, 173, 174, 184 200, 218, 219, 220, 221, 229n65; dialogue with 31, 46, 58, 61; family of 69, 76, 113, 115, 132, 203, 205; fate of 43, 68, 75, 77, 79, 80, 150, 162, 192, 193, 197, 198; relations with father 64, 70, 71, 139, 144, 146

death march 94

death camp 23, 46, 70, 71, 216

deceit, act of 102

defense 39, 112, 124; mechanism 16, 25, 35, 65, 228

delay tactics 33, 34, 99, 116

delusion 33, 34

denial 71, 74

dentist 117, 202, 204

deportation 8, 34, 57, 120, 142, 143, 164, 192, 219, 228n58; deportees 34, 91, 93, 110, 137; prior to 13, 31, 32, 210, 218; to Auschwitz 33, 46, 53, 136, 187

depravation situation 42

depression 29

deserter 66, 149

despair 10, 75

Destruction (Hebrew: *hurban*) 7, 8, 29, 110

deus ex machina 34

development 18, 25, 42, 90, 106, 225n4; town 116
dialogue 24, 58, 68, 87, 105, 119
diarrhea 140, 180, 189
diaspora 3, 16, 17, 116, 196
diaspora negation (Hebrew: *Shlilat Ha'Gola*) 11
diphtheria 146
dirty 35
dirty Jew 70, 151, 190
discourse 5, 7, 19, 20, 23, 24, 35, 44, 46, 59, 61, 84, 85, 90, 121, 129; expository 64; family 231n45; scholarly 29
disease 14, 51, 66, 73, 145, 182, 189, 201, 207, 219, 228n42
disinfection 36, 91, 138, 176, 184, 227n28
displaced persons 110, 186
displacement 32, 54, 65
dissident 80, 155
docudrama 90
documentary 8, 11, 16, 90
dogs 100, 159, 177
doom 10, 11, 34 93, 101, 176
dramatic impact 33
dream 26, 27, 28, 46, 54, 74, 124, 140, 165, 168, 195, 200, 214, 225n8

ego 54
Eichmann trial 16
electrified fence 158, 159
ellipsis 28
emancipation 12
emigration 14, 16, 67, 79, 168, 169, 195, 209
emissaries (from Israel) 198–99
emotions 11, 47, 52, 54, 65, 74, 75, 94, 119, 124; emotional 6, 26, 48, 55, 56, 70, 87, 125, 229n65
empathy 6, 12, 41, 54, 57, 133
empty life 80, 81, 156
empty stomach 42, 43, 165
encoded reader 88
enigmatic 49, 109
episode 76, 100, 101, 132, 153
Eretz Israel (Land of Israel) 194
Eros 42
esthetization 8

ethnic 16, 17, 28, 70, 226n16
euphemistic 50, expressions, use of 95
evanescent 29
excremental assault 46
expectations 28, 32, 64, 89, 114, 199

factories 14, 34, 65, 78, 93, 148, 149, 150, 153, 160, 195; airplane parts repair 35, 37, 132, 136, 137, 177; ammunitions 130, 141, 219; brick 174, 175, 185; cement 183; women working in 104–5, 106, 107, 108, 120, 129, 160, 161, 162, 178, 179, 191, 207, 208, 216
Fadayeen (terrorists from Jordan) 213
"failure in performance" 122
faith 8, 65, 88, 98, 211, 228n44; faithlessness 66, 192
fairy tale 25, 42, 43
family 15, 25, 27, 43, 60, 94, 131, 163, 181, 193, 194, 197, 199, 205, 210, 212; creating families 2, 117; folklore 2, 223; possessions 98, 181; religious 206, 208, 217, 218, 220, 221; Dora Ashkenazi 93, 129, 156, 163, 164, 167, 168, 170; Anna Bihari 121; Ernő Bihari 116, 118, 119, 120, 201, 205; Irma Fischer 58, 61, 62, 68, 132, 145; Aranka Friedman 24, 48, 49, 51, 54, 56, 57, 142; Zsuzsa Faludi 63, 64, 65, 66, 67, 69, 70, 147, 148, 149, 151; Rozsi Háger 41, 44, 45, 46, 47; Leah and Yoseph Heiman 111, 112, 113; Esther Israel 215, 216; Rachel Markowitz 95, 99, 174, 176, 181; Ruth Matias 186, 187, 193; Piri Meister 219; Ilana Rosen 1, 2, 24, 28, 51; GZ 78, 152, 153, 154, 155
famine 14
fantasy 34, 40
Fascist Party in Hungary 70, 74, 98, 105, 185
fasting 173
fate 2, 8, 12, 13, 16, 33, 36, 50, 54, 56, 58, 60, 93, 120, 132, 180, 185, 192, 196
father 25, 212; Dora Ashkenazi 156, 157, 167, 168, 174; Anna Bihari 120–21, 207, 208; Ernő Bihari 210, 205; Zsuzsa Faludi 63, 64–66, 69–72, 73, 132, 147, 148–49,

150; Irma Fischer 60, 144; Aranka Friedman 24, 49, 57, 58, 141; Rozsi Háger 41, 42–43, 45, 139; Yosef Heiman 115; Rachel Markowitz 175, 185, 186; Ruth Matias 103, 186, 187, 191; Piri Meister 218; Ilana Rosen 2, 3; Berta Wazner 209, 210; GZ 78, 152, 153

fear 54, 62, 100, 101, 125, 151, 176, 177, 184, 185

felicity of successful performance 122

female 1, 5, 6, 18, 33, 37, 39, 41, 121, 227n28; Holocaust survivors 7, 31, 128; prisoners 36, 109

feminine writing 41

feminist 30, 226n24

femininity 37, 41, 44, 106

fieldwork 4

figurative 30, 114

fill 11, 32, 43, 85, 89, 99, 188; fill in the blanks 89, 91

film 29, 90, 119

"final solution" 130

financial hardship 79, 80, 152

fish 187

fixation 42

flashback 29, 30

flour 135; mill 168, 180

focus 5, 6, 7, 27, 31, 35, 59, 62, 72, 87, 131, 226n9; focusing 3, 17, 26, 40, 90

folktale 31

folklore 2, 3, 16, 20, 25, 27, 51, 223n5, 225n4, 231n45; folkloristic 16, 20, 25, 109, 225nn3, 6, 230nn13, 28, 231n40

folk narrative 20, 24

food 6, 21, 42, 71, 142, 158–59, 174, 176, 182, 187, 189, 218; extra portions 9, 109, 128, 160; sharing 60, 96, 193; stealing 37, 59, 60, 137, 146; survival 49, 93, 96, 102, 136–37, 177, 188, 192; survivors 41, 43, 135, 138, 149, 155, 167, 179, 180–81

forced labor 2, 34, 43, 51, 120, 129, 130, 132, 133

form 5, 17, 18, 25, 27, 28, 33, 34, 42, 46, 47, 63, 64, 77, 84, 89, 92, 188

formalism 4

formula 43; formulaic 28, 31, 33, 34, 35, 43, 45, 48, 59, 63, 95; formulate 86, 93

Fortunoff Video Archives of Holocaust Testimonies at Yale University 10, 224n35

fragmentation 20, 131

frankfurter (food) 174

free association 26, 28, 54, 61

friendship 40, 129

French authorities 80, 155; citizens 155; ex-prisoners 163, 164, 165, 166, 192; language 19, 102, 104, 187, 188, 218; partisans 179

From the City to the Country 184

Front-Line Whore 140

frugality 32, 34, 44, 45

fruit 39, 138

fulfill/fulfillment 28, 32, 44, 183, 195

gabai (synagogue sexton) 186

gap of understanding 126

gas 144, 176, 191, 205, 219

gas chamber 14, 43, 53, 91, 92, 95, 99, 100, 118, 140, 158, 160, 205

gefilte fish 187

Gemara 103, 187

gender issues 3, 4, 30, 40, 43

genealogy 49, 56

genre 3, 16, 20, 61, 65, 90, 223n5, 230n28

Gentiles 33, 34, 67, 70, 98, 120, 139, 216

German 70, 96, 101, 121, 130, 161–62, 163, 165, 177, 186, 188; authorities 13, 36, 66, 98, 101, 102, 106, 140; culture 103, 107, 153, 187, 228n42; ghetto 7, 13, 46, 53, 73, 74, 109, 135, 141, 146, 148, 149, 153, 157, 209, 219, 221; guards 35, 36, 105, 109, 136; inhabitants 14, 33, 60, 136, 145, 185; invasion 18, 68, 71, 135, 152, 166, 218–19; language 19, 39, 102, 103, 104, 106, 109, 131, 161, 170, 181–82, 187, 194, 202, 218; liberation 52, 64–5, 142, 148, 149, 179; occupation 12, 13, 14, 77, 137, 150; outlook 106, 108, 110; soldiers 135, 140, 150, 152, 154, 159, 178, 187, 195; work manager/supervisor 37, 104, 108, 130

ghost chapter 89, 99, 122

glaucoma 147

God 8, 85, 139, 162, 164, 166, 167, 174, 178, 192
Greeks 140
grandchildren 10, 69, 70, 120, 144, 147, 157, 173, 185, 210, 214; grandfather 49, 146, 148, 170, 186; grandmother 44, 45, 49, 139, 141, 147, 150, 175, 198, 208; grandparent 10, 56, 149, 153, 215, 219; retelling Holocaust experiences 11, 15, 32, 215
grave 124, 191, 213
grotesque 36
group 4, 6, 15, 39, 75, 84, 92, 93, 95, 96, 99, 101, 108, 129, 130, 160, 194, 221; ethnic 16, 17, 28, 35; Jews and non-Jews 33; of narrators/narratives 83, 84, 90, 110; scholars 27; special prisoners 38
guilt 29, 30, 51, 54, 57, 66, 69, 151, 206
Gulf War 87, 184, 191
gynecological problems 66, 150–51
Gypsies 35, 36, 39, 69, 70, 140, 144; camp 21

hachshara (preparation for emigration to Israel) 169, 197
Haggana (defense movement) 197, 217
Halutz (movement) 219
hamechaye (Hebrew: thank God), 93, 94, 160
hametz (unleavened bread) 174
harassment 130, 135
hardships 16, 17, 20, 23, 41, 51, 80, 133, 147
Hashomer Hatzair (movement) 168, 169, 170, 218
hatred of Jews 97, 107, 120, 161, 206
healing 27, 28, 29, 50, 77
health 26, 51, 59, 68, 144, 154, 155
Hebrew 19, 79, 102–3, 106, 114, 154, 183, 187, 190, 193, 215
hermeneutics 83, 84–85, 86–90 intrusion 111; negotiation 93
helplessness 11, 29, 46, 131
heuristic 20
hide 49, 68, 160, 173, 178, 179, 185, 208, 211; hidden 62, 101, 128, 138, 157, 231n41; hiding 14, 25, 59, 77, 78, 96, 137, 139, 149, 154, 180
hierarchy 35, 36

history 3, 8, 11, 16, 20, 21, 79, 89, 91, 125, 131, 199; historical explanation 6, 23, 27, 34, 86, 87, 89, 131, 133
Hitler, Adolph 153, 213
Hitler Jugend 107, 161; Hitlerism 212
hope 33, 34, 41, 65, 102, 191
horrors of Holocaust 40, 124, 126, 131
hospital 55, 120, 143, 144, 145, 146, 152, 182, 202, 204, 207, 220
hostility 39, 68, 97, 98
housing 152, 155, 171, 183, 199
humiliation 12, 36
Hungarian 39, 43, 52, 66, 68, 71, 74, 76, 223n10, 224n.30; army 43, 73, 129, 135, 138, 174, 208, 211, 228n58; culture 12, 35, 194; Jews 4, 11–15, 17–18, 21, 33, 42, 60, 62, 63, 70, 77, 79, 88, 105, 114, 120, 128–29, 130, 140, 190; language 102, 103, 104, 130, 161, 194, 205; men 106, 162; name 78, 153; regime 80, 113, 130, 151, 156, 185, 211, 215, 216, 219–20; regulations against 195; 1956 revolution 80, 195, 197, 203, 207; soldiers 105, 142, 162, 201; song 105, 162; supervisors 35, 191, 192; women 103, 105, 106, 109, 128, 130, 161, 162, 177, 225n1, 232n appendix 1
hunger 8, 37, 40–2, 130, 135, 138, 180, 192
hurt 29, 30, 40, 67120, 132, 150, 151, 173, 190, 205, 208, 211, 221
husband 2, 5, 9, 55, 70, 90, 111, 116, 120, 124, 225n1; pseudohusband 170, 171; Dora Ashkenazi 167, 174; Ana Bihari 207, 208; Zsuzsa Faludi 150; Irma Fischer 69, 145; Aranka Friedmann 48, 50, 52, 53, 56, 57, 141, 142; Rozsi Háger 41, 43–44, 45, 138; Leah Heiman 113, 114, 198; Esther Israel 216; Rachel Markowitz 183; Ruth Matias 190; Piri Meister 219, 220, 221; Berta Wazner 210, 211, 212, 213, 214; GZ 78

identification 13, 37, 56, 66, 67, 77, 80, 87, 130, 228n54
identity 70, 77, 79, 114, 142, 229n65; Christian 3, 14; Israeli 16, 114; Jewish 15, 77, 97, 153, 229n64; national 12; personal 110, 151, 153

ideology 5, 109, 114; ideological 16, 20, 85, 114, 230n26
idiom 19, 35, 36 idiomatic 28
illness 40, 49, 56, 58, 66, 67–8, 141, 143, 144, 150, 154–55, 166, 207
illusion 65, 89
image 20, 35, 46, 47, 92, 157
immigrant 16, 19, 21, 115, 183
immigration 15–16, 19
impact 33, 70
implied reader 86, 87, 88
imprisonment 10, 14, 46
individuality, loss of 110
information gathering 99
inhibition 36, 40, 41, 118
inmate 14, 35, 37, 38, 126
insane 35, 157, 160, 164
instinct 58, 74, 75, 92, 149, 178
interaction 86, 90, 231n44; oral 77, 88; between narrators and audience 95, 111; between narrators and interviewer (researcher) 85, 86, 118–19, 126
interdisciplinarity 6, 90
intergenerational dialogue 24, 225n2
integration 91
interlocutor 8, 9, 10, 87, 126
interpretation 9, 20, 28, 75, 85, 88, 89, 90, 95, 109, 115, 121, 127, 128, 133; interpretive 84
intimation 111
intuition 73, 92, 120
iron curtain 23, 197
ironic 36, 37, 48; ironically 12, 39
Israeli army 173

Jewelry 96, 97, 175180
Jew-hater 96, 97, 98, 180
Jewish girls 39, 103, 130, 138, 161, 194
Jewishness 17, 62, 70, 88, 124
Jewish problem 77
Jewish women 38, 39, 40, 97, 105, 106, 109, 130, 137, 174, 177, 179, 180
Joint (Joint Distribution Committee) 166, 173, 198, 204, 212
joke 2, 105, 106, 128

journalist 76, 152, 153, 154, 155; journalistic style 8
Judaism 3, 17, 79, 193

kaftan (Hassidic coat) 186
kapparot (religious tradition of expiation) 183
Kásztner affair 13–14
keyword 118–19
kibbutz 115, 119, 200
kiddush (blessing over wine and *challa*) 174
Kiddush Hashem 8
kindergarten 201, 218
kinderlach (Yiddish: children) 104, 161
kitchen 37, 38, 42, 59, 137, 138, 146, 147, 166, 182
Kol Nidrei (prayer recited on eve of Day of Atonement) 164
kölyök (Hungarian: puppy/brat) 230n30
kosher 139, 174, 218
Krona (Czechoslovak currency) 169, 170
Kübel (German: huge pot) 106

labor battalions 2, 3, 13, 42, 43, 49, 53, 64, 65, 66, 73, 77, 112, 118, 138, 141, 142, 143, 145, 148, 163, 186, 195, 207, 208, 216, 219, 221, 223n3; brutalities endured 115, 119; conditions in 117, 203; labor camps 34, 115, 119, 130, 136, 186, 191, 200, 203, 204
Labor Service 9, 43, 77, 129
laconism 50
language 7, 8, 10, 11, 19, 21, 24, 28, 30, 31, 35, 76, 83, 118, 140, 203, 230n13, 231n36; battles between 130–31; function and meaning of 102; intermingling 90, 103, 110; German 103, 104, 105, 106, 109, 187; Hebrew 103, 114; Hungarian 2, 12, 104, 105, 106, 205
leading question 64
legends 34, 64, 65, 150
lei (Rumanian currency) 141
liberation 14, 52, 53, 58, 65, 78, 107, 110, 142, 189; post-liberation 97, 98, 108, 128, 133, 139, 153, 154, 179, 190, 219; women prisoners 96

lice 149, 175, 176, 189

Life histories: Dora Ashkenazi, 156–74; Anna Bihari, 206–8; Ernő Bihari, 201–7; Zsuzsa Faludi, 147–51; Irma Fischer, 144–47; Aranka Friedmann, 140–44; GZ, 152–56; Rozsi Háger, 135–40; Leah Heiman, 193–200; Yoseph Heiman, 193–200; Esther Israel 215–18; Rachel Markowitz, 174–85; Ruth Matias, 185–93; Piri Meister, 218–21; Berta Wazner, 208–15

life world 86, 229n8

lingual 20; metalingual 10, 20, 26, 47, 48, 52, 85; multilingual 103, 109

linguistic/s 6, 7, 10, 28, 31, 85, 101, 103, 104

lira (Israeli currency) 171, 172, 183, 184

listener 9, 11, 19, 26, 37, 85, 87, 90, 95, 98, 101, 131, 133

literary analysis 3, 5, 24, 27, 86; context 15; criticism 24, 26; memoirs 5 ; oral 16; principles 10, 18; studies 7, 89, 90; terms 18

literature, Holocaust 5, 7, 8, 227n28

Little Palestine 217

living conditions 51, 66, 104; improvement of 93–94

loose women 39, 138

lulav (palm branch) 88

ma'abara (temporary lodging) 217

magical 49; thinking 50

main text 19, 126

margarine 159, 161, 174, 179, 180

marked house 148

marriage 42, 43, 44, 150, 186, 202, 204, 212, 219 married couples 111, 122

mass violence 29

matriculation 185187, 220

maturity 18, 25, 26, 42, 61

meaning 2, 6, 8, 9, 11, 26, 28, 36, 37, 52, 54, 61, 62, 85, 86, 88, 93, 94, 95, 96, 102, 108, 110, 114, 129, 230n27, 231n41

meat 93, 104, 139, 160, 161, 166, 174

medication/medicine 49, 73, 145, 173, 182, 202

meister (work supervisor) 51, 107, 108, 130, 161, 162, 164, 173–74, 177, 178, 182

melting pot 11

memoir 5, 29, 40; Holocaust 6, 11, 16, 24, 96

memorial book 16; memorial candle 1, 223n1

Memorial Day 3, 15, 217

memory/memories 3, 7, 12, 29, 47, 74, 117, 122–23, 125, 128, 207; burdened with 93; coping with 15, 16, 121, 123, 214; lapse of 132; perpetuate 58; relationship with 120; repressed 110, 119, 123, 124

menstruation 40, 140. *See also* period

mental block 118

message 9, 15, 20, 32, 40, 61, 128

metamorphosis 34, 105

metanarrative 156, 118

metaphor 28, 110, 118, 231n44

metonym 28, 70

microcosm 54

mikve (ritual bath) 174

milk 160, 164

minimal 9, 13, 48, 119, 121, minimalist 5, 19, 52; minimally 2

miracle 44, 139

miraculous 50

mirror image 54

misery 20, 59–60, 62, 131

mitzvot (religious dictates) 200

Mizrahi (movement) 182, 193

modal 62

modesty 32, 34, 45

mosaic 83, 90

mother 7, 14, 43, 175, 193; mothers with children: separation of 93, 136;

mother-daughter relationship 7, 9, 18, 23, 24, 25, 26, 28, 44, 46, 58–59, 61, 77, 78, 79, 80, 87, 131, 132, 133, 193, 229n65; reconcilement 132; Dora Ashkenazi 92, 93, 156–57, 166, 174; Anna Bihari 208; Ernő Bihari 88, 118, 205; Zsuzsa Faludi 66, 68, 75, 129, 149, 150; Irma Fischer 9, 58–59, 60, 68–69, 73–74, 144, 147; Aranka Friedmann 49, 53, 57, 141; Rozsi Háger 31–33, 42–43, 44, 45–46, 47, 135, 139–40;

Leah Heiman 194; Esther Israel 215–16;
Ruth Matias 186; Piri Meister 218, 219;
Ilana Rosen 2, 3; Berta Wazner 209, 210,
211, 213; GZ 76, 77–78, 79–81, 152–55
mother's tongue 43
multiplicity 102, 110, 128
mumps 149
Muselmann 162
muteness 17, 19, 36
myth 40, 110

naked 94, 136, 157, 175, 176, 227n28
narrative event 46, 47, 76, 85, 87, 88, 101,
111, 115, 116, 118, 126, 127; narrated event
90, 101; narrators, interaction with
audience 95; with interviewer–
"client" 118
narratological 84
natural attitude 86
Nazi 7, 12, 13, 30, 33, 36, 46, 52, 53, 68, 70,
73, 93, 98, 106, 110, 130, 177, 178, 191, 204;
law 153; murderous intentions 106
needle 49–50, 100, 139, 159, 182
Neofascist 15
Neologist 12, 130, 147, 194
Nesher cement factory 183
never returned 3, 53, 142, 154, 188, 208, 221
nightmare 29, 62, 74, 123, 214
noodles 174
norm 54, 61
normal children 11; life 8, 41, 80; situation
30; times 54; 231n34
number 96–97, 142, 158, 159, 162, 164, 188
numbing/numbness 29, 30, 36, 48, 52
Numerus Clausus (quota system) 206
nurse 50, 56, 143
Nyilas. *See* Arrow Cross Party

objectivity 50
Odyssean 24, 39
offenses 38
omen 94, 101
ontogenetics 25
oppressors/oppression 37, 71, 72, 73, 77;
language of 104, religious 106
oral literature 4, 5, 9, 10, 11, 16, 17, 24, 29,

41, 65, 76, 77, 87, 88, 89; oral lore 65,
109, 231n40, 231n41; oral narration,
train of thought 94, 223n5
orientation 75, 229n62
orphanage 48, 58, 141, 142
Orthodox (religious way of life) 6, 103,
147, 186, 204, 218; birth rates 129; community 12, 14, 130, 139, 194, 208, 217,
224n30
over-critical reader 88
over-determined 88

Palestine Affairs Office 169
Palmach 173
"paradise" 94, 105, 160, 162
paralysis 26, 147
parapraxes 26, 28
parasite 35
parents 10, 31, 33, 212; Dora Ashkenazi 172;
Anna Bihari 202, 207; Ernő Bihari 201,
205; Zsuzsa Faludi 69, 72, 76, 143; Irma
Fischer 58, 60, 70–71, 144; Aranka
Friedmann 49–50, 56, 140; Rozsi Háger
31–32, 43, 45, 135, 139; Leah Heiman 198;
Yoseph Heiman 195, 200; Esther Israel
218; Rachel Markowitz 175; Ruth Matias
185; Piri Meister 219; Ilana Rosen 1–4,
11, 111, 115; Berta Wazner 208; GZ 78, 152
partisans 13, 39, 40, 137, 162, 179, 229n64
passive attitude 34, 52, 55; behavior 42, 43,
outlook 48, 54; passivity 26, 42, 48,
49, 75
Passover (Hebrew: *Pesach*) 164, 174, 196
passport 153, 169–70, 195, 196, 197
pathology 27, 226n12
perception 11, 29, 30, 75, 107, 114, 122, 125
performance 84, 92, 122, 225n44
period 140, 182. *See also* menstruation
persecution of Jews 4, 70, 135, 151, 153,
174–75, 202, 203, 211
personality 28, 32, 44, 98, 103, 119
personal narrative 15, 20, 223n5, 229n62
persuasive language 90
phenomenon 8, 17, 26, 54, 86, 118, 131,
229n64; phenomena 2, 10, 20, 25, 26, 27,
28, 29, 30, 61, 84, 225n4

phenomenological 84–90, 115; phenomenological-hermeneutic nego-tiation 93; phenomenology 18
philo-Semitism 205, 206
philosophy 3; philosophical 84, 89
phylogenetic 25, 225n4
physical-biological realm 49
picturing 89
pie 167
pitch 10
planet 8, 71
play 27, 31, 45, 84, 86, 98, 135, 181; down 74, 120, 229n64
ploy 3, 35, 37, 223n6
pluralism 103, 110
pneumonia 166
poetry 16; poetic 30; poetical 28
pogrom 125, 205, 216
point of view 20, 41, 47, 61, 71, 94, 96, 112, 115, 122, 154, 204; childish 31, 34, 62, 66, 72; viewpoint 37, 48, 51, 62, 63, 80, 116, 118, 151
Poles 140
police 143, 155; policeman 69, 70, 71, 72, 132, 144, 154
Polish survivors 142; refugees 152; women 109, 176, 177
political 11, 17, 34, 62, 67, 72, 90, 105, 106, 155, 206
polyphony of cultures and ideologies 110
pornographication 40
post-Holocaust 8, 10, 17, 18, 19, 23, 28, 83, 84; life 19, 111
Post Traumatic Stress Disorder (PTSD) 29, 30; post traumatic state 42
postmodern 16
potato 60, 93, 137, 146, 160, 164, 165, 174, 179, 180, 192
power 7, 36, 38, 49, 50, 55, 56, 105, 153, 187, 196, 206; figure 60; structure 71
pragmatic 56, 79, 114, 154
prayer book 49, 50, 100, 159, 173
pregnant 44, 5253, 139, 141, 150, 173; preg-nancy 4, 40, 54; in Auschwitz 91, 93, 140, 156, 160, 185
pre-Holocaust 18, 83, 133

premonition 58, 149
prisoner 14, 37, 38, 52, 71, 91, 100, 101, 102, 107, 136, 164; clothes 96; liberated 41, 110, 137; lives, evaluation of 94, 51; women 6, 36, 93, 96, 99, 105, 106, 109, 130
privacy 36, 41, 93, 227n42
privilege 15, 38, 59, 109, 136
proairetic 3, 35, 223n6, 227n26
professional training 68, 112, 129, 132, 139
prominenten 38
pronoun 19, 52, 61, 72
Protected House 73, 74, 145
protest, act of 102
proverb 16, 61, 107, 108, 113, 165
pseudonym 152
psychic 27, 29, 52
psychoanalysis 5, 24, 25, 26, 27, 28, 29, 226n6; psychoanalytical analysis 24–25, 30, 61, 86
psychology 1, 3, 17, 20, 90, 230n25; psycho-logical 6, 18, 28, 85, 86, 87, 104, 115, 122, 200, 211, 215, 227n41, 230n26
psychotherapist 25
public opinion 37, 40, 44

qualitative 90, 230n25
question-and-answer sessions 122

raid 132, 135, 149
rain 99, 100, 157, 158, 164, 175, 177, 179
ransom 13
rationalistic 48, 52, 56
rations 135, 148
reader 19, 20, 26, 27, 86, 87–89, 91, 93, 95, 98, 99, 101, 131, 133, 225n8, 226n9; reader-response 85
realism 50; reality 15, 20, 33, 34, 36, 40, 55, 66, 68, 85, 86, 92, 99, 102, 120, 131, 204, 214, 228n52
reciprocity 26
Red Army 14, 34, 65. *See also* Russian army
Red Cross 14, 143, 146
reflexivity 26, 27, 28, 31
refugee 13, 152, 153, 204

regression 37, 42, 43

rehabilitation 41, 50, 68, 117

relief 60, 101, 122

religion 8, 45, 69, 77, 139, 147, 148, 153, 154, 194, 196, 199, 200, 211, 217, 223n8; religious practice 144, 152, 156, 166, 173, 174, 192, 218; religious studies 194, 195

remained there 2, 24, 50, 51, 52, 95, 137, 142, 143, 145, 216

repetition 3, 10, 28, 30, 34, 41, 119; repetitious 11; repetitive 29

repression 16, 17, 34, 35, 37, 38, 41, 116, of memories 123, 124

rescue (noun) 13, 34, 68, 73, 76, 101, 106

resilience 51, 103

responsibility 9, 56, 93, 96, 111, 132, 170, 230n27, 231n41

reticent 9, 84, 90

reveal 3, 28, 35, 38, 39, 59, 61, 102, 112, 115, 116, 118, 119, 125, 127, 128; revealing and concealing 83, 84, 90, 110–11, 121

rhetoric 5, 88, 224n21

rickets 149

riddle 96

righteous 46

roll call 99, 100, 136, 157, 158, 159, 176, 177, 179, 185, 182, 185, 188. See also *appell*

Rosh Hashanah (Hebrew New Year's Eve) 104, 161, 198

Rumanian anti-Fascist movement 137; currency 141; Jewish leaders 143; language 19, 137, 191, 203; partisans 39, 137; regime 185, 220, 221

rumor 64, 65, 99, 101, 150, 229n64, 230n28; relying on 94

Russian army 38, 39, 74, 75, 112, 142, 149, 195

Russians 33, 143, 190, 193, 198; language 38, 137; prisoners of war 107, 108, 137, 165, 166, 188; soldiers/army 38, 39, 73, 74, 75, 96, 112, 136, 137, 138, 141, 142, 145, 149, 154, 167, 177, 178, 180, 195, 198

Sabbath 58, 139, 144, 192, 200, 211

sabra (native Israeli) 45, 139

sadistic 37, 136, 137

saintliness 47

salami 159, 161

sanatorium 141, 147, 219, 220

scene 26, 27, 35, 43, 50, 93, 101, 105, 106, 133; in Auschwitz 36, 92, 99

school 15, 32, 59, 68, 69, 103, 147, 148, 151, 201, 215, 220; Catholic 154, 185, 206; elementary 31, 48, 116, 135, 140, 144, 156, 195, 198, 208, 211; high 127, 141, 154, 187, 194, 202, 203, 207, 209, 218; Jewish 64, 67, 150, 194–95, 208, 209; school of thought 5, 225n44

science 50

scum 35, 136

second generation 1, 2, 223n1, 223n4

Seder 197

segregated 40

"selection" 8, 14, 35, 36, 91, 92, 106, 136, 156, 157, 176, 177, 178, 219

self-censorship, reasons for 94, 118

self-effacement 34

separation by Nazis of mothers with children 93

sewing 97, 135, 156, 168, 181, 218; machine 98, 138, 172, 182

sexual abuse 7, 40, 227n41; humiliation 106; sexuality 31, 41

Shabbat 174, 178, 186, 218

shame 37

sharing 12, 29, 89, 179

shave/shaving 36, 136, 138, 170, 175

Shavuot 33, 136

shelter 145, 149, 154, 162, 178, 180, 184, 204, 208, 217

shiva (mourning period) 157

shochet (ritual slaughterer of animals and fowl) 194

shoes 158, 175 181

shop (store) 104, 130, 141, 142, 161, 198, 201, 209, 211, 212, 216

shower 36, 91, 93, 99, 100, 101, 136, 158, 160, 177

shtreimel (Hasidic hat) 186

sickness 26, 67, 130

siege of Budapest 152, 154

sign 12, 20, 36, 80, 85, 94, 101, 102, 119, 216, 228n45

significant 6, 9, 16, 23, 27, 31, 34, 35, 44, 46,
  49, 52, 62, 83, 88, 94, 114, 117, 128, 132,
  153; significance 4, 19, 20, 26, 28, 29, 36,
  53, 56, 78, 79, 86, 116, 230n26; signifier
  102, 131; signify 93, 94, 102
silence 3, 15, 17, 123; silent 9, 151
Sinai War (1956) 213
single (unmarried) 53, 195, 212, 216
siren 178, 185
sister 1, 24, 38, 42, 94, 95, 129; Dora Ashkenazi 91, 92, 93, 99, 156, 157, 158, 159,
  162, 163, 164, 165, 166, 167, 169, 173, 174;
  Anna Bihari 208; Ernő Bihari 118, 201,
  202, 205; Irma Fischer 69, 144, 147, 156;
  Aranka Friedmann 55, 58, 14; Rozsi
  Háger 138, 140; Leah Heiman 197, 198,
  200; Esther Israel 216, 217; Rachel
  Markowitz 97, 98, 174, 175, 176, 177, 178,
  179, 180, 181, 182, 18; Ruth Matias 186,
  187, 188, 189, 192, 193; Piri Meister 218,
  219, 220, 221; Berta Wazner 209, 210,
  211, 212
sisters in sorrow 35, 37, 129
situational context 87
Six Days' War 184, 191, 193, 213
"skipping in time" 117
slander 70, 71, 132
slip 174, 179; slips of the tongue 28
small Palestine 217
snow 142, 165, 177, 178, 179
sob 26; sobbing 10, 192
Sochnut (Jewish Agency) 170, 171, 172, 183,
  184, 197
Socialist Party (Hungarian) 154
society 16, 54, 55, 61, 97, 98, 208, 213
sociology 3, 6, 20, 90, 230n25
Sonderkommando 95, 119, 231n48
soup 158, 161, 167, 174, 177, 192
Soviet Union 53, 57, 70, 142; units 154
speech 3, 25, 34, 37, 59, 61, 102, 123, 128;
  direct 103, 109; reported 109
SS 142, 157, 179, 188–89, 191
stagnation 42, 67, 227n36
stamp collecting, 78, 152, 153
Star of David 73, 146, 148, 149, 174, 187
starvation 51

Status Quo (Jewish religious community)
  12, 130
steal 35, 137, 146, 160; stealing 37, 59 96–97,
  180, 204
Stein-Lowenthal Syndrome 150
stepdaughter 44
stereotype, of Jews 107–8
sterile 67
stories 5, 10, 14, 19, 20, 21, 24, 28, 31, 64, 65,
  67, 83, 84, 85, 90, 100, 110, 118, 128, 150,
  151, 159, 227n28, 228n58, 229n64;
  Holocaust experiences 4, 15, 17, 40, 51,
  75, 96, 131, 133, 217; story 4, 11, 32, 33, 41,
  43, 44, 47, 48, 49, 53–59, 62, 63, 67, 69,
  70, 72–74, 76–79, 87, 96, 97, 111, 112, 116,
  119, 122, 125, 126, 127, 131, 39, 145, 153,
  168, 219, 225n44
structural analysis 27
style 8, 34, 43, 52, 56, 61, 76, 77, 78; stylistic 84
sub-critical reader 88
subordinate 19, 26, 76
suffering 30
sugar 135, 179
suicide attempt 128
Sukkoth 88
survival 6, 41, 50, 51, 52, 53–54, 65, 71, 129;
  chances for 94, 104; of infants 93,
  meaning of 102, 103, 114, 133
survivor 17, 18, 43, 63, 128, 223n3, 225n46;
  accounts of 8, 9, 11, 29, 35–36, 93, 96,
  133; survivor authors 46, 101, 131; community 3, 44, 57; identity 77, 114; lists
  2, 186; narrative 102, 121, 122, 125; narrator 9, 14, 26, 27, 30, 31, 60, 110, 118, 119;
  reintegration 24, 205, 209, 213; shar-
  ing/telling 15, 16, 20, 123, 126; women 7,
  23, 40–41, 71, 227n41; surviving 46,
  97, 163
suspense 101
swastika 188
Swedish Protection Pass 73, 145, 149
symbolic 11, 30, 44, 79
symptom 27, 29, 30, 42
synagogue 88, 117, 149, 156, 174, 186, 192,
  194, 211, 213, 214

syntax 26

Széchényi (Hungarian leaders) 206

Szolnok Jewish Youth 194

taboo 2, 25

Tachana Mercazit (Central Bus Station) 171

Talmud Torah 186, 195

Tape recorder 47

tapestry 210, 212

Technikum (Inst.) 154

Technological University of Budapest 155

Telefunken (company) 137

television 90, 218

tense (tension) 47, 69, 72, 101, 116, 148, 194, 209, 214

terminology, 8, 14, 19, 72, 86, 91, 102, 115; victims use of 95; Holocaust 110

testimonies 24, 27, 29, 33, 90; testimony research 225n46

text 7, 10, 26, 36, 43, 47, 67, 85–92, 99, 120–21, 131, 225n8, 226n8, 227n36, 228n44, 231nn38, 41; narrative 21, 25, 28, 29, 30, 34, 52, 77, 120

textual analysis 27

Thanatos (forces of death) 42

theme (thematic) 5, 7, 10, 34, 48, 60, 62, 77; repetition of 119

therapeutic 3, 29

therapist 26, 29, 225n8, 226n12

thieves 35, 136, 183

threat 27, 29, 66, 93, 98

TODT (organization responsible for roads and transportation) 189

toilet 140, 143, 144, 175, 176, 177, 179, 180, 184, 189, 227–28n42

tombstone 214

tone 15, 63, 64, 76, 92, 120; intonation 10

toothpaste 175

torture 14, 51, 112, 116, 117, 119, 175, 184, 195

totalitarian 15, 71

"Tower of Babel" 110

tragedy 26, 60

train: deportation 1, 33, 100, 136, 157, 158, 160, 162, 175, 177, 205; liberation 137–38, 143, 163, 164–65, 166, 168–69, 181

transmitting the Holocaust 9, 20, 40, 113, 231n41

transport 141, 143, 169, 170, 176, 177

trauma 16, 27, 29, 30, 36, 37, 48, 67, 71, 157, 209

tribulation 12, 24, 42

truth 10, 63, 69, 71, 72, 84, 85, 113, 132, 144, 148, 185; finding out 97, 188, 189; generation of 127; interpretation of 127, 131; ultimate 131

tuberculosis 49, 51

Tudor Vladimiresku anti-Fascist movement 137, 138

typhus 122, 157–58, 167, 189, 201, 204, 205, 207, 217

tzures (Yiddish: problems) 171, 184

ubi sunt 32

ulpan (Hebrew study course) 190, 199, 200

uncle 2, 4, 58, 63, 66, 72, 74, 135, 148, 149, 162, 163, 164, 165, 166, 201, 207

unconscious 28, 47, 57, 72, 106, 124

under-determined text 109

underground 6, 13, 151

understanding 27, 35, 50, 59, 74, 75, 88, 102, 107, 120, 121, 124, 130, 140, 191; meaning 28, 53, 95–96, 126; perception 66, 86, 120–21, 161

uniform 43, 154; prisoner's 96, 97

United Nations camp 155

unity of misery 20, 131

valid text 19, 126

vegetable garden 160

vegetables 181, 219

version 10, 25, 26, 71, 74, 81, 112, 114, 128, 132, 133

verstehen (German: understanding) 84

victim 11, 38, 72, 95, 162

video 10

Vietnam War 29

Vladimiresku, Tudor (anti-Fascist Rumanian movement) 137

vodka 167

volume 18, 92

vulgarization 40

war effort: contribution to 130; sabotage of 108
wavelike movement 118–19
weakness 11, 68, 108, 118, 133, 165; of Jews 107, 108
wealth 78, 97, 135, 153, 185, 207
welding 104, 187, 189, 190, 192
Wermacht soldier 162, 178
whip 157
whore 140, 160
wife 2, 3, 43, 50, 53, 55, 90, 116, 119, 121, 142, 143, 196, 202, 204, 205, 207
wine 165, 174
witch hunt 154
woe is me 59
work 40, 41, 55, 68, 94, 100, 129–30, 132, 159, 175, 177, 185; art 25, 26; book 5, 9, 10, 15, 17, 18, 20, 21, 31, 47, 48, 60, 63, 85, 86, 87, 88, 89, 106, 122, 128, 129, 225n1; by scholars 16, 25, 27, 46, 84, 85, 87, 89, 110, 131, 225nn6, 8, 226n24; in factory 37, 93, 106–9, 136–37, 160–62, 178–79, 187, 189, 219; after liberation 97, 104, 138–39, 143, 146–48, 153, 168–69, 172, 181, 199, 202, 204, 212, 217; physical 35, 51, 53
work camps 7, 14, 23, 43, 216, horrors of 109, 115; transfer to 99, 100; worldview 32, 50, 98, 106, 108

World War I 12, 128, 201–2, 205, 207, 227n25
World War II 2, 6, 15, 105, 129, 130, 156, 194, 202
wretched generation 60, 62
writerly 28, 226n17

xenophobia 12

Yad Vashem 127, 128
Yale University 10, 224n35
yellow badge 174, 187
yeshiva students 216
Yiddish 19, 95, 102, 103, 131, 139, 175, 194
Yishuv (Jewish community in pre-state Israel) 183
Yom Kippur (Hebrew: Day of Atonement) 104–5, 161, 173, 183; Yom Kippur War 213
Youth Aliya 168, 170, 193
youth movement 13, 64, 129, 168, 193, 220

Zehnnerschaft (German, group of ten) 6
Zionism 14, 17, 209, 218; movement 64, 150, 219; opposition to 112, 194
Zionist 114, 168–69, 190, 199, 212, 214

Name Index

Albee, Edward 52
Ashkenazi, Dora 49–50, 83, 91–93, 99–
    100, 102–8, 110, 130, 216; life history
    156–74

Babits, Mihály 151
Bakhtin, Mikhail 110
Barthes, Roland 27
Baumel, Judith (Esther) Tydor 6
Bettelheim, Bruno 2
Bihari, Anna 116–21; life history 206–8
Bihari, Dr. Ernő (Ernest) 83, 87, 111, 116–
    20; life history 201–6
Bitton Jackson, Livia 5
Blumenthal, Nachman 50
Bomba, Abraham 119
Brainer, Shoshi 83
Brooke-Rose, Christine 88, 89, 109
Brown, Laura 30

Cixous, Hélène 30, 41
Clemencau, Georges, President of France
    202, 206

Damari, Shoshana 183
Darnton, Robert 42
Des Pres, Terrence 46
Dilthey, Wilhelm 84
Dundes Alan 25

Eco, Umberto 84, 88, 89
Erzsébet, Queen of Hungary 205
Ezrahi, Sidra de Koven 7, 8

Faludi, Zsuzsa (Zsusánna) 9, 24, 25, 26,
    28, 58–76, 79, 129, 145, 146; life history
    147–51

Felman, Shoshana 9
Fischer, Irma 9, 24, 25, 28, 35, 46, 58–76;
    life history 144–47
Fischer, Sándor, 72, 145
Fish, Stanley 84, 88
Földvári, Ármin 117
Foley, Barbara 8
Frank, Gelya 86
Franz Jozsef 206
Friedmann, Aranka 9, 24, 26, 28, 47–58,
    129; life history 140–44
Friedmann, Jenő 48, 55, 57, 141, 142, 143
Freud, Sigmund 26, 27, 28, 66, 226n12
Fuchs, Dora (maiden name of Dora Ash-
    kenazi) 171–72
Fuchs, Shmuel 168
Fuchs, Yonah 159, 163, 168

Gadamer, Hans Georg 84, 85
Georges, Robert 27
Goethe, Johann Wolfgang von 187
Goldenberg, Myrna 6
Greenfeld, Ariella 75
GZ (anonymous narrator) 9, 24, 25, 26,
    76–81; life history 152–56

Habermas, Jurgen 86, 101
Háger Rozsi, 9, 24, 25, 26, 31–47, 53, 55, 59,
    59, 62; life history 135–40
Hasan-Rokem, Galit 3
Heiman, Leah (Julishka) 111–16; life his-
    tory 193–200
Heiman, Yoseph 83, 111–16, 117, 119; life
    history 193–200
Heine, Heinrich 187
Herman, Judith Lewis 27
Hershkowitz, Dr. 169

Hitler, Adolph 153
Husserl, Edmund 86

Ilona (Ilush) 1, 53, 57
Irigaray, Luce 30
Iser, Wolfgang 84, 86, 89, 91, 101
Israel, Esther 83, 111, 121–22, 125; life history 215–18

Jackson, Livia Bitton 5
Jones, Ernest 25
Jones, Michael O. 27

Karmel, Ilona 5
Kásztner, Israel 13–14
Kertész, Imre 96
Kirshenblatt-Gimblett, Barbara 15, 16
Kossuth, Lajos 206
Krausz, Károly 87, 117
Kremer, Lilian 6
Kun, Béla 206

Lacan, Jacques 28
Langer, Lawrence 7, 8, 10–11, 14, 19, 126, 127
Lanzmann, Claude 119
Laub, Dori 9
Lengyel, Olga 5
Lenin, Vladimir 206
Levi, Primo 38, 110, 224n21

Markowitz, Rachel 9, 83, 87, 91, 95–96, 102, 103, 108; life history 174–85
Masaryk, Jan 216
Matias, Ruth 91, 95, 103; life history 185–93
Meister, Piri 83, 111, 121–22, 125; life history 218–21
Mengele, Josef 91, 136, 157, 168, 175, 175, 176
Miklós, Baron Joszef 152

Mintz, Alan 7
Montgomery, General Bernard 186

Nagy, Klára 48, 55
Nietzsche, Friedrich 187

Poulet, Georges 85

Radnóti, Miklós 77
Ricoeur, Paul 84, 86, 101
Rosberger family 199;
Rosberger, Ilush (wife of Miki) 142
Rosberger, Jenő-Yaakov 48, 53
Rosberger, Miki (Miklós-Menachem) 48, 53, 57, 141, 142
Rosberger, Péter-Pinchas, 2, 49, 53, 142
Roskies, David G. 7

Salamon, Andor 49, 101–2
Salamon, Rika 49
Schiffrin, Deborah 7
Schiller, Friedrich 187
Schwartz, Gershon 192
Son, Dejő 190
Stalin, Joseph 206
Széchényi, Endre/Lajos 206
Székely, Magda 23
Szép, Mishka 2

Tátrai, Zsuzsánna 204
Timar, Hilda 77
Todorov, Tzvetan 87, 89
Trumpeldor, Joseph 191

Voigt, Vilmos 15, 16

Wazner, Berta 83, 111, 121–22, 123: life history 208–15
Wiesel, Elie 42, 46
Weiss family 176
Woolf, Virginia 29, 52

Place Index

Agrobank (Hadera neighborhood, Israel) 217
Alexandria (Egypt) 170
Allenby St. (Tel Aviv) 172
America 162, 163, 165, 166, 180, 192, 203
Augsburg (Germany) 100, 160
Auschwitz (Poland) 2, 8, 14, 23, 33, 34, 35, 36, 37, 38, 43, 45, 46, 50, 53, 54, 57, 71, 91, 92, 93, 140, 141, 142, 143, 156, 157, 158, 175, 186, 187, 205, 211, 216; conditions 160, 176, 182; entrance to 95, 98, 99, 175; food 176
Australia 4
Austria 103, 161, 195, 196, 197, 209

Bazera (Israel) 91, 123, 156, 173, 208, 210
Beer Yaakov (Israel) 210
Beit-Shemesh (Israel) 115, 199
Belgium 169
Belgrade (Yugoslavia) 155
Bergen-Belsen (Germany) 8, 64, 150, 168, 186, 188, 189, 216
Bergstadt (Poland) 104, 187
Bilu Hospital (Israel) 173
Birkenau (Poland) 14
Bor (Hungary/Yugoslavia) 41, 138
Bratislava (Hungary/Czechoslovakia) 125, 156, 166, 169, 170, 217. See also Pozsony
Brazil 214
Bucharest (Rumania) 190, 218
Buda 137, 204. See also Budapest
Budapest 14, 18, 23, 39, 48, 55, 58, 60, 64, 65, 73, 76, 77, 116, 120, 152, 193, 198; after liberation 97, 137, 138, 140, 143, 144, 147, 150, 155, 181, 201, 202, 206, 207, 208, 213, 219. See also Pest

Canada 200
Carpatho-Russia (Hungary/Czecho-slovakia) 103, 223n8
Champs-Elysées (Paris) 155
Chile 182
Csikmegye (Hungary/Rumania) 218
Cyprus 173, 182
Czechoslovakia 12, 169, 173, 196–7, 210, 211, 215, 216, 217

Dachau (Germany) 216
Danube, river 73, 75, 132, 149, 195, 197, 208
Dresden (Germany) 219
Dunajska Streda (Hungary/Czecho-slovakia) 156, 167, 168, 171, 173. See also Dunaszerdahely
Dunaszerdahely (Hungary/Czecho-slovakia) 91, 125, 156, 215. See also Dunajska Streda

England 170
Erdély (Transylvania, Hungary/Ruma-nia) 153
Essen (Germany) 186, 188
Europe 3, 4, 15, 109, 110, 123, 124, 127, 142, 203, 212, 213, 214, 215, 217, 226n16

Feldafing (Germany) 165, 166
Félegyháza (Hungary/Rumania) 140, 141
France 79, 80

Galanta (Czechoslovakia) 167
Galicia (Poland/Ukraine) 139
Galilee (Israel) 191
Gelért Hotel/Square (Budapest) 77, 152, 153

268 · *Place Index*

Gelsenkirchen (labor camp) (Germany) 186
Germany 12, 13, 68, 153
Givat Shmuel (Israel) 171, 172
Gutava (unidentified) 141
Gyergyóvárhegy (Hungary/Rumania) 125, 218
Gylafehérvár (Hungary/Rumania) 218
Györ (Hungary) 197

Hadera (Israel) 171, 217
Haifa (Israel) 170, 171, 173, 183, 184, 186, 210
Herzl Square (Tel Aviv) 173
Heviz (Hungary/Rumania) 219. *See also* Marosheviz
Hod Hasharon (Israel) 31, 125, 215
Holon (Israel) 200
Hulah, nature reserve (Israel) 184
Hungary 1, 2, 3, 4, 11, 12, 13, 14, 15, 16, 17, 21, 23, 33, 55, 62, 64, 65, 67, 68, 78, 79, 80, 87, 121, 139, 140, 155, 197, 201–2, 205, 210

Israel 17, 21, 139, 147, 169, 173, 203, 214, 215; immigration to 182, 183, 186, 193, 195–96, 197, 199, 209, 212, 216, 217, 220, 221
Italy 169

Jaffa (Israel) 173
Jerusalem 3, 111, 193, 199

Karkur (Israel) 171
Katona Jozsef St. (Budapest) 145
Kenyérmező (Hungary) 185
Kfar Achim (Israel) 210
Kfar Avraham (Israel) 193
Kfar Bilu (Israel) 173
Kfar Sava (Israel) 95, 185, 186, 193
Király St. (Budapest) 153
Kistarcsa (Hungary) 166
Komarno (Czechoslovakia) 166–67
Körmend (Hungary) 195
Krakow (Poland) 216

Landsberg (Germany) 62, 163
Latvia 141

Makarenko (day care center, Budapest) 146
Manara (Israel) 173
Marmarossziget (Hungary/Rumania) 142, 185. *See also* Sziget
Marosheviz (Hungary/Rumania) 218. *See also* Heviz
Marseilles (France) 170
Mattersdorf (Austria) 103, 161
Minsk (Soviet Union) 142
Mittelstein/Mittelsteine (Germany/Poland) 177
Montefiori (neighborhood, Tel Aviv) 71, 172
Moric Square (Budapest) 154
Munich (Germany) 164, 166

Nagybánya (Hungary/Rumania) 142
Nagymegye (Hungary/Rumania) 174
Nagyvárad (Hungary/Rumania) 33, 47, 50, 135, 138, 141, 219. *See also* Várad, Oradea
Nahariya (Israel) 147, 179
Netanya (Israel) 111, 210

Oradea (Hungary/Rumania) 31, 47, 140. *See also* Nagyvárad, Várad

Pápa (Hungary) 208
Pardess Hana (Israel) 171, 183
Paris (France) 155
Pécs (Hungary) 154
Pest 40, 138, 214. *See also* Budapest
Petach Tikva (Israel) 95, 174, 184
Pilsen (Czechoslovakia) 166
Plaszow/PIászow (Poland) 100, 101, 156, 158
Poland 9, 12
Pozsony (Hungary/Czechoslovakia) 137, 197, 209, 212, 214. *See also* Bratislava
Prague (Czechoslovakia) 170

Ra'anana (Israel) 125, 218, 220
Riga (Latvia) 14
Rosh Pina (Israel) 184
Rothchild St. (Tel Aviv, Israel) 172

Rumania 3, 4, 12, 14, 23, 31, 47, 48, 51, 54, 140, 144, 181, 190, 219, 221
Russia 12, 205

Sarafend (Hebrew: Zrifin) (Israel) 173
Sassen (unknown, may be Sachsen, Germany) 165
Seklers Road (Hungary/Rumania) 181
Silesia (Czechoslovakia/Poland) 177
Slovakia 209, 212, 213, 214, 215
Somlyo (Hungary/Rumania) 176, 181. *See also* Szilágysomlyo
Somorja (Hungary/Czechoslovakia) 123, 166, 168, 208, 209, 211, 212, 214
Sopron 211 (Hungary)
Soviet Union 53, 57, 142
Stalingrad (Soviet Union) 187
Stutthof (Germany) 141
Sudetenland (Germany/Czechoslovakia) 178–79
Sümeg (Hungary) 201
Sweden 168, 205
Switzerland 169
Szászregen (Hungary/Rumania) 195, 218
Szent István St./Square (Budapest) 146, 149
Sziget (Hungary/Rumania) 95, 185, 192. *See also* Marmarossziget
Sziládicse (Hungary/Rumania) 174
Szilágysomlyo (Hungary/Rumania) 95, 174. *See also* Somlyo

Szolnok (Hungary) 111, 193, 194, 195, 197
Szombathely (Hungary) 116, 201, 202, 204, 205, 208

Tel Aviv (Israel) 111, 171, 210
Tel Hanan (Israel) 183
Temesvár (Hungary/Rumania) 190
Tetk (Budapest) 146
Trans-Danube (Hungary) 195
Transylvania (Hungary/Rumania) 103, 195, 227n25. *See also* Erdély
Trumpeldor's grave (Israel) 191

Ukraine 216, 221
Ungvár (Hungary/Czechoslovakia) 163
United States 113, 193, 200, 224n30

Várad (Hungary/Rumania) 141, 143. *See also* Nagyvárad, Oradea
Vásárhely (Hungary/Rumania) 219, 220
Vienna (Austria) 202

Waldlager (Poland) 163
Weisswasser (Germany) 179
Wels (Austria) 195
West Germany 203

Yavne (Israel) 129
Yugoslavia 12, 138, 202

Zuglo (neighborhood, Budapest) 146

www.ingramcontent.com/pod-product-compliance
Lightning Source LLC
Chambersburg PA
CBHW050342270326
41926CB00016B/3577